Consumer Choice

The Economics of Personal Living

Consumer Choice

The Economics of Personal Living

Andrew J. Allentuck

Gordon E. Bivens
Iowa State University

Harcourt Brace Jovanovich, Inc.
New York   Chicago   San Francisco   Atlanta

TO BOB SYRON—without whom this book would not have been

ISBN:0-15-513456-6
Library of Congress Catalog Card Number: 76-42015

Printed in the United States of America

Original artwork by Allyn-Mason, Inc.
Cartoons by Sidney Harris

Other picture credits appear on pages 497–98.

PREFACE

Consumer economics is a vast field without neat borders, and consumer issues and problems reflect virtually all the components of contemporary life. In this book we make the philosophical and methodological assumption that the best way to understand consumer economics and to serve the consumer is not to shrink from those consumer problems that are adversary in nature; therefore, where necessary, we view consumer interests in opposition to the interests of the people and the firms that commit market abuses.

Each chapter deals with a particular market or problem area, such as food, clothing, or housing. After describing the legal, social, economic, and political forces that set the stage for the consumer's role in that area, we indicate what tools the consumer may use to advantage there. To do so, we draw heavily on the literature of home economics, law, microeconomics, industrial organization, and political science. Because the field of consumerism is changing fast, we also use interviews with authorities in various fields, legal and financial information services, and, in some cases, abstracts of information from broadcast media.

The components of consumer economics are presented within a conceptual framework that includes the concerns and the structure of the consumer economy as outlined in Chapters 1 and 2. Chapters 3–13 cover many topics that are conventionally taught in personal finance courses: career planning, budgeting, taxation and money management, credit, insurance, and estate planning.

Because money is not the only resource that the consumer controls, we have included a special chapter (Chapter 14) on the economics of leisure and recreation. In Chapters 15–20, we review several topics that are frequently taught in various fields of home economics and family management courses: nutrition (in an economic context), clothing and its technologies, home renting and buying, furniture and appliances, public and private transportation, and health care. Finally, in Chapters 21–24, we examine the social responsibilities of business, the adequacy of the American and other legal systems in solving consumer problems, and the accomplishments of the consumer movement to date.

Throughout the book, we have tried not to impose our own preferences about personal lifestyle on the subject matter or on those who study it. The particular tastes and values people bring to consumer economics are their own; we wish only to demonstrate that it is important for individuals to clarify what they want from life and how their selected lifestyles can best be achieved within the confines of the consumer market.

We could not have written about such a broad topic without the generous and expert help of many. In particular, the following people and organizations deserve thanks: Don Zasada, Director of Research and Planning, Department of Consumer, Corporate, and Internal Services, Province of Manitoba; Joe Locke, Rentalsman of the Province of Manitoba; Judy Divinsky, June Dutka, and Valorie Ward of The Elizabeth Dafoe Library, University of Manitoba; Pat Cherniack, Joyce Irvine, and Merle McLeod of the Manitoba Legislative Library; the staff of the Winnipeg Public Library; William Coco; Shelley Gurvey; Harcourt Brace Jovanovich staff members Judy Burke, Don DeLaura, Tad Gaither, Mary George, Arlene Kosarin, Jain Simmons, and Kay Ellen Ziff; reviewers Fred Culver (College of Marin), Elizabeth Dolan (California State University at Chico), and Eleanor Frasier (Florissant Valley Community College); cartoonist Sidney Harris; Daryl Kühl for help in preparing the index; and our families, without whose patience and understanding this book could not have been written.

ANDREW J. ALLENTUCK
GORDON E. BIVENS

CONTENTS

3 CAREER PLANNING: CHOOSING A VOCATION   19

4 CAREERS AND INCOME   35

5 BUDGETING: GIVING EXPRESSION TO LIFESTYLES   51

TAXES: A SLICE OFF THE TOP   63

SAVINGS 83

INVESTMENTS: CONCERN FOR THE FUTURE   101

9 CHECKING ACCOUNTS   131

10 CONSUMER CREDIT AND LOANS   147

11 LIFE INSURANCE   177

12 ESTATE PLANNING 201

13 AUTOMOBILE AND HOME INSURANCE 215

14 TIME AND LEISURE 235

15 FOOD: THE STRUGGLE FOR A SANE DIET 249

16 CLOTHING AND SELF-EXPRESSION 283

17 A HOME OF YOUR OWN: RENTING AND SHARING 305

18 BUYING AND OWNING A HOME   329

19 FURNISHING YOUR HOME   361

20 PUBLIC AND PRIVATE TRANSPORTATION   379

21 THE HEALTH-CARE INDUSTRY AND THE CONSUMER   411

22 CORPORATIONS AND THEIR SOCIAL RESPONSIBILITY   443

23 THE ISSUE OF CONSUMER SOVEREIGNTY   455

24 WHERE IS THE CONSUMER MOVEMENT GOING?   473

APPENDIX Federal and State Agencies That Help the Consumer   486

INDEX   499

Consumer Choice

The Economics of Personal Living

1

MONEY, LIFESTYLES, AND THE MARKET

> **A fool may make money, but it takes a wise man to spend it.**
>
> CHARLES HODDON SPURGEON

THE CONSUMER AND THE MARKET

We live in a materially abundant society, and while we cherish the range of choice that this abundance brings, we are often confused and unsure about how to make wise decisions given the choices that confront us daily, even hourly, as consumers. How can *consumers*—the people who use the goods and services that are ultimately produced for retail in an economy—function most effectively in an economy such as ours?

Consumer economics is an important and a useful means of analyzing and helping to clarify and to consolidate the multitude of sometimes difficult choices that different markets present to consumers. A *market* is a process that enables people who so wish to exchange goods or services that are of value. In a *product market* money is exchanged for goods; in a *labor market* labor services are exchanged for money. Some product or service is exchanged in every market, either for money or for some other product or service, and economics is a study of this process of exchange. The essential elements in the mechanism of the market are determined by the consumer, who decides whether or not to participate in an exchange and, if to participate, at what price. The buyer in every market must decide whether the object or service desired is worth what must be given for it in exchange (usually money). Thus crucial to an understanding of how our economy functions is an awareness of how money works as a medium of exchange. Money represents *exchange value;* that is, we can give up our earnings for housing or food, or we can trade a car for a boat or a Honda by using the medium of money.

Consumer economics focuses on how money can be used in *retail markets,* since consumers do not interact directly in wholesale markets or during the manufacturing process. Consumer economics studies the characteristics of these markets to determine how effectively or ineffectively they function for the consumer.

When we speak of markets, it is important to keep in mind that we are referring to the markets in a capitalist economy, which is only one of many economic systems throughout the world. Our concern here is with the market as it exists in the American economy and other so-called capitalist economies where exchange is voluntary. In noncapitalist economies, goods are often distributed to final users on the basis of social or political rank, need, or some other essentially noneconomic criterion. However, in this book we are primarily concerned with how market problems affect the consumer, and we reserve discussion of the consumer in nonmarket economies until Chapter 23.

THE CHANGING CONCERNS OF CONSUMER ECONOMICS

Consumer problems are probably as old as markets—and therefore as old as civilization itself—and history provides us with many examples of consumer legislation. Honest weight and measure standards, for example, were established by the rulers of ancient Babylon. Early Roman law was concerned with problems of deceit and fraud. And what we would call pure food and drug laws today sprouted in the wake of the many epidemics of plague and other diseases in Europe from about 1350 to 1850.

The study of economics itself has diverse roots. The Greek philosopher Aristotle (384–322 B.C.) was perhaps the first writer to be concerned with the problems of exchange. Aristotle analyzed the economy from the viewpoint of the household—a perspective that was subsequently ignored until recently. In the seventeenth, eighteenth, and nineteenth centuries, when basic modern approaches to economics were developed, Aristotle's concern for the household was disregarded. In its place, economists saw production and exchange from the perspective of the manufacturer and the seller. *Consumer economics*— examining exchange processes from the viewpoint of the consumer—developed

"Granted our commercials are a bit false and deceptive—but remember, Cyckle is *still* a good product."

only in the twentieth century. Of course, home economists have been concerned with many consumer economics issues, but these economists normally focus on elements of technology instead of exchange, and therefore on products instead of markets. Their work is valuable, for we need to know about fabric design characteristics, menu planning, and home design. But consumer economics goes beyond these specific areas to view the market as a whole.

Within the last 15 years, there has been a major departure from the old standards of consumer–producer relations. The ultimate precaution once rested on the consumer, and *caveat emptor*—may the buyer beware—was the merchant's defense. If a customer bought shoddy goods, it was the customer's fault. The concept of buyer self-protection is clearly inappropriate in markets where buyers and sellers do not know each other well or where complex or dangerous goods can be adequately tested only by skilled experts. Lawmakers are now willing to legislate product quality and safety standards. To the manufacturer or seller who would put shabby or unsafe goods on the market, they say *caveat venditor*— may the *seller* beware.

THE DIMENSIONS OF CONSUMER ECONOMICS

The new role of government in consumer affairs has changed the dimensions of the market, of consumer problems, and of the possible remedies for these consumer problems. New products and new laws have changed the frontiers of consumer economics. A current concern of consumers and pro-consumer groups is to ensure the accurate ingredient labeling of foods, drugs, and other ingestible products. Are health foods better than regular foods (this is really a nutrition issue), and are so-called organic foods an efficient way to spend food dollars (this is the consumer economics issue)? Why are drug prices so high, and what—if anything—can be done to bring them down? By their nature many products are unsafe or dangerous if misused. What are the costs and benefits of making products safer? Fabric and clothing prices have changed drastically due to the increasing costs of natural and synthetic fibers. How can a family clothe itself in the style it desires and remain within the confines of its budget? In some areas, the automobile is a major contributor to air pollution. Providing highways and police forces for this car traffic is also a large public expense. What public policies should be instituted regarding air pollution and transportation in general? Who should pay for traffic accidents, and how can automobile insurance be made more efficient? How can people be housed decently at prices they can afford? Can housing standards be changed to lower costs? Are there more efficient construction methods? What changes in credit laws could give people fairer access to mortgage money? How can tenants be guaranteed decent housing while landlords in most states hold all the cards?

Already the list of questions is long, but in fact it is still sketchy. Today all state legislatures are spending much of their time on long-overdue consumer reform. Congress and the courts face frequent demands for the correction of consumer abuses. There is a world of difference between the government that tells buyers and sellers to sort out their own differences and the government that intervenes in markets to enforce product standards. Which do we prefer? If government raises product standards to enable the consumer to choose from better products, this action may also reduce the number of products that are available. Thomas Jefferson said that the government which governs least governs best, but today the sheer complexity of products and markets may require more government presence than was necessary before the twentieth century.

In considering how, or whether, to reform a particular market, it is essential to understand why a reform does or does not work. Many markets can correct their own abuses. For example, a dishonest merchant may lose customers and be forced out of business if the public becomes aware of the unfair practices. But what if the merchant's potential customers don't find out or past customers are not aware that they've been injured until long after the product has been sold and used (as is the case with cancer-causing foods and drugs)? Government can issue licenses to manufacturers and merchants who are competent to protect public safety, but would other avenues of enforcement afford consumers even better protection?

The efficiency of regulation is only one dimension of consumer economics. It is relatively easy to specify the ways in which money can be spent for a given product or a particular form of law enforcement. But who is served when money spent on one product limits the buyer's and the society's choices elsewhere? The automobile is the best example of such a product interrelationship. Most motorists and truckers want more and better roads. But new roads cut through residential neighborhoods, affect land values, encourage air pollution, and take freight business away from railroads. For government, the issue is how to build the required roads in a way that is consistent with other social needs, such as maintaining quiet residential neighborhoods. For the consumer, the choices are what vehicles are necessary for different types of driving, how to ensure that a new car isn't a lemon, and, in many cases, whether to have a car at all or to rely instead on public transportation.

BASIC PRINCIPLES

Consumers must know more than simply which product is technically best. Budgets are limited, and spending more on one product means having less to spend on other goods or services. This is also true for government in the sense, for example, that every law-enforcement program costs money, changes market choices, and represents a further reduction in political or economic freedom for someone. This book attempts to deal with the broad problems of the market by applying consistent economic principles to various consumer problems. It is based on two very important principles. First, every purchase—or choice of an action or a career—costs something, either in money, time, or the foregone

opportunity to do something else. Second, peoples' needs are vastly different. Each person is unique; he or she has individual desires and concerns that others may not share. No one is *obliged* to eat meat; other diets sustain hundreds of millions of healthy vegetarians around the world. Every home does not need a family room or a swimming pool. Everyone does not purchase life insurance, although most of us do.

Personal finance books and consumer-problem surveys usually approach spending and earning decisions by isolating "problem areas." Using this approach, for example, the cost of operating a car is considered to be entirely distinct from the cost of housing. But having a house in the suburbs may involve a greater cash outlay due to commuting and consequent driving expenses than would having a house or an apartment in a city. Although it is simpler to regard problems as neatly distinct, conclusions drawn in this way are potentially false. For example, most consumer economics texts rely on standard family budgets and assume certain family values, such as the goal of owning a home in the suburbs. In this book, problem areas are approached in the context of assisting the student to realize his or her own values, not preestablished ones. Choices and solutions are not valid unless they relate directly to a person's needs. This book therefore indicates the ways in which personal values can influence market choices. Government regulation is not recommended without indicating its cost in reduced political and economic freedom. It is not our purpose here to teach a way of life; rather we attempt to show how a chosen way of life can best be achieved in the market for consumer goods.

VALUES AND LIFESTYLES

Much of the problem of how best to spend one's money can be resolved simply by becoming familiar with one's personal values. Unmarried people as a rule do not require suburban houses, and clearly, a family with several children would feel too confined in a downtown city apartment. Food budgeting, car buying, and wardrobe selection depend on knowing one's goals. Second-hand clothes and a rusty pickup truck are as proper for some lifestyles as current fashions and the latest model station wagon are for others. If a person values living alone with nature in a rural area, then his or her lifestyle should reflect this feeling. The point here seems obvious, yet how many people really pursue their own values instead of advertised ones? People accumulate useless goods and waste time and money on pursuits alien to their personal needs. To buy on a whim is foolish if the whim is indeed that and will pass in a few days or weeks. Some people equip themselves for a multitude of lifestyles, never knowing which one they are really seeking. We cannot and will not make value judgments in this book, but, where possible, we try to match economic choices with lifestyles and values.

SUMMARY

1 A market is a process that enables people who so wish to exchange goods or services that are of value.

2 Consumer law has a long history, but it has recently changed its emphasis from the theory that consumers must protect themselves to the theory that the producers or vendors may not manufacture or sell unsafe or unfair goods or services that are harmful to consumers.

3 Consumer problems and spending decisions must be approached with the understanding that each spending decision affects every other spending choice and opportunity; in other words, problem areas are not isolated from one another.

4 Spending decisions should be based on one's personal values and lifestyle.

Suggestions for Further Reading

* Buskirk, Richard H. and Rothe, James T. "Consumerism: An Interpretation," *Journal of Marketing* **XXXIV** (October 1970), 61–65.

* Mitchell, Wesley C. "The Backward Art of Spending Money," *American Economic Review* **II** (June 1912), 269–81.

Riesman, David. *The Lonely Crowd.* New Haven: Yale University Press, 1961.

* NOTE: Both of these articles can be found in Ralph M. Gaedeke and Warren W. Etcheson (eds.). *Consumerism.* San Francisco: Canfield Press, 1972. The Buskirk and Rothe article can also be found in Barbara B. Murray (ed.). *Consumerism: The Eternal Triangle.* Pacific Palisades, Calif.: Goodyear Publishing Co., 1973.

The Consumer Workshop

1 Define consumer economics.
2 What is *caveat emptor?* Compare *caveat emptor* with *caveat venditor.*
3 Discuss the relationship between values and lifestyles.
4 Almost every popular magazine espouses a particular lifestyle. Examine *Cosmopolitan, Ladies' Home Journal,* and *Playboy.* What values can you find in editorial policy, editors' concepts of readers, and (assuming editors know their audience) readers' beliefs and expectations about lifestyles?

2 CONSUMER DECISIONS IN THE ECONOMY

> **A typical buyer would find it difficult to make a selection if confronted with only the facts.**
>
> KEITH REINHARD,
> Broadcasting Magazine*

It is helpful, before discussing individual consumer problems and different markets, to have an overview of consumers' interactions with the economy. This chapter describes in general terms how consumer needs are met by the economy's production units, how consumers actually decide how much of what items they will buy, and the information that is available to guide consumers in their decisions.

THE BUYING PROCESS

There are two ways to examine the buying process. One may view the actual, rather casual, often haphazard ways in which many people choose particular goods and services; or one may examine the methods consumers can follow to get the most for their money. The results of the casual, haphazard approach are well known: Buyers fail to budget their money properly, they are unfamiliar with the technical qualities of the things they wish to buy, and they are misled by advertising. The reader of our book, we hope, will grow aware of these and similar errors of knowledge and judgment and learn to use money well. A good start toward such an understanding lies in knowing the five major elements that comprise the buyer–seller interaction:

1 Recognition of needs
2 Evaluation of these needs
3 Market opportunities
4 Decision factors
5 Consumer information sources

Need Recognition Consumers go to a market with needs or objectives, some more specific than others. The least specific motivations are those of shoppers who are merely window shopping or browsing for entertainment. In the middle are shoppers who want to buy something, maybe a gift, but don't know precisely what they

---

* Quoted in *Consumer Reports* **38** (January 1973), p. 6.

want. The most clearly motivated are shoppers who know exactly what they want to buy and perhaps are only checking prices and the competing products.

Need Evaluation Every product renders a service. The services of some products are long-lasting; for example, a washing machine may operate for a decade or more. Other products give only a few minutes or hours of service. As a rule, the longer a product's service life, or the more expensive the product, the more carefully consumers should evaluate it before purchasing it.

The important criteria for buying products include these questions:

1 How suitable is the product in satisfying the perceived need for it?
2 How much does it cost?
3 How long will it last?
4 What amount of service will it need and how much will this cost?

Suitability. The suitability of a product is not a simple matter; what a particular item actually is or does often depends largely on our imagination and vision. Some goods have very limited and specific uses; for example, any automobile needs a carburetor, and the work of the carburetor is limited to mixing fuel and air. An engine needs a particular carburetor and a carburetor for one engine can be used on a different engine only by modifying it, with much effort and expense. But another item, say, the brick, is infinitely more versatile: You can make a wall with it, a floor, a patio, or even a fence.

Cost. The market price of a product may be rigid or flexible. The more diligently one shops, the greater is the likelihood of finding varying prices and bargains. Some products are frequently on sale, others (such as used automobiles) are customarily purchased by bargaining. Sometimes the bargaining process involves a valuable trade-in. In other cases the trade-in is only a way for the seller to relieve the buyer of guilt at having to throw away a still serviceable product (a vacuum cleaner, for example).

There are many things that we buy in quantity. Groceries, socks, and automobile tires are typical products purchased in units of two or more. Economists have, for perhaps 200 years, been aware of a fundamental rule of consumer behavior, the *law of demand*. Simply stated, the law of demand is that, as the price of a commodity declines, people will buy more of it. Business people are well aware of this law, and a store that has overstocked an item can reduce its inventory by lowering the price for the item in question. Consumers should be aware that they may be able to obtain price reductions if they increase their purchases of a given item.

Durability. The length of a product's service life must be taken into account before buying. An inexpensive product that will last only a few months may be in the long run more expensive to use than a product that costs 50% more but that lasts three times as long.

Service Costs. Service requirements are an aspect of buying that consumers too often ignore. Many consumer products are not designed with service in mind, and any item that is mechanical and that is supposed to last for a period of years will in time probably need some service. How hard is it to change a light bulb in your refrigerator? Do you have to take it apart to do so? What sort of service is locally available? If routine maintenance is needed, what does it cost? Buyers of expensive foreign cars are often startled to find that tuneups cost a great deal and are required more often than on American cars.

Market Opportunities

The ease with which any article can be bought depends upon the:

1 Price
2 Amount of competition
3 Resale opportunities
4 Credit available

Price and competition are interrelated. If a thing is priced so low that there is little profit in making or selling it, many firms will leave the industry in which the product is produced. Then fewer firms will be left and each can, perhaps, charge a higher price. When the price is rising, however, more firms will enter the industry to share in increasing profits. A higher product price will usually induce any one firm to make more goods. All these facts can be summarized in what economists call the *law of supply:* Quantity produced by a firm rises when the price rises; quantity produced falls when the price falls.

The law of supply tells us that when a product is in heavy demand, producers will make more and raise their prices. But what about the industry that is controlled by one firm or by only a few firms? These firms may decide to keep production low and simply charge a lot for their output. When an industry is in this condition of *monopoly* (one seller) or *oligopoly* (few sellers), price increases will benefit sellers, not buyers. Government policy usually opposes monopoly. Consumers facing monopoly will do well to try to substitute a nonmonopolized product, if possible, for the monopoly good or shop in different markets. If a small-town drugstore charges high prices because it has no competition, the wise shopper will go to a larger town where there is competition, unless the added transportation cost more than offsets the saving on the prescription. If automobile dealers charge high prices for parts, as they do, one should try to buy needed parts from an automobile-parts supply firm independent of the dealer.

When an industry is very competitive, firms will try to increase their share of business and acquire more customers. Often they make credit available to customers, create resale markets (for example, for automobiles), and provide sales discounts to stimulate business. Generally, consumers should try to buy in the most competitive markets available. This means buying in locations where there are several sellers of the same item, and buying items made in competitive industries. It is a mistake to think of a product in such narrow terms that only one firm can supply your needs. The ability to substitute is the power to escape from noncompetitive markets.

Decision Factors

In examining a specific commodity for purchase, the consumer should ask:

1 Do I need it now?
2 Is it the right product?
3 Is the seller the best I can find?
4 Will the product last?

Urgency. Though a particular item may not be needed for immediate use, there may be other justifications for purchasing it. Perhaps the product is on sale; perhaps you anticipate that its price will rise in the near future. You may want to have a store of food or a reserve of spare parts. But if an item will not be used for a few years and will probably not increase in price in the interval, then you should consider banking its cost and earning interest on it.

Appropriateness. How well an item meets your needs is mainly a matter of how imaginative and flexible you are in understanding how a product functions and what your needs are. If curtains are too costly for your budget, you might be able to make a substitute out of fabric remnants or colorful sheets. A severely damaged plaster wall can be made respectable by expensive plastering or, inexpensively, by tearing away the remaining plaster to expose a potentially charming brick wall.

Quality of the Seller. There is usually a relationship between time spent shopping and the price you finally pay. Don't buy a major item without spending at least a few hours checking the price range of the product. Be aware that the purchase price does not necessarily include the cost of delivery, installation (if any), or subsequent service. Finally, one should consider the cost of the electricity or gas the product will consume and the product's price in adjacent towns or even in another state (adjusting, of course, for the added cost of transportation).

Some products, such as automobiles, are sold only by firms selected by the manufacturer and are thus, in theory, competent to give service, discuss the product's use, and so on. But most goods are sold by firms that may be unknown to the manufacturer. Personnel in many stores do not know their products well. It is worth going to a dealer who can help you make the right choice, even though you may often have to pay for the dealer's expertise. Discount stores, for example, tend to charge lower prices. But the sales clerks have to look after so many different kinds of merchandise that they are not able to understand each product. Specialty stores, such as hardware stores, paint stores, and furniture stores, usually have knowledgeable sales personnel. You pay more at these establishments but you may also receive valuable advice on product selection, care, and use. Particularly when buying a specialized product with which you are not familiar, it pays to go to a more expensive, but more knowledgeable, dealer.

Durability. Product life is always difficult to estimate. Many consumer goods are built to comparatively low standards; for example, washing machines for the home are less sturdily constructed than those for commercial laundries. One often does not realize how poorly built some products are until they break down. It is not always possible to judge durability from price or appearance. For example, production standards and labeling for tires are still vague. Kitchen or workshop tools usually have some relationship between price and quality, but not one firm enough to be dependable. Stainless steel lasts longer than aluminum; heavy sheet metal lasts longer than light sheet metal. But it is still difficult to determine the quality of a refrigerator's compressor or the type of sheet metal used in a stove. Of course, not every product has to be built to high standards. If you plan to use an electric drill only a few times a year, any drill will probably serve adequately (unless it has obvious safety hazards).

Consumer Information Sources

Once we understand our product needs, we must assess the market's choices. To do so we can use four kinds of information:

1 Our own judgment
2 Advertisers' claims
3 Casual information from friends
4 Assistance from government agencies, consumer groups, and accessible academic research

Personal judgment is probably the best guide in choosing a product and a dealer when you have experience with the product and firm. If the product is a minor one, say, some sewing tools or a box of screws, it would be foolish to invest much time in finding the very best thing at the lowest possible price.

Advertisers of name-brand goods could be helpful if their information were really informative, but advertising can be more persuasive than accurate. Consider advertisements for house paint: Every product is said to be easy to apply, long-lasting, washable, and so forth. Yet price varies by 300% on most brands of paint. The ads tell very little. Consider cosmetics: How many advertisers reveal the chemical composition of their products? Advertisements for men's colognes claim each fragrance will make the user irresistible to women. It would be more useful to know what's in the bottle. Examples of uninformative but persuasive advertising are endless: Automobile manufacturers don't promise that a car will be dependable (most aren't and they'd be sued if they promised they were); rather, they boast that the buyer will be popular, loved, or respected, if he or she purchases one.

Word of mouth information can be very revealing. It is difficult to find out what a car is like without having one, and you don't know a dealer well until you've had a problem. If a friend says a certain firm or product should be

"Whatever you do, don't let Ralph Nader discuss your sponsors."

avoided, it may be excellent advice; it certainly deserves to be investigated. Friends can also pass along news of bargains and make recommendations about such things as hotels, physicians, and dentists. The grapevine is an important source of information.

The last category of information is data from government, consumer groups, and published research. Some of this advice is valuable; some of it is not. The Consumers Union of the United States, located in Mt. Vernon, New York, tests products and published information in its important monthly magazine, *Consumer Reports*. Consumer groups in your area may be in touch with local problems. Before buying a car or a major appliance, it may be a good idea to check on the dealer's and the product's reputations. The Better Business Bureaus are supposed to provide this information, but their loyalties are invariably divided between the business community that supports them and the public whom they are supposed to serve. The Bureaus' main service appears to be keeping track of fly-by-night fraud artists.

Government agencies, both consumer agencies and all the other bodies of federal, state, and local government, can often be of some help to consumers. Every state has consumer assistance offices. See Appendix I for a list of some federal and state agencies of this kind. Your local telephone directory, the United States Government Manual (available at local libraries), your representatives in Congress, and your state legislative body can all lead you to the appropriate agencies for help with specific problems. We shall discuss specific agencies and their work in the appropriate chapters of this text.

Academic research can be useful if you can get to it. However, only large expenditures of money justify such forays. If you have a specific question, go to a good university library and ask the reference librarian for a listing of books and articles that address your particular problem or question. It is important, however, to have a precise question; if you don't, the research will not be worth-while.

Awareness of needs, market opportunities, decision factors, and information sources help consumers make better use of individual and family incomes. No one has so much money that everything desired can be purchased. To buy a product that is less than the best at the prevailing price or that is more expensive than other equally satisfactory goods diminishes economic opportunities in other areas. The consumer who budgets time to investigate the market before making important purchases will make the best use of economic resources.

SUMMARY
1 The five elements of the buying process are:
    1 Need recognition
    2 Need evaluation
    3 Market opportunities
    4 Decision factors
    5 Consumer information sources
2 Need recognition ranges from a vague motivation to a precise intention to buy a specific item.
3 Consumer needs must be evaluated in terms of:
    1 Product suitability
    2 Product cost
    3 Product durability or life span
    4 Service cost
4 The law of demand states that people will want more of a product if that product's price declines.
5 Market opportunities depend on:
    1 Price
    2 Competition
    3 Resale opportunities
    4 Credit availability
6 The law of supply holds that a firm will produce more of a good as the product's price rises and will produce less as the product's price falls.
7 Consumers facing monopoly markets should try to find substitute goods or sellers for the monopolized product.
8 Decision factors are:
    1 Urgency of need
    2 Appropriateness of product
    3 Dealer choice
    4 Product durability
9 Consumer information sources are:
    1 Personal judgment
    2 Advertisers' claims
    3 Casual grapevine information
    4 Information from federal, state, and local governments, consumer groups, and academic research

Suggestions for Further Reading

Packard, Vance. *The Hidden Persuaders.* New York: McKay, 1957.
——————, *The Waste Makers.* New York: McKay, 1960.
Rogers, A. J., III. *Choice: An Introduction.* Englewood Cliffs, New Jersey: Prentice-Hall, 1971.

The Consumer Workshop

1 Let us say that you have just rented a large, unfurnished six-room apartment and need to furnish it. You clearly recognize a need for furniture. Make a list of the questions you must answer—about the apartment and your lifestyle—before you can begin to accurately judge market opportunities?

2 Nancy and María have just met one another in their first week at college. They both are looking for an apartment and they feel they would like to share quarters. Now they must begin to evaluate their needs. What questions about their lifestyles should they discuss to begin planning their apartment?

3 We tend to perceive market opportunities through advertising and the opinions of others. Only in those cases in which we are repeat customers do we have direct, personal experience with specific products and services. Yet our lifestyles influence the effort we can put into examining what the market offers. A busy executive has less time to shop for personal needs than a retired person has. College students on fairly tight budgets have to be imaginative in stretching their incomes to meet their needs. Busy homemakers can create shopping time, and thereby get better values, if they cooperatively share child care and routine grocery shopping. Compare the opportunities for pre-purchase planning and market scrutiny that various lifestyles allow or require.

4 The process by which we evaluate our needs and compare them to market opportunities is both objective and subjective. Planning a lifestyle and achieving it in the marketplace require a good deal of imaginative thinking. You can, for example, buy furniture as advertisers would have you do, or you can extend your opportunities into other markets by making unusual objects substitute for ordinary products. For example, you can make a coffee table out of a few bricks and a door. Tin cans may be painted and then wired with light sockets to make single lights or even chandeliers. A discarded bed frame can become a garden trellis. What kinds of substitutions can you make within your lifestyle to stretch your budget further?

3
CAREER PLANNING: CHOOSING A VOCATION

3

" A journey of a thousand miles begins with a single step. "

LAO TZU

This chapter examines the value of careers, their purpose, and how they can be developed. We begin with a discussion of the importance and usefulness of making career commitments. Then we examine the problems of career selection, how one finds a rewarding job with a good future. Finally, we discuss how to prepare for a career, and investigate the usefulness of different courses of study for finding good jobs and earning good income.

ADVANTAGES OF CAREER COMMITMENT

There are many advantages to being committed to some kind of work or study. These include:

1 Economic satisfaction—the ability to support oneself or to lead a desired way of life.
2 Social satisfaction through meeting other people, being a respected co-worker, being recognized for the work you do.
3 A sense of accomplishment and usefulness, an ability to cope with new challenges or simply just the enjoyment of participating.
4 A sense of well-being, of inner resourcefulness and strength, an ability to overcome or ignore small problems.
5 Creativity in unusual or even routine tasks; pleasure in making something with one's hands, doing routine work with precision and speed, or just helping things to move along.

CHOICE IS NECESSARY

You will be responsible for your own career decisions. To make the best career choice, you must examine your abilities, limitations, and background. Consider your family life, education, hobbies, work experience, health, attitudes toward work, leisure, wealth, and life in general. Also consider your interests and your capacity to be involved with activities and people. Are you a loner or a joiner? Do you want to work with groups or to work alone?

Personal Values and the Job

Before making a commitment to devote years of your life to a particular type of work or to a certain firm it is necessary and helpful to learn to understand your needs and desires, your own individual characteristics. To avoid making the decision, no matter how difficult it may be, is to place yourself in danger of disappointment later in life. Some career frustration may be avoided by careful pre-career planning. Will your work be the center of your life or will it be simply a source of income? Will the work itself and the firm you work for (if you are not self-employed) be acceptable to your way of life and beliefs? Are you willing to modify the truth a bit, as a salesperson must do occasionally? Can you accept the danger that's part of the work of a police officer, firefighter, or soldier? The tension and responsibility that is a part of the work of an air-traffic controller? The long hours of labor and isolation that many farmers face?

Fortunately, we nearly always have several opportunities throughout our lives and careers to take new career paths. Jobs in related fields may open up, you may want to return to school for another degree, or you may be promoted or transferred into an entirely different environment. The important thing is to recognize the critical times when these opportunities for change arise and then examine the opportunities as new challenges, as important as the first stages of launching any career.

Work Objectives and the Job

Let's evaluate a few work objectives and the types of jobs that can satisfy them. If you feel a need for security, consider the jobs or employers that provide it. Civil service positions often have tenure, or protection from unfair and arbitrary firing, for employees after only a few months' service. Such positions offer permanence and stability. But if you desire adventure instead, consider some of the skilled construction and engineering jobs that provide travel opportunities and challenging work. Geologists, refinery-construction specialists, and related workers frequently spend years on assignment around the world. Perhaps you feel that contributing to others, or helping people in need, is important to your sense of accomplishment and personal worth. In that case you may wish to consider a career as a physician, nurse, social worker, or member of the clergy.

The Costs of Indecision

The costs of indecision can be very high. If a good job opening comes along as you are finishing your B.A. and you can't make up your mind to accept it, the job probably will go to someone else. Similarly, if you take a job with good prospects for promotion and a career, and while on the job you merely get by, hardly making a substantial effort to excel at your work, you may dim your future and eventually be dismissed.

The costs of indecision exist, of course, for every kind of human effort or experience. If you postpone making an investment, say, buying some bonds, you may lose interest they would have brought. A job is also an investment, and postponing, taking, or doing that job involves the same kind of loss of earnings and satisfaction. (The same may be said about waiting to buy consumer goods: The longer you wait, the less you may get.)

". . . and the recruiter from IBM—did you also tell *him* that at college you mostly sat on a rock by the sea, trying to find yourself?"

Economists call the "costs" of missed opportunities *opportunity costs*. If you take a job as an engineer at $11,000 per year and could have taken another as a plant manager at $14,000, then if all other elements are equal, your choice has an opportunity cost of $3000. Because opportunity costs are not simply financial, but also include hard to measure things like happiness, they are not easy to calculate. Yet the concept of opportunity costs is important. Making correct decisions involves analyzing these opportunity costs. When you have made the best choice, the opportunity cost of that decision is zero, for that is the difference between the value of what you decided and the value of what you chose not to do.

CAREER SELECTION: GROWING INDUSTRIES

Assuming that you have marketable skills or that you have a profession in which you can pick your place or work or type of employer, let's review some of the choices. Some fields are expanding in employment and importance. Others are losing people and are declining in significance.

Here are several occupations and fields that appear to have good futures:

1 Consumer goods
2 Public service
3 Medical and related services
4 Rental and leasing services

5 Security services, especially in cities
6 Goods and services for the elderly
7 Transportation, especially trucking, air freight, and urban transit
8 Waste management and recycling

RISING AND FALLING SECTORS

Any occupational goal is best furthered in an expanding business or industry, in contrast to an industry or business that is in decline. Getting in on the ground floor is a way of investing yourself, or your money, with the hope that the structure of achievement or profit will rise and pull your contribution up with it. To get in on the ground floor when nothing is going up—or when something is on the way down—is not a good idea.

For much of the twentieth century in the United States, *primary industries* (farming, mining, anything associated with the collection of raw materials) have been shrinking in terms of what they contribute to gross national product. Until the 1950s, *secondary industries* (manufacturing) were expanding their contribution to the GNP. *Tertiary industries* do not make products; rather they furnish services to people or businesses. An example of a primary industry is a company that mines iron ore. The company that processes the ore into sheets of steel is a secondary industry, as is the firm which makes computer cabinets from the steel. The firm that buys the computer to process the business records of other firms is a tertiary industry. Since the 1960s, tertiary or *service industries* have been the fastest growing sector of the economy.

This is not to say that the future is only in service industries. General Motors is in a secondary industry, and it will not be folding very soon. As GM's President, Edward Cole, said of the energy crisis, "General Motors' business is transportation, and GM will provide transportation machinery for America as long as Americans want to move." Primary industries benefit substantially from higher food, energy, and related commodity prices. Consider the embarrassingly high oil revenues being reported by America's largest petroleum firms. With more money to spend and invest, Exxon, Standard Oil of California, Gulf, Mobil, and the other oil producers will be expanding their operations for years to come.

SELF-EMPLOYMENT VERSUS BEING EMPLOYED

Is it better to be an employee or to be your own boss? Some professions lend themselves to self-employment or partnerships: doctors, lawyers, and accountants usually work for themselves or in small groups.   Other professions involve large collective efforts: chemical engineering in petroleum refining, mechanical engineering in locomotive manufacturing, and securities analysis in investment banking.

Working for a large firm may give one a sense of being a part of something large, powerful, and permanent.   Yet a person may feel trapped in a situation in which he or she is but one of a few hundred thousand employees.   Individuality may suffer or personalities may grow; it all depends on the person.   But large firms do offer a permanence that small firms do not.

The smaller the firm, the less likely that it will survive.   The rate of small business failure in the United States is substantial.   Each year about 400,000 firms are started and 350,000 are discontinued, of which 10,000 to 15,000 are involuntary closings due to bankruptcy or demands of creditors.[1]   For those thinking of establishing their own firms, the risk of business failure is substantial.   A small business often requires much more of its proprietor-operator than would the same job in a larger business.   For example, many small, "mom and pop" grocery stores produce less income for their operators than the same "mom and pop" could earn if each worked for a grocery chain as a clerk or cashier.   The Retail Clerks International Association, with 700,000 members, obtains a wage of $8000 or more per member in organized firms.   The annual return on most "mom and pop" stores is *less* than $2 \times \$8000$, or $16,000, per year. Teenagers over 18 years of age earn the adult wage.   "Mom and pop" stores can't buy in the bulk or variety to match the prices and selection of supermarkets and therefore do not do as well.

REGIONAL DETERMINANTS

Perhaps one should consider establishing a career in a growing region.   For some time the fastest growing areas of the United States, in terms of rates of increase of personal income, have been the suburban belts around the cities.   The energy crisis, however, suggests that people may begin to move back to inner-city dwellings to avoid paying the high cost of commuting.

Entire states occasionally exhibit rapid growth rates, often because they are moving from underdevelopment to economic equality with the more prosperous areas of the United States.   The rise of Arizona in the 1960s is an example. Some states have been in decline for decades.   For example, West Virginia went into an economic coma in the 1950s after coal began to lose out to oil as a preferred energy source.   But the high price of oil may change all this and bring an economic rebirth for the less expensive oil substitute—Appalachian coal.

[1] W. Rudelius, W.B. Erickson, and W.J. Bakula, Jr., *An Introduction to Contemporary Business,* 2nd ed. (New York: Harcourt Brace Jovanovich, Inc., 1976), p. 423.

CAREER PREPARATION

Deciding on a curriculum that will best prepare one for a career yet unchosen is obviously difficult. It is said that liberal arts studies, the humanities, teach analytical abilities and so provide a threshold to many careers. Specialized engineering degrees clearly indicate that their holders have accrued useful knowledge. But specialists can become outmoded by advances in the very technology they study.

To prepare for any career, any discipline with a well-developed method provides good training. Foreign languages, for example, have a grammatical structure to grapple with; philosophy pursues problems in need of sophisticated solutions. Fields such as mathematics lend themselves to rigorous analysis; other areas of study are conducive to intuitive or instinctive understanding. If you don't know exactly what you want to do with your B.A., then Greek is as instructive as electrical engineering. The best choice of a field of study is one that balances your career objectives with your academic likes and dislikes.

THE RIGHT COURSE OF STUDY FOR YOU

If you don't know what you want to do, you should analyze your abilities and pick an area of study or work in which they seem applicable. If you have chosen a field you want to pursue, then probably it's best to pick an undergraduate subject that is in some way connected to it. But choosing a course of study for a career needn't make you drop other interests. You can pursue them as avocations or hobbies while you follow a course of study leading to a desirable career. Ultimately, the question of whether your interests should be pursued as a vocation or as an avocation depends on the nature of your interests and career plans. Specifically:

1 If your career work requires formal laboratory training, then it's best to study in an area that offers the formal education required. Chemists must work in laboratories to gain practical knowledge of their field, and computer programmers must work directly with computers. Mere book study in such cases would be incomplete, like trying to learn to play the piano without an instrument on which to practice.

2 If your interests in a subject are very strong, you do yourself an injustice to struggle with a field you don't like.

3 But if the question is one of liking two or more things, one that offers practical application and requires formal training, and one that can as easily be studied as a hobby (history, philosophy, literature, art), then you have to look further into the economic and intellectual satisfactions that each field may offer. Engineering may be a more dependable career than history; if security

matters to you, engineering may be your choice. If you simply don't want to relegate a field to the status of hobby, you can try to work in both fields. Be a pharmacist by day and a potter by night. The decision ultimately will depend on your desires, imagination, and resourcefulness.

COURSES AND INCOMES

Does a college or a professional degree enable you to make more money? Generally speaking, the longer you go to school, the more money you can and will make. This does not mean that school actually makes more money for you, since it may be that only clever or goal-oriented people actually go to college or finish high school and such people would make more money than others even if they never went to college or finished high school. (The latter case is possible but rather unlikely.)

Let us consider some figures. For U.S. males 18 years and older in 1972, the total lifetime incomes for different levels of educational attainment are:[2]

Educational Attainment	Lifetime Income
Elementary school graduate	$421,136
High-school graduate	563,101
College graduate	975,799

This means that the total increase in lifetime income for elementary-school graduates as a result of finishing high school would be 35%. The increase of lifetime income for high-school graduates who finished college would be 64%. So it appears that more schooling, for whatever reasons, results in more money over a worker's lifetime. Does this mean that you should stay in school until you have a Ph.D.? Not necessarily.

Consider what you lose by going to school and for that time not participating in the labor force. While in school as nearly a full-time student, you don't have a full-time job, and you therefore lose the income you might have earned. If you go to college for four years after high school, you are out of four years of work at a wage for a high-school graduate of, say, $7000 per year (4 × $7000 per year equals $28,000 of lost income). By going to college for four years, you may earn more every year after graduation from college than you would have earned if you had not gone to college. For example, if the high-school graduate earns $8000 at age 40 and the college graduate earns $10,000 at age 40, then college is worth $2000 more a year at age 40. *But* if our typical worker is now 25 years old, what is the value of $2000 in 15 years? This all depends on the

[2] U.S., Bureau of the Census, *Current Population Reports,* Series P-60, no. 92, "Annual Mean Income, Lifetime Income, and Educational Attainment of Men in the United States, for Selected Years, 1956 to 1972" (Washington, D.C.: U.S. Government Printing Office, 1974), Table 7, p. 23.

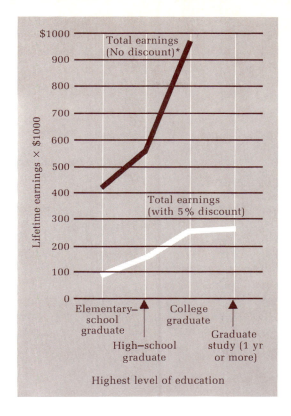

3-1
Education and Lifetime Income

rate of interest; for example, the rate of interest $2000 could earn in the bank in a savings account for 15 years. At 5% per year, compounded four times a year, $2000 is worth about $5000 after 15 years. Reversing this analysis, $5000 15 years from now is worth $2000 at present, given a 5% rate of interest or discount. That is to say, we can buy $5000 in 15 years at a present discount, and at 5% that discounted price is $2000.

Happily, it turns out that by going to school for a given number of years, you can more than make up for the income you lose by not working. (See Figure 3-1). Using a 5% rate of discount for all U.S. males at age 40 and assuming that no man's productivity improves, the lifetime incomes for different levels of educational attainment would be:[3]

Educational Attainment	Lifetime income (discount total)
Elementary-school graduate	$ 87,000
High-school graduate	151,000
College graduate	252,000
Some graduate school	269,000

[3] *Ibid.*, table 9, pp. 25–28.

At a higher rate of interest (say, 10%), the advantage of postponing income vanishes, at least in financial terms.

PERIL BY DEGREE: JOB PROSPECTS

We know that finishing high school or going to college can improve one's life income.   But how does furthering one's education affect the prospects for finding a certain type of job or for having a choice of jobs throughout life?   Are there hidden risks in going to college or graduate school?

Let's consider the position of the person who completes high school. Among 25–29 year olds in 1972, 79.8% had completed four or more years of high school.   In 1940, however, only 37.8% of 25–29 year olds had finished high school.   So we should not be surprised that high-school graduates with little or no work experience have a good deal of trouble finding work and entering the labor force. [4]

University education until recently was rare.   In 1940, only 5.8% of 25–29 year olds had completed college.   But today, 19% of all 25–29 year olds have finished college, and more than 53.3% of all high-school graduates complete one or more years of college. [5]

Some of the difficulty finding work which plagues high-school graduates now also affects the people who hold degrees from the approximately 1745 degree-granting institutions in the United States and Canada. [6]   As *The Wall Street Journal* notes, ". . . Colleges are turning out far more graduates than there are suitable jobs, especially in fields like teaching and many kinds of engineering. Thus they contend that . . . the job outlook for young college graduates may not [be] bright. . . ." [7]

College placement officials acknowledge the oversupply of degree holders and predict that many fields will soon be glutted with job seekers.   For the 12

[4] U.S., Bureau of the Census, *Current Population Reports,* Series P-23, no. 44, "Characteristics of American Youth, 1972" (Washington, D.C.:   U.S. Government Printing Office, 1972), table 18, p. 21.

[5] U.S., Bureau of the Census, *Current Population Reports,* Series P-20, no. 201, "Characteristics of Men with College Degrees" (Washington, D.C.:   U.S. Government Printing Office, 1970), table 4, p. 12; see *Yearbook of Higher Education,* 1974–1975, p. 541.

[6] (1) U.S., Department of Health, Education, and Welfare, Office of Education, *Survey of Educational Facilities,* 1971; (2) Gordon Campbell, *Community Colleges in Canada* (Toronto: Ryerson Press, 1971), p. 8; (3) Statistics Canada, *Universities and Colleges of Canada* (Ottawa: Queen's Printer, 1971), p. 3.

From these sources one gathers that in 1971 there were: 2,606 post-secondary institutions in the United States, including 931 two-year institutions and community colleges (see 1); 70 degree-granting institutions in Canada (see 3); plus 119 two year institutions and community colleges (see 2).   Thus we arrive at the figure: 2606 − 931 + 70 = 1745.

[7] *The Wall Street Journal,* January 21, 1972, p. 1.

years ending in 1980, the federal government estimates that there will be 10.5 million new entrants into the professional and working force—and only 10.4 million job openings.[8]

What do surplus college graduates do? Often they take jobs unrelated to their degrees. A U.S. Department of Labor survey of 1.1 million jobs in 1970 and 1971 showed that the work of 53.6% of the graduates wasn't directly related to their fields of study. Much depends on the graduate's field of study: 75.5% of the social-science graduates surveyed accepted positions that were not directly related to their degrees; for business students, this figure was 50.9% and for education majors, 31.4%. Most graduates taking jobs not related to their fields of study said they did so because it was the only employment they could find.[9]

It is not only an intense personal disappointment for teachers to run switchboards and chemical engineers to wait tables in restaurants, it is also a grave waste of human resources. And for many graduates, particularly those in highly technical fields, losing exposure to work in rapidly changing professions can mean obsolescence in only a few years.

Specialization

The preceding statistics may suggest that people with a broad, general education have more difficulty in finding the work they want than do people who have spe-

[8] *Ibid.*
[9] *The Wall Street Journal,* June 26, 1973, p. 1.

cialized training.   Yet many specialized graduates also have trouble finding work.   The most highly specialized degree holders—doctoral graduates—are currently experiencing the greatest difficulty in the job market.   In some cases, only one graduate in 20 can find a teaching or research job for which he or she has been trained.

Here is a rundown of the unemployment risks facing several types of degree holders:

1 Education degrees: Declining population trends have increased competition for existing jobs in education.
2 Science degrees: These depend on government budgets for research, and opportunities shift with changes in the priorities for various kinds of research.
3 Business degrees: The outlook is generally good, but finding the first job depends on the current stage of the business cycle; e.g., positions are difficult to find during a recession.
4 Home economics degrees: Here too the outlook is generally good, but this depends upon a continuing emphasis on consumer issues by business and government.

5 Engineering degrees: The outlook is good when business is prosperous, but there is the risk of training becoming outmoded by changing technology. There is also the danger of being locked into narrow jobs.
6 Liberal arts degrees: Although not a qualification for specific jobs (except in some areas of teaching), the degree indicates the holder's intellectual ability, accomplishment, and interest in learning.

This chapter has been written with the idea that each critical opportunity for career choice is unique for each person and should be treated as an event of great importance and having lasting consequences. In fact, as indicated previously in this chapter, most people have several chances in their working lives to make important career decisions. If a career or education choice that once seemed right no longer appears so, a person should reassess his or her needs and make the needed changes, if possible. Reassessing one's abilities and needs should be done periodically, perhaps every few years, to keep you continually aware of your own worth and the value of your work to you and to the community.

CAREER CHOICE AS A PATH TO A LIFESTYLE

As we indicated in the first part of this chapter, a career can help to define a personal lifestyle in three important ways:

1 A career as a *job* makes one financially independent.
2 A career as a *vocation* gives one's life meaning and importance.
3 A career as the substantial *use* of one's waking hours accentuates and increases the value of remaining leisure hours.

Contemporary American society has so many different values and encompasses such varied lifestyles that it cannot automatically teach specific values to its young. Some subcultures, such as the Amish, do offer definite values and tasks to their young people. But most Americans must seek and define their own values. Rollo May, in *Man's Search for Himself,* points out the great need for people to establish their center of values that can then serve to guide meaningful choices such as career selection, consumer spending, and use of time.

It is accepted and understood that contemporary Americans are defined by society in terms of their economic role. To drift from job to job without pattern or purpose is frowned upon and makes most people uneasy. It is both unfortunate and unnecessary that this is so, yet it is true. Accordingly, a career is viewed as a critical source of personal definition and lifestyle.

SUMMARY 1 There are five important advantages to being committed to a career:
  1 Economic satisfaction
  2 Social satisfaction

    3 A sense of accomplishment

    4 A sense of well-being

    5 The pleasure of creativity

2 One's career choice should be based on analysis of one's needs and resources.

3 Failure to choose a career or to choose the best career entails an opportunity cost. Opportunity cost is the difference between the value of the best opportunity and the one actually chosen.

4 Careers can be selected or pursued in growing industries (consumer goods, public service, medical services, waste management, and so on), rising sectors (primary: mining; secondary: manufacturing; tertiary: services), or developing regions.

5 The risk in being self-employed or in working for a small business is commercial failure or bankruptcy. Large firms are durable, but may stifle individuality.

6 Any course of study is beneficial if it is of interest to the student. But if in doubt as to what to study, practical subjects may offer employment opportunities unmatched by less directly useful subjects.

7 Incomes rise with education but the use of a time discount for future earnings reduces the apparent advantage of staying in school.

8 High-school graduation and college attendance are no longer rare attainments. Since both are common, neither offers one great assurance of employment. Many college graduates are forced to accept jobs in fields unrelated to their areas of study.

9 The broad liberal arts degree is not a credential of access to any one job or career, but a means of approaching many fields of endeavor. At the same time, specialized degrees may qualify holders for certain jobs, but they entail risks of being trapped in narrow jobs or being outmoded by changes in technology. Those with business degrees have good job prospects but may encounter trouble finding their first jobs during recessions. Jobs for science and home-economics degree holders partially depend on the government's budgets and priorities. The person with a degree in education faces declining job opportunities due to the slowing of the birth rate.

Suggestions for Further Reading

Cosgrave, Gerald P. *Career Planning: Search for a Future,* rev. ed. Toronto: University of Toronto Faculty of Education, 1973.

Goodman, Paul. *Growing Up Absurd.* New York: Random House, 1956. See especially chapter 1, ''Jobs.''

Lewis, Adele and Bobroff, Edith. *From College to Career.* Indianapolis, Indiana: Bobbs-Merrill, 1963.

May, Rollo. *Man's Search for Himself.* New York: New American Library, 1967.

Reich, Charles A. *The Greening of America.* New York: Random House, 1970.

The Consumer Workshop

1 Is a career an obstacle to self-development or a tool for achieving it? Give reasons for your answer.

2 "One can passively allow a job to become a career or actively build a career on one's needs and resources." Comment on this. Which is more likely to help achieve a desired lifestyle? Why?

3 Discuss career objectives with class members and friends. Evaluate your peers' ideas of post-school work. What are their income goals? Are they realistic? How well founded are their expressed career plans as a whole?

4 Discuss the advantages and disadvantages of working in a small enterprise versus a large one. Is it better to be one's own boss, to work with a few dozen acquaintances, or to be part of a staff of a hundred thousand persons in an industrial giant?

5 Your good friends, Sue and George, come to you just before going to college. Neither has a specific career plan or an intended study program. They want to have your views on what to study. What questions will you ask them about their values, needs, and resources? How will your advice depend on their answers?

4 CAREERS AND INCOME

> *Can you find a man who loves the occupation that provides him with a livelihood?*
>
> HONORÉ DE BALZAC

To avoid mistreatment in the labor market, you must understand how it works. To make the most of your own career potential, you must know the pitfalls of the system and what to do about them. Moving on from long-range planning and career choice, we focus in this chapter on wage and employment problems of people already in the labor market as employees or as job seekers. We study inequalities in pay, hiring, and promotion, and the solutions offered by unions, professional associations, and employment agencies. Finally, we review the sources of job information.

WAGE VARIATIONS

Two people doing the same job may be paid widely differing wages. When this occurs, there is a *wage differential*. A wage differential is thus the difference in wages between what different workers receive for identical work.

Regional Differentials

Across the United States there are significant wage differentials. A major, and traditional, differential exists between the North and the South. These regional differentials are persistent, though they have closed somewhat over the last few decades. An example of this differential is that in the mid-1960s, the average hourly earnings of workers in Southern meat packing plants were only 60% of the average hourly earnings of workers in the remainder of the United States.[1]

Why Differentials Persist

Wage differentials may persist due to surpluses of labor (that is, more people willing to work at given—and usually low—wages than there are jobs offering that wage), and differences in the extent of unionization, capital investment, and variations in the size of a given city. Unions tend to close regional wage differentials because they prefer having similar jobs pay similar wages. Large cities and urban areas produce competitive pressures for many types of labor that tend to close differentials. Finally, industries which are highly mechanized or

---

[1] Abraham Gitlow, *Labor and Manpower Economics,* 3rd ed. (Homewood, Ill.: Richard D. Irwin, 1971), p. 210.

capitalized make each worker very productive and therefore worth a substantial wage although, due to the mechanization, fewer workers may be required.

Other factors can be responsible for regional wage variations. Blacks have traditionally been paid less than whites for equal work. Therefore the high population proportion of blacks in Alabama and Mississippi reinforces their states' low rank on the income scale.

The Worker's Experience

Within any occupation there are extensive wage differentials. Two people doing exactly the same work may earn very different wages because of differences in experience or seniority, in the relative productivity of their places of employment, in their contracts or their length of employment, and so on. Many tasks can be done by both experienced and inexperienced people. The experienced worker may command an arbitrarily higher wage, as may the worker with more seniority, acquired by having worked more years on the job. Similarly, a worker in a rural poverty area usually cannot charge as much or earn as much as an equally qualified worker in, say, a wealthy suburb. Finally, as inflation pushes up the cost of living and as unions increase their wage demands to keep up with rising standards of pay, workers on older contracts may be paid less than those who are covered by more recent agreements.

Age Differentials

Age differentials are much the same as experience differentials, though they function on the assumption that the younger and older workers, often paid less than the middle-aged workers, are less productive. Young workers may lack experience and older workers may not have the stamina needed for certain kinds of work, but, in general, age discrimination is as arbitrary as religious, racial, and sex discrimination.

Current Trends

Today occupational wage differentials are narrowing due to five factors:

1 Union pressure
2 Restrictive immigration policies
3 Antidiscrimination laws
4 Job upgrading through mechanization
5 Minimum wage legislation

We discussed earlier the unions' desire to have their members earn equal wages for equal work. American immigration laws have been restrictive since the 1920s, preventing the accumulation of a large pool of surplus labor that could take very low-paying jobs. Federal and state laws improving the job and pay prospects of minority members and women have closed some differentials. And mechanization, like immigration policy, has eliminated low-wage, unskilled jobs in many industries and firms. Finally, by eliminating the lowest wages on the scale, minimum wage legislation has, by definition, raised the average.

"Of course we're an equal opportunity employer. Our Mr. Frisch is Catholic, Mr. Stamos is Greek, Mr. Mendez is Chicano, Mr. Green is Jewish, Mr. Ardwam is Protestant, Mr. Davis is Black, Mr. Kwan is Chinese . . ."

WOMEN IN THE LABOR FORCE

In 1972 women comprised $\frac{3}{8}$ of the total U.S. civilian labor force.[2] By tradition and current practice, women are paid less than men for equal work. Women tend to enter the labor force at a lower rate than men, and, in general, they tend to remain in any one career or job for a shorter time. A Bureau of Labor Statistics report found that continuous employment averaged 2.8 years for women and 5.2 years for men.[3]

Do Women Have an Equal Chance?

Let's examine some figures[4] that show the inequality accorded women in the labor force:

Though women constitute 50.5% of high school graduates, only 41% of all women high-school graduates enter college, as compared to 59% of all men high-school graduates.

[2] U.S., Department of Labor, Bureau of Labor Statistics, *Handbook of Labor Statistics,* Bulletin 1790, 1973, table 1, pp. 27—28.

[3] U.S., Department of Labor, Bureau of Labor Statistics, *Job Tenure of Workers,* Special Labor Force Report 77, January 1966.

[4] U.S., Department of Labor, Women's Bureau, *Underutilization of Women Workers,* 1971.

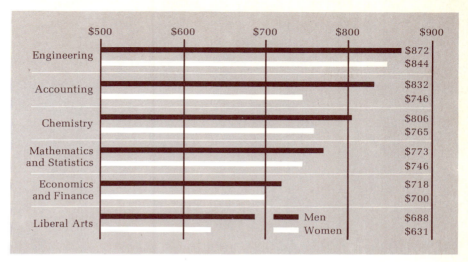

	$500	$600	$700	$800	$900
Engineering					$872 / $844
Accounting					$832 / $746
Chemistry					$806 / $765
Mathematics and Statistics					$773 / $746
Economics and Finance					$718 / $700
Liberal Arts			Men / Women		$688 / $631

**4-1   Starting Salaries of College Graduates Are Lower for
Women than for Men**

In American elementary education, 85% of the teachers are women, yet only
21% of the principals are women.   In high schools, the percentage of female
principals is only 3%.

The average annual income of a college-educated woman in the United
States is about $5000 less than that of a similarly educated man.   (See Figure
4-1.)   If she has a high-school education, she will make about $4000 less each
year than a man with the same certification.

**Women
in Society**
Part of the problem of women's disadvantaged position in the job market arises
from misunderstandings of woman's place in society.   From prehistoric times to
the twentieth century women were central and important in the home and the
economy.   When people lived in smaller settlements and the home was a farm
or workplace, a woman participated fully in the family's productive work and
reared, usually, a large number of children.   Society did not provide many alternate entertainments or occupations and women were not left out of the main-
stream of social and commercial life.

By the beginning of the twentieth century home had become a less important and central place in a family's life.   The husband and older children could
work far from home.   Factory or office work provided acquaintances the wife
usually could not share.   Compulsory education gave children activities outside
the home.   Freed from the many burdens of both helping produce family income and constantly watching her offspring, the wife was left with much free
time, including empty hours.   Unfortunately, the economy has not yet met the
opportunity and challenge of utilizing the skills and potential productivity of the
"underemployed" woman.

"Not bad, for a woman."

Overcoming Discrimination

Sex discrimination in the workplace, although illegal by federal law, remains widespread. Employers usually feel that most women who desire jobs are not earnestly pursuing full-time careers. The result is that, in order to get jobs that customarily go to men, a woman must show greater commitment than a man in her job interviews and her job record must show greater job stability.

Women and the Law

Since the early 1960s, much legislation has been passed to improve the job-finding and income-earning possibilities for women. While there is some evidence to suggest that the position of women in the job market may have actually gotten worse,[5] there have been important and historic settlements on behalf of women in antidiscrimination cases. For example, the American Telephone and Telegraph Company has agreed recently to pay its female employees over 40 million dollars for past job and pay inequities.

A woman who feels she has been unfairly interviewed or paid by an employer can appeal to the U.S. Equal Employment Opportunity Commission or the U.S. Department of Labor, Wage and Hour Division, to obtain relief under the U.S. Equal Pay Act of 1963 and Title VII of the Civil Rights Act of 1964. No woman should be reluctant to use legal means; before taking any important legal action, it is of course wise to consult an attorney either privately or through a campus or community legal assistance service.

[5] *Ibid.,* pp. iv, v.

YOUNG WORKERS IN THE LABOR FORCE

Young people between the ages of 16 and 19 suffer from a rate of unemployment three times higher than that of workers over the age of 20.[6] The rate of unemployment is higher among teenagers than among adults because the proportion of young job hunters is higher. Furthermore, teenagers' youth, limited education, life and work experience, usually bar them from jobs that require extensive prework training, the exercise of authority, or great responsibility.

Since employers tend to assume functional deficiencies among teenage job applicants, young people can obtain employment in many cases only by doing uninteresting, routine, or underpaid work. Employers hesitate to train teenage workers for career positions because they expect them to quit within a few weeks to several months. For young men and women who drop out of high school, the outlook for jobs is especially bleak: Employers don't expect them to hold jobs for lengthy periods and thus offer dull, futureless, underpaid work. It is a vicious circle: *Any* group would tend to leave such jobs; and having demonstrated their tendency to abandon these jobs, young people are barred from better work.

Self-help for the Teenage Job Seeker

In view of the rather difficult situation young job seekers face in pursuing part-time, temporary, or permanent, full-time jobs, let us suggest ways of improving the chances of finding work. The young job seeker should seek to distinguish him- or herself from the mass of young people looking for work. The young person should, in interviews, emphasize stability and willingness to remain at work; he or she should show maturity and seriousness.

The young person in the labor market must allow for the strong chance of being expected to accept lower wages than an adult for equal work. This will persist until the young person can convince the employer that he or she is a reliable and equally able worker. To get even these jobs, the young worker must explore job information sources much more thoroughly than his friends might and more thoroughly, in fact, than most workers in such lower wage jobs usually do.

Job and Work Information

Most young people tend to rely on informal sources to find jobs, mainly family and friends.[7] Next, young workers usually rely on job leads obtained through schools (dropouts of course haven't this source). State and private job referral agencies, such as government unemployment offices and employment agencies, are those least used for job-finding information. It appears that the only group

[6] *Handbook of Labor Statistics,* 1973, table 62.

[7] Edward Kalachek, *The Youth Labor Market,* Policy Papers in Human Resources and Industrial Relations, no. 12; Institute of Labor and Industrial Relations (Detroit and Ann Arbor, Mich.: National Manpower Policy Task Force, 1969).

which does use government or organized channels is white collar workers with some job experience, i.e., adults over 19 years of age. Family and friends are often excellent sources of job information. But they should not be a young person's only source.

UNIONS AND PROFESSIONAL ASSOCIATIONS

Unions and professional associations are charged with representing the economic interests of their members. For the various services they perform, unions and associations charge membership fees or dues ranging from a few dollars to several thousand dollars a year. In 1970, union members in the United States numbered 20,689,000, or 23% of the labor force.[8]

Unions and the Workplace

When employees of a given firm vote to be represented by a union, their decision usually is binding on all employees in a specialized department or in the plant as a whole. This means there is now a *union shop* in which all workers employed before the election or hired after the election are required to join the union within a month or two after the vote or after their initial hiring in the case of new workers. A union may require that all job applicants join the union *before* being hired. This illegal form of union membership recruitment and labor market control is known as the *closed shop*. In other situations an employee may not be required to join a union but will have to pay membership dues anyway. This arrangement is known as the *compulsory checkoff* or *agency shop*, meaning that everyone pays union dues, though not everyone must be a union member.

Professional Associations

Some professional associations are only vehicles for public relations, occasional parties, or giving status to people in a given trade. Many professional associations exist principally to publish the news of the profession or a journal by or of interest to association members. Academic associations are an example of the latter. Professional associations for dentists, accountants, and physicians do more; they issue or approve credentials for work in their fields. Often courts, hospitals, schools, and businesses will hire only persons certified by the trade's professional association.

The Benefits of Membership

The benefits that unions and professional associations provide their members vary. In general, unions make a strong effort to raise the wages of their members through periodic collective bargaining discussions and agreements

---

[8] *Handbook of Labor Statistics,* 1973, table 153, p. 345.

with management.   Unions also seek to provide health, insurance, and pension coverage in union contracts.   Other areas of interest to the unions include paid vacations and holidays, shorter hours, seniority benefits in promotion, grievance procedures, retention of workers during recessions, and improvement of working conditions.

In recent years, nonwage benefits such as those listed above have increased much more than have direct wages.   The cost of these nonwage benefits is significant.   In 1940, for example, only about 2 million union members, about 25% of the total union membership, were given annual vacations with pay; and it was rare for these workers to have more than one week of paid vacation.   By 1960, 91% of all workers covered by major contracts (those covering more than 1000 workers) were eligible for vacations with pay; 84% of the major agreements allowed workers to receive three weeks of paid vacation annually.[9]

To Join or not to Join

Should one join a union or professional group?   Often you have no choice if you wish to work in a certain trade or firm.   This is true for physicians and local medical societies, attorneys and their bar groups, and workers in unionized plants and firms.   But many professional groups are, as previously noted, voluntary in membership.   This makes it possible to bypass easily those groups that provide benefits only for members who go to conventions or who want to play pecking-order status games at the conventions.

An example of a voluntary (noncompulsory) group is the American Association of University Professors (AAUP).   It holds annual meetings, regional workshops, publishes several scholarly magazines, and occasionally issues comparisons of university salary scales.   The AAUP assists members who claim to have been wrongly dismissed, but the AAUP does this mainly for those who can show some ideological or otherwise politically acceptable reason (by AAUP standards) for dismissal.   If a college teacher is fired because of his or her unusual political views, the AAUP may take an interest in the case.   If the firing took place because of antagonism with faculty peers, the AAUP will probably do little.   In contrast, most unions would defend a member fired because of friction with the boss.

Union membership may have distinct disadvantages.   Some union workers in skilled trades are entitled to high wages negotiated by their unions.   Plumbers, carpenters, and electricians, for example, are hired from union lists for government construction contracts for which the law requires union men and women to have hiring preference.   Yet the wages of union workers may be too high for ordinary private work.   Nonunion personnel may thus, in effect, have a greater chance of getting lower paying but more abundant jobs.   Unions can freeze the promotion system in plants and firms where negotiated seniority systems prevail.   And in industries such as ship-loading and the construction trades, where contractors leave the chore of assigning workers to jobs to union

[9] Allan M. Cartter and F. Ray Marshall, *Labor Economics* (Homewood, Ill.:   Richard D. Irwin, 1967), pp. 336–46.

hiring halls, the work rights of members may be impaired by unfair or corrupt practices. Yet for most workers union membership has been beneficial, resulting in higher pay and greater fringe benefits.

JOB-FINDING ASSISTANCE: EMPLOYMENT AGENCIES

Employment agencies began during the Great Depression in the 1930s. Before the Depression, people seeking jobs used the traditional means of checking newspaper ads, visiting factory personnel offices, and asking friends about job openings. After 1930, when jobs became very hard to find, some unemployed workers and businessmen thought they could make money and perhaps help people by creating agencies to gather information about job openings and directing that knowledge to people looking for jobs.

The job market was not well-organized in the 1930s and is not now. Labor market communications still need to be improved. At times businesses are unable to find specialized personnel, yet there are poor performance records for the employment agencies, and especially those in which the potential employee agrees to pay a substantial portion (15–50%) of the first year's wages to the agency for placement.

Types of Agencies

There are five different kinds of employment agencies:

1 Agencies whose fees are paid by the employer
2 Agencies whose fees are paid by the employee
3 Specialized executive recruiters, often called "headhunters"
4 Employment counseling firms that prepare but do not place clients
5 Recruitment units of vocational schools and training courses

The Employer-paid Agency

A firm that does not have the time, staff, or the wish to handle its own staffing needs may engage an employment agency to secure its personnel. The firm pays for this work and the people interviewed or hired are not charged for it. Visiting such agencies is useful, for they can take information from firms, advise on whether placement is likely, and perhaps discuss alternate employment opportunities.

The Employee-paid Agency

The most common type of employment agency charges the people it places a fee for the service. While these firms may have no direct dealings with employers, they do offer some expertise and ideas in finding jobs suitable to their applicants' abilities and requirements. For job seekers, the question is whether fee-charging agencies should be used at all. State employment services offer the same kind of service but do not charge for it.

Headhunters   The executive recruitment specialty firm, often called a *headhunter,* is a special kind of employment agency recently developed.   These firms collect lists of experienced and highly trained people in various fields.   When a headhunter receives a request from a firm for, say, a packaging engineer with 10 years experience in paper chemistry, it contacts the men or women in industry who may be able to fill the job.   The headhunter may advertise in specialized journals or get in touch with universities.   In some cases, the desired candidate must be persuaded to quit his or her present job.   For all this effort the headhunters are handsomely paid, often into the thousands of dollars.   For recruiting at very high levels, for example, for a corporation president, a firm may pay the headhunter a fee of up to $50,000.   For the most part, headhunters aren't interested in inexperienced workers, even the recent graduates of colleges and universities.

Employment Counselors   Employment counselors coach and prepare clients for placement.   They may be paid by a firm trying to cushion the dismissal of its personnel.   Employment counselors can be of use but fees are charged for the assistance.   Commonly these firms charge from a few hundred to a few thousand dollars.   Recently it was reported that a man paid $50,000 before finding a satisfactory job.

Vocational Schools and Training Courses   Private, profitmaking vocational schools and training courses often advertise that they are able to place their graduates in high-paying positions for which the training they sell qualifies them.   These schools range from establishments advertised on the back of matchbook covers to large institutions operated by important American businesses. But Federal Trade Commission studies have shown that trade schools often are not dependable placement agencies and that most of such advertisements promising employment are deceptive. The studies indicate that private vocational training schools are, in many cases, able to place only a small fraction of the students who are "enticed" into enrolling by the promises of placement.[10]

Similar in ethical approach are some job placement services. In this category one finds "management-training positions" that are really low-wage, futureless jobs. When offered to teenagers by, say, fast-food chains and data processing firms, these positions often turn out to be nothing more than dishwashing and key-punching. The people hired are not expected to stay with the firm long enough to be eligible for promotion. Recently the Federal Trade Commission issued complaints against certain encyclopedia publishers for, among other things, advertising administration, marketing, and public relations jobs that were, in fact, simply the door-to-door selling of encyclopedias.

SOURCES OF JOB INFORMATION

The information available indicates that most people in search of new employment use very casual methods in their search for jobs. Especially among blue collar workers, the most common techniques used are knocking on doors within a dozen blocks of home, checking with friends, and looking through newspaper want ads. While these methods are hardly thorough techniques for investigating the labor market, they may work. Indeed, statistics indicate that a large proportion of jobs are located through direct application to employers and through information received from friends.

Finding a job is ideally, as we found in the last chapter, a matter of applying an understanding of yourself to the needs of the labor market. There is no substitute for understanding your own special skills, desires, ambitions, and plans. The ideal job search combines such self-understanding with a broad knowledge of the types of work and wages and salaries available.

Overviews of fields of work, income ranges, manpower needs, and entry qualifications are available in government publications. The U.S. Department of Labor, Bureau of Labor Statistics, annually revises the *Occupational Outlook Handbook* (Bulletin 1785). While this publication does not list specific job openings, it does provide a valuable analysis of job prospects and salary potentials.

Excellent job reference manuals are available for the college or university student. Each year the College Placement Council, Inc., publishes a 500-page

---

[10] Federal Trade Commission, *News Summary*, no. 6, 1973.

2 You have begun to work as a senior engineer for Blanktron Systems, Inc. You receive a letter from the union suggesting you join. What questions should you ask of fellow employees, the union representative, and the company?

3 "Teenagers have more trouble than anyone else getting jobs." Is this true or false? Defend your answer and comment on the ways in which antiteenager prejudice by employers can be overcome.

4 "A woman is never very secure in her job. The boss expects her to quit and uses her accordingly." Comment on this with respect to: different pay scales for women and for men; the chances of promotion for women compared to those for men; and the preference of some women to have a work schedule that fits into their responsibilities at home.

5 It is unjust that workers receive very different pay for the same work. Have you personally encountered a wage differential? Why do you think differentials persist in your area? What can be done to eliminate them?

5 BUDGETING: GIVING EXPRESSION TO LIFESTYLES

 Where I was brought up we never talked about money because there was never enough to furnish a topic of conversation.

MARK TWAIN

In this chapter, we develop a broad financial planning method that is useful for an individual or a family by:

1 Evaluating family spending
2 Constructing a method for the management of future spending
3 Examining spending plans in light of changing family needs and inflation

BUDGETS

A *budget* is a financial plan for matching future spending to future income. It may be a detailed schedule for every item a family wishes to purchase, or it may be a brief listing with categories of major income uses such as housing, food, clothing, travel, and savings. It can cover various periods of days, weeks, months, or years. Since daily budgeting is repetitious and time-consuming and lengthy five-year plans are insufficiently detailed for frequent use, we shall concentrate on the monthly budget. This budget is, of course, readily convertible by simple division and multiplication to weekly and yearly budgets.

Five Reasons for Budgeting

There are five principal reasons why an individual or family can benefit from designing and following a budget:

1 To plan for and implement a lifestyle
2 To live better in the present as well as in the future
3 To control expenditures
4 To maintain good financial records
5 To control debts

Planning for and Implementing a Lifestyle. If a family spends haphazardly, disbursing funds to meet needs which may be frivolous or unimportant, it may wind up with a lower standard of living than if it had a plan to spend for the things it considers useful and important. A financial plan is such a tool.

Living Better in the Present and the Future. Building a financial plan forces a family to evaluate its needs in terms of objectives. Planning sessions enable the family to consider the value of putting money to alternate uses. Is a given hundred dollars better spent on home repairs or new tennis rackets? Is ten dollars better spent on movies or put in the clothing budget? Questions such as these can only be answered in periodic budget planning and review.

Expenditure Control. Most people spend at least some money foolishly or on things which are not really important to them. The contents of the storage closets of most homes give ample evidence of thoughtless spending. A budget that is followed may help to eliminate such needless or foolish expenditures.

Record Keeping. Implementation of a financial plan will almost invariably call for record keeping. When a family budgets, it has to establish spending categories, examine past records, and generally organize its affairs. A budget can be the basis for managing and thus minimizing taxes. And tax savings are a means of getting more spending power out of current income.

Debt Control. Interest charges of up to 36% on consumer purchases seriously reduce the amount of money a person or family can spend on actual goods. If a family has more cash on hand, it can avoid paying high interest charges. Thus money can go further if its spending is wisely planned in advance.

THE CASH FLOW ACCOUNT

The construction of individual and family budgets should begin with an examination of personal and family *spending patterns.* This can be done by analyzing past income tax returns or other financial records (receipts, canceled checks, charge account and credit card statements), or by comparing one's own financial matters with typical family budgets available in various government home-economics and labor studies. It may be useful for the family as a whole to discuss spending patterns or to ask each person to make a list of past and current types and amounts of spending.

Then it is essential to make a list of the family's *income sources,* a tally of wages, salaries, payments in kind (services and goods provided by friends and neighbors, compensation in useful or saleable goods), profits, rents, and interest. Sometimes income sources are subject to uncertainty. For example, farm incomes are based on commodity prices subject to wide fluctuations. (See Figure 5-1.)

These two budget schedules—expenditures and income—together comprise the current *cash flow account* for a family or household. If more income is earned than is spent, it is carried forward into the next month's schedule. Deficits of spending in excess of income are also carried forward and applied to the next month's schedule. (Deficits should be paid from the planned cash reserve,

Source	Last Year	Estimate This Year	Actual This Year
Gross salary or wages			
Bonuses and commissions			
Dividends and interest			
Family Allowance			
Private Business			
Rentals and other			
Total			
Divide by 12 for Gross Monthly Income			
Less income tax and other salary deductions			
Monthly Take-Home Pay			

5-1   Total Income Chart

for it is better to borrow from one's savings than to take out a loan at a bank or finance company.)   Cash flow budgets do have some shortcomings.   If income or expenditures are lagged (for example, purchases are put on charge accounts), the current cash flow will not accurately reflect the family's earning and spending balance.

THE BUDGET PLAN

To ensure that the family does not lose track of *receivables* (income not yet received) and *payables* (bills due but not yet paid), it should construct a *budget plan*.   To do this, the family must actively decide how much money each category of budget expenditure will require and construct a ledger system to show whether spending in the category is above or below the amount allowed in a given month.   When a category is underspent in one month, a surplus can be carried forward within the category to the next period.   If a category is overspent in one month, two adjustments must be made: (1) another category should be debited in the current period to cover the overspending; and (2) the currently overspent category should be underspent in the next period and the saving used to restore the category which was debited in a previous period to cover the initial overspending.   When actual expenditures are in sum less than planned expenditures, the difference can be added to the *cash reserve*.   Needless to say, surplus funds that are in the cash reserve should be held in interest-earning accounts.   A sample monthly budget appears in Figure 5-2.

MONTH & YEAR _____

	Estimated	Actual
Food		
(Household and dining out)		
Total		
Housing		
Rent or mortgage payments		
Household taxes and insurance ($\frac{1}{12}$th)		
Fuel, light, water		
Household operation (telephone, supplies, laundry, baby sitters, etc.)		
Appliances ($\frac{1}{12}$th)		
Furniture ($\frac{1}{12}$th)		
Total		
Clothing		
Clothes and sewing materials for all the family		
Major items ($\frac{1}{12}$th)		
Total		
Transportation		
Car fare		
Gas, oil		
Parking		
Car payments		
Maintenance ($\frac{1}{12}$th)		
License, insurance ($\frac{1}{12}$th)		
Total		
Recreation/Education		
Membership fees		
Holidays ($\frac{1}{12}$th)		
Entertainment (subscriptions $\frac{1}{12}$th, sports, hobbies, tickets, books, personal allowances)		
Education ($\frac{1}{12}$th of school fees, books, lessons)		
Total		
Welfare and Miscellaneous		
Medical ($\frac{1}{12}$th of dentist, drugs, others)		
Contributions and gifts ($\frac{1}{12}$th of church, Christmas and occasional gifts)		
Total		
Savings Cash Reserve		
Pension, annuities ($\frac{1}{12}$th)		
Life and health insurance ($\frac{1}{12}$th)		
Loan repayments (including mortgage)		
Savings bonds and investments		
Bank savings ($\frac{1}{12}$th)		
Total		

Monthly Total _____
Take-Home Pay _____
Over Budget _____ Under Budget _____

5-2   Monthly Budget

[U.S. urban average costs = 100]

Area	Total Budget	Total Consumption	Food		Housing			Transportation[5]		Clothing	Personal Care	Medical Care[6]	Other Family Consumption[7]	Personal Income Taxes
			Total	Food at Home	Total[2]	Renter Costs[3]	Homeowner Costs[4]	Total	Automobile Owners					
Urban United States	100	100	100	100	100	100	100	100	100	100	100	100	100	100
Metropolitan areas[8]	102	102	101	100	103	103	104	101	102	102	102	103	104	104
Nonmetropolitan areas[9]	90	90	95	98	86	85	80	98	93	92	93	84	83	83
Northeast:														
Boston, Mass	118	115	108	110	139	119	154	103	116	100	103	98	110	146
Buffalo, N.Y.	105	104	104	104	106	105	107	108	103	109	99	89	105	111
Hartford, Conn	109	112	109	108	116	117	120	115	109	108	127	99	114	95
Lancaster, Pa.	98	97	103	104	89	96	86	98	94	105	94	87	98	106
New York-Northeastern, N.J.	114	113	114	110	125	115	134	94	106	100	102	109	113	132
Philadelphia, Pa.-N.J.	103	101	108	107	96	88	96	95	107	98	99	102	106	119
Pittsburgh, Pa.	97	97	103	102	88	83	86	98	96	100	102	87	103	102
Portland, Maine	101	102	106	108	101	101	98	104	99	97	95	94	108	91
Nonmetropolitan areas[9]	98	98	101	105	101	90	104	100	95	91	88	90	87	95
North Central:														
Cedar Rapids, Iowa	100	98	92	92	101	100	104	102	98	108	102	90	100	111
Champaign-Urbana, Ill.	103	103	99	101	107	129	105	101	96	115	100	101	98	99
Chicago, Ill.-Northwestern, Ind.	105	106	102	103	110	114	113	105	118	104	107	105	106	103
Cincinnati, Ohio-Ky.-Ind.	96	97	98	98	93	82	95	103	98	100	95	88	100	92
Cleveland, Ohio	101	103	97	96	108	88	115	102	101	101	116	100	105	96
Dayton, Ohio	93	94	97	99	86	88	82	97	92	97	95	89	103	84
Detroit, Mich.	101	101	103	103	97	94	99	100	99	101	110	104	102	107
Green Bay, Wis.	99	96	92	93	100	93	99	98	94	107	100	86	96	119
Indianapolis, Ind.	101	102	98	98	104	99	108	111	106	100	95	101	106	96
Kansas City, Mo.-Kans.	99	99	99	100	93	93	90	108	103	107	110	98	101	96
Milwaukee, Wis.	105	101	93	93	112	102	119	101	96	103	100	94	102	129
Minneapolis-St. Paul, Minn.	103	98	96	97	96	100	95	101	97	105	105	94	104	137
St. Louis, Mo.-Ill.	98	99	102	101	94	86	93	108	107	98	99	91	99	95
Wichita, Kans.	94	95	94	95	91	91	89	101	96	98	98	98	100	86
Nonmetropolitan areas[9]	93	93	94	98	92	97	88	98	94	96	96	83	85	93

Cost of Family Consumption

South:														
Atlanta, Ga.	93	94	97	97	83	86	76	99	95	97	103	96	104	82
Austin, Tex.	87	89	91	91	75	76	67	99	94	101	99	93	101	65
Baltimore, Md.	99	96	97	95	87	112	74	99	99	103	105	110	102	117
Baton Rouge, La.	90	92	99	99	80	76	76	99	94	90	101	88	100	75
Dallas, Tex.	90	93	91	88	84	88	79	100	96	95	103	115	100	70
Durham, N.C.	96	95	95	96	90	102	83	96	92	94	101	107	101	101
Houston, Tex.	90	92	96	94	79	78	72	100	95	96	102	106	99	69
Nashville, Tenn.	92	95	93	95	89	85	85	100	95	111	94	87	104	73
Orlando, Fla.	90	92	91	90	87	106	79	95	91	93	92	105	103	70
Washington, D.C.-Md.-Va.	103	102	104	104	102	108	101	103	102	104	98	101	104	115
Nonmetropolitan areas[9]	85	86	93	96	77	78	67	97	92	89	91	80	82	72
West:														
Bakersfield, Calif.	93	94	94	94	87	90	83	100	95	97	101	111	95	79
Denver, Colo.	96	96	94	94	90	88	86	99	94	116	96	96	98	94
Los Angeles-Long Beach, Calif.	99	100	94	92	101	106	101	102	102	102	98	123	97	87
San Diego, Calif.	97	98	91	90	97	98	99	104	99	104	97	117	96	83
San Francisco-Oakland, Calif.	106	107	98	97	115	144	112	106	106	109	114	113	103	98
Seattle-Everett, Wash.	100	103	100	99	105	104	106	102	98	108	103	106	101	83
Honolulu, Hawaii	118	115	113	114	128	144	129	115	110	100	109	105	105	151
Nonmetropolitan areas[9]	90	90	90	94	84	83	79	96	91	100	100	91	81	86
Anchorage, Alaska	131	129	112	117	156	198	155	122	116	118	133	154	95	160

[1] The family consists of an employed husband, age 38, a wife not employed outside the home, an 8-year-old girl, and a 13-year-old boy.

[2] Housing includes shelter, housefurnishings and household operations.

[3] Renter costs include average contract rent plus the cost of required amounts of heating fuel, gas, electricity, water, specified equipment, and insurance on household contents.

[4] The average costs of automobile owners and nonowners were weighted by the following proportions of families: Boston, Chicago, New York, Philadelphia, 50% for both automobile owners and nonowners; 65% for automobile owners, 35% for nonowners; all other metropolitan areas, nonmetropolitan areas, 100% for automobile owners.

[5] In total medical care, the average costs of medical insurance were weighted by the following proportions: 30% for families paying full cost of insurance; 26% for families paying half cost; 44% for families covered by noncontributory insurance plans (paid by employer).

[6] Includes average costs for reading, recreation, tobacco products, alcoholic beverages, education and miscellaneous expenditures.

[7] As defined in 1960–1961. For a detailed description of current and previous geographical boundaries, see the 1967 edition of **Standard Metropolitan Statistical Areas,** prepared by the Office of Management and Budget.

[8] Places with population of 2500–50,000.

[9] Places with population of less than 2500.

Source: U.S. Department of Labor, Bureau of Labor Statistics, *Monthly Labor Review* **47** (August 1974), p. 60.

5-3 Indexes of Comparative Costs Based on an Intermediate Budget for a 4-person Family,[1] Autumn 1973

BUDGET ANALYSIS

It is important to make periodic budget analyses. At intervals of three or four months one should examine the current budget to see if income and expenditures are fairly evenly matched. If income is greater than expenditures and planned savings, the family may be oversaving. Thus the family will exceed its *planned* savings and fail to manage all the expenditure objectives in its budget plan. If expenditures and planned savings greatly exceed income, the family could be already reducing its future spending power.

It may be helpful for a family to compare its budget with the budgets of typical one- to four-member families. Such budgets are available from the U.S. Department of Labor (see Figure 5-3). These indicate statistical averages representing families and households at various levels of low, middle, and upper income. These may indicate that one's family is greatly overspending in one area, but the purpose of the standard budgets is to be only a point of comparison. There is no need to conform to them. Indeed, the family whose budget conforms to the statistically average budget is truly unusual. Some families may require special purpose budgets to achieve early retirement, to pay for large past debts, or to build a reserve in case of recession or unemployment. No standard budget could possibly take into account the special needs of any one family.

Yet such budgets have their uses. There are several essential questions which can be asked of any budget in order to judge its suitability and efficiency in meeting family goals. How well does the budget balance present and future needs and take care of past debts? Are reserves adequate for emergencies or predictable risks such as unemployment? Have all important family requirements and goals been satisfied? Do some priorities need to be revised? Does the plan allow for flexibility for changes in family goals and future needs?

INFLATION

The ever-present problem of inflation is a compelling reason to reexamine budgets every few months. During 1974 and 1975 the rate of inflation in the United States averaged about 10% per year. A budget that sets total expenditures 10% lower than they actually are or that provides only 90% of the food a family needs isn't accurate or very helpful. Some incomes rise with inflation; typically, these are earnings that are continuously renegotiated or that rise via escalator contract clauses stipulating that paychecks go up with cost-of-living indexes. But many incomes do not rise with inflation and may even fall as inflation accelerates. Inflation is most damaging to people receiving fixed interest from past investments, profits from businesses hurt by inflation, or pensions.

Inflation in the later 1970s is not likely to be reduced to the levels of the 1960s, that is, to the comparatively comfortable range of 4–6% per year. It is likely that prices will continue to rise at rates of 7–12%. Even severe recession will not fully stop inflation. For any budget it is necessary at proper levels to add inflation markups to spending plans.

The bread which costs 59¢ a loaf today may be 79¢ in six months. The grocery bill which comes to $60 a week today may be $75 in six months. Such facts must be taken into account in budget projections. If one's income doesn't rise with the price level—and most don't—then it is necessary to be increasingly careful about how money is spent. For most Americans the purchasing power of their incomes declined by an average of 5% between February 1975 and January 1976. Stretching budgets by wearing clothes longer, buying fewer convenience foods and doing more cooking, stocking up at sales, delaying replacement of appliances, taking less expensive vacations closer to home, and eventually buying a more economical car—these are the things most of us have to do to cope with inflation.

SUMMARY

1 A budget is a financial plan for matching future spending to future income.
2 There are five reasons for budgeting:
    1 To plan for a lifestyle
    2 To live better in the present as well as in the future
    3 To control expenditures
    4 To maintain good financial records
    5 To control debts
3 Budgeting begins with the cash flow account, composed of two schedules, spending patterns and income sources.
4 The budget differs from the cash flow account in that
    1 The budget is an active plan, not a passive record
    2 The budget shows accounts payable, not simply cash outlays
5 Budgets should be analyzed periodically to see if they:
    1 Meet family needs, especially as these needs change during the family life cycle
    2 Are in balance
    3 Take into account changing money values (inflation)

Suggestions for Further Reading

Phillips, E. Bryant, and Lane, Sylvia. *Personal Finance,* 3rd ed. New York: Wiley, 1974.

U.S. Department of Agriculture, *Helping Families Manage Their Finances,* Home Economics Research Report, no. 21, June 1968.

_____, *A Guide to Budgeting for the Family,* Home and Garden Bulletin, no. 108, April 1972.

_____, *A Guide to Budgeting for the Young Couple,* Home and Garden Bulletin, no. 98, February 1973.
Moneyviews. New York: Bankers Trust Company, monthly.

The Consumer Workshop

1 Not every person has a single steady income. Some people have incomes composed of variable profits, stock dividends, and seasonal wages. What changes would you recommend in constructing a new monthly budget for a family accustomed to operating with a cash reserve of $400 out of a total after-tax income of $20,000?
2 The figure below is an average spending pattern for a family of four with take-home monthly pay of $400 to $800. Examine it closely and indicate how it can be changed for the following situations:
    1 A family living on a small farm and eating some of its own produce
    2 A couple without children living in the center of a large city and having no car (NOTE: Here transportation may be less than 12–16%; which categories may be higher?)
    3 A college student (Are the chart's percentages appropriate for housing, food, and education?)
    4 A retired couple that travels a good deal
3 Current budget accounts have a built-in bias: They tend to be accurate only for recurring, not one-time expenses. It is helpful for a family to have a financial plan to deal with expensive emergencies. Make a list of such problems; for example, house repairs for storm-caused damage.

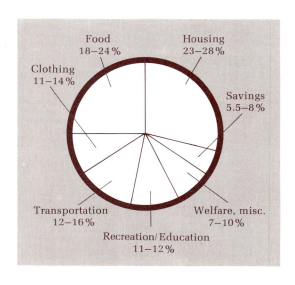

DISCOVERY NOTE: Although it is impossible to budget for *every* rare and expensive contingency, it is useful to know your *risk exposure*. Assume that you live in an area that is vulnerable to earthquakes (see *Scientific American,* May 1975, p. 14). Because quake damage insurance is expensive or impossible to buy for your home, you should develop a hefty contingency fund. Estimate your own risk exposure or the risk exposure of any sample household situation. Devise suitable reserves for each situation.

6 TAXES:
A SLICE OFF THE TOP

> **Taxation, according to its magnitude and the mode in which it is imposed, either makes men industrious, enterprising, and wealthy, or indolent, dispirited, and impoverished.**
>
> J. R. M'CULLOCH*
> (1789–1864)

Income tax returns appear complex and intimidating, but they can be handled with relative ease and to financial advantage if taxpayers understand the law and the tax forms in advance of filing. In this chapter, we present a broad overview of the basic income tax form, U.S. Individual Income Tax Return, Form 1040. We examine filing requirements, income definitions, deductions, and exemptions, and move on to a discussion of tax calculations and tax credits. Special reporting procedures are used for capital gains, income averaging, and foreign incomes and taxes, so each of these are discussed in detail. Many taxpayers prefer to employ others to help in preparing their returns and we examine the quality and usefulness of several kinds of tax preparation assistance. Finally, we cover two critical areas: the effect of income taxes on work incentives and the tax reform proposals currently being debated.

THE FEDERAL INCOME TAX

The Federal Income Tax for individuals is the most important tax in the United States for nearly all income earners. The body of laws and amendments comprising this tax, known as the Internal Revenue Code, is extraordinarily complicated, due to three major factors. First, the sources of income are themselves complex. Some people receive simple wages, others commissions which must or will cover some business costs; still others—farmers, for example—receive widely different incomes from year to year. Second, Congress has given some businesses and activities preferential tax treatment in the hope that they will ultimately produce more. The best example is the special accounting for oil and gas producers, the "oil depletion allowance," which increases the profitmaking powers of these firms and allows them to attract capital more easily. Third, many special interest groups have managed to acquire for themselves, through Congress and the Internal Revenue Service, special treatment on their tax returns.

---

* Quoted in C. Northcote Parkinson, *The Law of the Profits* (Boston: Houghton Mifflin, 1960), p. 87.

"That's the way it goes: Your peak earning years—our peak taking years."

Tax Rates Are Progressive

The most significant characteristic of the income tax is that its rate schedules are progressive. The more one makes, the higher the tax rates one must pay. For example, a single taxpayer with $10,000 of taxable income must pay $2090 in federal taxes. If one earns another $2000 (making it $12,000 in taxable income), one must pay 27% on the additional income. Should one earn another $2000 beyond that ($14,000 taxable income), 29% is due on *that* extra income. Income tax rates continue to rise to a maximum of 70% for taxable incomes exceeding $100,000 for single taxpayers and $200,000 for married taxpayers. The progressive tax rate structure does not work out in practice, however; middle income families wind up paying the highest of the income tax rates actually paid. Upper income taxpayers often have sources of income that are eligible for special tax treatment and are able to use the best tax experts, who very ably and legally cut their clients' tax bills. (Such expert tax advice, one should be aware, is rarely to be found in storefront tax preparation services that spring to life at tax time.)

The Tax Return

Citizens and residents of the United States are required to file the Federal Individual Income Tax Return, Form 1040, and its associated forms (usually called *schedules*) if they belong to these categories:

Taxpayer Status	Gross Income Above
Single, unmarried head of household, or surviving spouse with dependent child and under 65	$2350
Married, filing a joint return	$3400
Married, filing separate returns	$ 750

Filing Dates. Persons required to file must submit their tax returns to the Internal Revenue Service by April 15 of each year immediately following the year for which the return is submitted.   U.S. citizens living abroad have until June 15 to file their returns.

Gross Income. All tax return computations are based on *gross income*. As defined by the Internal Revenue Service, gross income includes all income in the form of money, property, and services that is not specifically excluded by law from taxation.   Examples of the types of income not taxed include accident and health insurance proceeds, cost of living allowances paid to U.S. government employees stationed outside the United States, scholarship and fellowship grants, Social Security benefits, veterans' benefits, and workmen's compensation payments.   Since these are not subject to tax, they need not be listed on a Federal Individual Income Tax Return.

Deductions. Deductions are expenses that may, by law, be subtracted from gross income to arrive at *adjusted gross income*.   Listed below are examples of types of deductions subtracted from gross income because for some taxpayers, they are disbursements required to produce the initial gross income.   Typical business deductions include salaries paid to employees, employees' fringe benefits, property rents, utility bills for business offices or factories, moving expenses due to job transfers, and payments by self-employed persons into retirement funds.

Other deductions are subtracted from the adjusted gross income to yield *income before exemptions*.   Many of these deductions are subtracted from adjusted gross income because Congress has determined to reduce the burden of certain expenses, such as medical bills and child care, or to encourage and reward philanthropy.   Many of these deductions involve elaborate rules, so it may be wise first to check with the Internal Revenue Service or to obtain other expert opinion before including these deductions on your tax return.

Examples of Deductions from Adjusted Gross Income

Alimony and separate maintenance payments
Child care expenses
Charitable contributions
Credit charges and mortgage interest
Fees for tax return preparation and for tax consultation
Fees paid for obtaining employment
Gambling losses up to the amount of gambling gains
Gasoline taxes (state and local)
Investment advisory fees
Medical and dental expenses and some drug expenses over 3% of adjusted
    gross income
Personal casualty losses over $100
Personal property taxes levied by state and local governments

Real property taxes levied by state, local, and foreign governments
Safe deposit box fees if box is for documents used to produce income, e.g.,
    stock and bond certificates
State income taxes

The Standard Deduction. A taxpayer may itemize (that is, list and add up) his or her deductions or take a *standard deduction* of a sum designated by IRS as equivalent to what itemized deductions usually are. The choice of whether to itemize or to use the standard deduction is made by picking the method that yields the larger deduction. The standard deduction can be calculated as either a percentage standard deduction or as a low-income allowance. The percentage standard deduction is one of up to 16% of adjusted gross income, to a maximum of $2600. On an adjusted gross income of $10,000, the standard deduction would be $1600. But on an adjusted gross income of $30,000 the maximum standard deduction would be $2600.

Taxpayers with adjusted gross incomes over $16,250 have an incentive to itemize their deductions in order to pay the lowest tax rates. But all taxpayers can maximize their deduction benefits by careful record keeping and judicious control of their payments of deductible expenses. Some medical and property tax bills may be prepaid before, or postponed until after, they are due to build up deductions and perhaps exceed the standard deduction permitted in a given year. Such treatment of bills must be made in conjunction with careful tax planning and analysis.

Exemptions. *Exemptions* are specific and precise amounts that may be deducted from income before exemptions to arrive at taxable income. The common exemptions are for oneself, for a spouse, and for dependents. To qualify as an exemption, a dependent must be accepted by law as such (most close relatives and adopted or foster children are) and have more than 50% of his or her total support furnished by the taxpayer who wishes to claim him or her as an exemption. The dependent must have a gross annual income less than $750, and the dependent must be a U.S. citizen or a resident of the United States, Canada, Mexico, the Panama Canal Zone, or the Republic of Panama for some part of the year in which the exemption is claimed. There are additional exemptions for persons over 65 and for the blind. The amount currently (on 1975 tax returns) allowed for exemptions is $750 each.

Tax Calculation. There are two basic ways to calculate the tax due on taxable income.

1 If adjusted gross income is less than $15,000 and deductions are not itemized, tax due may be calculated from the tax tables that accompany Form 1040. These tables include the standard deduction and the appropriate number of exemptions.
2 If adjusted gross income is over $15,000 and/or deductions are itemized, tax is figured from Tax Rate Schedules X, Y, and Z, also found on Form 1040.

Form **1040** US Department of the Treasury—Internal Revenue Service
Individual Income Tax Return **1975**

For the year January 1–December 31, 1975, or other taxable year beginning ...., 1975, ending ...., 19........

Please print or type

Name (If joint return, give first names and initials of both)	Last name
Present home address (Number and street, including apartment number, or rural route)	
City, town or post office, State and ZIP code	

Your social security number

Spouse's social security no.

Occu-pation Yours ▶
Spouse's ▶

For Privacy Act Notification, see page 2 of Instructions.

For IRS use only

Requested by Census Bureau for Revenue Sharing

A In what city, town, village, etc., do you live? ▶

B Do you live within the legal limits of the city, town, etc.?
☐ Yes ☐ No ☐ Don't know

C In what county and State do you live?
County _____ State _____

D In what township do you live? (See page 4.)

Filing Status (check only ONE box)

1 ☐ Single
2 ☐ Married filing joint return (even if only one had income)
3 ☐ Married filing separately. If spouse is also filing give spouse's social security number in designated space above and enter full name here ▶
4 ☐ Unmarried Head of Household (See page 5 of Instructions) ▶
5 ☐ Qualifying widow(er) with dependent child (Year spouse died ▶ 19___). See page 5 of Instructions.

Exemptions

6a Regular ☐ Yourself ☐ Spouse Enter number of boxes checked ▶ _____
b First names of your dependent children who lived with you _____ Enter number ▶ _____
c Number of other dependents (from line 27) . ▶ _____
d Total (add lines 6a, b, and c) . . . . . . ▶ _____
e Age 65 or over . . ☐ Yourself ☐ Spouse Enter number of boxes checked ▶ _____
 Blind . . . . ☐ Yourself ☐ Spouse _____
7 Total (add lines 6d and e) _____

8 **Presidential Election Campaign Fund** . . ▶ Do you wish to designate $1 of your taxes for this fund? . . . ☐ Yes ☐ No
If joint return, does your spouse wish to designate $1? . . . . ☐ Yes ☐ No

Note: If you check the "Yes" box(es) it will not increase your tax or reduce your refund.

Income

9 Wages, salaries, tips, and other employee compensation (Attach Forms W–2. If unavailable, see page 3 of Instructions.) · . . . . . | 9 | |
10a Dividends (See pages 7 and 14 of Instructions) $............, 10b Less exclusion $............, Balance ▶ | 10c | |
(If gross dividends and other distributions are over $400, list in Part I of Schedule B.)
11 Interest income. [If $400 or less, enter total without listing in Schedule B / If over $400, enter total and list in Part II of Schedule B] . . | 11 | |
12 Income other than wages, dividends, and interest (from line 36) . . . . . | 12 | |
13 Total (add lines 9, 10c, 11, and 12) . . . . | 13 | |
14 Adjustments to income (such as "sick pay," moving expenses, etc. from line 42) . . | 14 | |
15 Subtract line 14 from line 13 (Adjusted Gross Income) (If less than $8,000, see page 8 of Instructions on "Earned Income Credit.") | 15 | |

● **If you do not itemize deductions and line 15 is under $15,000, find tax in Tables and enter on line 16a.**
● **If you itemize deductions or line 15 is $15,000 or more, go to line 43 to figure tax.**
● **CAUTION.** If you have unearned income and can be claimed as a dependent on your parent's return, check here ▶ ☐ and see page 7 of Instructions.

Tax, Payments and Credits

16a Tax, check if from: ☐ Tax Tables ☐ Schedule D ☐ Tax Rate Schedule X, Y, or Z ☐ Schedule G **OR** ☐ Form 4726 | 16a | |
b Credit for personal exemptions (multiply line 6d by $30) . . . . . . | b | |
c Balance (subtract line 16b from line 16a) . . . . | c | |
17 Credits (from line 54) . . . . | 17 | |
18 Balance (subtract line 17 from line 16c) . . . . | 18 | |
19 Other taxes (from line 63) . . . . | 19 | |
20 Total (add lines 18 and 19) . . . . | 20 | |
21a Total Federal income tax withheld (attach Forms W–2 or W–2P to front) | 21a | |
b 1975 estimated tax payments (include amount allowed as credit from 1974 return) | b | |
c Earned income credit . . . . | c | |
d Amount paid with Form 4868 . . . . | d | |
e Other payments (from line 67) . . . . | e | |
22 Total (add lines 21a through e) . . . . | 22 | |

Pay amount on line 23 in full with this return. Write social security number on check or money order and make payable to Internal Revenue Service.

Balance Due or Refund

23 If line 20 is larger than line 22, enter **BALANCE DUE IRS** . . . . . . ▶ | 23 | |
(Check here ▶ ☐ , if Form 2210, Form 2210F, or statement is attached. See page 8 of Instructions.)
24 If line 22 is larger than line 20, enter amount **OVERPAID** . . . . . . ▶ | 24 | |
25 Amount of line 24 to be **REFUNDED TO YOU** . . . . ▶ | 25 | |
26 Amount of line 24 to be credited on 1976 estimated tax. ▶ | 26 | |

If all of overpayment (line 24) is to be refunded (line 25), make no entry on line 26. ▶

Sign here

Under penalties of perjury, I declare that I have examined this return, including accompanying schedules and statements, and to the best of my knowledge and belief it is true, correct, and complete. Declaration of preparer (other than taxpayer) is based on all information of which preparer has any knowledge.

▶ Your signature _____ Date _____

▶ Preparer's signature (other than taxpayer) _____ Date _____

▶ Spouse's signature (if filing jointly, BOTH must sign even if only one had income) _____

Address (and ZIP Code) _____

Please attach Copy B of Forms W–2 here
Please attach Check or Money Order here

Other Dependents	(a) NAME	(b) Relationship	(c) Months lived in your home. If born or died during year, write B or D.	(d) Did dependent have income of $750 or more?	(e) Amount YOU furnished for dependent's support. If 100% write ALL.	(f) Amount furnished by OTHERS including dependent.
					$	$

27 Total number of dependents listed in column (a). **Enter here and on line 6c** . . . . ▶ |

Part I Income other than Wages, Dividends, and Interest

28 Business income or (loss) (attach Schedule C)	**28**	
29a Net gain or (loss) from sale or exchange of capital assets (attach Schedule D)	**29a**	
29b 50% of capital gain distributions (not reported on Schedule D—see page 9 of Instructions) . .	**29b**	
30 Net gain or (loss) from Supplemental Schedule of Gains and Losses (attach Form 4797) . . .	**30**	
31a Pensions, annuities, rents, royalties, partnerships, estates or trusts, etc. (attach Schedule E) . .	**31a**	
31b Fully taxable pensions and annuities (not reported on Schedule E—see page 9 of Instructions) .	**31b**	
32 Farm income or (loss) (attach Schedule F)	**32**	
33 State income tax refunds (does not apply if refund is for year in which you took the standard deduction—others see page 9 of Instructions)	**33**	
34 Alimony received	**34**	
35 Other (state nature and source—See page 9 of Instructions) ▶		
	35	
36 **Total** (add lines 28 through 35). **Enter here and on line 12** . . . . ▶	**36**	

Part II Adjustments to Income

37 "Sick pay." (attach Form 2440 or other required statement)	**37**	
38 Moving expense (attach Form 3903)	**38**	
39 Employee business expense (attach Form 2106 or statement)	**39**	
40a Payments to a Keogh (H.R. 10) retirement plan	**40a**	
40b Payments to an individual retirement arrangement from attached Form 5329, Part III . . .	**40b**	
41 Forfeited interest penalty for premature withdrawal—see page 10 of Instructions	**41**	
42 **Total** (add lines 37 through 41). **Enter here and on line 14** . . . . ▶	**42**	

Part III Tax Computation (Do not use this part if you use the Tax Tables to find your tax.)

43 Adjusted gross income (from line 15)	**43**	
44 (a) If you itemize deductions, check here ▶ ☐ and enter total from Schedule A, line 41 and attach Schedule A		
(b) If you do not itemize deductions and line 15 is $15,000 or more, check here ▶ ☐ and: If box on line 2 or 5 is checked, enter 16% of line 15 but not more than $2,600; if box on line 1 or 4 is checked, enter $2,300; if box on line 3 is checked, enter $1,300 . .	**44**	
45 Subtract line 44 from line 43	**45**	
46 Multiply total number of exemptions claimed on line 7, by $750	**46**	
47 **Taxable income.** Subtract line 46 from line 45	**47**	

(Figure your tax on the amount on line 47 by using Tax Rate Schedule X, Y, or Z, or if applicable, the alternative tax from Schedule D, income averaging from Schedule G, or maximum tax from Form 4726.) Enter tax on line 16a.

Part IV Credits

48 Retirement income credit (attach Schedule R)	**48**	
49 Investment credit (attach Form 3468)	**49**	
50 Foreign tax credit (attach Form 1116)	**50**	
51 Contributions to candidates for public office credit—see page 10 of Instructions	**51**	
52 Work Incentive (WIN) credit (attach Form 4874)	**52**	
53 Purchase of new principal residence credit (attach Form 5405)	**53**	
54 **Total** (add lines 48 through 53). **Enter here and on line 17** . . . . ▶	**54**	

Part V Other Taxes

55 Tax from recomputing prior-year investment credit (attach Form 4255)	**55**	
56 Tax from recomputing prior-year Work Incentive (WIN) credit (attach Schedule)	**56**	
57 Minimum tax. Check here ▶ ☐, if Form 4625 is attached	**57**	
58 Tax on premature distributions from attached Form 5329, Part V	**58**	
59 Self-employment tax (attach Schedule SE)	**59**	
60 Social security tax on tip income not reported to employer (attach Form 4137)	**60**	
61 Uncollected employee social security tax on tips (from Forms W–2)	**61**	
62 Excess contribution tax from attached Form 5329, Part IV	**62**	
63 **Total** (add lines 55 through 62). **Enter here and on line 19** . . . . ▶	**63**	

Part VI Other Payments

64 Excess FICA, RRTA, or FICA/RRTA tax withheld (two or more employers—see page 10 of Instructions)	**64**	
65 Credit for Federal tax on special fuels, nonhighway gasoline and lubricating oil (attach Form 4136) . . .	**65**	
66 Credit from a Regulated Investment Company (attach Form 2439)	**66**	
67 **Total** (add lines 64 through 66). **Enter here and on line 21e** . . . . ▶	**67**	

Schedules A&B—Itemized Deductions AND Dividend and Interest Income

(Form 1040)
Department of the Treasury
Internal Revenue Service

▶ Attach to Form 1040.   ▶ See Instructions for Schedules A and B (Form 1040).

1975

Name(s) as shown on Form 1040

Your social security number

Schedule A—Itemized Deductions (Schedule B on back)

Medical and Dental Expenses (not compensated by insurance or otherwise) (See page 11 of Instructions.)

1 One half (but not more than $150) of insurance premiums for medical care. (Be sure to include in line 10 below) . . .

2 Medicine and drugs . . . .

3 Enter 1% of line 15, Form 1040 . . .

4 Subtract line 3 from line 2. Enter difference (if less than zero, enter zero) . .

5 Enter balance of insurance premiums for medical care not entered on line 1 . .

6 Enter other medical and dental expenses:

  a Doctors, dentists, nurses, etc. . . .

  b Hospitals . . . .

  c Other (itemize—include hearing aids, dentures, eyeglasses, transportation, etc.) ▶

7 Total (add lines 4 through 6c) . . .

8 Enter 3% of line 15, Form 1040 . . .

9 Subtract line 8 from line 7 (if less than zero, enter zero) . . . .

10 Total (add lines 1 and 9). Enter here and on line 35 . . . . ▶

Taxes (See page 11 of Instructions.)

11 State and local income . . . . . .

12 Real estate . . . .

13 State and local gasoline (see gas tax tables)

14 General sales (see sales tax tables) . .

15 Personal property . . . .

16 Other (itemize) ▶

17 Total (add lines 11 through 16). Enter here and on line 36 . . . . ▶

Interest Expense (See page 12 of Instructions.)

18 Home mortgage . . . .

19 Other (itemize) ▶

20 Total (add lines 18 and 19). Enter here and on line 37 . . . . ▶

Contributions (See page 12 of Instructions for examples.)

21 a Cash contributions for which you have receipts, cancelled checks or other written evidence . . . .

  b Other cash contributions. List donees and amounts. ▶

22 Other than cash (see page 12 of instructions for required statement) . . . . .

23 Carryover from prior years . . . . .

24 Total contributions (add lines 21a through 23). Enter here and on line 38 . . . ▶

Casualty or Theft Loss(es) (See page 13 of Instructions.)

Note: If you had **more than one loss**, omit lines 25 through 28 and see page 13 of Instructions for guidance.

25 Loss before insurance reimbursement . .

26 Insurance reimbursement . . . . .

27 Subtract line 26 from line 25. Enter difference (if less than zero, enter zero) .

28 Enter $100 or amount on line 27, whichever is smaller . . . .

29 Casualty or theft loss (subtract line 28 from line 27). Enter here and on line 39 ▶

Miscellaneous Deductions (See page 13 of Instructions.)

30 Alimony paid . . . .

31 Union dues . . . .

32 Expenses for child and dependent care services (attach Form 2441) . . . .

33 Other (itemize) ▶

34 Total (add lines 30 through 33). Enter here and on line 40 . . . . ▶

Summary of Itemized Deductions   **A**

35 Total medical and dental—line 10 . . .

36 Total taxes—line 17 . . . .

37 Total interest—line 20 . . . . . .

38 Total contributions—line 24 . . . . .

39 Casualty or theft loss(es)—line 29 . .

40 Total miscellaneous—line 34 . . . .

41 Total deductions (add lines 35 through 40). Enter here and on Form 1040, line 44 . . . . ▶

Income Splitting. Married persons are permitted to file a *joint return* that effectively splits or divides income between two taxpayers. This usually results in significantly lower tax if only one member of the family worked during the year for which taxes are due. The benefits of joint filing occur when spouses have very different incomes or when one spouse works and the other does not. Congress thereby rewards the traditional family in which one spouse tends the house while the other works. Advocates of full economic equality between the sexes should be aware that: (1) equal incomes for working spouses will increase tax burdens if all other tax characteristics of those filing are unchanged; and (2) if homemakers were paid the full market value of their services as servants, companions, teachers, and so on, the tax bracket and tax due for most families would rise greatly. These income boosts could entail major tax reform.[1]

Tax Credits. Once you have figured the amount of your tax bill, you can apply *tax credits* against the sum due. There are two types of credits, both of which give potentially large tax savings at filing time. The first type of credit is that which you or your employer deliberately accumulates to satisfy the legal concept of taxation, that tax is due on income as it is earned or accrued. At regular intervals employers pay the withholding tax due for employees. Employees receive notice of tax paid on the W-2 Form sent out at the end of each year to document the amounts of income earned, taxes paid, and Social Security payments contributed. If a person has $100 more tax due than will be withheld, he must file Form 1040ES. Form 1040ES and its instruction materials provide procedures for calculating income tax due above the amounts that may be withheld, and for making quarterly payments on such sums toward the total tax due. A penalty may be incurred by taxpayers whose estimated tax plus withholding is less than 80% of tax due or whose estimated tax plus withholding is less than 90% of tax due on income as earned in each quarter for which the estimate tax is filed and paid.

The second type of credit is based on taxes or payments made other than for the federal income tax. Tax laws permit dollar for dollar application of foreign income taxes paid, contributions for candidates to public office, federal taxes on certain gasoline and oil products, and certain investments, among other things.

Taxes on Capital Gains

Income received in the form of gains from the sale of such capital assets as real estate, stocks, bonds, rare coins, jewels, paintings, and the like is subject to taxation. A *capital gain* is the increase in value, realized at sale, over the purchase price of the good in question, after the deduction of commissions, brokerage fees, or other costs involved in selling the article or increasing its value. Capital gains may be of long or short term, depending on whether the asset in question was owned for more than one year prior to the sale producing the gain. A tax rate advantage may be applied to long-term gains. Capital gains qualifying as

---

[1] For an interesting and amusing discussion of the tax consequences of certain modern marriages, see *The Wall Street Journal*, May 3, 1973, p. 10.

long-term are taxed at a rate one-half of the regular rate for the gain if considered ordinary income. For such gains the maximum rate is 25% on the first $50,000 of qualifying income and 36.5% thereafter.[2]

Long-term Capital Gains. Long-term capital gains are clearly taxed at rates most beneficial to upper income taxpayers. A person in the top 70% bracket can never pay more than 36.5% on capital gains income. This is the difference between keeping 30¢ of every dollar earned versus keeping 64¢. Capital gains tend to be taken by the middle and upper bracket taxpayers. Is this form of tax relief justified? On the whole it is, although as we will see, the capital gains tax does produce distortions in the economy.

Long-term capital gains may be earned over a period of years. Assume that an asset appreciates at a rate of $1000 per year and is sold in the tenth year after acquisition. The sale would add $10,000 of ordinary income and be subject to taxation at bracket rates higher than the $1000 itself would have been if it were taken as a gain every year for 10 years.

The Risks of Capital Gains. Capital gains involve risk-taking. Especially in opening new enterprises or introducing new products, the failure rate is very high. To take as much as 70% of the fruits of success would penalize many private investors and make them reluctant to take such risks. Critics of the preferential treatment accorded capital gains justly assert that many workers and professionals take similar risks by investing their lives in their careers. An opera singer cannot take capital gains on his or her voice (nor depreciate it as an exhaustible asset, though it is exactly that), and a writer cannot use capital gains accounting on a bestseller, no matter how long the period spent writing it.

The capital gains tax advantage affects the attitude of stock market investors. Corporations pay maximum rates of 48% on their profits. Dividends when paid out are subject to taxation as ordinary income, so corporations have an incentive to retain earnings and thereby raise the prices of their stocks. (If a company has more cash in the bank, the company is in theory worth more. The company's shares should also be worth more in the stock market.) Upper bracket taxpayers will therefore prefer stocks growing rapidly by earnings retention, in preference to those paying dividends subject to ordinary rates of taxation. Thus the capital gains tax advantage encourages investment by the public in firms retainings earnings for future growth.

Income Averaging

Some people produce their work and incomes in relatively short periods of time—professional athletes, entertainers, authors of bestsellers, and so on. If instead of having their incomes taxed at peak rates while they are producing, they earned the same amounts of money over an extended period, their total tax bills would be much less. Since 1964, certain tax reforms have permitted in-

---

[2] Capital gains tax changes enacted into law in 1976 modify the holding times required for preferential tax treatment. See the Internal Revenue Service publication *Your Federal Income Tax* for 1977 or later years.

come averaging, that is the spreading of the tax of such incomes over several years. Almost all types of incomes qualify for averaging. While the computational procedure for income averaging on Schedule G is somewhat complicated, the essence of averaging is its effect in taxing income from the peak earning year, at the (lower) tax rate that applies to the first $\frac{1}{5}$ of the averageable income. To qualify for income averaging, one year's income must exceed average income for the previous four years by both $\frac{1}{5}$ and $3000.

Foreign Incomes Millions of American college students go abroad for holidays, for study, or to have the experience of living in other countries, and for many people living abroad is now a common experience. Therefore it is worthwhile to consider briefly the tax implications for foreign residence. Most countries have some form of income tax; virtually all industrialized countries do. American citizens are required by law to report to the IRS all income earned anywhere in the world. The problem, therefore, is how to avoid having to pay income tax twice—to the foreign country where you work and then to the United States as well. There are two main ways to avoid this sort of double taxation:

1 Claiming exemption of foreign income
2 Obtaining credit for foreign taxes paid

Exemption Qualifications. A U.S. citizen working in a foreign country may exempt a limited part of his or her income from U.S. taxation if certain requirements are met. First, the income must be *earned* by some kind of labor, as are salaries, wages, commissions, and professional fees. It may not be *unearned* in the sense of being produced by money working for the person, as are dividends, interest, capital gains, gambling winnings, and alimony. Second, the income must be received no later than one year after the year in which the services producing the income are performed. Third, the income must not come from the U.S. government. And, fourth, the income exemptable must be less than $20,000 per year for the first three consecutive years of foreign residence and less than $25,000 per year thereafter. In addition, the taxpayer must have been physically present in the foreign country for 510 full days during any period of 18 consecutive months immediately preceding the filing of the tax return on which exemption is claimed and/or must be a *bona fide resident* of the country.

A bona fide ("good faith") resident of a country is one who either has a permanent visa or immigration papers for that country and/or has established a home there with the intention of staying for a prolonged period, though not necessarily permanently. While the United States taxes its citizens on the basis of their citizenship, it should be understood that living abroad does not affect one's American citizenship. Americans living abroad who qualify for exemption of income may apply for exclusion on Form 2555, available from the Internal Revenue Service.

Foreign Tax Credits. An alternative method of avoiding double taxation on foreign income is the foreign tax credit. This credit may be used for all kinds of

"Last week I'm running an electronics plant in Ohio—today I'm a holy man in Kashmir. What won't my tax lawyer think of next?"

income, not only earned income. Any taxpayer who has paid foreign taxes may apply for the credit, for it is not necessary to have permanent or bona fide resident abroad to benefit from it. Basically the tax computation for the credit consists of an assessment of the total foreign tax as measured in U.S. dollars, the comparison of the foreign income taxed with total income from the United States, and, finally, the calculation of the credit as the lesser of either: (1) the foreign income tax paid multiplied by the ratio of the foreign income to total taxable income, or (2) the actual foreign tax paid measured in U.S. dollars. Thus the Foreign Tax Credit gives straight dollar-for-dollar savings against U.S. income taxes. A dollar of Belgian income tax paid, for example, can save a dollar of U.S. income tax due.

Deductions for Foreign Taxes. A final method for avoiding double taxation on foreign income is deduction of the foreign taxes on Form 1040 and Schedule A Itemized Deductions to reduce taxable income. This procedure, however, does not give dollar-for-dollar tax savings. If a taxpayer is in the 30% bracket, a dollar of reduction of taxable income will only save 30¢ of the tax. But deduction of taxes can still be used for foreign nonincome taxes, such as property taxes on land, houses, and other buildings and structures qualifying as real estate.

Foreign tax questions are very complex and may best be handled by competent tax counsel. The law contains loopholes through which certain qualified individuals and certain types of income can avoid the income tax entirely. Because of the complexity of international tax laws and treaties, it is doubtful that these loopholes can be eliminated entirely without causing hardship to some tax-payers who would, if the loopholes were closed, face the double taxation that IRS procedures are intended to avoid.

TAX PREPARATION SERVICES

The tax laws are, as we have begun to see, very complex. An individual is required by law to report all taxable income; to fail to do so and thereby evade taxation by concealment or deliberate fraud is a serious offense with possible criminal penalties. However, honest efforts to avoid high taxes and obtain lower tax bills by thoughtful use of the tax laws are legal.

Most taxpayers can prepare their own returns with a few minutes or a few hours work each year. There is no need for people with moderate incomes derived from wages and salaries and with no complex deductions to use tax preparation services. For those with larger or more complex incomes, competent tax counsel can be advantageous. There is a variety of tax advice available, ranging from friends and relatives with good will and common sense, to the storefront tax preparers that sprout like dandelions in the spring, to certified public accountants and firms of CPAs, to specialized tax practitioners, and finally, to attorneys and law firms specializing in tax law.

Storefront Services An honest friend's assistance can be useful, showing you the ropes and helping you over the hurdles, for the first time you prepare a tax return is the most difficult and the task usually looks harder than it really is. The storefront tax preparers are another story. Reports in both *The Wall Street Journal* and IRS policy statements indicate that their work can be inconsistent, inaccurate, and not always honest. The quality of their work is poor, but this is not surprising considering that many who work in the storefronts are only part-timers. Most have other jobs, often in fields far from bookkeeping and taxes. They become tax preparers by putting up a sign or buying a franchise. A few, however, do take short tax courses offered by the major tax preparation service franchise firms. The Internal Revenue Service regards all returns prepared by such outfits as questionable for the reasons outlined. It has attempted to improve and control the storefront operations, yet most remain essentially unregulated.

CPAs—Large and Small Certified public accounts often bring expertise to tax problems and may be helpful to taxpayers with complex or large incomes. Unfortunately, not all CPAs and accounting firms are interested in helping the individual taxpayer. Some simply take the taxpayer's fee and prepare a return replete with errors and omissions. Tax avoidance is not achieved by such methods. If you do

need competent help, a CPA can be consulted. The taxpayer would usually do well to try finding a CPA practicing alone or in a small firm. Some of the largest national firms may be too busy to take a serious interest in a person with "only" $20,000 of yearly income.

Tax Practitioners and Lawyers

Tax practitioners and tax lawyers have the special distinction of being the only tax preparers qualified to help you plead your case if the IRS challenges your return. Not all CPAs and virtually no storefront services can do more than hold your hand in an IRS investigation, called an *audit,* of your tax return. Qualified tax practitioners licensed to practice by the IRS and tax lawyers can defend the returns they prepare. Because they are specialists they are the most qualified tax advisors, but they are also the most expensive to hire. Yet for taxpayers with substantial incomes, the cost may be worthwhile.

TAXES AND INCENTIVES TO WORK

Two major investigations have been made of the impact of income taxes on the work effort of those in high tax brackets. T.H. Sanders of the Harvard Business

School interviewed 160 corporate executives and found that most had to work as hard as possible simply to perform their job and progress up the corporate ladder.[3]   Salary is as much a symbol as it is a spendable reward; consequently, it is pursued even if highly taxed.   Yet Sanders found the major impact of high income taxes to be on the willingness of top men to move to other companies or to change locations within their own firms.   Older executives build up associations, pension rights, and feelings about their work for which moving allowances and heavily taxed salary increases cannot compensate.

G.F. Break of the University of California at Berkeley interviewed 306 lawyers and accountants in England.[4]   This group is well-suited to a tax study because of the United Kingdom's very high rates of taxation and the ability of these group members to control the amount of work they do.   They can take on fewer or more clients, adjust their weekends and holidays, or retire early or late.   Break found three different responses.   Of the 306, 40 said that taxes definitely reduced their efforts and led them to have fewer clients or to do less work.   But 31 said that they had to work longer or harder to maintain the standard of living they preferred.   And 235 reported only negligible effects on their work.

Summarizing this evidence, Professor Otto Eckstein notes:

> If our tax system were simpler, with lower rates and fewer loopholes, the keen intellectual qualities of [tax experts and tax-wary business managers and professionals] could be devoted to other purposes.   And increasing tax avoidance constitutes a threat to the system itself.   As taxpayer morale weakens, the tax base erodes, and tax rates need to be kept high to produce necessary revenues.[5]

TAXES AND INCENTIVES TO SAVE AND INVEST

The present structure of income tax rates has significant effects on the supply of investable funds.   The progressive rates our system imposes fall most heavily on the wealthy, those with the most funds and incentive to invest.   Income taxes reduce their investment resources, although there is still a great deal of wealth in the hands of this group.

The tax system also distorts the pattern of private investment.   Investors are forced to consider the tax implications of investments and to search not for those with the highest return, but rather for those with the highest after-tax return.   Certain investment opportunities, such as tax-free municipal bonds and capital gains taxed at half the rate of ordinary income, are particularly attractive, as are resource investments covered by depletion allowances.   These tax distortions

---

[3] T.H. Sanders, *Effects of Taxation on Executives* (Cambridge, Mass.: Harvard Graduate School of Business, 1971).

[4] G.F. Break, "Income Taxes and Incentives to Work," *American Economic Review,* 47 (September 1957), pp. 529–49.

[5] Otto Eckstein, *Public Finance,* 2nd ed.   (Englewood Cliffs, N.J.: Prentice-Hall, 1967), pp. 6–7.

make it possible for cities to finance public works at lower rates than otherwise possible and, to a limited extent, they encourage long-term investments.

ALTERNATIVE TAX SYSTEMS

The present income tax structure has undesirable effects on people's incentive to work, to save, and to invest. Recently it has been suggested that other tax systems could overcome these problems. Currently the programs being discussed as theoretical replacements for the income tax are the value-added tax and some form of a federal sales tax.

Value-added Taxes

A *value-added tax* would levy a fixed rate of taxation on the additional worth firms give their machines, labor, and raw materials by working them to produce goods and services. A steel mill may turn $100 of iron ore into $1000 of steel and the value added by production, $900, would be subject to this tax.

It has been estimated that a value-added tax would raise as much money as the present corporate income tax with rates only $\frac{1}{3}$ those of the present system. Its flexible form would allow it to be levied on all businesses, expanding the tax base and thus permitting even lower rates. The advantages of the value-added tax lie in its neutral attitude toward capital: It taxes all factors of production at equal rates. The disadvantages are simply the other side of the coin. By taxing labor added to products, the value-added tax is a payroll tax and amounts to double taxation of incomes received by workers (on which they will presumably pay income tax). Firms that make high profits may have reduced taxes to pay with value-added accounting, but firms that only break even or have poor years can be put out of business by it. The tax has proven quite inflationary when it has been used, for it is easily passed on to consumers in the form of higher prices.

Federal Sales Taxes

A federal sales tax levied at rates of a few percent would raise enough revenue to replace personal and corporate income taxes. Yet this tax would be rather difficult to administer. It would be regressive (that is, it would bear more heavily on persons with lower incomes) in comparison to the progressive character of the present income tax.

The Single Tax

Another alternative is the *single tax*. If the myriad federal, personal, and corporate income taxes were replaced with a single rate for each type of return, enormous amounts of work would be saved. A straight 10% rate taken on all income—no fancy accounting and everybody pays 10% on everything—would be as progressive as the present system. It would fall harder on lower incomes, so a basic exemption could be allowed for these situations. But for all taxpayers it would take increased amounts as income rises.

THE NEGATIVE INCOME TAX

There is widespread belief that America's system of welfare payments is expensive and inefficient. For all the money that the welfare bureaucracy absorbs, it assists only half the families in the United States below official poverty levels. As an alternative to piecemeal welfare schemes, the negative income tax would pay the difference between a designated adequate income and the taxpayer's lower reported income. If the poverty level were $4000 for a family of four and a family had a reported income of $2500, a 100% supplement plan would give the family $1500 to bring the income up to the designated $4000 level.

The main objection to the negative income tax is its potential effect on the incentive to work. Many unskilled workers today have poverty level incomes. If they were assured incomes higher than those they presently earn, they well might leave the labor force. A fractional supplement plan would not eliminate the incentive for the poor to work. A fractional supplement of 30% would, with an official poverty level of $4000 for a family of four, increase reported income of $2500 by $\frac{3}{10}$ of the $1500 deficiency or $450. A recent New Jersey income maintenance experiment did not seem to result in the reduction of incentives to work on the part of the main earner. But reductions were more pronounced in the second and third earners in the household.

If the negative income tax replaced the welfare bureaucracy and its massive inefficiency, it would save the present exorbitant administrative costs and it would restore dignity to people whose lives are now open records for numerous investigators and administrators. Finally, it could eliminate the distortions in family life that some welfare systems have created in the name of morality.

SUMMARY

1 Taxable income is gross income less business expenses less itemized deductions, or the standard deduction less individual exemptions of $750 each.
2 For single persons, the federal income tax rises progressively from 14% on $500 of taxable income, to 70% of taxable income over $100,000.
3 Married taxpayers may file a joint return and so split their incomes. The resulting lower tax rates are particularly advantageous in cases in which spouses have very different amounts of income or in which one spouse works and the other does not.
4 Long-term capital gains are taxed at rates half as high as those for similar amounts of ordinary income up to maximum rates of 25% for the first

$50,000 of long-term gains and 36.5% thereafter. The tax prevents gains that have grown over a period of years from being taxed at peak rates in the year in which the gain is taken and reported.

5 Income averaging spreads peak incomes over a period of years and protects them from higher income tax rates.

6 U.S. citizens with foreign incomes may avoid excess taxation by:
    1 Claiming exemption of the foreign earned income on the basis of bona fide or permanent residence abroad for the required periods
    2 Obtaining a tax credit for foreign income taxes paid to foreign countries

7 The present structure of income taxes affects incentives to work, save, and invest. Alternative taxes on the value added to materials in production or on retail sales could raise sufficient funds to reduce or eliminate the present income tax. A value-added tax could fall more heavily on small or less profitable firms. A retail sales tax would be regressive.

8 A negative income tax would bring families to minimum income levels. A 100% compensation plan would eliminate economic work incentives for unskilled and other low income workers earning less than the compensation target. Fractional compensation would only diminish the economic incentives to work.

Suggestions for Further Reading

Eckstein, Otto. *Public Finance,* 2nd ed. Englewood Cliffs, N.J.: Prentice-Hall, 1967.

Parkinson, C. Northcote. *The Law and the Profits.* Boston: Houghton Mifflin, 1960.

Your Federal Income Tax. Revised and published annually by the Internal Revenue Service as Publication 17. Available at local post offices, IRS offices, or by mail from regional offices of the Superintendent of Documents.

The Consumer Workshop

1 It's possible to file income tax returns with minimum effort and a passive attitude, or you can actively plan your life to minimize taxes, perhaps refocussing your lifestyle to achieve tax reductions. What are some of the modest ways taxpayers can alter their lives to reduce taxes without sacrificing the lifestyles they desire?

2 It's early April and time to prepare your tax return. You'll need some help this year because your income has risen to about $20,000 gross, and you've little time. What sort of assistance will you seek? What questions concerning ability, experience, service, and cost will you ask of the various types of tax preparers?

3 "It's paradoxical that both the income tax and the negative income tax can discourage people from working." Explain this paradox and comment briefly

on the meaning of work to you. Do you work just for money or for other rewards?

4 Tax reform is a frequent subject of government and public interest. Which parts of the Form 1040 return would you modify in its complexity or unfairness? Why? With what would you replace these taxes?

5 The present system of income taxation, with its complexity and due to the actual cost of paying taxes, affects incentives to save, work, and invest. Interview a few local business owners on their responses to taxes; ask them if they'd run their firms differently if there were fewer, lower, or simpler income taxes.

7 SAVINGS

7

> **Money is like an arm or leg—use it or lose it.**
>
> HENRY FORD

Savings are an important element in nearly all lifestyles. This chapter examines the role of savings in achieving lifestyle goals and discusses the ways in which different methods of savings can assist in attaining the goals. We examine the principal vehicles for saving: bank savings accounts, government savings bonds, cash value life insurance policies, and new high-interest devices in the stock market. And we conclude by discussing inflation's impact on savings and suggest what one can do to reduce this impact.

WHAT ARE SAVINGS?

The act and habit of saving is essential to fulfill any need that we cannot realize out of current income. Defined briefly and in practical terms, *saving* means not spending. To save is to retain some amount of one's current income, possibly for future use or to pay off debts. There are five elements to consider when determining how much to save:

1 The level of one's income
2 The dependability of one's income
3 The current stage of one's household life cycle
4 The state of the economy
5 The level of available interest rates

Income Level

The ability to save increases as income rises. The more we earn, the more we can and do save. The poor must use most of their income for current expenses, so they can save little. Middle-income earners, on the other hand, are able to accumulate funds for such things as vacations, payments on a home or a car, and retirement. The wealthy often spend a relatively small percentage of their income and save the rest.

Income Dependability

Many people have incomes that are unstable. Profits of a small business may rise and fall seasonally; professional stock market speculators have both good months and very bad months. Good financial planning means that one should save for bad times by not spending all income immediately. Sudden or windfall income, such as a stock market profit or a jackpot in a state lottery, should be saved for a time when you may need it for essentials and not just luxuries.

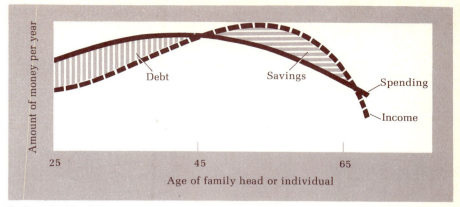

Early in the life of a household, income is usually less than what is spent; thus debt is incurred. After age 45, income is greater and savings accumulate. In the illustration the area marked savings is equal in area (i.e., in amount) to that of debt. Some households may save more than their past debts and thus accumulate retirement funds or estates.

7-1   Cycle of a Household's Earning and Spending

Stage in the Household's Life Cycle

In most households, the early years call for the purchase and furnishing of a house; expenses are great in comparison to income and loans and mortgages are necessary. In the "middle years" of family life, typically from 35 or 40 to 55 years of age, the expenses of house and furnishings (including the mortgages and loans) are usually paid off; if there are children they come to maturity and leave home; income rises relative to spending, and savings increase. Finally, during retirement years, the householder's income tapers off to pension levels; spending declines but not as much as income does, so savings are consumed. Figure 7-1 illustrates these trends.

State of the Economy

"Saving for a rainy day" is a popular phrase that indicates how people respond to the business cycle. People tend to save more when a recession is in sight or in progress. They are uncertain about their future incomes and tend to hold back on some of their spending. In better times, many income earners, especially salaried middle-income people, tend to ignore the possibility of recession or other kinds of misfortune.

Level of Interest Rates

When interest rates for savings are high, saving is a better "deal" than when the rates are low. Studies of consumer behavior do not indicate that the amount of money in savings increases along with rising interest rates; rather, they indicate that whatever savings are available are *placed* where interest rates are highest. When U.S. Government Treasury Bills pay very high interest rates, people do buy them to save. When the banking system or savings and loan associations pay relatively well, money does flow into them. Thus consumers respond very intelligently to interest opportunities. It appears that savers operate in the money market to obtain the highest returns consistent with the low risk that is characteristic of most of the popular forms of saving.

VEHICLES FOR SAVINGS

There are six important factors to consider when choosing a means to save:

1 Safety—the assurance of receiving back all the money put into the savings vehicle. Almost all bank and savings and loan association accounts are insured by a U.S. government agency, the Federal Deposit Insurance Corporation (FDIC), or similar agencies, to a limit of $40,000 per depositor per institution. Account holdings up to this limit are therefore safe.
2 Yield—the annual interest or growth of savings.
3 Liquidity—the speed and ease of cashing in or withdrawing cash from the account or other vehicle.
4 Capital gains and losses—not all savings instruments are free of risk. The principal balance of a U.S. Savings Bond cannot change, and interest is paid at a constant rate. Common stocks, on the other hand, rise and fall in price and thus expose their principal balance or price to the advantage of a price rise or to the disadvantage of a price decline.
5 Costs—the charge made for placing funds in the specific vehicle chosen. Stocks and bonds, for example, usually have brokerage fees the customer must pay. Savings accounts and U.S. Savings Bonds, on the other hand, have no fees on purchase, deposit, encashment or withdrawal.
6 Convenience—the amount of work necessary to place funds in savings or to watch their growth. A bank near home or work is convenient in most cases. Savings bonds purchased through payroll deductions are also convenient. But common stocks and corporate bonds need to be watched daily or weekly lest they fall in price.

Once these general ideas about savings are firmly in mind, one may think more precisely and consider the different kinds of savings vehicles.

Cash The most primitive way to save is simply to hold on to one's money. We learn the habit of holding cash with piggybanks in childhood, and some people persist in hoarding their money in special hiding places throughout their lives, always in fear of the collapse of the banking system. During the Great Depression some banks did fail, but most large U.S. banks survived. Today there is, as a result of the Depression, government bank account insurance, so bank failure need not be a motive for holding a great deal of cash. Pocket money is needed for our daily use, but keeping large amounts of cash at hand may be a temptation to spend it. In any case it is dangerous, for such funds are subject to theft, fire, and other kinds of loss. It is difficult and quite expensive to insure cash in the home, and the cash itself, of course, pays no interest.

Checks

A check is a written instruction to a bank holding one's money in a designated account to pay a part or all of it to a party when the check is presented at the bank. (Checks are often called *drafts*.) The use of checking accounts to save is a safer means than holding cash. They provide a convenient means of paying for purchases or investments, and checking accounts usually include monthly statements, so it is easy to keep track of how much money is spent or held. Further, since with few exceptions checking accounts pay no interest in the United States, there is no temptation to think that one's purchasing power is protected from inflation. If you keep some savings in a checking account, you must find other means—good investments for still other extra funds in the bond market, the stock market, or in other vehicles—to keep up with inflation. If you fail to keep up with inflation, to get at least 7% interest when inflation is 7% a year, then your money is slowly losing value.

Savings Accounts

The most popular means of saving in the United States, with the possible exception of U.S. Savings Bonds, is the savings account at commercial banks, savings and loan institutions, and credit unions. There are many kinds of commercial banks, among them national banks, state banks, and mutual savings banks. At the end of 1973 there were 14,132 commercial banks in the United States, of which 5722 were national banks or members of the Federal Reserve System and 8341 were nonmembers.

Commercial Banks. National banks bear the word "national" in their titles. They operate under rules established by the Federal Reserve Board—the manager of the U.S.'s money supply—and must hold certain reserves behind their deposits. They are subject to frequent audit by the Controller of the Currency, the "watchdog" of the national banks. While the initial assets needed to start such a bank are not large (currently $25,000), the process of obtaining charters is sufficiently complex to weed out many of those who haven't the experience or resources to make their work successful.

The 9213 state banks in existence in mid-1973 were chartered under much looser rules by the various states. In some states in the past a person of no previous banking experience and with only $5000 could start a bank. Today $5000 is hardly enough to rent a shabby storefront, have a sign painted, buy a desk and a typewriter, and hire a teller. Small state banks are prone to failure. They tend to flourish where there isn't enough business to maintain a national bank or where branch banking isn't allowed by law. To compete, small banks of this kind must pay more interest than big banks and make riskier, higher interest loans. Most state banks (all but 204 of them in 1973), however, belong to the Federal Deposit Insurance Corporation and don't pose a substantial hazard to depositors who individually keep less than $40,000 in any one bank. In the event of failure, arrangements are usually made within a few days for depositors to redeem their funds. But the delays can be much longer in the case of banks that make every account holder a stockholder (for example, mutual savings banks).

Savings and Loan Associations. Savings and loan associations (S&Ls), which were originated by nineteenth-century building societies, finance residential home construction. There are nearly 7000 S&Ls in the United States, with nearly 50 million depositors. Deposits held in S&Ls tend to rise when S&Ls are paying higher interest rates than low-risk bonds or bank accounts and tend to fall when S&L interest rates are lower than those available on low-risk bonds or bank accounts. Nevertheless, among all S&Ls in the United States there are usually over $100 billion in deposits at any given time.

Savings and loan associations may be chartered by federal or state law. About one-third of S&Ls have federal charters, while the remaining two-thirds have state charters. Also, two-thirds of the S&Ls hold government insurance provided through the Federal Home Loan Bank System's Federal Savings and Loan Insurance Corporation (FSLIC), that insures against loss in a way similar to that offered by the FDIC, in the amount of $40,000 per depositor at each of the subscribing S&Ls. Most of the remaining one-third S&Ls not insured by the FSLIC have private insurance coverage. But a few hundred S&Ls, like the few hundred state banks not covered by the FDIC, have no insurance coverage.

The safety of insured S&Ls is comparable to the safety of commercial banks, but rules may vary about a depositor's ability to have his or her money on demand. For example, S&Ls operate on the premise that each depositor is a shareholder. In the event of bankruptcy, the FSLIC can delay covering accounts on the grounds that it is necessary to have an audit (a rigorous examination of accounts to ensure that all financial laws have been obeyed) to see how much each "share" in the S&L is worth. This process, similar to that used when a bankrupt firm prepares to settle its accounts, no longer causes much delay to depositors, though it did in the past when payout delays of six months occasionally occurred.

But even without bankruptcy there may be delays. Commercial banks operate true "demand" accounts and will instantly pay out a demand for money because the Federal Reserve System provides cash to its member banks if the volume of withdrawals in a given bank exceeds the cash and deposits the bank has on hand. The Federal Home Loan Bank provides a similar service to participating S&Ls facing large withdrawal demands but S&Ls may require a period of one to three months before honoring such withdrawal requests. Delaying withdrawals for such a long time is up to the individual S&L, though it almost never happens. Yet the power is there so no S&L can ever run out of money.

Mutual Savings Banks. Mutual savings banks differ from commercial banks in that their only stockholders are the depositors who in turn receive the banks' dividends on their accounts. The concept of the noncommercial savings institution had its origin in the eastern United States in the early nineteenth century, when savers wanted banks that would look after the interests of people with only small amounts of money to deposit. Today the mutual savings banks include very large institutions such as the Union Dime Savings Bank of New York. In the late 1960s there were over 500 of these banks in 16 eastern and midwestern states and Oregon. Mutual savings banks are permitted by law to hold a wider range of assets than savings and loan associations and thus they often are able to pay slightly better dividends and rates of interest. Most mutual savings banks are insured by the FDIC and therefore are safe institutions for savings.

Credit Unions. Credit unions began in Germany in the mid-nineteenth century. They represented a response by middle-class savers to have a banking alternative to the huge banks that served the needs of government and big business. Then and now they are associations of people who work together in the same firm or plant, who live in a certain area, or even people who, say, attend the same church. Over 20 million people in the United States belong to nearly 25,000 credit unions, with each credit union having an average membership of about 900 persons and assets approaching $500,000. Credit unions receive savings from members and lend money to other members at comparatively low rates. The overhead expenses of credit unions are fairly low and thus they can pay to depositors interest rates higher than those paid by commercial banks. Similar to the FDIC, the National Credit Union Administration insures accounts to a limit of $40,000 per depositor in the participating federal- and state-chartered credit unions.

THE RANGE OF INTEREST RATES

Congress and the Federal Reserve Board—the government agency charged since 1913 with regulating the money supply and the banking system—controls the rates paid on bank deposits. Generally, the Federal Reserve Board imposes an upper limit on the amount of interest that can be paid on bank savings accounts. In 1975, for example, the Federal Reserve Board's limit on savings deposits was 5% per year. For deposits under $100,000 committed to banks for fixed periods without withdrawals, the Federal Reserve's interest limit ranged up to $7\frac{1}{2}$%. In comparison, unregulated interest paid on deposits over $100,000 during 1974 ranged from 8 to 12% (see Figure 7-2).

Interest Rate Competition Banks do not always compete in the interest they pay. Regular passbook accounts can vary by as much as 400% in the amounts of interest paid. The actual interest you can receive is governed by three factors:

1 Rate of interest
2 Method of calculation
3 Frequency of compounding of interest

Type of Account	Commercial Banks	Thrift Institutions
Regular savings	5%	$5\frac{1}{4}$%
90-day	$5\frac{1}{2}$%	$5\frac{3}{4}$%
1-to-$2\frac{1}{2}$ years	6%	$6\frac{1}{2}$%
$2\frac{1}{2}$-to-4 years	$6\frac{1}{2}$%	$6\frac{3}{4}$%
4-to-6 years (minimum deposit, $1000)	$7\frac{1}{4}$%	$7\frac{1}{2}$%
6 years or more (minimum deposit, $1000)	$7\frac{1}{2}$%	$7\frac{3}{4}$%

7-2 Interest Rate Ceilings by Type of Institution

Rate of Interest. The Federal Reserve Board limits the amount of interest commercial banks and competing "near banks" (the savings and loan associations, mutual savings banks, and other thrift institutions) can pay. The regulation, known as Regulation Q, the operating interest rate ceiling, is periodically revised. In 1975, it was 5% for passbook accounts in commercial banks and $5\frac{1}{4}$% on passbook accounts held at savings and loan associations.

Regulation Q holds interest rates to levels comfortable for the banks. They may borrow at 5% and make consumer loans at 9–14%. Yet not all banks are content with borrowing from depositors at 5%. In February 1975, *Consumer Reports* found that a quarter of all commercial bank savings deposits were in institutions paying below the Regulation Q rate ceiling. (A few banks paid as little as 2%!)

The banks paying the highest interest tend to be the smaller institutions trying to expand their business by offering better terms than the larger banks in their respective areas. Least generous are the banks having a monopoly of business in a town or region, and the largest institutions in a given area. Depositors tend to favor big banks on the theory that they are safer. But today's FDIC insurance makes the safety issue less important than it once was. Among insured banks, accounts under $40,000 are government-guaranteed, no matter what happens to the bank. Depositors who choose the psychological comfort of big banks often must pay for it dearly. Note that, with few exceptions, you get a better return at a savings and loan association than at a commercial bank. *Consumer Reports* has indicated that the vast majority of savings and loan institutions pay at the legal ceiling for each kind of deposit.

Method of Calculation. There are several ways to calculate interest. Going from the most generous to the most deceptive methods, *Consumer Reports* found a variation of 171% in accounts supposedly paying 6% interest. The variations arise when a savings account shows much deposit–withdrawal activity. The method of calculation would be unimportant for an account with balances with no withdrawals over long periods of time (roughly spans of six months). But most savings accounts have constant activity and the method of interest computation is therefore significant. In general, the depositor benefits

These four banks all pay the same interest rate— yet interest payments range from $44.93 to $75.30.

There are many ways of computing interest, as the text of our report indicates. Here are four passbooks showing the identical deposits and withdrawals (made on the same days), with explanations of how the interest has been computed under four common methods. All four assume a six per cent interest rate and quarterly crediting and compounding.

Passbook 1

	DATE	WITHDRAWAL	DEPOSIT	INTEREST	BALANCE	TELLER
1	JAN-1		**1,000.00		**1,000.00	
2	JAN 10	- . .	**2,000.00		**3,000.00	
3	FEB-6	- . . .	**1,000.00		**4,000.00	
4	MAR-3	*1,000.00			**3,000.00	
5	MAR 20	**500.00			**2,500.00	
6	MAR 30	**500.00			**2,000.00	
7	APR-1			*14.79	**2,014.79	
8	JUL-1			*30.14	**2,044.93	
9						
10						

LOW BALANCE
Under this method, interest is paid only on the smallest amount of money that was in the account during the interest period. Despite a balance that reached $4000 during the first quarter, this account earned interest only on $1000— the lowest balance during that period. (There are no withdrawals during the second quarter, so the low-balance formula is not important there.) This method, which tends to discourage deposits, is the most punitive to savers. Yet 30 per cent of commercial banks still use it, according to a study last year by the American Bankers Association.
Interest: $44.93

Passbook 2

	DATE	WITHDRAWAL	DEPOSIT	INTEREST	BALANCE	TELLER
1	JAN-1	. . . .	**1,000.00	. . . .	**1,000.00	
2	JAN 10	. .	**2,000.00	. .	**3,000.00	
3	FEB-6	. .	**1,000.00	. .	**4,000.00	
4						
5	MAR-5	*1,000.00			**3,000.00	
6	MAR 20	**500.00			**2,500.00	
7	MAR 30	**500.00			**2,000.00	
8						
9	APR-1			*22.19	**2,022.19	
10	JUL-1			*30.25	**2,052.44	
11						

FIRST-IN, FIRST-OUT (FIFO)
With this method, withdrawals are deducted first from the starting balance of the interest period and then, if the balance isn't sufficient, from later deposits. This erodes the base on which your interest is figured and means you automatically lose interest on withdrawals from the start of the interest period rather than from the dates on which the withdrawals were actually made. Another variation of this method is to apply the first withdrawal to the first deposit, rather than to the beginning balance; this would earn $53.93. About 16 per cent of commercial banks use the FIFO methods, according to the ABA.
Interest: $52.44

Passbook 3

	DATE	WITHDRAWAL	DEPOSIT	INTEREST	BALANCE	TELLER
1						
2	JAN-1	. . .	**1,000.00	. . . . .	**1,000.00	
3	JAN 10	. .	**2,000.00	. . . . .	**3,000.00	
4	FEB-6	. .	**1,000.00	. .	**4,000.00	
5						
6	MAR-5	*1,000.00			**3,000.00	
7	MAR 20	**500.00			**2,500.00	
8	MAR 30	**500.00			**2,000.00	
9						
10	APR-1			*28.10	**2,028.10	
11	JUL-1			*30.34	**2,058.44	
12						

LAST-IN, FIRST-OUT (LIFO)
Under this plan, withdrawals are deducted from the most recent deposits in the quarter and then from the next most recent ones. This method, which does not penalize savers as much as the two FIFO methods, is used by about 5 per cent of commercial banks.
Interest: $58.44

Passbook 4

	DATE	WITHDRAWAL	DEPOSIT	INTEREST	BALANCE	TELLER
1						
2	JAN-1	. . . .	**1,000.00	. . .	**1,000.00	
3	JAN 10	. . .	**2,000.00	. .	**3,000.00	
4	FEB-6	. .	**1,000.00	. .	**4,000.00	
5						
6	MAR-5	*1,000.00			**3,000.00	
7	MAR 20	**500.00			**2,500.00	
8	MAR 30	**500.00			**2,000.00	
9	APR-1			*44.71	**2,044.71	
10	JUL-1			*30.59	**2,075.30	
11						
12						

DAY-OF-DEPOSIT TO DAY-OF-WITHDRAWAL
Under this arrangement, the bank pays you interest for the actual number of days the money remains in the account. This method, which is sometimes called daily interest, instant interest, or day-in day-out, is the fairest to consumers. It is used by almost 50 per cent of commercial banks and 60 per cent of insured S&Ls (there are no industry figures for savings banks). It yields the greatest return.
Interest: $75.30

(Source: *Consumer Reports*, February 1975, p. 93.)

7-3 Same Interest Rates—Different Interest Payments

the shorter the calculation period. Some accounts pay on the lowest balance during any calendar quarter or three month period. In this case, if in one quarter your account goes from a balance of $1000 to a balance of $4000, you'll receive interest only on the $1000. Better than this lowest quarterly balance method, or a lowest monthly balance method, are methods which use an average periodic balance over a span longer than a quarter. Best of all is the day-of-deposit-to-day-of-withdrawal system that pays interest on each dollar for the number of days it's actually on deposit. Four methods of computing interest as reported in *Consumer Reports* are shown in Figure 7-3. All assume a 6% interest rate and quarterly crediting and compounding.

Frequency of Compounding. Compounding is the method by which interest is figured on previous interest that has been paid and added to the principal balance of an account. For example, if you deposit $1000 at 8% annual interest paid once a year, then one year later you will get $80 interest. Two years later, if the entire amount is left on deposit, you will earn $86.40 total interest ($80 on the $1000 plus $6.40 on the $80 earned at the end of year one at 8%). Three years later your interest for the year would be $86.91 if you made no withdrawals. Most savings accounts are compounded twice a year or more often. Accounts can be compounded quarterly, monthly, or even daily. Term deposits, in which you agree to leave a sum on deposit for a prearranged term of days, weeks, months, or years, often compound only at the end of the term.

If a bank offers daily or monthly interest calculations but only adds that interest to your account quarterly or semiannually, compounding really occurs only at the longer interval, quarterly or semiannually, and not daily or monthly.

Fine Points of Savings Accounts

There's more to getting the best deal on your savings than simply picking the institution with the best interest for your situation. American banks customarily offer many frills that may be of value to you. Some banks also have hidden charges that may be costly to the unwary saver.

"You just can't expect much interest when your day-of-deposit and your day-of-withdrawal are the same day."

Hidden Extras. By law and practice, savings and loan associations pay $\frac{1}{4}$% more than do commercial banks. But there are greater differences between the two. Some S&Ls provide free safe deposit boxes, traveler's checks, and sometimes even checking accounts at cooperating commercial banks. (As we indicate in Chapter 9 (pp. 137–42), free checking can be worth a lot.)

Gift Horses. Because of their relatively low rates of interest, banks and thrift institutions often promote their savings accounts by offering "gifts" to new depositors. The gifts usually vary from fountain pens to toasters to color televisions. By law these gifts may not be the main return on the account. (One Illinois bank, however, did try, without much success, to entice deposits by offering no cash interest and, as a substitute, Cadillacs and yachts, on sufficiently large accounts left for lengthy contracted periods.)

Is it wise to put your money in a bank for 5 years at 6% plus a "free" color TV? Let us assume the TV has a retail price of $200 and you wish to deposit $10,000. In 5 years at 6% interest, $10,000 will earn $3165.85 if the interest is compounded once a year. Add to this the $200 television and you will have a return of $3365.85. In contrast, a 5-year corporate note at $8\frac{1}{2}$% will provide

$4250 (with some risk of gain or loss if the note is "negotiable," or saleable, in its market).   One should apply similar general rules to evaluate any bank offering gifts along with the regular interest.   If you really desire a gift that is offered, estimate the interest on the deposit for the given period, add to this the retail value of the gift (or the price at which you could buy it with careful shopping), and compare this sum to what your money could bring if invested in ways that offer higher interest in the first place.

Grace Days.   Competitive institutions may allow a depositor to make a deposit as late as the tenth day of a month and receive interest as though the funds had been placed since the first day.   A similar provision may allow funds withdrawn a few days before the end of a month to receive interest for the entire month. This feature is most important with monthly balance interest calculations because it makes it possible for you to get a full month's interest even if you are a day or two late with a beginning-of-the-month deposit or if you need to make a withdrawal before the end of the month.

Penalties.   Some commercial banks charge fees of 50¢ to $1 for withdrawals that number more than two or three per quarter and banks may charge $1–5 if an account is closed in the first month or quarter after it is opened.   In other cases, a bank may deny interest unless a sufficient balance is maintained to the end of the bank's quarter.   The oddest and most unfair penalty provision is the "maintenance fee" some banks charge for inactive accounts.   Though such accounts in fact require very little administration, banks may charge from 50¢ to $4 per month for merely carrying them on the books, according to a *Consumer Reports* February 1975 survey.

SAVINGS BONDS

Savings bonds are among the most popular vehicles for savings.   Like other bonds, U.S. Savings Bonds either gain in value (with Series E, the initial $18.50 paid for the bond results in a bond value of $25 at maturity) or pay a series of coupons or timed interest payments (Series H pays 6% semiannually until the bond is redeemed or matures).   Income tax due on interest earned from Series E bonds may be reported annually or deferred until the bond is redeemed or matures.   Savings bond interest is taxed as ordinary income at regular income tax rates but is not subject to state income taxes.   An unusual feature of savings bonds is that one usually can hold the bonds beyond maturity, continue to receive interest, and continue to defer the taxes due on them.   This tax postponement is useful if you are experiencing a sudden increase in taxable income and are being pushed into higher tax brackets.   Such postponement can also be done with the assistance of knowledgeable bond dealers and other specialists, by means of certain legally tax-free exchanges of ordinary corporate bonds.

TREASURY BILLS

U.S. Treasury Bills are short-term promises (two years or less) made by the U.S. Treasury to repay a given sum (the face value of the bill) on a certain date. They are sold in weekly Treasury auctions and the price at which they are sold is less than the face value. For example, if a $1000 treasury bill has a one-year life and is sold for $930, the $70 difference is its yield.

Treasury bills are not subject to interest rate regulation; they reflect current market interest rates. In 1974 they paid over 9% and in 1975 they paid as little as 5¼%. Minimum purchase amounts are set variously at $1000 or $10,000. When treasury bills yield more than savings bonds, they are an equally safe alternative (although they lack the tax postponement feature of savings bonds). If sold before maturity, treasury bills may vary in price, rising if interest rates fall and falling if interest rates rise (this relationship is explained in Chapter 8).

LIFE INSURANCE AS SAVINGS

Some insurance companies sell their life insurance with the proposition that with each premium paid the cash value of the policy grows and thus the policy holder accumulates "interest." This is discussed in depth in a later chapter on life insurance. For the present, it is enough to say that ordinary life insurance is not a good way to save unless you lack the discipline to save on your own, without the compulsion of having to pay premiums at regular intervals.

The cash value of life insurance builds slowly because most firms charge high management fees, deduct large amounts (typically 30%) of premiums in the first few years of the policy's life for salesmen's fees, and pay very low rates of interest. The usual life insurance company pays about 4% on the accumulated cash value, or savings balance, of the policy. Admittedly, the cash value is gravy on top of the insurance coverage (and savings for people who could not save without being "disciplined" by a life insurance policy) but it's quite expensive.

If you want to buy a life insurance policy, you will do better to buy it "stripped down." The least expensive form of life insurance, known as term insurance, does not build up savings upon which you can later draw. But it costs as little as 25% of the cost of ordinary life insurance with its fancy trimmings. When you buy term insurance you in effect make a bet with the insurance company that you won't live out the life of the policy: Term policies are sold, usually, for a period of one to five years, and people in their 20s and 30s have a good chance of living for some time; consequently, their premiums are quite low. People of the same age who contract to buy ordinary life insurance and its savings accumulation features take 4% interest on a part of their premiums at a time when inflation is running at two or three times that rate. Thus it's cheaper to buy term insurance and put the 75% you can save into things that return 8% or more.

MONEY MARKET FUNDS

Money market funds are mutual funds into which people pool deposits and buy large-denomination, high-yield bonds, bills, commercial paper, or other negotiables in the international money market. Investing this way makes it possible for the saver with $1000–5000 in deposits to obtain yields usually available only to the wealthy investor. During the summer of 1974 these funds paid over 9%, compared to the commercial bank passbook rate of 5%. In 1976, it appears that this historically unusual amount of advantage will not prevail. Nevertheless money market funds will continue to be advantageous in comparison to commercial bank accounts.

There are risks involved in money market funds. First, their rates of interest are not guaranteed and, indeed, these change daily as the market rates paid vary. They are not necessarily insured. But many funds offer unusual advantages: daily calculations of earnings, free expediting of withdrawal orders by telegraph, and, in one case, free checking against deposits.

You can enter a money market fund by means of load or no-load funds. The names load and no-load mean that sales charges are added on (the load fund) or that there are no such sales fees (no-load fund). Load funds have salespersons, no-loads are sold in a less costly way, by telephone and mail. Load funds charge a sales fee averaging $8\frac{3}{4}\%$ of purchase price. No-load funds charge no sales fee. It is important to note that a fee of nearly 9% of the purchase price of the fund's shares will cancel out most of, all of, or *more* than the first year's interest, because *both* types of funds charge, in addition to the sales fee, an average of 1% of the total assets as a management fee. Since no-loads can do as well as load funds, there is no reason to pay the extra expenses involved in load funds. (Each issue of *The Wall Street Journal* lists suitable load and no-load funds.)

SPECIAL PURPOSE SAVINGS

Many banks and department stores offer plans to save toward specific goals or purchases. Such plans, commonly known as "lay-aways," holiday clubs, and deposit accounts, pay no interest or at most 1–2% per year. They seem to appeal to people with a weak sense of thrift who won't save except to achieve a very tangible goal. In the mid-1960s, an average of 15 million persons put a total of $1.8 billion into holiday clubs. This represents $90 million in foregone interest at 5%.

Lay-away Plans Lay-away plans are offered by stores to customers who make regular payments until they pay the full price of an article, after which they receive it. During the lay-away process the article involved is "laid away" in storage for the purchaser.

Merchants who offer lay-aways gain much by it. There is no risk of credit loss and no chance that the buyer won't pay the bill. Once the lay-away begins the customer is captive and is unlikely to go elsewhere for a better deal. The store has free use of the customer's money and, in fact, collects the interest on it. Yet for consumers who can't hold on to a dollar or manage to get to the bank with it, lay-aways may be helpful in buying needed appliances and other durable goods. In any case, lay-aways are cheaper than interest rates on installment loans.

An unusual but not uncommon variety of lay-away are "forced saving" investments offered by some insurance companies and mutual funds. Under these schemes a person agrees to make periodic contributions and failure to make an agreed-on payment results in a small deduction from the principal accumulated, or in a suspension of the usually low interest payment. These plans thus have a built-in penalty for failure to be thrifty.

These schemes may help those with no incentive or initiative to follow a savings or investment plan of their own, under their own self-discipline, those who need a kind of punishing parent to nudge them toward their goals. But the cost is high: Forced savings plans often pay only half the interest or gain of comparable, unforced plans, not to mention the losses caused by failure to stick to the plan. The greatest problem of contractual savings plans, as of lay-aways and prepurchase deposit accounts, is the absence of flexibility. When you commit yourself to a certain store or investment company, you usually don't shop as carefully as you did before. It may be possible to change the savings commitment or lay-away arrangement, but often that is inconvenient.

A HOME FOR YOUR MONEY

It pays to shop around to select a place to save. You should determine whether a particular bank, credit union, savings and loan association, or mutual savings bank has federal or other account insurance. Insured institutions usually advertise their coverage protection for depositors, and this should be easily verified. If in doubt, you can write to the appropriate government agency active in the field, the FDIC or the FSLIC.

When choosing commercial banks and other institutions, it is important to know whether it operates under federal or state regulations. Federal rules are tighter and national banks are often more solid than some state-regulated institutions. Dividend and interest rates vary among the different types of institutions and even among competing firms of the same type. It pays to shop around and to compare the rates of return. Sometimes smaller banks and S&Ls offer higher rates of interest on savings—but rates *far* above the prevailing level for its type of institution may indicate the firm is desperate enough to pay very high rates to maintain incoming funds.

Depositors often can make equally good use of each type of savings institution. In some cases it may be helpful to deal with a commercial bank offering comparatively low interest rates but which has such needed services as foreign

branches.   Beware of banks in countries with notoriously lax banking laws.
Banks in the Bahamas, for example, have in the past taken deposits and never
returned them to depositors.   Some European banks offer very high rates of
interest; for example, 12% at British "building societies" (similar to our S&Ls)
and 14% in Denmark.   These and other European financial institutions may
not have FDIC-type account insurance and may be in very inflationary environments.   In 1975–1976 Britain had a 24% annual inflation rate.   So 12% in a
building society was a losing proposition.   Before putting deposits in foreign
banks such as these, check the reputation of the bank and the rate of the
country's inflation.   The United States requires disclosure of deposits in foreign
banks and reporting of transfers of sums over $5000 to foreign countries.
Check with the Internal Revenue Service for further information.

SAVING DESPITE INFLATION

Many family financial-planning experts suggest that a family plan to save at least
5% of its income after taxes, food, clothing, shelter, and other family needs have
been covered.   Such rules of thumb must be viewed as applying only in some
instances, however.   And simply keeping money idle in cash or a checking account is wasteful when inflation steadily eats away at it.   We must carefully look
for ways to keep our purchasing power strong, or purchase needed items before
prices rise even higher.
    We know that savings instruments that pay less than the prevailing rate of in-
flation lead only to losses.   What's more, those saving vehicles which pay less

---

SAVINGS VEHICLES: A COMPARISON

Type of Vehicle	Safety	Liquidity	Ability to Pace Inflation	Interest or Yield
Cash holdings	good (except for risk of theft)	excellent	poor	0
Checking accounts	excellent	excellent	poor	0
Savings accounts	excellent, if insured	good	fair	to 5½%
Certificates of deposit over $100,000*	good	good	good	to 10%
Life insurance	fair	fair	poor	4%
Savings bonds	excellent	excellent	fair to poor	6½%
Treasury bills†	excellent	excellent	good	
Money market funds‡	variable	good	good to very good	about 8%

* $100,000 minimum
† risk of price decline, chance of profit
‡ funds should be investigated before purchase

than the sum of inflation plus the taxes of one's own tax bracket don't maintain purchasing power. For example, if the rate of inflation is 10% per year and you pay an average of 20% of your incomes in income taxes, you need to get 10% plus 20% of 10% = 2%, which is 12%, to keep up with inflation's erosion of your purchasing power.

It's difficult to find secure savings vehicles in the United States that pay more than 7–8%. If you have, say, $100,000 to place, you can easily get 10%. But of course few people have such amounts to save. Nevertheless, there are three basic things every saver can do to ensure that inflation takes the smallest possible bite out of his or her savings:

First, avoid the sure-fire losers for long-term savings or for large amounts, the commercial bank savings accounts paying less than 5%, excess cash balances in checking accounts and cookie jars, and low interest, special-purpose deposit accounts.

Second, keep at hand only as much cash as you need for convenience. Put emergency reserves and funds for future spending in essentially low-yield savings accounts or certificates that can be cashed on 30 days notice or less.

Third, keep in mind the long-term goal of savings: To have a better life in the future. Watch for safe but high yielding savings instruments such as term deposits, money market funds, and some U.S. government securities.

SUMMARY

1 Savings are monies not spent out of current income.
2 There are five things to consider when determining how much to save:
    1 Income level—the ability to save rises as income rises
    2 Income dependability—people with uncertain incomes should save more
    3 State in the household's lifecycle—debt is incurred during the formation of the family household; later it is paid off with net savings
    4 State of the economy—people save more when they anticipate hard times
    5 Level of interest rates—savings flow to vehicles offering the highest interest rates
3 There are six factors to consider in choosing a savings vehicle:
    1 Safety
    2 Yield
    3 Liquidity
    4 Potential for capital gain or loss
    5 Costs of placing saved funds
    6 Convenience
4 The vehicles for savings are:
    1 Cash and Checks—these pay no interest
    2 Savings Accounts—interest varies depending upon six factors:
    a Interest rate
    b Calculation method

      c Frequency of compounding
      d Hidden extras (checks, safety deposits, etc.)
      e Grace days
      f Penalties
   3 Savings bonds—pay 6% at present
   4 Treasury bills—rates vary with market conditions
   5 Life insurance—yields about 4% but can help one to save
   6 Money market funds—rates vary with market conditions, now 8%
   7 Special purpose savings—lay-away plans pay no interest; the forced savings they encourage tend to pay below the market rates

5 Savings Accounts held in commercial banks, saving and loan associations, mutual savings banks, and credit unions are usually insured up to $40,000 per depositor in each institution participating in government account insurance programs.

Suggestions for Further Reading

Phillips, E. Bryant, and Lane, Sylvia. *Personal Finance,* 3rd ed. New York: Wiley, 1974.

Federal Reserve System, Board of Governors, *Federal Reserve Bulletin* (monthly). Note: This journal is written at an advanced level.

Consumer Reports, February 1975, pp. 90–97, and May 1975, pp. 306–309.

Dow Jones and Company, *The Wall Street Journal.* Published each business day. Articles on personal budgets, savings, and investment frequently appear in the *Journal.*

The Consumer Workshop

1 Do the general motives for saving, as outlined in this chapter, correspond to your own reasons for saving? How might savings behavior vary with the age and lifestyle of different people, different households?
2 Is inflation an impersonal, statistical force or does it reach into each person's pocket and home? Discuss your own experiences with inflation as it has affected your ability to achieve savings goals.
3 What are the forms in which we can save? How is each affected by inflation?
4 How safe are the various institutions in which one can keep savings?
5 What differences are there in the need to save of someone whose income varies a great deal, compared with someone whose income is quite stable and predictable?

8 INVESTMENTS: CONCERN FOR THE FUTURE

 In investing money, the amount of interest you want should depend on whether you want to eat well or sleep well. ""

J. KENFIELD MORLEY
*Some Things I Believe**

An investment program needs planning, and a single model can't serve everyone. In this chapter, we therefore consider many variables and endeavor to:

1 Relate investment goals to one's lifestyle and needs
2 Determine which investments will satisfy the goals desired
3 Examine the basic financial media—bonds, preferred stock, and common stock
4 Develop basic rules for selecting basic financial media and mutual funds
5 And examine investments in nonfinancial media such as land, gold, and physical wealth

INVESTMENT

In Chapter 7, saving was defined simply as not spending. We limited our discussion to those types of saving that do not produce high interest or other high gains. In this chapter, we assume that funds already have been saved and are now to be invested in vehicles with somewhat greater risks than the savings devices covered in Chapter 7. Since these risks also provide a far greater potential for gain, we define *investing* as putting saved funds to profit or high interest-earning uses.

Types of Investment

Investments may:

1 Produce only capital gains, the increases in their market value
2 Yield periodic gains in the form of interest or dividends, such as corporate profits distributed to shareholders
3 Yield both periodic payments and capital gains at the time of sale

Most stocks and bonds fall into the third category, for they have a variable market price and, as well, yield in most cases periodic income. Other investment vehicles investors may use include agricultural commodities, gold and other precious metals, jewels, fine art, stamps and coins, antique objects of many

---

* Quoted in Burton G. Malkiel, *A Random Walk Down Wall Street* (New York: Norton, 1973).

A MENU OF INVESTMENT CHOICES

Type of Asset	Annual Pretax Return	Time Needed for Return	Risk Level
Savings account	±5%	Minimal (some banks and S&Ls pay daily interest)	Slight (accounts insured to $40,000)
Term deposits	6–10+%	30 days–6 years	Slight (accounts insured to $40,000)
Commercial paper	6–12+%	1 day–5 years	Variable (depends on issuer)
Government bills, notes, bonds (taxable)	5–9%	1 day–30 years	Low if held to maturity (risk increases with time)
Municipal bonds	6–8%	5–35 years	Same as taxable issues
Corporate bonds (high quality)	7–10%	5–35 years	Low if held to maturity (risk grows with time)
Corporate bonds (lower quality)	12–20%	5–35 years	Substantial
Preferred stocks	6–9%	Average return can be calculated only over periods of many years	Low
Diversified portfolio of blue-chip stocks	±9%	Same as above	Moderate to substantial (can fall substantially in down market)
Diversified portfolio of risky growth stocks	10–20%	Same as above	Substantial (can fall 90%+ in poor market)
Commodities	25–500%	Contracts can mature in days or months	Very high (losses can exceed investment because of margins)
Gold, other precious metals	0–25%	Can hold for days or years	Moderate (high interest losses and storage fees)
Land	25–100%	Same as above	Same (also property tax costs)
Art, antiques, stamps, coins, jewels	10–35%	Investors tend to take long-term positions	Interest losses and insurance fees

kinds, and land. All have potential for capital gains and none pay interest. (One must always keep in mind that what can yield a capital gain can as well yield a capital loss.)

CORPORATE DEBT ISSUES: BONDS

When a firm needs money it can raise it in a number of ways: by borrowing from banks, by incorporating and having a public sale of stock, or by issuing long- or short-term promises to repay the sums borrowed. In the last category are long-term promises, typically for one to 30 years, that are called *bonds,* and short-term promises, usually for less than a year, known as *commercial paper.* When issued for intermediate terms of 2–5 years, corporate repayment promises are called *notes.* Within these categories are numerous instruments that have guaranteed claims against a given piece of salable property (for example, mortgage bonds and railway equipment trust certificates).

All such corporate debt issues rest upon a firm's promise to repay, and upon the public's appraisal of the worth of the promise. Corporate bondholders are the first to be paid after wages, salaries, and materials have been covered, while holders of *commercial paper* are simply treated as other creditors if the firm goes bankrupt. Since bondholders have greater security than do holders of commercial paper, they usually receive a lower rate of interest on the bonds they hold.

Physical Appearance

Most corporate bonds are printed on large pieces of heavy paper and often are elaborately engraved with figures and pictures, much like a unit of paper currency, to make forgery difficult. The bond usually has a tail of coupons to be clipped at regular annual or semiannual intervals and cashed in at banks. Bonds registered to the owner (that is, the company has a record of the owner's

SAMPLE OF A CORPORATE BOND

name and address) for both principal and interest have no coupons, for the corporation mails an interest check at appropriate times to the registered holders. Some government bonds have this no-coupon form. The value of the bond is printed on the main certificate and each coupon bears the promised interest repayment. At maturity the issuing corporation repays the face value of the bond, or prior to maturity the bond may be sold at face value to anyone willing to buy it.

Tax Status

The interest on corporate bonds is subject to the federal income tax and to many state and local property and income taxes. To enable local governments to borrow at less than market cost, the Treasury exempts interest on state and local debts from federal income taxation. State and local governments make the same exemption for their own bonds from their own taxes. These tax-exempt bonds, known as *municipal bonds,* have an appearance similar to corporate bonds but bear lower interest yields that may be equal to corporate interest after the individual in the upper tax brackets (35% or over) pays his or her income taxes.

Capital Gains and Losses on Bonds

With a few exceptions, such as U.S. Savings Bonds, all corporate and government debt of any term may be sold in the open market at any time or used as collateral for a loan; this means it is *negotiable.* But all negotiable debt is subject to change in price, as we will see.

Let us say that a corporation issues a "perpetual" bond that never comes due for repayment of the face value of the bond and each year the bond pays one coupon. At the time of issue the coupon is set to pay a rate of interest of $80 per thousand dollars of face value. The bond has a face value on issue of $1000, so the interest coupon is 8%. One year later the rate of interest rises to 10%. You can get 10% on another perpetual bond, so that $1000 buys a $100 annual coupon. If you have the perpetual with its 8% coupon and you wish to sell it, what is the price you'll get? No one will pay more than that sum for which $80 is 10%, or $800. Note what happened: The market interest rates rose and the price of the existing bond fell. *Bond prices and prices of other negotiable debt move reciprocally to interest rates.* If our $80 coupon bond had to be sold when interest rates fell to 6%, what would be the sale price? (Answer: $1334, for $80 is 6% of that amount.) Thus negotiable debt is subject to capital gains and losses. (It is worth noting that perpetuals have an unfortunate history, as do most long-term bonds. First issued by the British government to finance the Napoleonic Wars and occasionally issued by other governments (for example, Canada in 1936), perpetuals have fallen steadily in price as interest rates have steadily risen. The 1936 Canada perpetual bore a 3% coupon and is today worth $370 on its face value of $1000.)

Speculative Bonds

Some bonds are subject to additional risks. The price of a bond whose repayment and interest coupons are absolutely certain moves only with interest rates. But bonds whose repayment and coupons may be affected by the business cycle have a speculative element and thus are known as *speculative bonds*. If it appears that a company will go bankrupt before its bonds are due for repayment, say, in 1998, people will not buy its debt unless it is available at a large discount to compensate for the risk. Defaulted (interest unpaid) bonds will have a rising price if new management appears able to rescue both the firm and the bondholders.

Some bonds are purely speculative; this category includes East European railway bonds that went into default during or after World War I. Occasionally, Poland, Rumania, and the other East European countries announce settlements of a few cents on the dollar for these bonds and their prices rise a bit. This is also where one finds the general debt obligations of the bankrupt Penn Central Railroad, once America's largest rail mover of freight and people.

Effects of the Business Cycle The prices of bonds and other debt issues move with the business cycle. When the economy flourishes and unemployment declines, interest rates rise. Businesses need more money to invest in expanding production, and it can afford to pay more interest. New bonds come out at higher interest rates; old bonds fall

8-1 Corporate Bond Yields, by Ratings

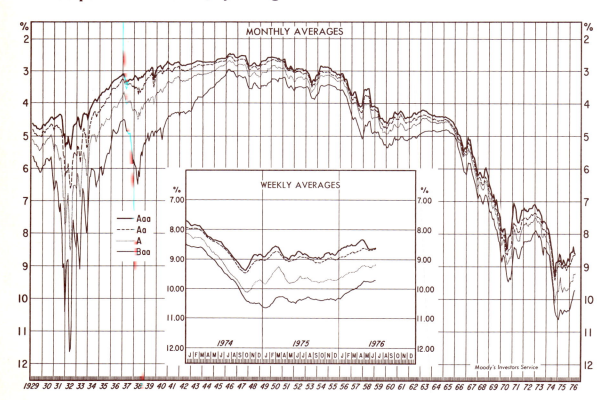

	Rating			Meaning and Rank
	Moody	Standard & Poor's		
Highest safety, lowest yield	Aaa Aa	AAA AA		The highest grade obligations with the highest degree of protection of principal and interest.
	A	A		Upper medium grade. Considerable investment strength but not entirely free of adverse effects of changes in economic conditions. Interest and principal are safe.
	Baa	BBB		Medium grade. Borders between sound obligations and those in which the speculative element begins to dominate. Are susceptible to changing conditions, particularly to depressions; require constant watching. The bonds are more responsive to business and trade conditions than to interest rates.
		BB		Lower medium grade. Interest is protected only by narrow and uncertain profit margins.
	Ba	B		Speculative issues. Payment of interest cannot be assured under difficult economic conditions.
	B Caa Ca	CCC CC		Very speculative, interest uncertain.
Least safety, highest yield	C	C DDD DD D		In default, rating indicating relative salvage value if bankrupt company's assets are sold to pay off liabilities (including bondholders).

(Between the rating columns and the Meaning column: vertical arrows labeled "Security Increasing" and "Yield Increasing")

8-2 Relative Bond Ratings and Meanings

in price. As a recession approaches, interest rates fall. Business no longer needs large amounts of money for plant expansion since additional sales and production are in doubt. Interest rates decline, causing old bonds to rise in price. Speculative bonds, however, may fall in price as their firm's outlook darkens.

It is possible to make capital gains on changing bond prices. The investor must understand economic conditions and buy the appropriate types of bonds. Various rating services provide evaluations of bond quality (see Figures 8-1 and 8-2).

CORPORATE OWNERSHIP: STOCKS

A corporation may issue *preferred stock* in addition to or instead of bonds. Preferred stockholders are first, after bondholders, to receive the marketable assets if the firm goes bankrupt or is otherwise liquidated. Preferred stock is therefore more secure than common stock. But unlike common stockholders, preferred stockholders do not vote to elect corporate officers or to judge overall management policy.

In exchange for greater security and a position ahead of the common stockholders in bankruptcy proceedings, holders of preferred stock receive guaranteed dividends nearly as secure as the interest accruing to bondholders. Bondholders receive interest whether or not the corporation earns a profit; preferred stockholders are paid only if there are sufficient profits; common stockholders are third in line for earnings. No common stock dividends may be paid unless and until all preferred stock dividends have been paid. If preferred stock is *cumulative,* the issuing corporation must make up at a later date any preferred stock dividends skipped in profitless years. *Noncumulative* preferred stock exposes holders to the year-to-year risk of nonrecoverable defaults of dividends. If the preferred stock is *participating,* holders may participate in greater earnings generated in especially good years.

Determining of Preferred Stock Prices

The market price of straight, noncumulative, nonparticipating preferred stock will move reciprocally to interest rates, as will prices of high-grade bonds. When preferred stock has cumulative and participation features it can jump in price if a good year follows a very bad year in which a dividend is skipped, for the holders may then receive the extra-large compensating dividends. Similarly, recessions that severely jeopardize corporate earnings will make preferred stock take a speculative drop in price, for investors will be reluctant to miss a dividend.

Common Stock

Common stock is created by a corporation's board of directors. The value of all the corporation's assets can be divided into so many thousand, or million, shares and sold to the public as common stock. If a person owns all the common stock he or she owns the firm. But 51% of the common stock is enough for the "controlling interest" in a corporation, for it usually gives one control of a majority of seats on the board of directors of the firm. Since the board is the top authority by law, *its* word is final.

Bonds and preferred stock impose fixed long-term interest and dividend obligations on a corporation. The issuing firm must agree to pay its creditors a fixed sum for many years, although its obligations can be reduced through repurchase of preferred shares or redemption of outstanding bonds.

Common stock, on the other hand, imposes no fixed dividend obligations on a company. Indeed, many small or "growth" companies retain all earnings and pay no dividends. Any dividend is, as we will see, an incentive to buy a common stock, but it is not the only incentive. Dividends are taxed at ordinary income rates, after an exclusion of $200 ($400 for married persons filing jointly) from U.S. Federal Income Tax liability. Capital gains from stock are, however, taxed at a rate lower than ordinary income. Thus a firm which retains earnings and grows in sales and output, building cash reserves, will be worth more. Ownership is vested in a fixed number of shares and the value of this ownership will increase. The stock will be worth more and will therefore be eligible for capital gains tax treatment if sold. Given all this, common stock is an attractive way for a company to finance its growth. It sells ownership of itself to the public, by "going public," but makes no firm commitment to pay anything to anyone. Only if outsiders buy up 51% of the stock and thereafter order dividends to be paid can the company be obliged to pay out its earnings.

Life Cycle of a Common Stock

We can better understand common stocks if we examine the financial history of a fictitious small corporation, General Wheel. Founded in 1900 by Thomas Squire, it was by 1920 a bustling producer of steel wheels and related goods. The founder then decided to expand from his market base of tiny Rhode Island. To do this he needed great amounts of cash, more than banks would lend, and for an unduly long period. Thomas went to his stockbroker cousin for help. The broker suggested that Thomas incorporate as General Wheel with a capital base of $100,000, the approximate value of the firm in 1920. Then 100,000 shares would be issued at $1 each. The brokerage house would sell the stock, telling each prospective customer of the glowing prospects for growth and hinting at the chance for grand dividends. Thomas became chairman of the board.

GW's sales grew rapidly, 20% per year. The firm bought more factories, built a steel plant, and hired an advertising agency, to build its "image." Word got to Wall Street and GW became speculative. The firm was worth more each year, and the stock grew even faster. If the company earned $5 profit per share one year when its stock was selling for $50, the next it would earn $6 and the stock would sell for $70. The *ratio of price to earnings* (or P/E ratio) was growing, reflecting the confidence of investors in the firm's future.

By 1930 things were less rosy. Sales had leveled off after GW came to dominate the American market. In every village store there was a pile of GW products; it had penetrated the market. Foreign sales prospects were dim, growth had come to an end for GW, and the price of its stock tumbled. During the Great Depression its stable earnings were better than those of most firms, yet GW's price fell to $21 on earnings per share of $7. But Thomas still needed money to replace new machine tools. He decided to declare a dividend of 70¢ per share. Banks that had not failed were paying 1% on savings accounts. Yearly return of 70¢ on $21 equalled 3.34% and the public bought GW once more. Thomas released previously authorized stock that hadn't been sold, more money came in, and GW's coffers were full again.

The story of General Wheel illustrates the trend of stock prices over the life cycle of a corporation. Typically, when firms are young, vital, and growing, price–earnings ratio are high. Later, when firms mature, the ratios fall. If management thinks its stock is priced too low, it can issue a higher dividend and thus induce an increase in the stock's price.

The Role of the Stock Market

There is, however, more to the price of a stock than its price–earnings ratio and the stage of the corporate life cycle. The stock market's condition affects *every* stock and the market, because it trades on business news, tips, rumors, and suspicions, is known to be mysterious, oversensitive, and maybe a little "crazy." Every hint of change quickly becomes public knowledge. President Eisenhower's heart attacks tumbled the market in the 1950s as Watergate news did in the 1970s. And the market feeds on itself; it can generate booms and busts on its own. If investors fear a bust, they will sell as fast as they can, driving down stock prices and producing the expected disaster. If they expect a boom, they will buy as fast as possible, driving up prices and producing the good days expected. At every price there are as many buyers as sellers, for no one knows when or where the market will peak or bottom out.

BASIC RULES FOR SELECTING A STOCK

Know the Company

There are approximately 2000 stocks listed on the major stock exchanges in the United States and thousands more not listed but available "over the counter," that is, at the broker's desk. It is difficult to find the stock that will perform in a desired period of time (for investors a few years, for speculators a few days).

To choose wisely, it is imperative to know a company's products and what each contributes to the company's sales and profits. One must also know the firm's major costs and how economic developments can affect the firm. A 1969 survey indicated that the majority of amateur investors did not even know their firms' main products, much less the profit potential of those products. The survey, taken in the late 1960s, when the market seemed to have nowhere to go but up, showed that there were many investors who had bought stock on the sheer hunch that any company with "Electronics," "General," or "Aerospace" in its name must be good.

The 1970s have witnessed some extraordinary bankruptcies: the Penn Central Railroad, Equity Funding, and National Student Marketing, to name only a few. Close reading of the annual reports of these companies would have told cautious investors of the bad news to come. Losses could be found between the lines of glowing profit reports of the Penn Central Railroad and National Student Marketing, and sheer skepticism could have kept one from investing in Equity Funding, an insurance company that grew faster than had any in history.

The theory of the majority of investors seems to be the "momentum" of the moment or "what goes up must go up." But common sense tells us otherwise, that some things must come down eventually. To buy a stock because it is "performing," or going up, is to jump in *after* everyone else. Good investment decisions are made only after reading a company's annual report to stockholders, followed by the Security and Exchange Commission's extensive 10-K report, available either directly from the company or from a stockbroker (if one insists, a copy will be found). It also does no harm to examine the massive research by individual brokerage firms, although the prediction record of much of it is rather poor.

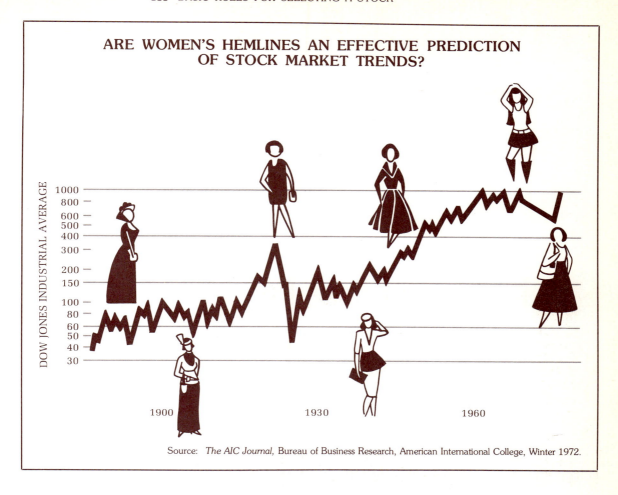

ARE WOMEN'S HEMLINES AN EFFECTIVE PREDICTION OF STOCK MARKET TRENDS?

DOW JONES INDUSTRIAL AVERAGE

1000
800
600
500
400
300
200
150
100
80
60
50
40
30

1900   1930   1960

Source: *The AIC Journal,* Bureau of Business Research, American International College, Winter 1972.

Know the Management

A good firm is, by definition, a well-managed one with at least a recent history of good management. How can the small investor get to know management? Investment bankers and stock analysts can have lunch with corporation presidents, perhaps pick up some tips, and beat the public to buying good stocks and dumping bad ones. The law, however, says otherwise. The Securities and Exchange Commission has a consistent record of prosecuting for the use of such "inside" information that is not available to the public. The SEC requires that if any broker gets inside information he must disclose it to the stock market. If the broker trades on it he or she risks prosecution for securities laws violations. But inside tips are not essential for investing. If a company shows profit in good times and bad, one can assume the management is competent.

Feel Out the Market

A good company's stock can be run down drastically in a bad market. And a bad stock can be run up in a rising market. Eventually things tend to right them-

selves, but it helps to have a sense of where the market is going generally and specifically in the stock you're considering.

Two questions to be asked about any stock are Who owns it? and Why is it being traded? Some stocks have widespread ownership, often referred to as *depth,* while others are dominated by institutions such as bank trust departments and pension and mutual funds. Institutions hold 24 million shares of American Telephone and Telegraph, but this is less than 4% of its outstanding shares. A few mutual fund managers can't throw AT&T into a tailspin all by themselves, though they can easily drop the price of a stock with less depth.

Trading patterns in particular stocks are often initiated by research reports published by major stock brokerages. A report that predicts that the next quarter's earnings of a firm will be sharply down can begin a sell-off, with price dropping accordingly, and a favorable report can begin a price run-up. Occasionally the stock analysts buy a stock, write a good report, wait for the run-up, and then sell out. This is illegal stock manipulation but it does happen. In the fall of 1972 it happened in *Value Line,* a major investment reference publication, when an executive editor touted Power Conversion, a maker of lithium batteries, in exchange for a $15,000 bribe. Power Conversion was $5 per share in March 1972 and $38 just before the favorable analysis; it was $45.25 immediately after the analysis, and $5 when the scheme burst.[1]

Measure the Stock's Price

There are two schools of thought about stock market analysis. One holds that the market and individual stocks perform in a complex but consistent fashion, and the other holds that there is no consistency and yesterday's activity tells nothing about tomorrow's.

The Chartist School. Those of the former school are believers in history and are called *chartists* because they track their stocks on graph paper, relating prices, dividends, and P/E ratios. They draw "resistance lines" connecting historical peaks and bottoms and say that the stocks won't go through them. (If a stock does go through a resistance line, they draw another line and play on.)

Charting a stock's movements is often helpful but not always so. For example, the years 1973 and 1974 held unpleasant surprises: Arab oil boycotts, wars in the Middle East, and the Watergate scandals. The market fell due to politics, not economics, although a recession loomed as early as the late spring of 1974. Chartists could not incorporate sheiks, Palestinians, and the Nixon government in their graphs.

The Random Walk School. Stock analysts who operate on the *random walk theory,* that insists that the price movements of a stock are more random than predictable, form the second school. Random walkers, as practitioners of the theory are called, do not deny that stocks have short- and long-term trends but they hold that the trends cannot be predicted at any given moment. The poor market performance of most mutual funds and their highly paid "expert" managers offers some confirmation of the theory. If anyone could predict the market, these experienced people should have been able to do so. Considering that politics and mass opinion affect a stock's price as much or more than a company's performance, the random walk approach must be considered in any investment analysis.

Apply the Beta Theory

The random walk theory, backed by massive and persuasive research, holds that stock prices fluctuate randomly about the market's trend. Stocks will show random upward and downward movement around a downtrend in falling markets, random movement about an uptrend in good years, and equally random movement about vague horizontal lines in "stable" markets.

Yet some stocks fluctuate more than others. Stocks (and, for that matter, negotiable bonds) may show an average amount of movement, or less than

---

[1] *The Wall Street Journal,* October 25, 1974, p. 14.

A NOTE TO THE PASSIVE INVESTOR

If intelligent people are constantly shopping around for good value, selling those stocks they think will turn out to be overvalued and buying those they expect are now undervalued, the result of this action by intelligent investors will be to have existing stock prices already have discounted in them an allowance for their future prospects. Hence, to the passive investor, who does not himself search out for under and overvalued situations, there will be presented a pattern of stock prices that makes one stock about as good or bad a buy as another. To that passive investor, chance alone would be as good a method of selection as anything else.

—Paul Samuelson,
Nobel prize-winning economist[2]

---

average movement if they are quiet and uninteresting issues, or more than average movement if they are speculative. Stock analysts can compute a stock's *volatility*, or tendency to fluctuate, by measuring the changes in a major stock average (for example, the Dow Jones Average or Standard and Poor's Index) and comparing any one stock's changes against this basic index. If a stock has 1.5 times the change of the average, it is 50% more risky. The *volatility index*, popularly called the *Beta*, will be 1.5.

Stock analysts have measured the Beta of all major stocks, mutual funds, and market averages and compared the risk to the average return yielded by the stock. The conclusion is powerful, persuasive, and yet obvious: *The return of any stock is proportionate to its risk.* Investors often behave as though they are trying to beat the market by buying at a low price a stock with much potential. A few experts can do this but most people simply buy the "risk exposure" they desire. The chart in Figure 8-3—based on mutual funds with low risk (balanced income funds), average risk (growth and income funds), and high risk (growth funds)—shows that each fund gives a rate of return consistent with its risk. The central star is the market average. Standard and Poor's Index of 500 stocks gained about 10% per year in the 1957 to 1962 period and had, by definition, an average change (that is, *Beta* = 1.0).

Measure Intrinsic Value   For all the uncertainties of the market, conservative investors can avoid excess risk and do well in the long run by buying a stock not because it has been rising, not because it's cheap, and not because it's been recommended by a stock broker, but because it has what is called *intrinsic value*. There are seven determinants of intrinsic value:

1 *The company must offer a useful product, a basic good, or a service with an essential or proven role in the economy.* The stock of companies whose products are not used by necessity or by habit are inherently speculative.

[2] Quoted in Burton G. Malkiel, *A Random Walk Down Wall Street* (New York Norton, 1973), pp. 167–68.

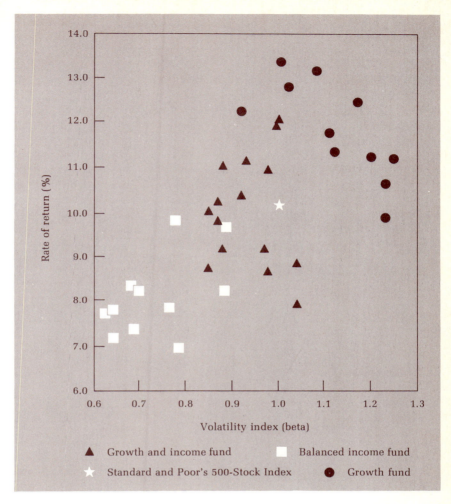

8-3 Performance of Selected Mutual Funds: 1957–1972

2 *The company should be well-established but not past the prime of its life cycle.* Some aging industry giants are locked into patterns of low return on invested capital. If a firm's gross rate of profit is less than what the assets of the firm would earn if sold and put into a bank, the firm is basically a poor buy. One should never hold stock in a company whose product or service is dying.

3 *There should be no serious adverse factors in view.* If energy problems, union negotiations, foreign takeovers, or government regulation endanger the firm's profits, it is not a sound buy.

4 *The company should not have a debt load so heavy that it can only pay a profit to stockholders in good times.* The Chrysler Corporation is an example of a firm whose bonded debt is so large that little is left for stockholders' divi-

"What I really want is a stock with no risks that will quadruple in four weeks."

dends except in the best of years. In high-profit years, Chrysler pays a decent dividend and its stock soars; the dividends plummet when profits drop. Chrysler is, therefore, good for speculation but rather poor for investment.

5 *The firm must have a history of paying dividends steadily over a long period.* The dividends should be fairly steady and not drop too much in years of recession. They should show a solid trend up during the past decade.

6 *The stock's price/earnings ratio should be reasonable and not out of line with the market.* In boom years a P/E ceiling for safe investment-grade stocks may be about 20. In recession years one may find very good companies with P/E ratios of 3–5.

7 *The market participation in the stock should have some depth;* that is, a few institutions should not be able to make the stock's price drop severely.

These seven rules for intrinsic value will not lead you to "hot" stocks about to take off. And they will not lead you to a company that is about to become another Xerox or IBM of the 1980s. But they will keep you away from many of the kind of stocks that, sadly, fall from ratios of $50–5 per share in two weeks.

The basic method for prospering in the stock market is to buy low and sell high. No person is bright enough to guess a stock's peak and trough prices but an investor who studies the market can sense when the peaks and troughs are coming. One does this by holding few enough stocks so that one can keep track of each. One must read the annual reports, quarterly income statements, SEC 10-K reports, and published brokerage research information. One must acquire a perspective on the market and not trade on momentum alone; that is, gleefully buy when a stock is up and glumly sell when it is low. One must not follow tips or ''recommendations,'' regardless of their origin—unless it is clear the tip is good advice. One must have the wisdom to know mistakes can be made. And one must try to spread risks by dealing in several stocks when possible.

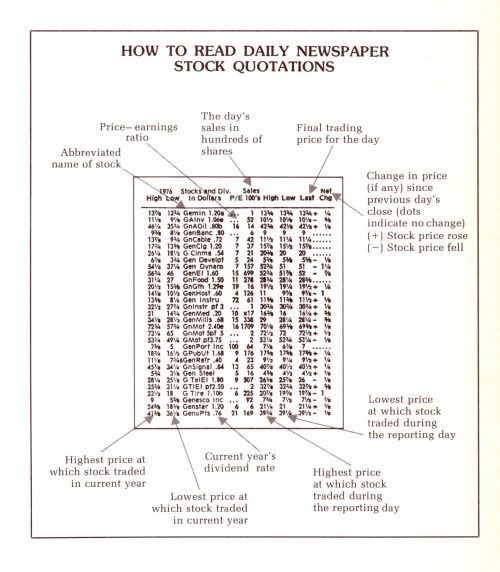

HOW TO READ DAILY NEWSPAPER STOCK QUOTATIONS

THE RISK OF BROKERAGE FAILURE

People who trade in common stock for speculation, as opposed to long-term appreciation or dividends, often prefer to leave their stock certificates with their brokers or, as the brokers call it, in *street name*. Unfortunately, stock certificates bought with money lent by brokers and left with them for safekeeping may be given as collateral to banks that supply credit to the brokerage firms. This hocking of an investor's stock is called *rehypothecation*. An example of this occurred in November 1963 when a large, well-established Wall Street brokerage firm, Ira Haupt and Company, was helping a Mr. Anthony de Angelis to speculate in salad oil. Mr. de Angelis in fact had very little salad oil on his New Jersey tank farm.[3] When this was discovered, Haupt went to bankruptcy court, losing many millions of dollars of its customers' money, and Mr. de Angelis went to jail. Another of the backers of Mr. de Angelis, American Express, lost $60 million on the scandal and the value of its stock fell by over $80 million.

Haupt was only the first of the failed brokerages. In the 1970 market decline dozens of firms, large and small, collapsed, mostly from financial mismanagement, and even from the inability to find or deliver the stocks of goods their customers had ordered. This number of brokerage failures made insurance companies reluctant to cover brokers for theft and other losses. From 1956–1959, 57% of every dollar paid in premiums by brokers was paid out to cover losses and theft of their customers' stock. From 1960–1963 it was 67%. It escalated to 79% between 1964 and 1967. Loss claims have stayed very high since 1967 due to the collapse of many brokerage firms in the 1970s recessions.

Today a quasi-government agency, the Securities Investor Protection Corporation (SIPC), insures individual accounts for up to $50,000 ($20,000 for cash not currently invested in securities) in the event of brokerage house failure. But the insurance guarantees only return of the securities held by the broker, not the return of their dollar value at the time of the broker's failure. This means that if the customers' stocks fall in price in the several months the SIPC takes to sort out the brokerage's affairs, the customers will be unable to recover the full value of their shares.

MUTUAL FUNDS

Some investors feel they haven't the time or ability to handle their own investment portfolios and they seek expert management and diversified holdings to

---

[3] de Angelis claimed he had salad oil holdings that in fact exceeded the known world market supply, as a verification would have revealed. See Norman C. Miller, *The Great Salad Oil Swindle* (New York: Coward-McCann, 1965).

avoid having all their money in relatively few stocks. *Mutual funds* are a potential solution for such investors. A mutual fund is a grouping of many investors' funds in one portfolio of a few dozen stocks. Several friends may each contribute, say, $1000 to a portfolio under their own or professional management, or thousands of investors may contribute to a permanent, ongoing fund.

Organization of Mutual Funds

There are many types of mutual funds. If 12 friends each place $1000 into a portfolio, they can issue shares, perhaps 1200 shares at $10 each, buy their stocks, and watch how their money makes out in the market. If one of the members wants to get his or her money out, the fund may choose from two methods of redemption. A *closed-end fund* may simply instruct the member to find someone else who wants to buy the shares. Under this method, the capital base of the fund is closed until it dissolves, and shares can only be transferred, not actually cashed in. On the other hand, an *open-end fund* may be open to new money or redeeming stock at any time, charging or giving back money on the basis of what a share (1/1200 in our case) is worth at a given time.

Most mutual funds are open-end. They have ongoing management, accept new investors without question (but usually with a minimum $1000 initial investment), and have their net asset values published daily or weekly. They may be found in the mutual fund listings in *The Wall Street Journal* or on the financial pages of many newspapers.

Sales Fees

Some open-end funds have large staffs of salespeople; others sell through stockbrokers. There is a sales charge, usually $8\frac{1}{2}\%$ of the fund share value. This *sales fee load* can wipe out the first year's gains, for few funds' management do better than $8\frac{1}{2}\%$ per year growth in the long run. Some funds have no salespeople and charge much smaller management fees. These funds, known as *no-load funds,* sell and redeem their shares through the mail and often have toll-free, long-distance lines for customers.

Fund Objectives

Mutual funds may have many different goals. Some aim for high capital gains, others for dividend income. There are high-risk, high-performance funds, often called *go-go* or *hedge funds,* that reach for very high capital gains through trading options to buy and sell stocks. The record of most mutual funds, and especially of high-risk funds, is dismal. Most have done no more than drag their investors along with the market. Random stock selection is a better investment than most fund portfolios, yet investors pay management and sales fees and get bumbling service. A few closed-end funds offer better performance. For example, "dual purpose" funds give their members income shares or capital gains shares. If a dual purpose fund has a 50-50 division of shares, then the holders of income shares will get twice the dividends their money could buy in an identical portfolio in a conventional fund. The capital gains shareholders get twice the risk exposure and gains (or loss) opportunity they would have in an ordinary fund. For income shareholders in recent years the dual purpose fund has been largely satisfactory. Yet the record of funds as a whole is not positive.

A mutual fund composed of risky stocks will outperform the market in good years and fall more than the market average in bad years. The mutual fund which reaches for the heavens in a boom will plunge horribly in a bust.

Each public fund has a prospectus with extensive disclosures, for the Securities and Exchange Commission ensures that essential information—about management, purpose, risk exposure, fees chargeable—are clearly set forth. A prospectus should be read with care, with attention to the fund's performance record, and bearing in mind that high gains often become high losses.

Scandals   With most mutual funds, the maximum risk is the ordinary one of poor decisions on the part of management: The fund may buy the wrong stocks, lose money, and pass the losses along to the fund's customers. But also possible is the risk of investing in a dishonest fund or one so poorly managed that there is not enough money left in the fund to pay every customer if all demanded their money.

IOS: A Case History. Between 1971 and 1974 most funds had more withdrawals than new deposits. Investors became aware of the poor performance of mutual funds and decided to put their money elsewhere. One of the world's largest funds, Investors Overseas Services (IOS), managed from Geneva, Switzerland by Bernie Cornfeld, suffered massive withdrawals, as did other funds. IOS had been so badly run and had lost so much money on its own (even apart from its poor market performance) that it could not pay off its obligations. Investors demanded their money, not enough cash could be found to pay them, and the Swiss government put Cornfeld in jail for a number of charges related to fraud and mismanagement. During its heyday IOS directors and officers lived like princes: there were castles, private jets, much gold and other jewelry held in private warehouses. Investors in the fund didn't know of the mismanagement because IOS was, as a New Brunswick (Canada) corporation managed from Switzerland, not subject to stiff, SEC-type disclosure requirements. Because no security can be sold in the United States without meeting SEC guidelines, few Americans were touched directly by the IOS disaster. But many Europeans were wiped out. Even after Cornfeld's fall in 1970, with IOS already in its death throes, no regulatory powers came to save its customers. Robert Vesco then gained control of IOS and sold the remaining IOS stocks in exchange for securities of little value in shell companies he organized for that purpose. The "shells" were "paper companies" in tolerant little countries and received IOS' remaining good stock.

The sad story of IOS can teach us that flashy sales representatives and impressive letterheads, promises of gain and records of performance mean nothing if you cannot check the people who make the claims and the accounting behind the figures. SEC disclosure standards are not perfect but they do give an investor a good chance for protection—if one takes the time to investigate.

PHYSICAL WEALTH

Some investors shun marketable securities, believing that they are not sufficiently tangible to provide the safety the investors demand. At the same time other investors feel that physical property, which is both personal and tangible, has greater potential for capital appreciation than paper securities do. Physical wealth may be land, antiques, cars, gems, works of art, houses, or other real estate. People have been known to speculate in scrap steel, industrial chemicals, and cattle feed. One can invest wisely in physical goods but such investments need not be made on the false belief that paper securities are unsafe or that commodities or real estate have a better chance for gain. Paper securities represent ownership or claims to businesses with valuable services to sell. And stocks and bonds can provide any amount of risk and performance potential the investor wishes.

REAL ESTATE

The Advantages

Real estate has a strong ability to counterbalance against inflation and to provide long-term capital gains. U.S. land prices have a long-term upward trend, yet land can go down in price. The value of real property is determined by many factors, of which adjacent use is one kind. For example, if some buildings in a neighborhood turn to slums, the property surrounding it will probably fall in value.

Real estate may provide rental income, and rented land or houses on one's property can provide rents to cover the costs of ownership. Investors often borrow money via mortgages on their real estate and the yield of rent or capital gains is magnified by the amount borrowed. A $1000 annual yield on a rented house is 10% of $10,000 if the owner paid cash in full, or 50% if the owner put down 20%, or $2000, and financed the remainder with a mortgage. Investors in real estate may also benefit from favorable tax treatment of depreciation.

The Disadvantages

The disadvantages of real estate investment are its risks, the high entry costs, its need for management, its tax burdens, and the difficulty in selling. Land is riskier than savings accounts or high-grade bonds held to maturity. Settlement and closing costs (to be discussed in Chapter 18) can run to thousands of dollars. Land must be inspected in person before purchase and developed land needs continual management. Most communities levy property taxes. And land cannot always be sold at the owner's price at the moment he or she wishes to sell.

Your Own Home

What about investing in your own home? House prices have climbed steadily since 1945 and most homeowners have been able to take a paper profit if they've sold in good markets. But there is a fallacy in these profits. *All* houses go up in price, so it would cost proportionally more to replace the house on which a homeowner takes a "profit." One four-bedroom ranch house on a half-acre in a good neighborhood may have gone from $30,000 to $60,000 between 1960 and 1970, but *every* four-bedroom ranch house did so too. One's home does protect one against rising rents, but it is not really an investment in the same sense as property that is held only for rentals or later sale.

COMMODITIES

Trading in commodities—sugar, cocoa, wheat, copper, zinc, and so on—offers the chance of large, quick profits; it also exposes one to large, quick losses. A U.S. Department of Agriculture survey of the record of 8782 speculators in the grain market showed that only 25% made a net profit.[4]

Profitable trading in commodities calls for high skill. All commodity trading is a speculation on the future price of the commodity in question. A contract can be purchased to buy or sell, say, 10,000 tons of oats in nine months. The profit or loss of the trade will arise from the accuracy of the future price estimate as well as the timing of the price change.

Let us examine a typical commodity process. Mr. Stevens, an investor, agrees to sell 50,000 pounds of Maine potatoes in six months for a given sum. He borrows 90% of the price of the contract from the commodities broker and puts up 10% himself. He hopes that potatoes fall in price so that he can buy them to cover his position in which he is, in fact, short of the potatoes he needs to fulfill his contract. If the price change takes too long or is too small, interest charges will erode his profits. In an opposite trade Mr. Stevens can buy 50,000 pounds of Maine potatoes for future delivery. He is "long" on potatoes and hopes they rise in price and thereby make his profit. Either way the return on the investor's actual cash (the 10%) will be 10 times what he'd gotten if he had not used borrowed money.

Commodity prices are volatile; they rise and fall rapidly on changing news of world supply and demand. The sudden scarcity of Peruvian anchovies, from which fishmeal for animal feed is made, sent the price of a substitute feed, soybeans, soaring. A day of bad weather in Iowa can inflate the price of corn. To play in this market an investor must be alert to every rumor. At any moment the commodity price is adjusted in terms of what is known of the world's supply and demand. The only way to beat the market is to know "more" about the world than the consensus of investors. Since few speculators have such knowledge, most take many positions in their favorite commodities, dispose of unprofitable contracts, and hold profitable positions (those in which the price changes are

[4] *Trading Techniques for the Commodity Speculator* (New York: Association of Commodity Exchange Firms, Inc., 1972), p. 4.

going in the direction hoped for) long enough to cover losses and earn additional profit. Of every ten average contract positions held, successful speculators take small losses on six or seven, compensating for these losses with good profits on the remaining three or four.[5]

Commodities speculation is only for farmers or processors who deal in the physical commodity as well as the future, or for those who like risk and have enough money to be able to afford high-risk investing. It requires expertise, good nerves, and fast responses to changing markets. Fortunes are made and lost on a few pennies of price change, for 50,000 pounds of potatoes means there will be $500 profit or loss for every penny per pound change. If the market is going against your position, you have to pay the broker the potential loss of $500 per penny change. So although you can put up as little as 10% on potatoes, you can be wiped out by a few cents' movement in the wrong direction. If you bought when they were too high or too low, or if they don't change price quickly enough, you may lose many times your original investment. These risks are far greater than those of the average stock and bond investment.

GOLD

From 1970–1974 gold went from about $50 per ounce in the free market to around $200. Then it fell to a stable range of $120 to $150 before rising as 1974 ended. In 1975 and 1976 it is trading in a range of $120–135. A few people had claimed for years that gold would rise over $100; suddenly their prediction became respectable. One gold "bug," Harry Browne, wrote a best-selling book which urged everyone to horde gold, bury some under the floor-boards of a mountain cabin (nothing too conspicuous, lest the mob attack), and wait for the fall of currency and civilization. Browne and his colleagues scored a publishing success, yet only the momentum theory endorses their advice. The theory that what goes up, goes up, or at least stays up, doesn't work for the stock market, or for that matter any economic market, any better than it works for a world subject to gravity. As supply and demand change, so the market price changes.

Apart from ornamental uses, gold has very little usefulness except as a medium of exchange. It is rare and therefore can offer a better guarantee of value than some inflated paper currencies. But gold earns no interest, entails some safekeeping expense, and must be bought and sold with substantial fees if it is traded in units smaller than 400 ounce bars (a 400 ounce bar costs $50,000 for gold at $125 per ounce, about the current price).

Since the beginning of 1975 U.S. citizens have been able to hold gold legally for speculative purposes. If gold behaves like silver, then its price will be volatile. Citibank of New York calculated a long-run price for gold in the vicinity of $120. If gold is purchased in this range it should afford some security and

---

[5] *Ibid.*, p. 7.

opportunity for gain. Yet one must not forget that gold is mainly a medium of exchange with few other uses, expensive to hold, and earns nothing before it is sold. The dividend or interest on a good stock or bond will repay its purchase price in seven to ten years. If gold doesn't keep doubling steadily every decade, you will be in a position of loss relative to the earnings available in high quality securities.

FOREIGN CURRENCIES, ACCOUNTS, AND OTHER INTERESTS

Foreign currencies rise and fall against the U.S. dollar. It is possible to speculate on this by taking a commodities-type position in a foreign currency or property. If, for example, you buy Belgian Francs and they rise in respect to the dollar, then your Belgian Francs can be sold for a dollar profit (that is, you bought BFs for less than you sold them). Or you can buy a contract to deliver a large quantity of British pounds in six months and profit if the pound falls.

Foreign currency movements tend to be small and the cash itself pays no interest. Banks and currency brokers take a profit in the spread between what they pay to buy a currency and the price for which they sell it. A broker's buying price is always less than the selling price. You can get interest by putting foreign money into a bank account in that currency, but such accounts may have to be quite large to qualify for interest. To earn interest on Belgian Francs, for example, you must have $2 million worth on deposit in major Swiss banks. Certain foreign bank accounts are subject to exchange controls from time to time. Once you put your money into a foreign country you cannot always take it out easily. There are other risks. The majority of U.S. banks and savings and loan associations have accounts insured up to $40,000. But most banks in the rest of the world don't have account insurance. German bank failures in 1974 jeopardized many accounts. Finally, there is the danger of dealing with a bank that takes deposits but doesn't give them back to customers, as a few banks in the Caribbean have done. Not every country protects customers as zealously as do the United States and Canada. In sum, foreign financial interests can yield profits but they require knowledge of foreign banking operations and likely future currency movements.

ART AND ANTIQUES

The cultural monuments of the past are valued for their importance, uniqueness, and rarity. The major paintings of the Renaissance, surviving copies of important documents, critical manuscripts, and so on, have intrinsic value. Their market value, however, depends on what potential buyers are willing to pay. Works in museum collections are not for sale and have no price. Other, usually less important works, sell for what buyers are willing to take out of other investments. If the stock market is in good shape, fine paintings will command better prices than when the market is depressed.

Important works of art and significant antiques have substantial value but many collectable items have only the value which collectors assign them. Contemporary paintings, comic books, most stamps and coins, old guns and cars command high prices because they are currently desirable. But fashions change. Paintings of a stature less than Rembrandts can and do fall in price. The coin and stamp markets have such large spreads between dealers' buy and sell prices that it is quite difficult for ordinary investors to profit from them.

To invest in paintings or anything old, fine, or rare you must know what you're doing. Art is much more easily forged than most people realize. Whether a painting by Raphael is really by Raphael depends not only on the easily copied style and signature but also on the opinions of art historians. Expert opinions do change and art investors are thus subject to the debates of scholars. You can ask a living artist if he or she painted a particular picture, but this check is only as good as a person's memory.[6]

Only a few living artists have firm markets. The news that 30,000 excellent works by Picasso were to be auctioned following the artist's death dropped their price substantially. Contemporary American art is largely without direction. Signed soup cans and pieces of structural steel painted safety orange cannot command high prices indefinitely. It is the authors' opinion that acquisition of such pieces is risky investment, and art is perhaps best bought for sheer enjoyment. In art as in every other investment medium, the investor must have extensive knowledge of what is being bought and what the future market's condition will be.

Art and antiques pay no interest. They must be insured and can usually be sold only in major cities or when auctions are held. To many Renoirs on the market at one time can depress their price, for art markets haven't the depth of the stock market with its millions of investors. The only security in art, stamps, coins, and jewels is, therefore, their compactness; great value can reside in a stamp or small painting. The fugitive investor can appropriately buy diamonds and small, old master canvases. Everyone else should stick to less exotic investments.

GEMS AND JEWELRY

Jewels and rare gemstones have, as we indicated, the advantage of compactness. Like works of art they can provide for their owner a sense of beauty.

---

[6] Sent a forged "Picasso" for authentication, Pablo Picasso, himself unsure of its origin, asked "How much did the dealer pay for it?" Told that it had cost $100,000, Picasso replied, "Well, if he paid that much, it must be real." See Clifford Irving, *Fake!* (New York: McGraw-Hill, 1969), p. 227.

But fine gems, whether set into jewelry or unset as cut stones, have important disadvantages. The prices of rare gems are maintained at artificially high levels by governments, such as South Africa's, that restrict gem sales. A change in political conditions in South Africa or in the South American nations that provide most of the world's emeralds can result in vast stores of fine stones being dumped on world markets. The person who wishes to buy stones for investment must buy at retail prices but will have to sell them at wholesale prices. The level of wholesale to retail price increase in the jewelry trade is very high, perhaps 300%. Price must, therefore, appreciate a great deal beyond this to compensate for lost interest, storage costs, and insurance. In this field again the buyer must be expert. Those lacking substantial knowledge or not having a very reputable source to guide them, expose themselves to unusually high risk. Of course, fashion greatly affects jewelry; set stones may have constant value but their settings can fall in price as styles change. Finally, technology may create synthetic diamonds, emeralds, and other gems that are indistinguishable from the natural equivalents. If such synthetics are inexpensive, the market will be devastated.

A good rule for buying gems is to buy only the finest and with expert guidance. Risk is high, costs (including lost interest) are substantial. Thus we conclude that jewels offer distinct advantages of portability but little else as investments.

ON PROFESSIONAL ASSISTANCE

A famous European statesman once said that war is too important to be left to generals. The same may be said of investments and professional managers and advisors: It is indeed valuable to have competent professional guidance or management but the chosen person or firm must be monitored. If you wish to hire an advisor, get a list of previous recommendations he or she has made. Check out this track record against stock quotations or other market price information. If you wish to buy a mutual fund's shares, check one of the excellent mutual fund scorekeeping services available at most libraries. No manager or advisor is infallible, but the chosen advisor's record should be better than average.

It is important when seeking investment advice to ensure that the goals of the professional or firm are the same as the investor's. A growth-oriented mutual fund or investment advisor will be unsuitable for an investor who needs current income and safety. Very safe short-term debt issues will be unsuitable for the investor who needs the tax advantages of long-term capital gains.

Above all, one must know the vested interests of the person or firm whose advice one seeks. A stockbroker wants to trade stock, mortgage brokers want to sell their wares, art galleries want to move their merchandise. Well-meaning advice from any "house" advisor is colored by a firm's needs. Independence is thus a valuable but not essential quality in seeking an advisor; it is not essential because many advisors with vested interests are honest and do take to heart the interests and goals of the investor.

SUMMARY

1 Investment is the process of putting saved funds to profit or high interest-earning uses. Investment bears higher risks than pure saving and may expose investors to risks of capital loss or capital gains.
2 Investment serves three basic needs, the need
   1 For current income
   2 For future income
   3 To preserve or build capital
3 Corporations can finance their operations by bank borrowing, stock or bond sales, or issuing unsecured commercial paper. If a corporation goes bankrupt, the order of priority for claimants (after the suppliers and workers are paid) is: bondholders, preferred stockholders, common stockholders and other creditors (including holders of unsecured commercial paper).
4 Bond prices and prices of other negotiable debt move reciprocally to interest rates.
5 The price of a firm's common stock is influenced by its price/earnings ratio, the dividend yield, the stage in the corporation's life cycle, and the general stock market condition as it influences investors' attitudes toward the company's future.
6 Before buying a stock, an investor should be familiar with the company, its management's record, the state of the stock market, depth of public ownership, and the current opinion of stock analysts.
7 Chartists believe stock prices follow historical patterns. Random walk theorists claim there are no predictable patterns to stock price movements.
8 Risk (Beta) is proportionate to return.
9 Intrinsic value is a method for identifying low-risk stocks with profit potential. It requires that the company
   1 Make a useful product or provide a useful service
   2 Be established but not past its prime
   3 Have no severe internal or external problems
   4 Be free of heavy debt loads
   5 Have a long history of steady or rising dividends
   6 Have a P/E ratio less than 20 and not out of line with the market generally
   7 Have widespread ownership (depth)
10 Brokerages can and do fail. Investors can hold stock certificates or leave them in street name. The Securities Investor Protection Corporation insures individual accounts up to $50,000 ($20,000 of it in uninvested cash) in the event of brokerage house failure.
11 A mutual fund places many investors' funds in one portfolio. A fund offers each investor a share in more stocks than he or she could afford or manage. In spite of their professional guidance, the record of most funds is very poor.

12 Physical assets can be investment vehicles. None pay interest and all have holding costs.

13 Land does rise in price in the long run but may be costly, speculative, and hard to sell in the short run.

14 One's own home can be sold at a paper profit. This profit vanishes in practice since the costs of a replacement home will rise proportionately.

15 Commodities are risky but offer high profits through use of borrowed funds. Only 25% of all commodity traders have net profits.

16 Gold is a speculative commodity like any other.

17 Art and rare objects bought as investments are speculative and risky. Gems and jewelry entail a similar risk.

Suggestions for Further Reading

The nonprofessional investor will do well to begin with the charming, sophisticated books by the pseudonymous Adam Smith, *The Money Game* and *Supermoney.* New York: Random House, 1968; 1972. To acquire up-to-date knowledge of the market, *The Wall Street Journal* (a daily) and *Barron's* (a weekly), both published by the Dow Jones & Company, are good sources of investment data. Company financial information is published continuously by Standard and Poor's and Moody's services. Read the prospectuses, annual, and quarterly financial reports of the firms you're considering. Look at stock trends published by *Value Line* or similar services. Consider the research reports that brokers issue. Read *Business Week, Forbes,* and, *The New York Times,* to get general information affecting the economy.

Investors beyond the beginning stages of understanding can benefit from Benjamin Graham, David L. Dodd, and Sidney Cottle, *Security Analysis: Principles and Techniques,* 4th ed. New York: McGraw-Hill, 1962. The annual reports of the Securities and Exchange Commission are useful, as are the annual reports of the major stock exchanges. Broad economic trends can be discerned in the monthly *Federal Reserve Bulletin* and the publications of the U.S. Department of Commerce. A fine commodities bibliography may be obtained without charge from the Chicago Mercantile Exchange, 444 West Jackson, Chicago, Illinois 60606.

Every investor should know something about the horrors of past investment. See Christopher Elias, *Fleecing the Lambs.* Chicago: Regnery, 1971; John R. Daughen and Peter Binzen, *The Wreck of the Penn Central.* Boston: Little, Brown, 1971; and Norman C. Miller, *The Great Salad Oil Swindle.* New York: Coward-McCann, 1965.

The Consumer Workshop

1 List and describe how your own needs implicitly contain your investment goals.

2 Given your investment goals, what kinds of investment media should you select?

3 Let us say that your brother-in-law has profited in the stock market and now considers himself an expert investor. He tells you of a good opportunity to make some fast money in a new firm's stock. As a prudent investor-to-be, what do you want to know about the stock?

4 Assume that you inherit $250,000 in stocks. You recognize a need for professional management help, and to find the right person or organization you interview a variety of advisors. What kinds of questions should you ask about each candidate's methods, interests, goals, and products (mutual funds)?

5 How is risk related to the yield of investments? To pursue this question in depth, in terms of stocks, see Burton G. Malkiel's readable, basic book *A Random Walk Down Wall Street.* New York: Norton, 1973.

9 CHECKING ACCOUNTS

Checking accounts often make for a great deal of trouble for both those who write checks and those to whom they are paid. Since nearly everyone uses checks, it is useful to know how they work, what they cost, and how they can be used safely with a minimum of inconvenience and risk. In this chapter we examine the mechanics of writing and processing checks and the costs of using checks. Then we investigate the problems of protecting oneself from bad checks and from having one's checks misused. Finally, we discuss the recent idea that checks may be replaced by credit cards.

WHAT IS A CHECK?

A *check* is a negotiable obligation created by a payer (the person who writes the check) to convey a certain sum of money to a payee (the person who receives the check) drawn upon an account in a given bank. The word *negotiable* describes the essence of a check. A mere written contract that Smith is to pay Jones and Jones alone $100 for laying a brick wall is not negotiable. If the wall is satisfactory, Smith must pay Jones and the promise to pay is not subject to any further discussion or modification; only Jones is to be paid and Jones is to receive $100. A negotiable instrument or check, in contrast, is a written promise, signed by the maker of that promise, to pay unconditionally a sum of money at a definite date or upon demand (when presented to the bank's cashier) to the payee or any person legally holding the check.

Endorsement   A negotiable instrument may be endorsed over to any other person. For example, if Smith's check specifies that John Jones is the payee, Jones may endorse the check on its reverse side with the words "pay to bearer" or "pay to Sam Brown." In the case of the former endorsement, any bearer may walk into Smith's bank and demand payment. In the case of the latter endorsement, Brown may present the check for payment or, if he likes, endorse it "pay to the order of Henry James" and James could present the check for payment. The check may be sold or negotiated from one party to another and Smith is required in any event to make good on it. All such subsequent holders of the check are called *holders in due course* and are generally entitled to get their money from

Smith's bank. (A number of exceptions to this arise in the case of checks and other promises to pay for consumer goods; see Chapter 10.)

All subsequent holders or endorsees of Smith's check are holders in due course, provided that the check is complete and regular on its face, that the holder took it in good faith in exchange for something of value, and that the holder had no notice of any defect in the check or in the right to hold it of the person who conveyed it.

If a check is payable to "bearer" it need have no endorsement. But when one holder in due course accepts a check, endorses it, and passes it on to yet a third person, the first holder in effect guarantees that the check is genuine and good for payment, that he or she has proper title to it and no knowledge of any defect in the check, and that he or she will make good for it to the person to whom it is conveyed or to any subsequent holder if the original issuer doesn't pay the check when presented.

Forms of Endorsement

One must be careful in accepting checks and even more careful endorsing them. There are three forms of endorsement: (1) *blank endorsement,* (2) *specific endorsement,* and (3) *restrictive endorsement.* If Tom Schultz receives a check from Bill Hauser and blank endorses it "Tom Schultz," the check becomes payable to any holder. If Schultz endorses it specifically "pay to T. Schneider on order," the check cannot be negotiated further without Schneider's endorsement. And if Schultz endorses it restrictively "pay only to Schneider," the check ceases to be negotiable.

"I paid my garage with this check, they endorsed it over to the electrician, he paid the hardware store with it, and they have paid their bill to me with it."

Restrictive endorsement is a means of self-protection. If you receive a check in the mail and plan to deposit it or even to hold it a few days before cashing it, there are several rules to follow. First, never put a blank endorsement on a check unless you plan to deal in negotiable obligations, as banks and finance companies do. Since almost no one apart from specialized credit firms does this, you should use the blank endorsement rarely. The best endorsement for subsequent deposit is the restrictive form, "pay only to the order of [your bank]" along with your signature. If on the other hand the check is to be cashed, it is best left unendorsed until the moment you present it. Then you should endorse it specifically and leave the matter of deposit to the person or firm accepting it.

Because checks are negotiable instruments, any writing on a check becomes binding on all holders. For example, you may write on its face "issued in full payment for one 1974 Ford automobile, serial number . . ." and tender it to the dealer from whom you buy a car. If you don't get the car you specify or if the dealer asserts that you owe still more money, the statement on the check is your claim and defense. Similarly, if you endorse a check on its face "[your name]; buyer Smith [who tenders the check] still owes $50," you could claim $50 against Smith if Smith fails to pay.

Handle Checks With Care The "holder in due course" process makes all endorsers potentially liable to subsequent holders if the issuer of the check fails to pay. If a dentist gets a check from a patient and endorses it over to a landlord, then, if the landlord presents it to a bank for collection and the check bounces, the landlord is entitled to payment from the dentist and the dentist in turn is entitled to claim against the patient. To avoid responsibility for the bad checks others may write, you can do three things:

1 Refuse to take checks that have strings of endorsements
2 Refuse to endorse checks and pass them on, except to your bank for collection
3 If you must for any reason endorse a check other than for deposit or cashing, write "without recourse"—this limits your responsibility if the issuer of the check can't make good on it

HOW CHECKS ARE PROCESSED

About 25 billion checks were processed during 1975 by United States banks. Almost all checks are quickly routed through clearing houses maintained by the Federal Reserve System for the commercial banking network. Let's follow a check through this clearing process.

Suppose that a manufacturer in Hartford, Connecticut sells $1000 worth of electrical equipment to a dealer in Sacramento, California and receives in payment a check on a bank in Sacramento. Clearing takes place as follows. The

Hartford manufacturer deposits the check in a Hartford bank. The Hartford bank sends the check together with other checks to the Federal Reserve Bank of Boston for credit to its reserve account. The Boston Reserve Bank sends the check to the Federal Reserve Bank of San Francisco, which in turn sends it to the Sacramento bank. The Sacramento bank charges the check to the account of the depositor who wrote it and has the amount charged to its own reserve account at the San Francisco Reserve Bank. The Federal Reserve Bank of San Francisco thereupon credits the Federal Reserve Bank of Boston.

Banks and the Federal Reserve thus cooperate in forwarding checks to major clearing centers for processing. In many cases checks move by nighttime air taxis between cities and banks. During the time that a check has been deposited to one customer's account but not deducted from the account, the issuer's money supply is enlarged. This temporary swelling of funds available to one is called the *float*. Between the time you issue a check to have an account paid, and the time that the check arrives at your bank for payment, you have the use of twice the amount of the check. The float for most consumers dealing with major firms is only a few days. In winter and during bad weather, however, the float grows as transportation slows down.

SPECIAL TYPES OF CHECKS

The person who presents a check for payment may have difficulty getting it accepted if he or she is not known to the firm or person with whom he or she is dealing because many checks are either *NSF* (meaning *not sufficient funds* in the payer's account) or simply *bogus* (written on a nonexistent account and/or by a person using a false identity). To overcome this problem, the special checks listed below are available. All surmount the problem by having payment guaranteed by a reputable institution.

Cashier's Checks and Money Orders

Rather than write a check on your own account, you may have a bank or post office issue one. If the check is a bank's own promise to pay, then it is a *cashier's check*. If issued by a post office or a currency exchange, it is a *money order*. Sometimes banks also issue money orders.

Certified Checks

You can write your own check and have your bank certify that it is authentic and backed by sufficient funds. To certify a check, a bank marks it "certified" with a rubber stamp and sets aside funds from the customer's account to cover the check.

Letters of Credit

A letter of credit is an elaborate variation of the certified check or cashier's check. To establish a letter of credit a bank accepts from a client a sum of money, say

$10,000, and issues a certificate saying that the person has $10,000 available to be drawn on.   The certificate may be presented at other branches or other banks, at which time each advances cash on the letter, notes the amount advanced on the certificate, and thus lowers the sum available for further advances.   The certificate of credit is, in other words, a sort of variable guaranteed check.   Business executives use them extensively when traveling.   Banks traditionally charge 1% of the issue amount for establishing them.

Traveler's Checks

Traveler's checks are cashier's checks issued in fixed amounts of $10, $20, $50, $100, and so on, on which the name of the payee is written before the payer signs the check to make a payment (see Figure 9-1).   They offer protection against loss or theft for the usual purchase price of 1% of face value.   Many large banks and financial institutions issue them and they are acceptable to merchants to the extent that the names of their issuers are well known.

The main reason people buy traveler's checks is to protect themselves from loss or theft.   Yet there are some little-known requirements that make the claims procedure difficult.   If you lose checks or report them stolen, the issuing firms have several requirements.   Often you must produce a written record showing the date and place where each check not stolen or lost was used.   Then you must provide a bond of indemnity assuring the company that you will reimburse their losses if it turns out that you spent your checks and that they were not lost.   Some firms will not replace lost or stolen checks until you have given a very detailed account of yourself and the firm as ascertained such things as your reputation in the community.   Some firms make it a practice to delay refunds for large losses (usually those over $2500) until they have been able to look over the claimant's background and the story of the checks' loss.

Traveler's checks are, on the whole, useful.   The customary 1% fee, however, is excessive; the issuing firms make vast profits on their float, investing much of this money (that they will later pay out) in high-yield, short-term money

9-1   A Specimen Traveler's Check

market certificates. Most of the 1% fee goes to the firm or bank that sells the check to you. (Each spring the Citibank, formerly First National City Bank of New York offers checks at a substantial discount. Citibank is a very large bank with offices all over the world. Its checks are worth considering, if you are able to get its discount. Also, Barclay's Bank, a British firm, sells traveler's checks without fee all year long. But the checks may be hard to cash in parts of the United States where Barclay's Bank is not well known.)

One must *never destroy* any cashier's check, certified check, or letter of credit. The only way you can have such an instrument refunded is to return it to the bank or issuer. If you destroy your own certified check, you may have to wait 20 years before you can withdraw the funds your bank prededucted from your account to cover it.

HOW TO RECONCILE A CHECKING ACCOUNT

Once a month your bank sends you a statement of your checks paid and deposits received. To reconcile the account, the statement should be compared with the register of checks written that you update each time you write a check. The five-step procedure is simple:

1 Examine all canceled checks returned with the statement to ensure they are bona fide and as issued. Tick off each on the register and statement and verify that each deposit made in the statement period is listed.
2 From your check book register, total all checks issued but not appearing on the statement. Deduct this sum from the statement balance and deduct the service charges, if any.
3 Add any deposits made since the closing date of the statement.
4 The resulting sum should agree with your register. If there is a discrepancy, verify all the arithmetic in your register and on your statement. A frequent problem is the failure to deduct the service charge from the register, causing the statement to appear deficient.
5 If there is still a problem, call your bank promptly.

COST OF A CHECKING ACCOUNT

The cost of maintaining a checking account has two components: charges levied by the bank, and interest foregone on account balances. Before 1933 many banks did pay interest on checking accounts but in that Depression year the Banking Act compelled banks henceforth not to pay interest on checking accounts. Rampant bank failures were, it was thought, in part due to excess interest payouts and the consequent weakening of bank finances. Today most

A CONVENTIONAL CHECK
AND THE MONTHLY STATEMENT
ON WHICH IT APPEARS

All spaces filled and lined— to make kiting impossible

Magnetic numbers indicate clearing route, payee, and amount

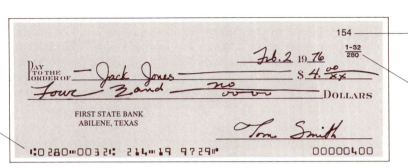

Number of check in payer's record

Bank's Federal Reserve Number

FIRST STATE BANK ABILENE, TEXAS	PREVIOUS BALANCE	$100.00		
	TOTAL CHECKS	134.00	4	NUMBER OF CHECKS
	TOTAL DEPOSITS	460	2	NUMBER OF DEPOSITS

ACCOUNT NAME & NUMBER: _____ TOM SMITH _____

CHECKS	CREDITS	DATE	BALANCE
4.00		2/5	96.00
	150.00	2/6	246.00
30.00		2/8	216.00
10.00		2/10	206.00
90.00		2/12	116.00
	310.00	2/13	426.00
Service charge - 0			
			Closing balance 426.00

Statement Period: From 1/15/76 to 2/14/76

banks pay no interest on checking accounts, though many offer side benefits such as promotional gifts for opening accounts, free checks, and assorted services.

There are about 13,000 commercial banks in the United States and 6000 "near banks," including savings and loan associations and mutual savings banks. Most near banks can now compete with commercial banks in offering checking accounts, so there are many kinds of checking accounts available. In January 1975 *Consumer Reports* published an analysis of checking account costs showing that there are six categories of account costs:

1 *Activity or "Per-Check" Plan:* This type of account has a flat fee for maintaining the account plus a charge per check. Assuming a maintenance fee of 75¢ per month and a fee of 10¢ per check, the annual cost for an account with 20 checks per month would be $33.

2 *Analysis Plan:* All transactions in this plan, both checks and deposits, bear a charge and at the end of a month charges are reduced by credits based on balances maintained during that month. A plan that charges 12¢ for each check and 6¢ for each deposit and provides a 20¢ credit for each $100 balance maintained, would cost $28.20 for an account with $2\frac{1}{2}$ deposits and 20 checks per month and an average balance of $100.

3 *Minimum Balance Plan:* With this type of account, customers enjoy unlimited checking for charges that vary with the minimum monthly balance. The large New York banks tend to require $500 for the waiver of such charges. CR found that smaller banks had lower no-fee requirements. Some banks use a lowest-account-balance method to figure monthly balance. Others,

more favorable to the consumer, measure account balances as the average of daily balances. If savings account interest rates are 5%, then a $500 minimum balance carried each month costs $25 per year in lost interest.

4 *Unconditional Free Checking:* According to *CR*'s published estimate, 13% of American banks, mostly in the Northeast, offered no-charge checking to any and all customers. Other banks offer them to students, the elderly, and good customers of other services.

5 *NOW Accounts:* These are checking accounts that pay interest. In 1972 banks and near banks in Massachusetts and New Hampshire began to offer a *Negotiable Order of Withdrawal,* a check that isn't quite a check. The NOW account is a legal runaround that works to the consumer's advantage. Conventional checks must be paid on demand. NOW account checks have a savings-account-type provision giving the bank the right to require 30–60 days notice before paying a check. So a NOW check isn't technically a check and thus escapes the 1933 Banking Act rule against interest being paid on checking accounts. Few banks have invoked the time delay rule, so the difference isn't significant.

CR found that NOW banks pay an average of 5% interest on checking account balances. Many offer free checking while others charge 10–15¢ per check. Obviously, for the consumer the NOW account is the best thing that has happened to checking accounts since the 1933 rule was made. Under considerable pressure from the public and some parts of the banking community, Congress appears willing to allow NOW accounts to spread to other states. New York, New Jersey, Illinois, and Wisconsin have already been added to the list of states in which NOW accounts are currently in operation.

"I'm afraid that despite the term 'free checking', you still have to deposit funds in your account."

CHECKLIST FOR CHECKING-ACCOUNT SHOPPERS

This checklist is intended as a guide for consumers comparing the cost of services from bank to bank. Don't try to get information for every type of account and service listed below; ask only about the account, or accounts, that seem most likely to suit your particular needs. Use the same approach for miscellaneous services. (We used data from First National City Bank, the largest bank in New York City, to demonstrate how to fill in the form.) You may find that banking institutions in your area offer variations of the accounts listed below, or, alternatively, do not offer the accounts we describe. In such cases, use this checklist as a guide to draw up your own questions. The object is to find out how much a given service costs, what you get in return for your money, and what the limitations are.

← fill in for your bank

Name of Bank — *First National City Bank*

Name of Officer Providing Information — *Christopher Reid, Asst. VP*

ACCOUNT COSTS

Activity Plan
- Monthly Maintenance Fee — *25¢ (not applied for 10 or more checks)*
- Cost per Check — *15¢*

Analysis Plan
- Monthly Maintenance Fee
- Cost per Check — *not available*
- Cost per Deposit
- Credit per $100 Balance

Minimum Balance Checking
- Balance Required — *$500 average balance*
- Service Fee if You Fall Below — *$2 for $300–$499; $3 under $300*

Unconditional Free Checking
- Available — *no*

NOW Account
- Balance Required
- Cost per "Check" — *not available*
- Rate of Interest Paid

Package Accounts
- Available — *yes*
- Cost per Month — *$4*
- Services Provided — *unlimited checking + checks; travelers + cashiers checks; money orders; $10 safe deposit box; lower loan rates*

CHECK COSTS

- Free nonpersonalized — *only occasionally*
- Free personalized — *yes (name only)*
- 200 Personalized — *about $2.50*

MISCELLANEOUS COSTS

- Stop-payment Order — *$3*
- Overdraft Charge — *$5*
  - Notify Before Bouncing? — *for charge of $6/yr.*
- Deposited Check Returned — *$1.50*
- Free Two-Way Postage — *no*
- Travelers Checks — *$1 per $100*
- Safe Deposit Box — *$16–$60 depending on size*
- Money Orders — *40¢ under $500; 68¢ above*
- Certified Checks — *$2.50*
- Cashier's Checks — *$2.50*

6 *Package Accounts:* For a flat fee of a few dollars a month, a bank may provide unlimited checking, no-charge travelers' checks, a free safety deposit box, a bank credit card (after a credit investigation), and overdraft privileges (that is, the right to have a check that would otherwise be NSF covered with a loan). These accounts are useful only to the people who write a substantial number of checks, say 20 or more each month.

Checking account costs vary not only in terms of the type of charge plan a bank uses but also by the cost of such incidental services as overdrafts, stop orders, and books of personalized checks. Each of these extras may cost $2–4. It is of interest that Canadian banks have both activity and package accounts. They offer 3% interest on activity plans and usually don't charge for checkbooks and stop orders.

Finding the best or least expensive checking account is often difficult. One should investigate the different types of banks in the community and if mail delays are not a problem, you may be able to use a bank in another community. Most banks pay mailing costs for out-of-town customers.

HANDLE CHECKS WITH CARE

Checks may be misued, causing substantial inconvenience and loss. All holders of checking accounts should, therefore, be aware of five ways to protect themselves against losses due to checks:

1 *Never sign a blank check.* The amount payable should be written on any check you sign. If you do sign a blank check or leave the payee's name blank, *anyone* who finds the check can legally cash it—at your loss.

2 *Fill in every part of the name and amount spaces when writing out the payee's name and the amount of money payable.* If, for example, you write "Four   Dollars," a person could easily write in "teen" and collect $10 more than you intended to pay. A "1" in front of the "4" in the space where the amount is written numerically would make the amount agree. This fraudulent raising of a check's amount is called *kiting* (making the paper fly higher). *Avoid kiting by writing the number of dollars very close to the dollar sign in the number space and against the left margin in the word space.* Draw a line from the end of the number to the end of each space. Do the same in the payee space, thus making it impossible for the holder to write in "or bearer" after the name of the proper payee.

3 *Keep deposit slips and canceled checks in a safe place.* Compare them with your monthly checking account statements. When destroying old deposit slips and unused or canceled checks, especially those with specimens of your signature, rip them up carefully or destroy them by some other means. If for some reason a check is returned to you or you don't use a check you've written out, either destroy it or write "VOID" on its front and back.

4 *You can have your bank stop payment if you find that a merchant cannot deliver goods as promised or has otherwise seriously breached a contract.* To stop a check, call the bank (it's faster and more reliable than a telegram), explain the situation and advise them of the amount of the check, the name of the payee, the date and number, and other particulars they ask for. Then put all these details into a letter and send it to the bank by certified or registered mail, or special delivery if necessary. Some banks have special stop-order forms and some charge fees for this service. Do not, however, stop checks frivolously—you can be liable for an unjustified stop order if the payee, properly entitled to be paid, sues you and/or your bank for payment.

5 *Do not issue or accept checks with erasures or other evidence of alteration.* Most checks are printed on special safety paper that makes alteration by erasure or chemical means obvious. If you issue checks with erasures, they will be suspect. If you receive or are offered an erased or altered check, investigate it carefully.

BAD CHECKS

Some people write bad checks. Usually they haven't sufficient funds in their accounts and the banks bounce such checks back to depositors with an NSF ("not sufficient funds") notation. In other cases people write checks on nonexistent accounts or forge other people's names as account holders. NSF checks can result from error in good faith, for example, if a person forgets that he or she hasn't quite enough to cover a check. But the second type of bad check is usually of criminal origin, though there may be exceptions (for example, if you write a check on an account you've forgotten you closed or you improperly sign someone else's check because the payer had a broken arm and asked you to help).

Bad checks may be handled two ways. A good faith NSF check can be collected by a phone call or letter reminding the payer of the mistake made. If the payer doesn't make good on the check and it is for a small amount, you can go to small claims court, though this costs time and a few dollars for a filing fee. Fraudulent checks should be turned over to police authorities, though a phone call to the issuer, if you can find the person, may help if you mention your intent to call on the police.

THE UNIVERSAL CREDIT CARD

There is some talk today that the personal check will be replaced by a universal credit card. Computers, it is said, will automatically collect wages, deposit them in designated accounts, and pay bills. The individual account holder will be free of the labor of writing checks, reconciling statements, tracking down bad checks, and so forth. Human error will diminish, the float will vanish, and business will be more efficient.

So goes the fable. Writing checks and reconciling accounts may be troublesome but each step is an opportunity for one to check and thereby control one's money. Do you want your bill paid automatically, even if it is wrong? Wouldn't you rather examine it for error and then pay it? What if the computers necessary for such a large task break down, send wrong bills, or lose part of your paycheck? And what will this mixed blessing cost? Will people be obliged to use a fee-for-service card instead of no-fee cash? Or will merchants be charged for service and so have to raise their retail prices? (See the further discussion of credit cards in Chapter 10.)

Perhaps most important, what will happen to privacy if a national data bank knows one's full financial history? Will businesses have access to one's spending habits, the better to cast advertising and promotions? Will creditors have instant access to a debtor's history or will a no-questions-asked authority be able to take a part of a person's paycheck? The implications of the cashless, checkless society must be explored, but it as well may be true that some inefficiency is a low price to pay to protect the little privacy an industrial society like ours allows us.

SUMMARY

1 Checks are important to nearly all lifestyles.
2 A check is a *negotiable* contract.
3 Endorsement of a check upon accepting it controls subsequent negotiability. There are blank, specific, and restrictive endorsements.
4 One who receives a check in good faith and for value received is a holder in due course and is presumed to deserve payment regardless of any defects in the merchandise or services for which the check was issued or accepted by subsequent endorsers.
5 The Federal Reserve System maintains check-clearing facilities for the American banking system.
6 After a check is deposited into a payee's account but before it is deducted from the payer's account, there is an increase in the money supply known as the float.
7 All special checks (certified, traveler's, cashier's, and letters of credit) are guaranteed promises by reputable institutions to make full and prompt payment on presentation of a check. These instruments solve the problem of anonymity for people when they are not well known to those with whom they deal.
8 Checking account fees vary considerably. Checking accounts tend not to pay interest in the United States, though often they do in Canada.
9 Checks must be carefully issued, reconciled, and stored.

Suggestions for Further Reading

Chandler, Lester V. *The Economics of Money and Banking,* 6th ed. New York: Harper & Row, 1973, Chs. 1 and 2.
Consumer Reports, January 1975, pp. 32–38, and May 1975, p. 307.
Markstein, David L. *Manage Your Money and Live Better.* New York: McGraw-Hill, 1971.

The Consumer Workshop

1 Checking accounts facilitate paying for things, but they're not the only way to pay. Discuss which lifestyles don't call for such accounts and what methods they do use.

2 A checking account carries advantages but also poses risks for the person who uses a checking account frequently. What are these risks? Does the risk of forgery or kiting increase with certain ways of living? What are sensible rules, appropriate to any lifestyle, for managing checking accounts safely?

3 The businessperson must handle many more checks than the average student. Every day a business makes payments and receives them, and a businessperson has to know a good deal about endorsements. If you were in business, what would be your policy on endorsements?

4 Not all banks are the same. Some banks charge quite a lot for checking, others levy no charges. How would you go about finding the checking account which provides good service at lowest cost? Refer to the checklist in the text.

10 CONSUMER CREDIT AND LOANS

" Americans often overpay for credit because they don't know how—or won't take the time—to shop for the best deal. "

MORTON C. PAULSON*

This chapter examines the problems of securing the credit and loans that consumers often need. We begin by analyzing the role of credit in family and personal financial planning, defining the nature of the credit available and the levels of debt characteristic of American families. Then we examine the types and sources of consumer credit and the mechanics of loan agreements. Next, we look at recent federal legislation concerning credit administration, bankruptcy, and the credit problems that affect women, the young, and the poor. Finally, we review government regulation of the credit industry and recommend some reforms.

CONSUMER DEBT

Between 1950 and October 1975, consumer debt in the United States rose from $21.5 billion to $190.8 billion, an annual rate of increase of about 9%. Breaking down the figure for October, 1975, we find that the total was composed of $156.9 billion in installment loans and $33.8 billion in noninstallment loans. Installment loans included $52.7 billion in automobile loans, $45.5 billion in personal (unsecured, signature-only) loans, $8.1 billion in home improvement loans, and $50.6 billion in miscellaneous loans.[1] (see Figure 10-1).

Thus consumer debt has risen at a very rapid rate even in comparison to corporate debt. In the 24 years following 1950, consumer debt rose about 9 times, while corporate debt rose only four and a half times. The increasing tendency of people to go into debt may be attributed to important changes in the age, income, and location of the population. Young married people make heavy use of credit. When they are forming their households, their needs exceed their current income and credit allows them to meet current needs by drawing on their future income. Between 1950 and 1971 the number of persons aged 18–24 years, the average age of these young married people, grew from 18.6 million to 28.2 million, an increase of about 50%.

* Quoted in *The National Observer,* February 3, 1973, p. 3.
[1] National Commission on Consumer Finance, *Consumer Credit in the United States* (Washington, D.C.), December 1968, p. 9 (hereafter cited as CCUS); *Federal Reserve Bulletin,* December 1975, p. A-45.

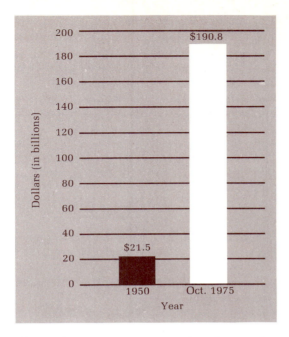

10-1   Consumer Debt in the United States, 1950 and 1975

Changing Lifestyles

The amount and stability of family income has increased substantially since 1950, allowing many families to incur future income obligations in exchange for consumption goods in the present.   In 1950 15% of the U.S. population lived on farms; by 1970 less than 5% did.   The shift to cities, together with the influence toward cultural homogenization produced by the mass media, has probably induced a greater reliance on credit to achieve what is conceived of as the "American way of life." [2]

The rise of credit coincided with the social conditions of the United States at the end of World War II.   Soldiers came home, married, and produced a baby boom that called for more homes, clothing, transportation facilities, and so on. Land and houses were available and relatively inexpensive in rural areas that quickly became sprawling suburbs.   The automobile made it possible to commute from city fringes to downtown offices and factories.   To acquire these new houses, cars, and so on, young families needed to spend money they didn't actually have.   Credit made it possible for them to mortgage their future incomes for present prosperity.

The number of people living in their own homes rose from 55% of the population in 1950 to 64% in 1970.   In addition, the shift to people living in their own homes, especially in the suburbs, has resulted in a great demand for household equipment purchased on credit: for washing machines, refrigerators, lawn

[2] CCUS, pp. 5, 6.

mowers, and so on. As well, suburban living, together with the decline in urban transit systems, produced a need for families to have more than one car, and the proportion of families owning two or more cars rose from 16% in 1950 to 30% in 1970. Overall there has been a trend toward what is called *asset ownership,* in which consumers prefer, for example, to have their own washing machines instead of making use of laundromats, to have their own cars instead of paying for public transportation, and to use the television at home instead of going to movies.[3]

MAKING USE OF CREDIT

When one has decided that one's available cash is not to be used for a current purchase, the decision to use credit or, alternatively, to forego the purchase until later comes down to asking, Is it more beneficial to have the thing now or in the future? Or, in other terms, does the cost of credit outweigh the benefit of having the commodity now rather than later?

Economists call the value of a missed opportunity the *opportunity cost.* The cost of credit may exceed the value of its current use or, on the other hand, the value of the product's use may exceed the cost of credit. For example, the 36 months of rental charges one saves by buying a lawnmower on a 3-year loan may exceed the interest charges for the loan. Ignoring any repair costs and gas for transporting the lawnmower, the opportunity cost indicates credit costs less than waiting to purchase. Only when the opportunity cost is zero has the consumer made the best of credit opportunities.

Let's look at some examples of how credit can work to the advantage of the consumer and how the failure to use credit can cause the consumer to bear an opportunity cost for the lost chance to use the credit. Let us say that a young family decides not to use the cash it has on hand to buy a washer and dryer. It then has two choices, either to use the laundromat a few blocks away, thereby renting the washer and dryer service, or to buy the needed machines on credit. A study prepared for the National Commission on Consumer Finance indicates that the annual rates of the consumer's "profit" from owning a washer and a dryer ranged from 6.7% annually, with three loads per week, to 29.0% with seven loads per week.[4] If the yearly interest is less than 6.7% for the three-load family or 29.0% for the seven-load family, the use of credit would be efficient. But credit is difficult to find at 6.7% (except on life insurance policies), so the three-load family would do better to use the laundromat if it wants neither to use cash on hand nor to borrow on the value of its life insurance to buy the units. But the seven-load family can very likely find credit at a rate less than 29% annually and thus can use the credit efficiently.

[3] CCUS, pp. 6, 7.
[4] CCUS, p. 7.

There are a number of other circumstances in which credit can be employed efficiently. For example, if prices are rising faster than the prevailing rates of bank interest, it pays to buy on credit. Let us say that you expect automobile prices to rise 25% next year and you need to replace your 10-year-old car immediately. Then, even assuming that your present car will have no repair expenses and has as well a constant (or zero) trade-in value, you can use credit efficiently as long as the interest rates on car loans are less than 25% per year.

Yet there are dangers in extending one's credit obligations. Recessions can cause layoffs and reduce a family's ability to repay its debts. And price change estimates are only educated guesses. If you buy a three-year supply of canned beans on credit at 15% annually and bean prices rise less than 15%—you've lost. If the car you buy on credit turns out to be a lemon, you may still have to pay for it. Worst, the consumer who learns to depend on credit or uses it by habit may become a captive of the stores that extend it, buying only where credit is available and overlooking stores where prices in fact may be lower.

INTEREST IN GENERAL

Lenders set interest rates to provide some profit and to compensate themselves for the cost of acquiring their funds, the length of the desired loan, the administrative cost of carrying the loan, and the risk of losing some or all of the loan if the borrower defaults on the obligation to repay. Long-term loans to risky borrowers should and do bear higher interest than short-term loans to safe borrowers. A loan for which the borrower puts up no security or collateral will cost more than one secured by the creditor's right to take the collateral if the borrower defaults.

Interest Regulations

Governments often have felt it necessary to set limits on the interest rates lenders charge. We can find examples of interest ceilings being imposed by governments from as early as the 24th century B.C.[5] Yet most interest ceilings don't work. Lenders become more secretive about their loan rates, reword their contracts so that interest is called something else, and paradoxically raise their rates to compensate themselves for the additional bother of evading the law. Legitimate lenders may be driven out of the market and be replaced by those who disregard the law. Most of all, interest ceilings tend to make it more difficult for borrowers to obtain credit.

Laws regulating interest rates or putting ceilings on various loan markets do, nevertheless, have some appropriate uses. Governments should not attempt to control interest rates through ceilings, but they can use regulations, together with good law enforcement, to eliminate loan racketeers from the credit market.

[5] CCUS, p. 91.

Where high-risk borrowers are forced to pay 100–200% per year to gangsters on penalty of being beaten or murdered if they default, government can use interest regulations as a part of the effort to eliminate these loan-sharking practices. But, as we have shown, interference with the process of the supply-and-demand determination of interest rates works poorly and produces as many problems as it solves.

REVOLVING CREDIT

A firm can offer its charge account customers the chance to renew and add to existing balances by making periodic payments on past balances due. Such continuously renewable, or *revolving charge,* accounts are said to "revolve" as they are paid off. A firm may offer a customer the privilege of paying a balance due after a certain period, usually 30 days, with no charge for the credit if the account is paid strictly within the time allotted. In this case you could buy a suit for $100, charge it, receive a bill for $100, and pay it within 30 days; each month you could repeat the process and never be obliged to pay an interest charge. Other kinds of revolving accounts charge interest but renew the credit as past balances and interest are paid.

Revolving credit accounts are commonly issued by department stores, gas companies, and the major credit card firms such as Master Charge and Bank-Americard. It is estimated that there are 300 million cards for revolving credit in use today and as such they constitute a form of "near money."

While many revolving accounts charge interest only if they are not paid within the customary 30-day period, others charge interest as soon as an item is charged. In this case the amount of interest charged depends on the rate of interest and the method of calculating interest. It is important to be aware that even assuming that the rate of interest is set at $1\frac{1}{2}$% per month, or 18% per year (common figures), the amount of interest actually charged will vary greatly, depending upon the billing practices of a given company.

For example, under the *previous balance* method of account computation the customer pays interest on the balance due at the beginning of a given period. This means that even if he or she has paid off the balance due during the current period, full interest still is charged, as though the account were not cleared. So, if you have a $500 balance and pay off $250 in 15 days, at the start of the next billing period you will be billed for the full interest on the $500 balance, 5 times $1.50 per $100, or $7.50. But your true outstanding balance would have been $250, on which interest should have been $2\frac{1}{2}$ times $1.50 per $100, or $3.75. This is in effect a 100% "overcharge."

Under the *average daily balance* method of calculating interest, balances outstanding at different times of the month are added up and divided by the number of days in the period. If the $500 balance were reduced to $250 at mid-month, say, the credit calculation would be

$$\frac{\$500 \times 15 \text{ days} + \$250 \times 15 \text{ days}}{30 \text{ days}} = \$3.75$$

The *adjusted balance* method of billing, on the other hand, charges only for amounts due after the current payments are made. The $500 balance reduced to $250 bears interest only on the outstanding $250. At $1\frac{1}{2}$% per month this would be $3.75.

The best deal for the account holder is the *past-due balance* method, under which credit charges are based only on balances not paid during the *next* billing cycle. A $500 balance thus has two billing periods beyond the current one to be paid off without charge. Credit charges are not levied until the $500 has been unpaid for 60 days, or 55 days if the accounting system needs 5 days to catch up.

Problems of Credit

Errors. Computer-generated bills are often in error but it is difficult, of course, for the consumer to get the machine or its attendants to correct mistakes, for notes and protests are often ignored. Vast overcharges can be sent to collection agencies and the customer, and friends and associates, may sometimes be subjected to illegal harassment, all for bills not really owed. Under the Fair Credit Billing Act of 1974, a creditor is required to answer within 30 days a customer's inquiry about a charge, and while the discussions continue, the creditor is not allowed to initiate collection of the bill. If a company cannot explain its bills within 90 days, the charges up to $50 are forfeited. For a $200 unexplained bill, only $150 would be payable after 90 days. The harassed consumer can bring a civil suit for damages and collect a minimum of $100 from a firm that violates the Act.

Failures to Refund. A problem with revolving charge accounts has been the failure of some stores to refund overpayments by customers or even to notify the customers of their outstanding credits. A September 1974 complaint by the Federal Trade Commission charged some prestigious major retailers, including Bonwit Teller, Neiman-Marcus, and Gimbel Brothers, with failing to notify customers with outstanding credit balances of their right to request cash refunds. Some firms also have ceased to notify customers of their outstanding credits after certain periods of account inactivity. The FTC estimated that between 1969 and 1974 Gimbel Brothers kept $1.2 million of its customers' money and that all firms charged held back a total of $2.8 million of customer funds.

Hidden Costs. Credit never comes free. If you take out a "free" 30-day loan on a revolving charge account, the company extending credit must itself obtain the money and pay on it the going commercial rate of interest for business loans. Alternatively, universal charge cards giving customers 30 days to pay before interest is levied, such as American Express and BankAmericard, collect a 5% surcharge from merchants to cover the free credit they extend to cardholders. 5% per month for purchases means 60% per year, a great deal of income for the credit card companies and a great loss to consumers.

It has become a common business practice for merchants to bury the cost of credit by advancing the selling price of an item by about 5%, and American Express and other universal charge card issuers traditionally have required participating merchants (that is, those displaying the BankAmericard or other such decals in their windows) to refuse to give discounts for cash. Prompted by a Consumers Union lawsuit and subsequent Federal Trade Commission intervention, the American Express Company stopped coercing merchants and now allows them to give discounts for cash payment. The legal precedent appears to apply throughout the United States, although in Canada and elsewhere outside of the United States merchants and restaurant owners still may be bound by their contracts to refuse to give cash discounts.

Currently, one may offer a merchant payment either by way of a universal charge card or in cash with a 2–5% discount. A merchant who takes the cash is really ahead, for he or she has the money immediately and, at any discount less than 5%, makes additional profit on the spread between the real price and the price inflated by the charge-card system. Some consumer groups offer cash discount cards and lists of participating merchants. And it does no harm simply to bargain on your own.

The Layaway or Delayed Purchase Plan

There is an odd variant on credit buying in which the buyer pays in installments for goods before being allowed to have them. The customer makes a series of payments until they add up to the purchase price of an article (plus, perhaps, a service charge) during which time the merchant "lays away" the article for the buyer until its price is fully paid. Although no interest is charged, the customer in fact bears an additional cost because he or she is providing his or her own credit. The merchant holds the customer's money, earning interest on it while the customer earns nothing. Layaways are thus inefficient for the consumer, yet it appears that some people feel the need for this parentlike form of disciplined saving.

Credit Card Loss and Theft

The so-called universal credit cards were perhaps an inevitable consequence of the modern computer's ability to handle billions of charge sales with great ease. Equipped with these computers, thousands of retail firms in the past sent unsolicited credit cards to millions of people, who had never asked for them. Some of the cards were lost or misused and the recipients were billed for items they'd never bought or seen. Deluged by complaints from angry consumers, Congress passed a bill, in force since January 1972, that limits the liability of credit card holders to $50. This means that if a card issuer fails to provide a method for notification of loss (such as a stamped, self-addressed envelope), there is no liability for loss. Further, the cards must bear some means of identifying the proper holder, such as a signature, and unsolicited cards may not be issued to people who don't desire them.

Credit cards, in spite of these new laws, still must be used with the care that one accords currency. If a credit card is lost, the issuing firm should be notified by phone or telegram and followed up by a registered or certified letter. It is also possible to buy credit card loss and theft insurance. Frequently, credit card firms provide this insurance free or at a low fee, and many homeowner and tenant insurance policies have it built-in at no extra cost.

INSTALLMENT CREDIT

Installment credit is extended when a lender and a borrower make a special agreement that a certain sum lent will be repaid in a given number of payments with interest set at an agreed-on amount. This installment credit may be *secured* or *unsecured*. Secured credit is issued against a *lien* (a right of seizure or repossession) against some kind of property. Secured consumer loans are usually issued on houses (as mortgages), on cars, and on recreational devices such as pleasure boats and snowmobiles. Unsecured loans, on the other hand, are those issued on a "signature only" basis.

When deciding on what kind of loan you want, it is well to remember that, generally, the more security a lender has, the lower the interest charges can be. For example, during 1965–1975, typical lending rates on house mortgages varied from 6–9%, on cars and boats 12–14%, and on unsecured loans 15–36%—usually depending on the amount of security one could offer.

As we shall see in the next section, when we examine the laws requiring "truth in lending," a loan's annual rate of interest can be figured easily by taking account of the length of its full life. But how does one determine the rate of interest on a loan that is paid off well before it is due? Many lenders recoup the interest charges before beginning to apply loan repayments to the outstanding principal. Suppose that a person borrows $200 at an annual rate of 16%, to be repaid in 24 installments of $9.79 each. If the loan contract says that all interest due is to be paid before the principal is credited, it will be necessary to wait until about 4 payments have been made before any dent can be made in the $200 principal outstanding. If the $200 is repaid after ten months, not a penny in interest will have been saved, for all the interest due was repaid by the end of the fourth month. Borrowers would do well to modify loan agreements to apportion interest to the time their loans are actually outstanding, but sadly, most borrowers do not have the knowledge, ability, or courage to bargain this way.

Consumer Loan Sources

Consumers may obtain loans under varying conditions and widely differing rates of interest, depending on the source (see Figure 10-2). Seven commonly used sources are:

1 Life insurance firms
2 Commercial banks
3 Savings and loan associations
4 Credit unions

5 Finance companies
6 Pawnbrokers
7 Illegal lenders

Life insurance firms make loans on request on the cash value of life insurance policies. Interest is usually charged at 5–6% of the outstanding loan balance with no time limits on repayment. These loans are the least expensive to obtain since the insurer is merely lending the policyholder his or her own money.

Commercial banks make secured and unsecured loans at their prime rate or higher. In 1975 loan rates ranged from 9–18%, depending upon the type of loan and the nature of its security, if any. Interest rates and repayment periods are arranged individually for amounts and times agreeable to both the bank and the borrower.

Savings and loan associations make nonmortgage loans on a fraction of funds the borrower has in his savings account, with interest usually running from 9–12%. Repayment schedules are usually set up to a limit of 3 years.

Credit unions make loans to their members at reasonable rates. Since they do not operate for profit, credit-union loan rates are low, usually around 9–12%, though sometimes they rise to 15%. Some credit unions, due to their small size, do not have the monetary capacity to make large loans. Others, those with funds comparable to those of the medium-sized commercial banks, can offer the same service as commercial banks.

Finance companies make secured and unsecured loans at 12–36% per year. Typical rates are around 21–24%. Finance company installment repayment contracts usually work on the basis of "first repayments to interest only," so that a borrower may be penalized (depending on the state in which the finance company operates) if the loan is paid off well ahead of time. Some states and Cana-

10-2 Sources and Rates for Consumer Loans

Source	Who May Borrow	Rate	Maturity	Credit investigation
Life insurance companies	Policyholders with cash value life insurance	5–6%	None	no
Commercial banks	Anyone meeting bank credit standards	9–18%	Short-term; 1–3 years	yes
Savings and loan associations	Savings-account holders or shareholders	9–12%	1–3 years	yes
Credit unions	Members	9–12%	10 years	no
Finance companies	Anyone meeting credit standards	12–36%	5 years	yes
Pawnbrokers	Anyone with personal property	25% to over 125%	1 year	no
Illegal lenders	Anyone	very high (100% per week, for example)	Indefinite	no

dian provinces require interest rebates for a loan prepayment of this kind. Most finance companies use 60-month installment contracts on which interest is in fact substantial if the loan is carried to its maturity.

Pawnbrokers take a borrower's goods as security on loans. Their rates range from 25% to over 125%, depending on their appraisal of the goods' worth (which is often far less than the replacement or the original cost). Some pawnbrokers deny that they charge interest, claiming instead that they charge "storage." In fact, this is a ruse to help them evade legislation requiring disclosure of their true interest rates.

Illegal lenders are those unregulated or unlicensed lenders who do not obey the "truth in lending" and/or other regulations. Sometimes called loan sharks, these may be persons or firms that try to make a borrower sign a loan agreement with blank spaces or that try to avoid giving a copy of the loan agreement to the borrower. Loan sharks are lenders of last resort for those with no established credit or those who have exhausted their credit. Their collection methods are often vicious and, since they are unlicensed and unregulated, they have little to lose by using extortion and brutality.

"The masked man? He's the Loan Arranger."

FORMS OF CREDIT AGREEMENTS

When credit for goods or money is extended by a store, bank, or other lender, a written contract must be signed assuring the lender of repayment of a specific amount within a given time. These contracts usually specify the penalties that can be levied on the borrower for failure to repay on time. Because the conditions for loan agreements vary greatly, it is important to understand how they are written and how they work. This way, the borrower knows what he or she is getting and thus can both shop for credit more wisely and bargain to strike out unusually hard conditions.

Finance Charges

The basic element of a loan agreement is what the loan will cost. If you borrow $100 for one year and pay $6 interest for it, repaying $106 365 days later, you have had the use of $100 at an annual percentage rate of 6%. But if you have to repay the $106 in 12 equal monthly installments, you do not have the use of the $100 for the entire year. In fact, over the entire year you have the use, on the average, of only about one-half of the full $100. So the $6 interest charge becomes an annual rate of 11%.

In the past many lenders engaged in shady practices, for instance, using clever arithmetic to conceal from borrowers the true costs of interest. Alert to this, Congress created a series of laws known as Truth in Lending that, at many levels of enforcement and supervision, went into effect in mid-1969. The basis for Truth in Lending is Federal Reserve Regulation Z, requiring that all forms of consumer credit transactions under $25,000, and all real estate transactions involving property for personal, family, or agricultural use, be subject to honest disclosure of interest rates (see Figure 10-3). If Regulation Z is violated the borrower may sue the lender for twice the amount of the finance charge for a minimum of $100 or a maximum of $1000 plus the court costs and attorneys' fees. Willful evasion of Regulation Z subjects the lender to penalties of up to one year in jail and a fine of $5000. Nine different federal agencies enforce Truth in Lending.

All loans made under Regulation Z must state their borrowing costs as a finance charge, expressed in terms of an annual percentage rate. These borrowing costs include interest, loan fees, finders' fees, discounts, service and carrying charges, mortgage points, appraisal fees (except in real estate transac-

10-3 A Disclosure Form for Regulation Z

The Merchants Bank of New York 434 BROADWAY • NEW YORK, N.Y. 10013 • (212) 966-5500

BRANCH NO. _____
APPLICATION NO. _____
LOAN NO. _____ DATE _____

CREDIT LIFE INSURANCE COVERAGE UP TO $5,000 IS PROVIDED BY THE BANK UNDER A GROUP POLICY AT NO ADDITIONAL CHARGE.

STATEMENT OF DISCLOSURE

FEDERAL CONSUMER CREDIT PROTECTION ACT
The above law requires the disclosure of certain matters with respect to consumer credit transactions. The note which you have tendered to the bank with your application for a loan contains the following provisions in addition to those at the right.

ATTORNEY'S FEES IN THE EVENT OF SUIT
You agree that if the bank institutes action to enforce or collect the note or any other of your "Liabilities" for non-payment at maturity, the actual expenditures for such action, including attorney's fee of 15% of the amount due thereon, shall be added thereto and will be paid by you.

DELINQUENCY CHARGES IN THE EVENT OF LATE PAYMENTS
If any of the payments under your note, the maturity of which has not been accelerated, shall become due and remain unpaid for a period in excess of ten days thereafter, you promise to pay immediately a fine of five cents per dollar on each such unpaid instalment, provided that no such fine shall exceed five dollars. The aggregate of such fines shall not exceed 2% of the Total of Payments and, in no event, $25. Bank may accelerate the obligation and declare the entire indebtedness due and payable, without notice or demand, upon failure to pay any monthly instalment when due or upon borrower's death, insolvency, bankruptcy, entry of judgment or tax levy, termination of employment, or any breach of this or any other note or agreement with Bank.

The Federal Equal Credit Opportunity Act prohibits creditors from discriminating credit applicants on the basis of sex or marital status. The Federal Agency which administers compliance with this law concerning this Bank is the Federal Reserve Bank, 33 Liberty Street, New York, N.Y. 10045.

1. AMOUNT FINANCED DATE:		, 19
a. LOAN PROCEEDS		$
b. FILING AND OFFICIAL FEES		$
PRIOR LOAN	$	
LESS: INT. REBATE	$	
c. AMOUNT REFINANCED		$
TOTAL AMOUNT FINANCED (A+B+C)		$
2. FINANCE CHARGE		$
3. TOTAL OF PAYMENTS (1+2)		$
4. ANNUAL PERCENTAGE RATE		%
5. NUMBER OF PAYMENTS		
6. MONTHLY PAYMENT		$
7. DATE OF FIRST PAYMENT		19

Note that under the security interest described above and the terms of the Security Agreement, (a copy of which is part of your note), after acquired property will be subject to the bank's security interests and other future indebtedness is secured by any such security interest. In addition, you are required to pay and the Security Agreement secures all taxes, assessments, and charges levied on the property for the use, storage, maintenance or repair thereof, all charges and expenses in connection with or incidental to the repossession, any attempted repossession, holding, storage, preparation for sale and the sale, including a reasonable attorney's fee and legal expenses (which are agreed to be 15% of the amount recovered), paid by or incurred by the bank and all premiums paid by the bank for insurance required to be maintained under such agreement.

The bank may also obtain a security interest in other collateral by virtue of security agreements with you, given in connection with other "Liabilities." You may choose the person through which any insurance against loss or damage to property covered by the security agreement is to be obtained.

SECURITY INTERESTS
You give the bank a lien on, security interest in and right to set-off of all of your moneys, securities and other property, now or hereafter delivered to or permitted to remain with the bank, or coming into possession of the bank in any way, and also any balance of any of your deposit accounts and credits with, and any and all of your claims against, the bank at any time existing as collateral security for the payment of your note and of all other liabilities and obligations now or hereafter owed by you to the bank (all of which are collectively called "Liabilities").

REBATE OF FINANCE CHARGES AND PENALTY CHARGES IN THE EVENT OF PREPAYMENT
The unearned portion of the finance charge will be rebated pursuant to S 108 of the New York State Banking Law, which provides that borrower may prepay a loan in full or, with the consent of the bank, may refinance the loan. In the event of such prepayment or refinancing, the bank shall refund: (1) a rebate of precomputed interest computed under the Rule of 78's provided, however, that if the amount of interest previously deducted (i) was less than $10 no refund shall be required; or (ii) that if the interest previously deducted exceeded the sum of $10 and the earned interest is less than that amount, the bank may retain such an additional amount as will bring the earned interest to the sum of $10 and refund the remainder, and provided further, that unless the loan is refinanced, no refund shall be required if it amounts to less than $1.

tions), credit life insurance premiums, and investigation or credit-report fees. The lender must also list the cash price, down payment, unpaid balance financed, and penalties for late payments. (In real estate transactions, closing and settlement costs are exempt from inclusion in the finance charge disclosure statement.) Regulation Z also gives a three-day cancellation privilege to borrowers who have signed for real estate loans. And Regulation Z requires stores and finance companies to itemize charges and credits on their monthly or periodic statements to account holders so that borrowers know exactly what they are paying.

Timing

Loan agreements must also include a statement of the method of repayment, the frequency of required periodic repayments, and the total number of repayments required. If repayments are due on a certain day of the month, the contract must say so. But contracts are not required to set out the apportionment of repayments between interest and principal. If the lender first applies the repayments to the interest and, after all the interest is actually prepaid, only then to the principal, the borrower will lose if he or she prepays the loan and fails to receive a refund of interest charges for the time the loan was not outstanding. If there are prepayment penalties, the contract must indicate them. If the prepayment costs are not readily disclosed, you should get them stated in writing. And if they are substantial, you should shop around for a loan with lesser penalties.

Balloon Payments

Some interest contracts have what are called *balloon payments*. These are final payments "blown up" to a size larger than previous payments. They can be used to make figures come out evenly. For example, if total interest charges are $50 and each of 23 payments has included $2 for interest, then only $46 has been paid toward the $50 in interest due. The final payment, number 24, will have to include a $4 balloon. When used to keep repayments amounts in round numbers, thereby avoiding odd cents, they are a legitimate convenience to borrower and lender. But balloons have been used by some lenders to make the borrower in effect unable to make a final loan payment, thereby allowing the lender to repossess the goods for which the loan was made, resell the merchandise, and start all over again. In automobile and appliance sales, balloon clauses were set so that final payments were many hundreds of dollars higher than previous payments. Many buyers couldn't meet these huge payments and defaulted, thus allowing the sellers to resell the merchandise on other loan agreements.

Contracts of Adhesion

Installment contracts are written by creditors, not by borrowers. It would be difficult for the consumer-finance industry to administer millions of variations of contracts, each written especially for a given transaction. To reduce such an administrative problem, lenders write standard contracts and expect borrowers to sign them without requesting special conditions. Yet convenience is only a par-

"Truth-in-lending?
Do we ask you for
truth-in-borrowing?"

tial explanation for the use of such standard contracts. The lenders and their attorneys wish to protect themselves as much as possible; they are less concerned about the welfare of their borrowers than about their own profits. So most lenders write contracts that give them a wide range of heavy weapons to use against borrowers who fail even in a slight way to live up to their agreements. Because a person can do little but sign the standard contract or look elsewhere for credit, a borrower is forced in effect to *adhere* to a contract he or she has had little influence in writing. These contracts are called *contracts of adhesion.* Such adhesion clauses are the source of most of the unfairness in debtor-creditor relations and the reason why the person unable to make even a small payment on time may have almost no power for protection against having wages attached and property seized or life and work disrupted by vicious collection practices.

Acceleration   *Acceleration clauses* give the creditor the right to declare all principal and interest due on the loan to be payable immediately when the debtor fails to make a payment on time or as soon as the creditor determines that the loan has become "insecure." When the creditor exercises the right to accelerate, he or she can either repossess the goods if the loan is secured by collateral, or sue for full repayment. Once acceleration begins the debtor must prove that he or she did not *default,* that is, fail to make full and timely payment. In some states, if the creditor is repossessing goods, seizure can occur without giving the debtor any notice of the intended repossession. Statistics indicate that banks begin acceleration an average of 12 days after default of a timely payment and that finance companies wait 16.5 days to do so. Acceleration ought to require written notice to the debtor of the intent to accelerate, allowing the debtor the right to make up all payments due. Unfortunately, the law does not usually provide this.

Confession of Judgment

Many installment agreements contain a clause authorizing the creditor to appoint an attorney to appear in court to confess judgment (admit error or guilt) on the part of the debtor. When any slight breach in the debtor's contract occurs, the creditor can initiate suit to recover the loan or collateral. Using the *confession of judgment clause,* he or she hires an attorney to "represent" the debtor, obtains a confession of judgment, and then takes all that's possible of the debtor's goods or wages. Confession of judgment clauses, in other words, force the debtor to admit error before any default actually occurs, thus giving one no recourse to self-defense. And, in almost every case, these clauses are accompanied by statements in which the debtor agrees to pay all the legal fees of the debtor's own appointed lawyer as well as the creditor's lawyer and all court and collection fees.

Venue

Venue is the place within a jurisdiction in which a trial takes place. Some creditors, by choosing an inconvenient venue for their legal actions against debtors, make it difficult for debtors to explain their situations or to defend themselves. Some very large retailers choose, for their own convenience and the debtor's inconvenience, to hold trials many hundreds of miles from the debtor's home. This is an obviously heavy burden for the person who must take leave of a job to defend him- or herself against what may be entirely wrongful accusations.

Holder in Due Course

It is a common practice for stores and firms that issue credit to customers to sell installment contracts to finance companies. This way the merchant gets paid quickly and is able to avoid being in the business of running a small-loans office. It is an old principle of law that one who takes a promissory note in good faith is entitled to have it honored. This theory, that the *holder in due course* is entitled to his or her money, means in practice that once a loan agreement is sold to a third party, the loan must be paid off exactly as the contract specifies regardless of any defects in the merchandise sold.

Let us look at a case of fraud. A car dealer deliberately sells a "lemon" to an unsuspecting buyer who signs a loan agreement that in turn is sold to a finance company. The car breaks down but the buyer is stuck, for the holder-in-due-course doctrine requires the buyer to pay off the loan as though the car is good, even though the dealer has fraudulently sold junk.

Because the holder-in-due-course procedure has been widely used by disreputable merchants to cut off the consumer's ordinary defenses against bad merchandise, many states have ruled it illegal in consumer finance agreements. By 1975 Alabama, Arizona, California, Colorado, Connecticut, Georgia, Idaho,

Indiana, Maine, Maryland, Massachusetts, Michigan, Minnesota, Missouri, New Hampshire, New Jersey, New York, North Carolina, Ohio, Oregon, South Dakota, and Wisconsin had ruled that third-party buyers of consumer loans are not holders in due course, and that the right to contest bad merchandise or nonperformance by a seller extends to those who obtain consumer loans.[6]   In May 1976, the Federal Trade Commission adopted a special rule that forbids a seller from taking loan proceeds as payment for a sale unless the loan contract signed by the consumer contains a notice that permits the consumer to assert legitimate claims and defenses for bad merchandise or nonperformance against the lender. This rule appears to give consumers throughout the United States an effective defense against the holder-in-due-course doctrine.

The effects of abolishing the holder-in-due-course policies are very healthy. While the consumer may have only occasional or one-time contact with merchants, the finance companies that buy consumer loans are continuously in contact with them.   If finance companies can suffer losses through legal nonpayment of loans for bad merchandise, they will take care to buy consumer loans only from those merchants who satisfy their customers.   The holder-in-due-course procedure has not been used in commercial loan agreements for many years because businesspeople cannot be coerced into signing adhesive contracts.   A businessperson can shop around for a loan under acceptable terms.   And buyers of commercial loans have traditionally checked the reputations of sellers to ensure that they don't buy loan paper on defective goods or from irresponsible businessmen.[7]

Attachment of Goods and Wages

One of the least expensive methods for a creditor seeking to recover the principal and interest on a loan in default is to repossess goods, in the case of a secured loan, or to attach the debtor's wages, in the case of an unsecured loan.   In the past repossession of goods (called *replevin*) or attachment of wages (known as *garnishment*) has been available to creditors without prior notice given to the debtor.   Often goods seized have been household goods unrelated to the loan in default.   Both garnishment and replevin are severely disruptive to the debtor, even if an effective and inexpensive method for the creditor.

The easy remedy of replevin was severely impaired by the United States Supreme Court in an important 1972 decision, *Fuentes et al. v. Shevin.*[8]   And the garnishment of wages has, since July 1970, been subject to the U.S. Consumer Credit Protection Act that limits garnishment to whatever is the lesser: 25% of a worker's weekly earnings after taxes, or the amount by which such earnings for

---

[6] United States, Executive Office of the President, Office of Consumer Affairs: *State Consumer Action, Summary '71* (Washington, D.C., 1972), pp. 52–55; and *State Consumer Action, Summary '72* (Washington, D.C., 1973), pp. 132–33.   United States, Department of Health, Education, and Welfare, Office of Consumer Affairs: *State Consumer Action, Summary '74* (Washington, D.C., 1975), pp. 105–106.

[7] CCUS, pp. 34–38.

[8] 407 U.S. 67 (1972).

the week exceed 30 times the federal minimum hourly wage. (The multiple of 30 may be too low. The National Commission on Consumer Finance recommended 40, and some states—Alabama, for example—exceed the federal multiple with a base of 50 times the federal minimum wage.) The Consumer Credit Protection Act also forbids firms to discharge an employee whose wages are garnished for any single debt.[9]

Contracts ought to require creditors to choose the remedy they will use to get their money back from defaulting debtors. Loan agreements that allow a creditor to repossess goods *and* to attach wages are obviously unfair. Several states require creditors to pick one remedy and be limited to it. Such reforms are obviously of benefit to debtors. Creditors claim they need a full stock of resources to protect themselves from losses. But the social harm and injustice resulting from free use of garnishment and replevin exceed the benefits business derives from such use.

CREDIT RATING

Before extending retail credit to a customer, retail firms and financial institutions attempt to evaluate how likely a customer is to live up to the terms of the loan agreement. Using information provided by the applicant and obtained through a credit reporting agency, the merchant, loan company, or bank attempts to draw a picture of the would-be borrower's life insofar as it affects his creditworthiness (see Figure 10-4).

Unfortunately, the process of credit rating or credit scoring (the latter term is used when performed with numerical standards) is an arbitrary process in which the rating depends on how well the subject's lifestyle fits into the mold (usually conventional) ideas of the credit grantor. If a person is male, between 25 and 55 years of age, has a steady income, has lived in one dwelling for some time, has property, life insurance, a few children (but not "too many"), and a long, respectable history of borrowing and repaying on time, he will probably get a loan or credit. But if a person is female, or "too young," or "too old," or self-employed, or doesn't bother with life insurance, or unmarried, or divorced, or separated, or moves a lot, the person will have much difficulty obtaining a loan. No matter that the predictable wage earner can't find $100 to buy a television without visiting a loan company, or that the more independent person is quite wealthy and seeks $10,000 as a bridge to the time when some superior bonds are ready to be cashed, the rather mindless credit rating industry will tend to trust the "family man" and act cautiously toward the independent person.

In the past women found it especially difficult to obtain credit. Credit grantors thought that divorce always led to financial irresponsibility and they would

---

[9] CCUS, p. 33; *State Consumer Action, Summary 1971*, p. 57.

Here's How You're Rated

	Favorable	Unfavorable
Employment	Stable, has skilled job with established firm. Has worked two or more years at present job.	Unstable employment, perhaps seasonal. Changes job often.
Income	Stable, adequate for all regular needs.	Unstable, may come from occasional work. Inadequate for regular needs, debt service.
Home	Homeowner or renter in good area. Stays in one residence for long periods.	Transient behavior. Lives in furnished room, poor neighborhoods.
Financial Behavior	Has a savings account, property, investments, life insurance.	No bank relationship. No identifiable assets.
Debts	Able to service debts easily. Pays regularly and promptly. Makes large downpayments on loans for constructive uses.	Irregular payer. May have record of past delinquencies. Tendency to borrow increasing amounts.
Legal Situation	No court actions.	Has past debt collection actions. Possibly a bankruptcy.
Personal Traits	Mature person, involved with family. Fewer than five children, few other dependents.	Immature, no family ties. May have many dependents to support.
Application Conduct	Applies for loan at regular bank or other financial institution	Seeks loan where he or she is not known. Past credit troubles denied when asked. Application errors. In a hurry for money.

10-4   What Factors Affect Your Credit?

not, in many cases, even grant credit to married women except with the husband's permission. But beginning in October 1975, the Equal Credit Opportunity Act prohibited discrimination by credit grantors on the basis of sex or marital status. Now creditors cannot in most cases even ask a credit applicant's sex. Credit grantors used to ask about credit applicants' child-bearing plans and use of birth control methods; they can no longer ask such questions. A woman's income, if any, must be counted dollar for dollar with a man's; in the past only half of a married woman's income was counted in calculating ability to pay. The Equal Credit Opportunity Act has improved women's rights in the credit market, but it leaves large gaps in the rights of divorced women, who may still have to reveal the sources and amounts of alimony and child support or maintenance payments to obtain credit.

Credit Reporting   Today credit reporting has become a major industry, dominated by Dun & Bradstreet, which prepares reports on businesses for businesses, and Equifax, Inc., based in Atlanta, Georgia, which prepares reports on individuals. The nature of the credit reporting industry is such that a great volume of information must be generated in little time, and the resulting inaccuracy and the use of unconfirmed information can be, and has been, damaging to entirely creditworthy firms and individuals.

Known as Retail Credit before January 1976, Equifax has been the subject of much recent public attention, for with its 13,000 employees and 1800 offices in the United States and Canada it prepares over 30 million reports each year for its 62,000 business customers.[10] Retail Credit has a quota system that *requires* its investigators to generate a certain percentage of *unfavorable* information. Until mid-1974 the company refused to allow the people investigated to see their reports, though it now does permit direct access to most of the files.

Perhaps the heaviest price one must pay in having credit is the loss of privacy that accompanies it. Credit investigators can make even deeper penetrations into one's life when jobs paying over $20,000 per year or life insurance policies are involved. In these cases credit investigators can and do interview friends and neighbors about marital relations, drinking habits, and anything else that could in some way cast doubt on one's character in the view of a severe critic. These companies refuse the obvious wisdom that a person's private life and business life must be viewed separately and that what goes on in one's home should be the concern of no one except the individual him- or herself.

The Fair Credit Reporting Act. Due to the abusiveness of the credit reporting system, Congress passed the Fair Credit Reporting Act, in effect since April 1971. This law gives consumers the right to be told the name and address of a credit bureau responsible for preparing a report that was used to deny credit, insurance, or employment or to increase the cost of credit or insurance. It gives one the right to obtain a statement of the "nature, substance, and sources" of the information about oneself in a credit bureau file. The disclosure must be made without charge following a report which results in failure to get a job, credit, or insurance or causes the credit or insurance to be more expensive. If no adverse consequences of a report are involved, one may obtain one's file material for a nominal fee (the Federal Trade Commission appears to permit charges up to $25; Equifax may charge $3.25–6.00). Unfortunately, disclosure of "nature and substance" means only that you can have a credit bureau employee read your file's contents to you; there is no way to know whether the oral reading truly reflects what is in the file. Equifax now allows one to examine the file directly, but information obtained in detailed personal investigations through hearsay (alleged drinking, extramarital affairs, and so on) need not be disclosed.

Any person who hopes to obtain credit, insurance, or employment has an interest in having a credit file that does not do injustice to his or her personal history. Although the Fair Credit Reporting Act does not at present allow the subject of a credit report to see the file directly, you should contact your local credit bureau, accessible through the classified telephone directory (the *Yellow Pages*),

---

[10] *The Wall Street Journal,* January 16, 1974, p. 1; Equifax, Inc., *Annual Report 1975.*

and have your report explained to you. Only such vigilance by consumers can guard against the potentially great harm erroneous credit reports can cause.

The Fair Credit Reporting Act gives one the right to have incomplete or incorrect information reinvestigated and, if the information is found to be inaccurate or unverifiable, to have such data stricken from the file. You can obtain the names of creditors who have received inaccurate reports in the last six months and of employers within the last two years. You can have corrected reports given to all firms that have received the inaccurate or incomplete information in the last six months (or within the last two years in the case of potential employers). If you and the credit bureau do not agree on facts, you can have a brief statement of your version put in the file and included in subsequent reports. Adverse information must be stricken after seven years but a bankruptcy notice can be retained for 14 years. If a credit reporting firm willfully or negligently violates the Fair Credit Reporting Act, a person who is the subject of a credit report can sue for damages and, if successful in the case, collect attorney's fees and court costs.

The Fair Credit Reporting Act is an improvement over a bad situation. Yet you still can be injured by sloppy investigation methods and you surely will lose some of your privacy if you apply for credit, insurance, a job, or a loan. It is essential that "nature and substance" disclosure be changed to the actual presentation of the file, with opportunities to obtain copies at a reasonable charge. Credit bureaus have protested that forcing them to disclose files wastes their time and harms their business. In fact it appears that few people bother to see their files.[11] The right to sue for violation of the Act should be turned into a meaningful option by addition of minimum penalties, say $500 per willful or negligent violation, and/or by the imposition of triple damages on offending credit bureaus. Invasion of privacy should be allowed only within the bounds of laws that effectively discourage abuse.

BANKRUPTCY

When a person is no longer able to pay debts out of current income or realizable cash (for example, by selling some stocks and bonds), the person becomes insolvent. At this point the person, or the person's creditors, can begin an orderly liquidation of his property, formally known as *bankruptcy*. Bankruptcy has sinister connotations but it is little more than a reorganization of assets, usually involving their sale, to pay off creditors. Under the Federal Bankruptcy Act a debtor may choose one of two methods of discharge the debts. Under *straight bankruptcy* all assets (except certain personal possessions, depending on the state in which one resides) are sold to pay creditors. Even if less than half of one's valid debts can be discharged with the results of the sale, a person is freed

---

[11] *The Wall Street Journal,* June 5, 1974, p. 23.

from those debts. One can then begin with a clean slate, except for the credit record, which can carry notice of bankruptcy for 14 years. (Also, a bankrupt cannot declare bankruptcy again for 7 years.) Under the wage-earner plan, a newer form of bankruptcy, a federal bankruptcy referee may leave most of a person's possessions intact and instead arrange income and debts so that they can be paid off in a certain period of time, often extending the debt period and calling for payment of only a fraction of the outstanding debt.

For a number of reasons, bankruptcies are becoming more frequent.[12] The population is more mobile and a person can go bankrupt in one place, move to another, and begin anew. Urban life has reduced our direct dependence on property. Where the farmer faces destitution if a farm is lost in bankruptcy, an employee of a business may face little more than inconvenience and embarrassment.

The rising volume of personal bankruptcies is often cited today as evidence of the decline of the puritan ethic and social morality. No longer in direct contact with the shopkeepers and craftspeople who once served us, one's escaping from the debt of the anonymous credit card through bankruptcy is not a matter of honor but of convenience. People may be foolish to extend their indebtedness to within one or two paychecks of insolvency, but calling such folly immoral means imposing one's own morality on others.

CREDIT AND THE POOR

The operations and methods of the credit industry pose many difficulties for all consumers. Yet the problems the middle-class person faces are small compared to the desperate situation into which many poor consumers are placed by abusive businesses and inadequate laws. The Federal Trade Commission in 1966 made an important study of installment credit and retail sales practices in the furniture and appliance trade in the District of Columbia. The results, published two years later, demonstrate the ways in which the poor are treated differently than the average buyer, and in the remainder of this section we make use of this FTC data (see Figure 10-5).

The FTC study indicated that in general the poor use credit more frequently and in larger amounts, when figured as a fraction of their incomes, than do middle-class families. Some District of Columbia retailers specialize in selling to low-income shoppers. Such firms make use of installment credit in 93% of their sales, in comparison to 27% of all sales for general-market retailers. Retailers specializing in the poor had higher markups and gross profit margins (60.8%) than did general-market retailers (37%). On the average, goods with a wholesale cost of $100 sold for $255 in the low-income market, compared to $159 in

---

[12] *The Wall Street Journal*, August 14, 1974, p. 28.

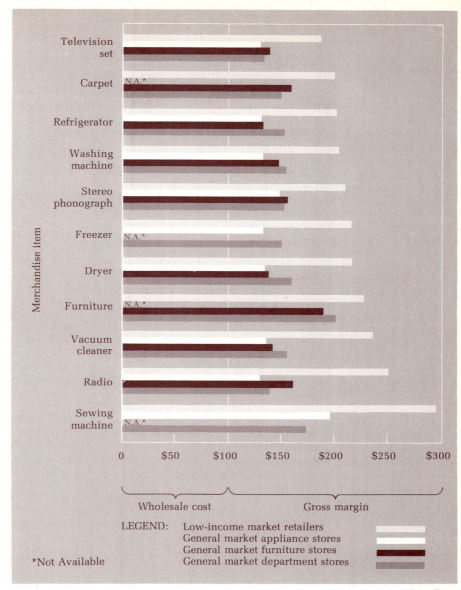

Source: Federal Trade Commission, *Economic Report on Installment Credit and Retail Sales Practices of District of Columbia Retailers* (Washington, D.C., 1968).

10-5   Gross Margins, Prices, and Profits

general-market stores.   In a case of a clothes dryer with a wholesale cost of $115, the low-income retailer would sell it for $300, in contrast to $150 in the general-market store.

Low-income retailers usually did not sell their credit agreements to third-party finance companies, according to the FTC study.   Low-income market stores retained 80% of their finance contracts, although general-market retailers retained only 2% of their finance contracts. Restating these results, we can conclude that low-income retailers are in fact also in the finance business, using merchandise as little more than an inducement for the customer to borrow money at high interest rates. Needless to say, low-income retailer finance contracts had higher interest rates in the study than did general-market retailers.

Perhaps the most striking finding of the FTC study was that low-income retailers use the courts as a regular means of bill collection. In the FTC study 11 low-income market retailers were found to have obtained 2690 judgments against their debtors in 1966. Their legal claims resulted in 1568 garnishments and 306 repossessions. In contrast, general-market retailers reported very few judgments. Eight furniture and home furnishings stores reported only 70 judgments for 1966. Low-income market retailers obtained nearly that number of judgments in an average *week*. One large department store, whose 1966 sales far exceeded the total for the entire low-income group, reported only 29 judgments for 1966. In terms of suits filed, 3030 actions begun by 18 low-income market retailers amounted to one lawsuit for every $2599 of net sales. Among the general-market retailers in the FTC survey, 47 general-market retailers filed 616 suits, an average of one lawsuit to every $232,299 of net sales. Summing up, low-income market retailers were 89.38 times more likely to go to court against a customer than were general-market retailers. As the FTC study says, "A number of low-income market retailers have come to view the courts as an integral part of their credit-collection system and in so doing have put a heavy burden on our legal system."

If the position of the poor at the hands of credit grantors specializing in the low-income market is one of serious disadvantage, it is not wholly different from the position of anyone who uses credit. The general-market retailer can use the same credit-collection methods. So lifting the burden of onerous collection methods from the poor will help all consumers.

SUPERVISION AND ENFORCEMENT

Enforcement of the many laws dealing with consumer credit has been spread among the consumers themselves, as well as a multitude of federal and state bureaucracies. There are, indeed, so many laws and enforcement agencies that *effective* enforcement of these laws has been hindered.

Persons injured through improper credit investigations or illegal lending tactics may themselves sue for damages in appropriate courts. Yet to expect that poor or timid debtors and credit applicants will engage lawyers and pursue compensation is wishful thinking.

Some financial institutions and credit grantors are well-regulated, others are hardly so. Finance companies are diligently supervised by state authorities. Banks, on the other hand, are supervised by bank examiners who are primarily concerned with the solvency of the bank, not the correctness of interest-rate charges and disclosures. Retailers issuing credit are often unsupervised. Credit granted by railroads and airlines to passengers is subject to Truth in Lending laws, as administered by the Interstate Commerce Commission and the Civil Aeronautics Board. Not surprisingly, these two agencies apparently have not found a single violation in credit administration, for the ICC and the CAB are decayed bureaucracies more interested in protecting the transportation industry than in protecting the public. At the absurd extreme of regulation, packers selling bulk meats to consumers are subject to Truth in Lending law enforcement by the federal Packers and Stockyards Administration, a less-than-famous government agency.

The National Commission on Consumer Finance recommended that credit regulation be consolidated in one agency with broad powers to enforce all pertinent legislation.[13] While in general we do not usually favor an expansion of the federal bureaucracy, we do believe this recommendation is worthwhile. Removing a few lifeless appendages of existing government offices and concentrating power in one agency with broad and substantial powers of civil and criminal enforcement would make it easier for consumers to obtain redress for wrongs. Complaints could be voiced to an authority responsible directly to the public and injured borrowers or credit applicants would not need to search through government organization charts and find lawyers to have their rights enforced. There is, of course, the risk that such an agency would wind up, as do most federal regulatory agencies, protecting the industry it is supposed to regulate; yet the value of having enforcement concentrated in a single, conspicuous, and powerful agency does, we believe, outweigh this risk.

RESOLVING THE CREDIT DILEMMA

Perhaps because credit is so readily available, it has been so greatly abused by both borrowers and lenders. Borrowers do often ignore the role of credit in their lifestyles. People willingly enter the "cashless society" and go into debt with little thought about the costs of carrying their debts and few concerns about their ability to repay them should the economy take a turn for the worse.

Meanwhile, the administration of credit has grown haphazardly. Dependent on credit, borrowers have willingly signed one-sided credit agreements that only favor the lender. Armed with many ways to get back their money, the credit-granting industry has not hesitated to use ruthless tactics, especially on the poor. Faced with the task of compiling tens of millions of credit reports each year, the credit reporting industry has relied on shabby, brief investigations and in the process has accepted rumor and gossip as evidence, ruining many careers and lives.

[13] CCUS, pp. 58–59.

Government regulation of credit concentrated in the past on maintaining interest ceilings that, as we have seen, only disrupt markets and drive people into the hands of loan sharks. Recent reforms, including Truth in Lending and the Fair Credit Reporting Act, are either enforced by a patchwork of sometimes unconcerned agencies or left to the initiative of the injured individuals. But the future need not be so corrupt as the past. Consolidating enforcement powers in a single national agency would reduce the diverse bureaucracies now charged with overseeing credit laws. Penalties for violations should be increased, particularly in the case of credit reporting, so that agencies will be encouraged to guard, not injure, people's reputations.

SUMMARY

1 The use of consumer credit should be determined by one's preferences for having things now or in the future, and by one's lifestyle in general.

2 Consumer debt increased rapidly in the United States after World War II due to important changes in the age, income, and residence patterns of the population. Young married people increased in number and borrowed heavily to form households and to buy houses, furnishings, and equipment. Higher incomes allowed discretionary spending to carry additional interest charges. The urban lifestyle disseminated by the mass media brought more people into a pattern of high consumption, often on credit. People evidenced a preference for ownership of transportation, entertainment devices, and utility devices over renting equivalent services.

3 The opportunity cost of credit use is the future use of the interest one must pay for a loan. But if the value of current use exceeds this cost, or if you correctly expect prices to rise faster than interest, net opportunity costs will be zero.

4 Interest rate ceilings should not be set above equilibrium interest rates lest credit markets be disrupted. Such ceiling laws either drive sources of money to lenders or honest lenders themselves from the market.

5 Revolving credit is credit that is continuously renewed as past credit balances are paid off. Many issuers of revolving credit do not charge interest for the first 30 days.

6 There are four basic forms of calculating interest due on revolving credit accounts. The previous balance method ignores current account payments and charges as though no payments have been made. The average daily balance method charges daily interest on daily balances outstanding. The adjusted balance method bills interest on the unpaid balance only. The past-due balance method gives an additional billing period's grace before charging interest on the past period's still-outstanding charges.

7 People who shop or eat at businesses accepting universal charge cards pay an implicit 5% interest charge, for firms accepting such cards must pay 5% of all card billings to the card issuers for their service and prices are raised to cover this cost. Under a recent Federal Trade Commission settlement, uni-

versal charge card firms may no longer prevent participating businesses from giving cash discounts.

8 Layaway plans are credit in reverse. The merchant holds the goods the customer wants and takes periodic payments from the customer until the purchase price is paid. In this interval the customer loses the use and interest on the money paid.

9 Credit-card loss exposes the holder to a maximum $50 liability, and this only if he or she has been given a means of notifying the issuer of the loss.

10 Installment credit is credit issued to be repaid with interest in a stated number of payments at given intervals. Secured installment loans arise when the lender acquires a right to seize a specific piece of property if the loan is not repaid. Unsecured installment loans do not have this lender's right of seizure of specific property.

11 Federal Reserve Board Regulation Z is the Truth in Lending statute. It requires lenders to disclose annual percentage rates of loans, cash price, down payment, unpaid balance financed, and penalties for late payments. It applies to all consumer finance transactions under $25,000 and to all real estate transactions involving land for personal or family residential, recreational, or agricultural use.

12 Installment credit contracts are written by lenders to favor themselves. The buyer in need of credit usually lacks the knowledge and courage to bargain for better terms, and due to their disadvantageous position, buyers are forced to adhere to these unfair agreements. Among typical features of such contracts are:

1 *Acceleration*—a lender's right to make all payments immediately due
2 *Confession of judgment*—the borrower agrees in advance to plead guilty to breach of contract
3 *Venue*—the lender's choice of the location for trial
4 *Holder in due course rule*—the demand—abolished in many states—that a third-party buyer of a finance contract must be paid, regardless of the merchant's bad performance
5 *Garnishment*—the right to seize debtor's wages for the payment of a contract
6 *Replevin*—the right to seize the debtor's goods for repayment

13 Credit rating is a process by which a potential borrower's life patterns are measured against an arbitrary standard of social conformity to see if he or she is a good credit risk.

14 Credit reporting is a large industry devoted in investigating applicants for credit, life insurance, and jobs. Its methods are slipshod and often injurious to credit report subjects. Under the Fair Credit Reporting Act a person may sue for damages if a credit reporting agency fails: to correct factual errors in its files; to include a subject's own version of contested file information (if desired) in its reports; to amend its past incorrect reports; or to disclose the "nature and substance" of a credit file to its subject. Persons have the right

to be told the name and address of the agency responsible for reports having adverse consequences in a given situation.

15 The poor depend on credit, use it more frequently, and pay more for it than does the middle class. Low-income specialty retailers appear to be in the finance business, using highly overpriced merchandise as a front for their loan operations. A sample of retail firms specializing in merchandise aimed at the low-income buyer sued customers in court 89 times more often than did general-market retailers.

16 Truth in Lending and Fair Credit Reporting laws are enforced by a patchwork of agencies, not all of them interested specifically in consumer credit. Each statute permits self-enforcement by injured consumers, through civil suits for damages, but the poor are unlikely to use this remedy. The administration of these statutes would be more effective if consolidated in a single agency with broad and substantial powers of civil and criminal enforcement.

Suggestions for Further Reading

Whiteside, Thomas. "Credit Bureaus," *The New Yorker,* April 21, 1975, pp. 45–101.

Caplovitz, David. *Consumers in Trouble: A Study of Debtors in Default.* New York: The Free Press, 1974.

—————. *The Poor Pay More.* New York: The Free Press, 1963.

Federal Trade Commission, *Economic Report on Installment Credit and Retail Sales Practices of District of Columbia Retailers* (Washington, D.C., 1968).

National Commission on Consumer Finance, *Consumer Credit in the United States* (Washington, D.C., 1968).

Consumer Reports, March 1975, pp. 171–78; May 1975, pp. 306–309.

The Consumer Workshop

1 Mark and Sally are about to graduate from college. They're discussing their living and working plans after graduation. Mark says he hopes to have a career in sales, marry, have a family, and live as orderly a life as possible. Sally replies that she prefers to travel inexpensively, live rather simply, and continue her education part-time. How does credit fit into each of these persons' lives? Who will most likely be the heavier user of credit? Why?

2 Let us assume that you have an income of $12,000 per year, rent an apartment at $200 per month, have a number of universal charge cards (including BankAmericard, for example) and store charge accounts. You have $6000 in cash value paid-up life insurance on which you can borrow. You have no debts and you have a good credit rating. A power boat recently caught your eye; it costs $5000. You haven't the cash to pay the entire $5000 but you can put down $1000. Discuss the advantages and disadvantages of the means available to finance the boat.

3 Jack Bianco has applied for a bank loan to buy a new car. He hasn't heard from the bank for a week but a neighbor told him that an investigator had

been around asking neighbors questions about his lifestyle and habits.   Jack calls the bank, asks what's happened to his application and is told that a credit investigation has produced an unsatisfactory result.   Quite disturbed about the situation, Jack comes to you, his friend, for advice.   What will you tell him about his means for complaint?   What precisely should he do now?

4 When you establish your first home, how much do you anticipate you will trade future goods and services for present satisfactions?   In doing this, analyze your own lifestyle as a series of changing needs, not simply as a single way of life.

11

LIFE INSURANCE

11

Life insurance is a vast industry with about 2000 firms operating in the United States and Canada. To help consumers find their way in this plethora and get the best insurance for their needs, in this chapter we will:

1 Examine the individual's need for insurance
2 Learn how life insurance works
3 Develop a process for determining how much life insurance to buy
4 Investigate the types of life insurance policies that are appropriate for various needs
5 Study two of the biggest problems for life insurance buyers, sales fees and inflation
6 And determine the methods for comparing policies and costs

INSURANCE NEEDS AND YOUR LIFESTYLE

Not every person needs life insurance. For example, it may not be needed by people living alone without dependents, retired couples with ample and accessible savings and investments, and families fortunate enough to have sufficient investments and current cash to see them through the death of breadwinners and beyond until the children (if there are any) leave home and the spouse dies.

Most families, however, have the greatest need for such insurance at the very time when their financial means are lowest. Most families experience maximum liability when they are young. In a family with two parents and two children, the need becomes greatest when the second child is born. Death of the breadwinner would expose the family to financial problems for 18 years (or more, if the children's education is prolonged). As the household develops, however, its assets should grow. By the time the parents are middle-aged (say in their 50s), the children probably will have left home, thus reducing the family's needs to only one spouse's requirements, in the event of the other spouse's death. As parents grow older, the maximum cost of their total future living expenses should also decrease. We can illustrate the relationship of need to financial means with the diagram in Figure 11-1. In part A we see that family needs decrease over time from a high initial level. In part B we see that assets grow as the family develops. And in part C, parts A and B are combined to show the period of net (unmet) family needs.

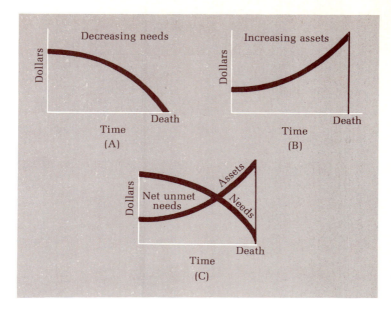

11-1 Family Financial Needs Change Over Time

HOW INSURANCE WORKS

Life insurance provides financial protection against the risk of premature or untimely death. The basic elements in the insurance agreement are:

1 The probability of the insured person's death at a given time
2 An insurable interest
3 The period of the agreement; that is, the risk that the insured person will die within one year, five years, 20 years, and so on

Probability Statistical tables showing the life expectancies and death rates for various groups and populations have been compiled to provide the data that determines the price for setting life insurance. Assembled by actuaries (mathematicians specializing in insurance probability theory and statistics), these mortality tables and their data form the foundation of life insurance. The most widely used general table is the Commissioners Standard Ordinary (CSO) Mortality Table, published by the National Association of Insurance Commissioners (see Figure 11-2). It begins with a base of 10 million people, at birth, and follows them through age 99. For each year it calculates how many of the 10 million will remain alive, how many will die, and translates the difference into a death rate per thousand.

Age	Number Living	Number Dying	Death Rate Per 1,000	Expect-ancy, Years	Age	Number Living	Number Dying	Death Rate Per 1,000	Expect-ancy, Years
0	10,000,000	70,800	7.08	68.30	50	8,762,306	72,902	8.32	23.63
1	9,929,200	17,475	1.76	67.78	51	8,689,404	79,160	9.11	22.82
2	9,911,725	15,066	1.52	66.90	52	8,610,244	85,758	9.96	22.03
3	9,896,659	14,449	1.46	66.00	53	8,524,486	92,832	10.89	21.25
4	9,882,210	13,835	1.40	65.10	54	8,431,654	100,337	11.90	20.47
5	9,868,375	13,322	1.35	64.19	55	8,331,317	108,307	13.00	19.71
6	9,855,053	12,812	1.30	63.27	56	8,223,010	116,849	14.21	18.97
7	9,842,241	12,401	1.26	62.35	57	8,106,161	125,970	15.54	18.23
8	9,829,840	12,091	1.23	61.43	58	7,980,191	135,663	17.00	17.51
9	9,817,749	11,879	1.21	60.51	59	7,844,528	145,830	18.59	16.81
10	9,805,870	11,865	1.21	59.58	60	7,698,698	156,592	20.34	16.12
11	9,794,005	12,047	1.23	58.65	61	7,542,106	167,736	22.24	15.44
12	9,781,958	12,325	1.26	57.72	62	7,374,370	179,271	24.31	14.78
13	9,769,633	12,896	1.32	56.80	63	7,195,099	191,174	26.57	14.14
14	9,756,737	13,562	1.39	55.87	64	7,003,925	203,394	29.04	13.51
15	9,743,175	14,225	1.46	54.95	65	6,800,531	215,917	31.75	12.90
16	9,728,950	14,983	1.54	54.03	66	6,584,614	228,749	34.74	12.31
17	9,713,967	15,737	1.62	53.11	67	6,355,865	241,777	38.04	11.73
18	9,698,230	16,390	1.69	52.19	68	6,114,088	254,835	41.68	11.17
19	9,681,840	16,846	1.74	51.28	69	5,859,253	267,241	45.61	10.64
20	9,664,994	17,300	1.79	50.37	70	5,592,012	278,426	49.79	10.12
21	9,647,694	17,655	1.83	49.46	71	5,313,586	287,731	54.15	9.63
22	9,630,039	17,912	1.86	48.55	72	5,025,855	294,766	58.65	9.15
23	9,612,127	18,167	1.89	47.64	73	4,731,089	299,289	63.26	8.69
24	9,593,960	18,324	1.91	46.73	74	4,431,800	301,894	68.12	8.24
25	9,575,636	18,481	1.93	45.82	75	4,129,906	303,011	73.73	7.81
26	9,557,155	18,732	1.96	44.90	76	3,826,895	303,014	79.18	7.39
27	9,538,423	18,981	1.99	43.99	77	3,523,881	301,997	85.70	6.98
28	9,519,442	19,324	2.03	43.08	78	3,221,884	299,829	93.06	6.59
29	9,500,118	19,760	2.08	42.16	79	2,922,055	295,683	101.19	6.21
30	9,480,358	20,193	2.13	41.25	80	2,626,372	288,848	109.98	5.85
31	9,460,165	20,718	2.19	40.34	81	2,337,524	278,983	119.35	5.51
32	9,439,447	21,239	2.25	39.43	82	2,058,541	265,902	129.17	5.19
33	9,418,208	21,850	2.32	38.51	83	1,792,639	249,858	139.38	4.89
34	9,396,358	22,551	2.40	37.60	84	1,542,781	231,433	150.01	4.60
35	9,373,807	23,528	2.51	36.69	85	1,311,348	211,311	161.14	4.32
36	9,350,279	24,685	2.64	35.78	86	1,100,037	190,108	172.82	4.06
37	9,325,594	26,112	2.80	34.88	87	909,929	168,455	185.13	3.80
38	9,299,482	27,991	3.01	33.97	88	741,474	146,997	198.25	3.55
39	9,271,491	30,132	3.25	33.07	89	594,477	126,303	212.46	3.31
40	9,241,359	32,622	3.53	32.18	90	468,174	106,809	228.14	3.06
41	9,208,737	35,362	3.84	31.29	91	361,365	88,813	245.77	2.82
42	9,173,375	38,253	4.17	30.41	92	272,552	72,480	265.93	2.58
43	9,135,122	41,382	4.53	29.54	93	200,072	57,881	289.30	2.33
44	9,093,740	44,741	4.92	28.67	94	142,191	45,026	316.66	2.07
45	9,048,999	48,412	5.35	27.81	95	97,165	34,128	351.24	1.80
46	9,000,587	52,473	5.83	26.95	96	63,037	25,250	400.56	1.51
47	8,948,114	56,910	6.36	26.11	97	37,787	18,456	488.42	1.18
48	8,891,204	61,794	6.95	25.27	98	19,331	12,916	688.15	.83
49	8,829,410	67,104	7.60	24.45	99	6,415	6,415	1,000.00	.50

Source: National Associa-
tion of Insurance Com-
missioners, *Proceedings of
the NAIC* I (1959),
composite of tables on
239, 240.

**11-2   1958 CSO (Commissioners Standard Ordinary)
Mortality Table**

At the age of 30, for example, 9,480,358 of the original group of 10 million people are still alive. Within the next year 20,193 can be expected to die. This translates into an annual death rate of 2.13 per 1000. Using this mortality rate as a basis for calculation, a group of ten thousand students or workers, all 30 years of age, can compute the rates to charge one another for insurance policies to provide a given benefit to any group member who dies during the coming year. Let's say that the group decides a member's family should have a $10,000 benefit payment if he or she dies. The death rate of 2.13 per thousand is the same as 21.3 per ten thousand. So the group of 30-year-olds would have to pay out 21.3 × $10,000 or $213,000 within 365 days. To make this possible, each group member must contribute $21.30. If each member pays his or her share at the first opportunity on day one (that is, before anyone has a chance to die), and if the reserve of $213,000 draws no interest, and if no one is to be paid to administer the fund or sell insurance policies, and if no one receives profits—then the $21.30 is the correct premium. In practice, though, insurance companies invest the reserve in low-risk securities and charge substantial sums for administrative and sales expenses.

Insurable Interest

A person may insure his or her own life, or a member of a family may take out a policy on another member's life. A creditor may take out insurance on a debtor's life, or a business may insure the life of an important employee. What is essential is that the person buying and benefitting from the policy have an insur-

"Sure I'm depressed. According to the latest actuarial figures, I've only got 63.27 years to live."

able interest in the life that is insured. A wife loses by a husband's death and a business partnership may lose if a partner dies. But a person cannot take out a policy on someone with whom he or she has hardly any or perhaps no business or family relation whatsoever, for the beneficiary then has nothing to lose and everything to gain by the death of the insured. Insurance companies also do not pay benefits if a beneficiary has murdered the person whose life was insured. This rule of insurable interest in life and property coverage, and all other types of insurance, serves to guarantee the legitimacy of the insurance relationships and to minimize sheer gambling, fraud, and crime.

Period of Agreement It costs less to insure the life of a 10-year-old than that of an 80-year-old. The more likely the timing of death, or the sooner it will occur, the higher will be the cost of the insurance agreement. Referring again to the CSO Mortality Table (Figure 11-2) a person at age 85 will have to pay $161.14 + $172.82 + $185.13 + $198.25 + $212.46 = $929.80 for coverage to age 91. If interest on the premiums is added, the sum will exceed $1000 in total premiums over the five-year term.

HOW MUCH LIFE INSURANCE TO BUY

The question of how much life insurance to buy is complicated by the current high rates of inflation, for they make the future even more difficult to predict. In anticipating a household's needs one must try to seek out a course of probable costs. No one, of course, can predict or even anticipate every possible need or outcome after one's death. To measure the quantity of insurance benefits that your family will need, estimate their assets and yearly income and subtract their liabilities and yearly living costs after your death. The variations of yearly income to yearly expenses should then be averaged over the probable life spans or periods of dependency of the intended beneficiaries and adjusted to the difference of the yield, after taxes, on the family's insurance proceeds and other assets, minus the reduction of purchasing power caused by inflation. The result is the principal sum that must be produced by insurance to meet the beneficiaries' needs over their expected lifetimes or periods of dependency. This procedure is in fact a seven-step calculation, the assumptions behind which should be changed as circumstances require. The questions and methods are these:

1 *Funeral, probate, and estate tax expenses:* How much will the funeral cost (or how much does the family wish to pay)? What legal fees are charged in your jurisdiction for the settlement of the deceased's estate (a legal process known as *probate,* in which the dead person's assets are collected, debts paid and creditors satisfied, and any surplus paid to the heirs)? What estate taxes may be charged where you reside?

2 *Discharge of liabilities:* What debts may be expected to remain after the insured dies? Can these be handled by advantageously priced credit life insurance that pays off any revolving or installment debts in existence at one's death? Leave only those debts not protected by credit life insurance.

3 *Education:* Expenses for college, graduate school, and related or similar special training for children should be added together over the expected duration of such training. Undergraduate college costs are not readily deferred by scholarships, although student loans are available. Graduate students in nonlicensed professions and medicine can usually obtain substantial financial assistance. Currently, undergraduate expenses in state-supported and public universities are $2600–3000 per year, in private universities and colleges $3000–7000 per year. To allow for inflation add 15% annually each year until each college-directed beneficiary may be expected to begin college and 15% for every year of undergraduate training.

4 *Annual living costs:* Allow for three months' current income to cover expenses in the period of transition, when the family begins to live without the deceased. Then total the family's different levels of monthly living expenses as various children grow older, acquire part-time jobs (and so become partially self-supporting) and later leave home. Multiply the different levels of expense by the number of years (and multiply by 12 for the 12 months of each year). And using the standard mortality tables, terminate the calculation at the expected death date of the spouse or the other life beneficiaries.

5 *Total 1 + 2 + 3 + 4:* The result is the schedule of the total post-death expenses for the beneficiaries of the deceased.

6 *Estimate the total income:* This is the total income that can be expected by the family at different life stages. Include Social Security, investments, company pension plans, fraternal lodge benefits, and so forth. If benefits are to be received in a lump sum, calculate their yield if invested prudently and add the yield to the monthly income of periodic payments from Social Security and periodic payment benefit plans.

7 *Subtract needs from income (5 − 6):* If the result is negative, then projected needs exceed projected income and the family should have life insurance protection. To determine the face value of the policy to buy, compare the yield that can be realized on secure investments over the period of need with the estimated rate of inflation. For example, if you expect a secure yield of 6% on bank deposits or 8% on high-quality bonds for the next 20 years, multiply the insurance need by the reciprocals of .06 or .08; that is, 1/.06 or 1/.08, which are 16.6 or 12.5, respectively. This is the no-inflation principal sum needed to pay the required annual insurance. Then adjust for inflation, estimating the probable inflation trend over the needed period of insurance benefits. (Today 8% is a fair, conservative figure.) The value of money will fall at a rate determined by the equation $P = (1 - r)^n$, where P is future purchasing power of the money, r, is rate of inflation per year, and n is the number of years until need will end. To find precalculated reductions in purchasing power for a $10,000 initial sum, see Figure 11-5.

TYPES OF LIFE INSURANCE

All life insurance policies protect the beneficiaries against the possibility that the insured may die before reaching his or her estimated year of life expectancy. The protection can take many forms, from insurance against dying within a specified period of time, to more elaborate forms in which the insured can receive back some premiums paid and/or use the insurance policy as collateral for loans. The different types of policies available must be examined individually to determine which best meets a household's needs.

In spite of the thousands of different policy features and combinations one may encounter, there are basically five fundamental variables:

1 *Duration of insurance:* Protection may be for the length of one airplane flight, one life, a 30-day vacation, one year, five years, or from the present to the commonly used age of 65. The longer the period of protection and the older the insured when the policy is taken out, the greater is the risk of death, and consequently, the higher the premium.
2 *Premium schedule:* The risk of death increases with age. Policies can charge suitably increasing premiums but most people prefer to have their premiums averaged over the life of the policy. Premiums may also be set to start low and grow with income-earning ability, to start rather high but to pay for the policy in a short period, or to decrease as need and coverage decline.
3 *Face value:* The face value of a policy may grow, decline, or remain constant.

4 *Savings accumulation:* Savings accumulation builds in a policy through a surcharge over the pure risk premium. This surcharge goes to a reserve and may be drawn upon by a loan or used as a payment to the insured if he or she reaches retirement age.

5 *Risk covered:* The risk covered by insurance is greatest per dollar with term insurance and least with an endowment policy that builds to a specified cash value. In the case of cash-value life insurance the total premium paid into the cash-value reserve eventually approaches the death value of the insurance. Of course, as the cash value grows, the risk covered by the insurance company and paid for by the insured declines.

Term Insurance

Term insurance is the most direct form of protection against unexpected or premature death. In its most common form, the insured is covered for one year against untimely death. Since the mortality tables indicate that almost anyone under 65 has a very good chance of living one more year, term insurance is inexpensive. Term insurance is built into every form of life insurance, but unlike other forms, term insurance pays nothing if death does not occur within the period of the policy. Term insurance contracts may be taken out for any period of time, and they are commonly issued for terms of 1, 5, 10, and 20 years or to a given age, such as 65. Naturally the longer the period of insurance, the higher the risk of death. Higher death risk carries higher premiums.

Term-Insurance Options. Term policies are available with options to buy higher coverage, to renew at given intervals, and to convert to other forms of life insurance. Each of these extras costs more. One feature enables the insured to renew the policy when it expires without taking another physical examination. This gives the policyholder the advantage of renewing the insurance in spite of deteriorated health. A young person with limited funds to invest in insurance can maximize insurance per dollar of premium by buying, say, the coverage of a five-year renewable term policy. If we assume that yearly income grows significantly over the five years, the insured can then be assured of a continuing ability to buy coverage, although he or she will have to pay the higher premium associated with being five years older. The option to buy higher coverage is a more expensive form of renewability. Another feature allows a term policy to be converted into a cash-value policy, usually bearing a lower total value of insurance. Again, this feature gives maximum protection for a young person who may want to think today of retirement cash values for the future.

Premium Control. Term policies may be written to average out premiums over a lengthy insurance term. For example, the commonly used "level term to age 65" is term insurance renewed automatically every year until the insured reaches age 65, with premiums averaged out so they are constant. Level-term insurance initially costs more than straight-term, but less than straight-term after the insured reaches the later years of the insurance period.

Decreasing term insurance provides maximum protection in the beginning, when the death risk is lowest, and less insurance in the future when the death risk is higher but when the insured may have accumulated enough assets to provide for his or her family. Special applications of decreasing term insurance are *credit life* and *mortgage life* insurance, the death values of which decline as the unpaid balances of loans decline. Credit and mortgage life thus protect the family from having to pay off debts left over after death and ensure that the goods or house bought by the insured will remain in possession of the family.

Cash-value Insurance

All cash-value life insurance is basic term insurance plus a charge for savings. The savings are used to pay the insured on retirement or expiration of the insurance period, if the insured lives that long. Cash-value life insurance can be purchased in three basic forms: *continuous premium whole life, limited payment life,* and *endowment.*

Continuous Premium Whole Life. This is sometimes called *ordinary life.* Under either name it is cash-value insurance, the premiums for which are paid as long as the insured is alive or as long as the policy is in force. Because it spreads the premiums over the longest possible period, it gives the most cash-value insurance protection per dollar of premium. On the other hand, the obligation to pay on a contract until death is a possible peril to limited income during retirement and a nuisance for some people.

Limited Payment Life. These policies are commonly written in the form "10 pay life," "20 pay life," and "30 pay life," meaning that the life insurance policy cost is paid up after 10, 20, or 30 years. The insured pays the full premiums due in the shortened period. Naturally, the result of condensing the total policy cost into a shorter period is an increase in annual premiums. But a condensed payment period may appeal to the person who wishes to buy insurance during peak income years and then leave retirement income unencumbered. A special form of limited payment life is *single premium life.* It may be chosen when a grandparent wishes to make a gift of insurance to a grandchild, or an investor, perhaps for tax reasons, decides to convert some assets to life insurance. The investor's decision can be wise if estate planning is a concern, for life insurance usually takes a large jump in value on the death of the insured.

Endowment Policies. These are cash-value policies in which the savings accumulation builds very rapidly, for term protection decreases quickly as savings build. The policy typically reaches full face value at age 55, after which retirement payout, when taken, equals face value plus interest. Endowment policies thus feature quickly expiring death protection together with large quasi-compulsory savings charges. Some people view the endowment policy as a way to benefit whether they live or die, but the charges for endowment coverage are higher than what one would have to pay to an insurance company for a pure endowment (in which you pay a given sum and get it back, with interest, if you live long enough) or for term insurance.

11-3 Estate Buildup of Term Insurance if the Difference Is Invested*

Age	Premium for Term	Difference	Invested at 5%†	Total Estate
30	$ 325	$ 1,152	$ 1,210	$101,210
31	331	1,146	2,484	102,484
32	338	1,139	3,804	103,804
33	346	1,131	5,182	105,182
34	356	1,121	6,618	106,618
35	371	1,106	8,110	108,110
36	391	1,086	9,656	109,656
37	414	1,063	11,255	111,255
38	441	1,036	12,906	112,906
39	472	1,005	14,607	114,607
40	504	973	16,359	116,359
41	540	937	18,161	118,161
42	577	900	20,014	120,014
43	616	861	21,919	121,919
44	661	816	23,872	123,872
45	708	769	25,873	125,873
46	762	715	27,917	127,917
47	821	656	30,002	130,002
48	884	593	32,125	132,125
49	954	523	34,280	134,280
50	1,028	449	36,465	136,465
51	1,108	369	38,675	138,675
52	1,194	283	40,906	140,906
53	1,285	192	43,153	143,153
54	1,385	92	45,407	145,407
55	1,492	− 15	47,662	147,662
56	1,610	− 133	49,905	149,905
57	1,739	− 262	52,125	152,125
58	1,882	− 405	54,306	154,306
59	2,037	− 560	56,433	156,443
60	2,202	− 725	58,498	158,498
61	2,378	− 901	60,472	160,472
62	2,581	−1,104	62,336	162,336
63	2,813	−1,336	64,050	164,050
64	3,081	−1,604	65,568	165,568

* The straight life policy premium for the same $100,000 in coverage is assumed to be $1,477.
† Savings compounded annually.

| | Age at Issue | | |
Type of Policy	25	35	45
10-year renewable term	$ 4.93	$ 6.84	$12.89
Straight life (ordinary)	12.71	17.07	25.18
Payment to 65	14.37	20.79	35.30
20-payment life	23.33	27.97	35.30
Endowment at age 65	16.94	24.97	42.64
20-year endowment	39.35	39.73	42.64

11-4   What Various Policies Cost ($1000 Policy) a Mutual Company

"Forced Saving" All forms of cash-value insurance involve what is often called "forced saving." Because premiums exceed cash value until rather late in the policy's life, there is a sense of loss if one defaults on premiums and faces cancellation of the policy. Thus there is a pressure to keep up a policy whose rate of savings growth may be poor compared to what one could earn by buying term insurance and investing the difference of high whole-life premiums and lower term-insurance premiums (see Figures 11-3 and 11-4).

FEATURES OF INSURANCE CONTRACTS

Beneficiary Options The *primary beneficiary* is the person selected to receive the payout of the insurance policy.   Should the primary beneficiary die, *contingent beneficiaries* may be appointed to receive the benefits.   Extending payment over additional lives into the future either increases the policy's cost or reduces annual benefits that are paid under the policy.

Settlement Choices The proceeds or cash value of life insurance policies may be distributed in one of four ways, as the insured desires.   Proceeds and cash benefits may be received in one lump sum, taken in any number of fixed installments, left with the insurance company in an annuity to be paid as long as the recipient of the proceeds lives, or left with the company to bear interest until a future date.   The worst choice is to leave the proceeds to draw interest, for life insurance firms traditionally pay submarket interest rates and therefore offer no hope of keeping the principal's purchasing power equal to inflation.   Taking the proceeds as a lump sum and then investing them wisely is a good choice if the beneficiary or recipient has some knowledge of investments.   The life annuity and fixed number of payments choices are subject to erosion by inflation but may be necessary if the primary or contingent beneficiaries are themselves infirm, immature, or otherwise incompetent to look after the funds.

Loan Options (Cash-value Policies)

Whole-life policies accumulate a savings fund on which interest is paid at a low rate. The insured may borrow against this sum at very low interest rates with few or no questions asked. Since the company is in fact advancing the insured his or her own money, the formalities are quite properly minimal. Although the very low interest rates charged for these loans are attractive (typically 6%), and repayment is at the borrower's convenience, the situation is one of paying someone else for your own money. It should be noted that if the insured dies before repaying the loan, the loans against accumulated cash value are subtracted from the face value of the policy. Once the loan is repaid the policy returns to full face value. One may, finally, regard the loan feature of a cash-value policy as compensation for the susceptability to inflation of a whole-life policy. You can borrow your own money more cheaply than you can get money elsewhere, but you'd have been further ahead to have bought term insurance and invested the difference between the term rate and the whole-life, cash-value policy rate in a form that provides high yield and quick cashability.

Renewability and Convertibility

At extra cost on term life policies one may buy the option to renew or increase coverage without further medical examinations or other proof of insurability. This feature is valuable if, for example, you find you have a serious illness and wish to give more protection to your family. Multiyear policies can also be written to include the option to convert to whole-life policies. Whole-life policies can be traded for 20 pay life policies, and the premiums can be adjusted upward to match the shorter payment period. Whole-life policies may also be traded for term policies, although in this case the insurance companies often require proof of continued insurability. Choice is in itself a valuable thing, and these options are worth noting because their usually low cost gives one the right to change coverage to meet new situations in the future.

Default and Reinstatement

If the insured fails to pay the premiums promptly or within the grace periods stipulated by the policy, the insurance company may do one of several things: it may terminate the policy and pay its accumulated cash value to the insured, or apply the cash value to a fully paid up policy of the same duration but lower amount, or apply the cash value to a term policy with the same face value but of shorter duration than the whole-life policy. When a policy conversion occurs on such a default option, any new policy issued is valued at the age of the insured at the time of the default and this tends to be disadvantageous to the insured. If the insured wants to have the original policy reinstated and has not already drawn its cash value, he or she must within a stated period pay all back premiums, interest due on unpaid back premiums, penalties (if any), and submit to a new medical examination and background investigation.

INFLATION—A GUARANTEED LOSS

Consumer prices rose in the United States during 1975 at average annual rates of 8–10%. The index of consumer prices was 67% higher in January 1976 than it was on average in 1967. The trend of prices since 1945 has been very inflationary, with rates of inflation rising from 2–3% in the 1950s, to 5–6% until about 1968, to 7–8% until about 1972. Since 1973 prices have risen at double-digit rates. The trend is clear: Prices are rising and they are rising faster all the time. On the other hand, the purchasing power of the dollar is falling, and falling faster all the time.

The life insurance buyer must be concerned about what the beneficiaries will receive if he or she survives to retirement or to the policy's maturity. A 25-year-old man can buy a $10,000 20 pay life policy for a premium of $220 per year. Assuming that he lives to be 45, pays his last premium, and only then dies, he will have paid $4400 in premiums. His beneficiaries will receive the $10,000, the purchasing power of which will then be equal to $1216, assuming a 10% rate of annual inflation sustained for 20 years. To some extent this fall in the value of the policy's proceeds is softened by the declining value of the premiums paid as the 20-year payment term of the policy progresses. The harsh fact is, nonetheless, that it is possible under such inflation to pay more in premiums than is returned to the beneficiaries (or to the policyholder in the case of endowment insurance) in buying power.

As long as inflation rates remain less than about 15% per year (not a fantastic figure considering that Great Britain had an annual rate of inflation of 24% in 1976), almost any insurance policy will pay its proceeds in a good measure of purchased value if the insured had term coverage or an extended cash-value policy payment period and died within a few years of the policy's beginning. In short, the life insurance policyholder can beat inflation by dying promptly after buying the policy. Such knowledge, of course, isn't useful as a strategy.

PLANNING FOR INFLATION

A good defense against the ravages of inflation is renewable term insurance. It costs less than whole life, and the difference in cost can be placed in investments that pay a good deal more than the insurance companies do on the accumulating savings of whole-life and endowment policies. Traditionally, the insurance companies have paid interest rates of about 3–4% on the savings portion of life policies, whereas the companies themselves have earned 5–6% on their policies since the mid-1960s. A wise insurance shopper will do well to stick with term policies with renewal options and invest the difference between the term premium and the whole-life premium in a form that pays or grows at a

Inflation Rate	Years			
	10*	20	30	35
6%	$5386	$2901	$1563	$1147
8%	4344	1887	820	540
10%	3487	1216	424	250
12%	2785	776	216	113
14%	2213	490	108	51
20%	1074	115	12	4

* Data for full years elapsed since beginning year.

11-5 Residual Purchasing Power of $10,000 after n Years

rate geared to current inflationary conditions. Term premiums should not even be averaged more than five or ten years, for if the rate of inflation is increasing, the reduced purchasing power value of premiums later in the term will not offset the higher purchasing power value of premiums early in the term. A 5-year renewable term has fairly level premiums without averaging as long as the policyholder is under 45. After age 45 premium averaging can become useful, for the premiums then rise rather quickly.

For a given sum P inflated at annual rate r purchasing power after n years is

$$P(n) = P(1 - r)^n$$

See Figure 11-5.

SALES AND ADMINISTRATIVE FEES

Insurance companies spend a great deal of money to persuade people to buy life insurance and to help them plan their coverage. Salespeople must be paid generous commissions, often 50% or more of the first year's premiums and 20–25% of the subsequent premiums. There are, however, two important classes of life insurance in which the sales and administrative fees vary significantly from the norm.

Group Life Insurance

Group life insurance is usually bought by a business for its workers, or by a fraternal order, club, or other organization for members; it thus is able to offer reduced premiums because sales charges are significantly lower. Group-life policies also eliminate a problem of bad risks for insurers and the consequent cost of medical examinations, since members of large groups naturally have average and predictable health. Group life is usually level premium term to age 65 with the employer carrying some or all of the premium. Frequently, group life may be converted to paid up whole life when a group member reaches retirement age. Because the employer may pay part of all of the premiums and because the premiums are reduced by low sales and administrative costs, group life is almost always a good deal as long as you stay with the company or group. Unfortunately, many group-life programs are not mobile, either between jobs or employers. Therefore, if you change jobs or employers, you may lose your life insurance coverage.

Credit Life Insurance

Credit life insurance is decreasing term insurance. The death value of credit life policies falls as the unpaid balance of loans declines. Credit life may be a good buy or a very poor buy, depending on the issuer. Some consumer loan firms use overpriced credit life to squeeze out of borrowers an extra interestlike charge. Many large financial institutions, however, offer inexpensive credit life to borrowers at low group rates.

COMPETITION AND COMPARISONS

There are about 2000 life insurance companies in North America. Some are owned by stockholders, others by policyholders. The policies they offer vary so much in hidden costs, special features, services, and privileges that price comparisons are difficult to make. We can, nevertheless, discern meaningful differences in costs resulting from the form of an organization and we can use an index of costs to determine levels of true cost of policies (see Figure 11-6, pages 194 and 195).

Dividend Participation

Two classes of life insurance are available in extended term and whole-life coverage. Participating policies distribute an annual dividend to policyholders based on better than expected performance, lower than expected administrative costs, or better than expected loss and payout experience. Originally, only mutual companies (those owned by their policyholders) paid dividends on policies. Later, in order to appear competitive, companies owned by separate stockholders not necessarily having insurance in force with their company began paying dividends. Today, dividend-paying policies are available from both types of insurers. The dividend-paying policy has a higher premium than the nonparticipating policy. If the firm paying dividends does well, the annual dividends may lower the net premium cost (actual premium *minus* dividends) of the participating policy to a cost beneath that of the nonparticipating policy. If it does rather poorly, dividends may not make up the difference in premiums between the two types of policies. The dividend history of the company, available on request, can be a rough guide to what can be expected.

Sales Fees

Life insurance sales commissions and administrative expenses consume 17% of a life insurance company's income (see Figure 11-7, page 196). Excluding nonpremium investment income, sales and administrative fees consume 22% of premium income. This is a substantial sum, nearly three times as high as the 8% sales and service fee charged on shares in (mostly ill-fated) mutual funds. Insurance companies, of course, perform more services than do mutual funds.

Sales fees tend to be highest for those policies that require the greatest customer service (including hustling sales) per dollar of premium income. The standard sales commission is about 50% of the first year's premium on whole-life policies, with significant annual residuals going to salespeople for the remainder of the time the policy is in force. Term-insurance fees are about 30% of premiums. Concrete figures are difficult to obtain because the insurance companies are often reluctant to release them. Basic sales fees do not vary greatly between participating and nonparticipating policies issued by mutual and stock companies, because both types of company have to make similar sales efforts to attract business. Sales fees can be reduced when large amounts are purchased at one time ($100,000 of term insurance, for example) because the sales cost per dollar of insurance sold is lower than if the same coverage were sold to 10 separate policyholders. Group insurance rates are low for the same reason—lower sales fees per dollar of insurance sold.

Exceptional bargains in life insurance are available to people who live or work in Massachusetts, Connecticut, and New York State. Some mutual savings banks in these states offer *Savings Bank Life Insurance* (SBLI) subject to maximum coverage ceilings of $41,000 in Massachusetts, $30,000 in New York, and $30,000 in Connecticut. For example, a $10,000 renewable and convertible term participating policy for a man at age 35 has a typical high first annual premium of $75. The Massachusetts Savings Bank Life Insurance first premium is $48, which is 64% of the expensive stock company's first premium.[1] Savings Bank Life Insurance, like group insurance, costs less because sales fees are small. To obtain SBLI you must apply for it at a member institution; no salesperson will come to you. SBLI coverage is presently limited to people who work in or live in the three eastern states. Consumers Union is attempting to have the coverage made available throughout the United States and to have the relatively low coverage limits eliminated.

Cost Comparisons

The more complex the features of an insurance policy, the more difficult it is to determine its cost. In the simplest case, that of nonparticipating, nonconvertible, nonrenewable term insurance, the annual cost is the annual premium. For whole-life policies with growing cash value, however, the calculation must take into account the possibility of policy surrender. Insurance sales representatives often use the *Net Cost Index* to demonstrate that their policies cost "less than nothing." This index subtracts dividends and cash values at the end of a

[1] *Consumer Reports*, January 1974, p. 51; February 1974, pp. 136–37.

Premiums and Insurance Cost for the Ten Lowest-Cost $10,000 Straight-Life Cash-Value Insurance Policies[2]

Company[4]	Male Age 20 or Female Age 23[3]			Male Age 35 or Female Age 38[3]			Male Age 50 or Female Age 53[3]		
	Annual Premium	Average Yearly Cost of Insurance	Ranking[5] at Age 20/23	Annual Premium	Average Yearly Cost of Insurance	Ranking[5] at Age 35/38	Annual Premium	Average Yearly Cost of Insurance	Ranking[5] at Age 50/53
1. Bankers Life Company (Iowa)	$149.70	$24.70	4	$229.10	$42.00	1	$400.30	$119.20	2
2. Home Life Ins. Co. (NY)	150.70	23.10	3	228.40	43.10	2	405.10	125.90	5
3. National Life Ins. Co. (VT)	152.70	28.30	10	230.30	46.30	5	389.80	125.80	4
4. Connecticut Mutual Life Ins. Co.	135.00	22.40	1	218.50	46.70	6	397.70	132.70	11
5. Phoenix Mutual Life Ins. Co.	157.00	26.60	7	233.60	48.60	7	392.50	127.70	6
6. Northwestern Mutual Life Ins. Co.	157.40	28.70	11	234.80	45.50	3	405.40	129.40	8
7. Central Life Assurance Co. (Iowa)	155.10	22.90	2	235.70	46.10	4	404.00	136.00	15
8. State Mutual Life Assurance Co. of America (Mass.)	149.50	28.80	12	231.60	49.00	9	408.30	132.70	11
9. Modern Woodmen of America[1]	138.80	27.50	9	214.10	48.90	8	377.80	134.80	13
10. Lutheran Mutual Life Ins. Co.	144.80	27.30	8	226.10	49.50	10	394.90	135.00	14

[1] Fraternal organization; policy available only to members.
[2] The ten lowest cost policies of those sold by 166 larger companies licensed in Pennsylvania.
[3] Usual premiums for a female are the same as those for a male three years younger.
[4] Listed according to the average of the interest-adjusted costs at the three ages.
[5] Ranked at each age according to the average yearly cost of insurance over a 20-year period.

Note: All are participating policies.

Source: A Shopper's Guide to Life Insurance. © Pennsylvania Insurance Department. Harrisburg, Pennsylvania, April 1972. NOTE: These rates quoted as of 1972 are no longer in effect but illustrate price differentials between companies.

Premiums and Insurance Cost for the Ten Highest-Cost $10,000 Straight-Life Cash-Value Insurance Policies[3]

Company[5]	Male Age 20 or Female Age 23[4]			Male Age 35 or Female Age 38[4]			Male Age 50 or Female Age 53[3]		
	Annual Premium	Average Yearly Cost of Insurance	Ranking[6] at Age 20/23	Annual Premium	Average Yearly Cost of Insurance	Ranking[6] at Age 35/38	Annual Premium	Average Yearly Cost of Insurance	Ranking[6] at Age 50/53
1. Georgia International Life Ins. Co.[1]	$119.20	$61.00	166	$192.20	$94.50	166	$344.90	$202.40	165
2. The State Life Ins. Co. (Ind.)	155.70	55.70	165	237.00	88.70	165	410.60	199.60	162
3. Valley Forge Life Ins. Co.[1]	120.20	51.80	154	195.70	87.80	163	354.00	201.70	164
4. The Employers Life Ins. Co. of America (Del.)[1,2]	119.60	50.70	145	194.00	84.30	150	361.00	205.20	166
5. Old Republic Life Ins. Co. (Ill.)[1]	122.00	52.30	158	196.30	85.90	157	357.90	201.00	163
6. Wabash Life Ins. Co.[1]	120.30	52.80	159	192.90	86.70	159	348.70	199.30	161
7. Pennsylvania Life Ins. Co.[1]	110.40	53.60	162	183.60	86.40	158	340.40	198.30	160
8. Puritan Life Ins. Co.[1]	114.60	53.00	160	188.00	86.90	160	338.70	193.50	152
9. Security Life and Accident Co. (Colo.)	164.50	49.50	140	250.40	88.30	164	417.30	194.60	155
10. Travelers Ins. Co.[1]	118.00	53.10	161	190.90	84.70	154	348.10	194.40	154

[1] Nonparticipating policy: no dividends, guaranteed costs. All others are participating.
[2] Policy includes Waiver of Premium for disability at no extra cost. Costs have been adjusted to remove the estimated charge for this benefit.
[3] The ten highest-cost policies of those sold by 166 larger companies licensed in Pennsylvania.
[4] Usual premiums for a female are the same as those for a male three years younger.
[5] Listed according to the average of the interest-adjusted costs at the three ages.
[6] Ranked at each age according to the average yearly cost of insurance over a 20-year period.

Source: A Shopper's Guide to Life Insurance. © Pennsylvania Insurance Department. Harrisburg, Pennsylvania, April 1972. NOTE: These rates quoted as of 1972 are no longer in effect but illustrate price differentials between companies.

11-6 High and Low Costs of Premiums and Insurance

Income	
Premiums	77.9¢
Net investment earnings and other income	22.1
	100.0¢

Use of Income	
Benefit payments and additions to reserves	
Benefit payments in year	51.8¢
Additions to reserves and surplus	26.5
	78.3¢
Operating expenses	
Commissions to agents	6.6¢
Home and field office expenses	9.9
	16.5¢
Taxes	4.2¢
Dividends to stockholders (nonmutual companies)	1.0¢
	100.0¢

Source: The American Council of Life Insurance, *Life Insurance Fact Book 1976* (New York: The American Council of Life Insurance (formerly Institute of Life Insurance), 1975, p. 58.

11-7   The U.S. Life Insurance Company Dollar, 1974

period from the sum of premiums to that date, and then divides by the number of years in the period.   In a typical hustle to a 23-year-old male prospect, an insurance sales representative may suggest that a $25,000 whole-life policy with a $36 monthly premium would be worth $2400 more than the sum of the premiums and reinvested dividends after 20 years.   But the Net Cost Index ignores the interest that the dividends and savings portion of the premiums could earn.

The *Interest-Adjusted Net Cost Index* overcomes the problem of lost interest by adding it at a constant rate to the premiums and dividends.   From this sum, the constant cash value at a given date is deducted.   Then the value of the money is adjusted upward to its future value at the end of the time for which the calculation is made and this interest adjustment is divided into the adjusted premiums *plus* dividends *minus* cash value.   Finally, the result is divided by a constant to get the Interest-Adjusted Net Cost Index.

To show the important difference between the two methods, take a sample $20,000 policy issued at age 35 with an annual premium of $400.   Annual dividends are $28 at the end of the first year and increase by $10 each year to $218 at the end of 20 years.   Cash values are zero for the first two years and then increase by $340 each year to $6120 for the twentieth year (see Figure 11-8).

Life insurance companies like to use the Net Cost approach in their sales appeals because it tends to understate the cost of coverage.   A number of states, however, including Arkansas, California, Pennsylvania, and Wisconsin, all noted for their rigorous regulations, require insurance sales representatives to disclose costs based on the interest-adjusted method.

Which method is best is of course more than a squabble among actuaries and statisticians, for insurance companies' rates are not as competitive as they ought to be. Because policies vary so much in their details it is difficult to make extensive and conclusive comparisons among the nearly 2000 life insurance underwriters in North America. The difficulty of comparison permits some firms to charge premiums consistently 100% higher for the same basic coverage. Insurance shoppers thus need accurate unit pricing. Yet two policies at the same price may be very different. The Interest-Adjusted Net Cost Index is only a rough measure of cost and benefit. It doesn't include important policy benefits such as a premium waiver during periods of disability, speed of customer service, and so on. Of course, determined insurance shoppers can find nearly identical policies from companies of similar size and perform their own cost calculations with a book of compound interest tables and a slide rule, but most shoppers don't bother.

Insurance companies protest that compulsory use and disclosure of interest-adjusted data will force the better (and presumably high-cost) firms to cut back on important policyholder benefits and to give all-around poorer service. Industry investigators insist that the interest-adjusted method will save billions of dollars for policyholders.[2] As an interim judgment, we may expect that more honest and meaningful disclosure will save consumers large amounts of money, eliminate excess premium ripoffs, and force the industry to aim its advertising, selling, and services at the significant differences between competing firms and policies.

[2] *The Wall Street Journal,* March 8, 1974, p. 24.

11-8   Comparative Cost Indexes (first 20 years' cost)

	Net Cost Index	Interest-Adjusted Net Cost Index
Sum of premiums	$8000	$13,888
Minus sum of dividends	2460	3,539
	5540	10,349
Minus cash values	6120	6,120
	−580	4,229
Divided by 20 equals cost per year	−29	
Cost per thousand	−1.45	
Accumulation of $1 per year at 5% interest		34.719
Interest-adjusted net cost per year		121.81
Interest-adjusted net cost index per $1000		6.09

Note: The Interest-Adjusted Net Cost Index differs from the Net Cost Index in that (1) instead of being added, premiums and dividends are accumulated at a given rate (5%), and (2) instead of dividing by the number of years, the accumulated premiums *minus* accumulated dividends *minus* cash value is *divided by* the amount to which $1 paid at the beginning of each year will accumulate during the period using the same interest rate in (1), or 5%.

TRUTH IN SELLING

The consumer is in a difficult position when buying life insurance. The structure of premiums and benefits is very complex and few buyers, whether naive or sophisticated, are able to evaluate accurately the true costs of coverage. The life insurance industry has been essentially noncompetitive in selling cash-value insurance and the nature of level premiums in whole-life policies has tended to obscure major cost differences among policies. The life insurance industry has developed largely without regulation of its pricing practices and until recently without meaningful requirements or incentives to disclose actual costs to the buyer.[3]

If and when price disclosure does come to the industry in a uniform fashion, the high-cost companies will be forced to change their ways or to go out of business. There might be a good deal of policy switching by existing policyholders. These reallocations of coverage and revenue, no matter how inconvenient for the industry, would be of major benefit to consumers.

Until accurate rate reporting is done by all insurance firms, life insurance buyers would do well to concentrate on straight term insurance (perhaps with renewability and convertibility features), the costs of which are pretty well out in the open. The forced savings inherent in cash-value insurance is the major problem in assessing its true cost. Because the insurance premiums usually can perform better if one reinvests the price difference between term and whole life, cash-value insurance should be approached cautiously.

SUMMARY

1 Life insurance basically protects beneficiaries against the economic consequences of the early or otherwise untimely death of the insured.

2 Life insurance fills a gap in income resulting from death. If the gap is small or if survivors otherwise have ample income, life insurance need not be carried.

3 Life insurance rates are based on the probability of the death of the insured, the length of the agreement, and the guarantee that an insurable interest exists between the insured and those who benefit from the death of the insured. The probability of death increases with age and the length of the insurance period. Insurable interest requires that a beneficiary lose something by the insured's death.

4 The amount of life insurance a household needs is calculated by estimating its assets and yearly income, subtracting liabilities and yearly living costs after the death of the insured. The variations between yearly income and yearly expenses are averaged over the probable life spans and periods of dependency of the intended beneficiaries and adjusted to the difference of after-tax

---

[3] Joseph M. Belth, *The Retail Price Structure in American Life Insurance,* Indiana Business Report No. 40 (Bloomington, Indiana: Indiana University, 1966), pp. 242, 245.

yield that can be achieved on the insurance proceeds and other assets *minus* the reduction of purchasing power caused by inflation.

5 The two basic types of life insurance are term and whole life. Term insurance is pure risk coverage and leaves no monetary benefit if death does not occur in the policy period. The whole-life policy has a savings feature and does accumulate a cash value whether or not death occurs in a given time.

6 The five fundamental insurance policy variables are:
  1 Duration of insurance
  2 Premium schedule
  3 Face value
  4 Savings accumulation
  5 Risk carried

7 Term insurance offers the most insurance per dollar of premium. It can and should be bought with renewability and convertability guarantees in order to ensure that the insured and family can obtain coverage in the future, regardless of health. Term-insurance premiums are higher as the insured grows older, but multiyear coverage can be bought with level averaged premiums for the duration of the term. Decreasing benefit term insurance offers a method of covering mortgages and other debts.

8 Cash-value, whole-life policies are available in forms requiring premium payments for the life of the insured or limited periods requiring higher payments condensed into 10, 20, or 30 years. Continuous premium whole life spreads payments out for the longest possible time and thus yields the most cash-value insurance per premium dollar.

9 Inflation brings a guaranteed major loss on whole-life, cash-value insurance. It carries only a modest loss on five-year term insurance.

10 Sales fees average 50% of a first-year premium on individual cash-value policies, 30% of a first-year premium for term insurance, and much less for group insurance.

11 Life insurance policies are sold by 2000 companies in North America. Cost comparisons are hard to make, but can be done accurately via the Interest-Adjusted Net Cost Index. Where sales fees are lowest, as in Savings Bank Life Insurance or in group coverage, net interest-adjusted costs tend to be lowest. The interest-adjusted net cost calculation fails, however, to make valid comparisons among policies that are in any way different. Accordingly, true unit pricing of life insurance must await reform by the insurance industry itself.

Suggestions for Further Reading

General:

Bickelhaupt, David L. and Magee, John H. *General Insurance,* 8th ed. Homewood, Illinois: Richard D. Irwin, 1970, Chs. 22–26.

Belth, Joseph M. *The Retail Price Structure in American Life Insurance,* Indiana Business Report, No. 40. Bloomington, Indiana: Indiana University, 1966.

Mehr, Robert I. *Life Insurance: Theory and Practice.* Austin, Texas: Business Publications, 1970.

Rate Comparisons:
Consumer Reports, January, February, and March 1974.
Best's Insurance Reports—Life/Health. Oldwick, N.J.: A.M. Best Co., *annual.*
National Underwriter Life Reports. Chicago: National Underwriter Co., *weekly.*

Consumer Pamphlets:
Bankers Life Company. *How to Select the Right Insurance Company.* Des Moines, Iowa: Bankers Life Co., 1971.
Canadian Life Insurance Association. *Considerations in the Comparison of Life Insurance Policies.* Toronto: CLIA, n.d.
Cohen, Jerome B. *Decade of Decision.* New York: Institute of Life Insurance, n.d.

The Consumer Workshop

1 "A young and growing family is more likely to need life insurance than is the family that has seen its children through college." Evaluate this statement in terms of the family financial planning criteria developed in this chapter.
2 A good friend, slightly confused by too many life insurance sales presentations, comes to you for unbiased guidance. She wishes:
   1 To assure for her children the financial means to go to college in the event of her death
   2 To buy some immediate insurance coverage
   3 To establish a retirement plan
You recognize that her dilemma centers on the differences between whole-life, term, and endowment coverage.
Which form will be most suitable for your friend? Explain your choice in detail.
3 Why is it very difficult to compare cash-value life insurance policies? What tools can the consumer use to analyze various policies and their costs?
4 Inflation complicates the purchase of life insurance. How should consumers adjust their buying plans for life insurance to compensate for expected reductions in the future purchasing power of the dollar?
5 "Life insurance is the best investment a family can make." Analyze the validity of this statement. Does life insurance offer returns higher than other investments? If not, how may life insurance be superior to other forms of investment that admittedly offer higher yields?

12 ESTATE PLANNING

12

In this chapter we examine the problems and methods of estate planning. We begin with a discussion of the objectives of estate planning and consider the forms of property that are subject to inclusion in the estate of the deceased. We then concentrate on the process of estate transmission—the will and its administration after the maker's death. We examine trusts and estate and gift taxes and conclude with advice about avoiding the pitfalls of estate planning.

THE IMPORTANCE OF ESTATE PLANNING

An *estate* consists of personal property, interests, and rights that may be inherited or divided when an individual dies. *Estate planning* is the process of arranging this transfer of interests. It is important to understand and to plan this transfer so that one's instructions about the division of property will be implemented, or at least not frustrated, when death ends one's personal control over the property. The most common planning objective is, of course, to ensure adequate income for a surviving spouse and family during their period of dependence.

Estate planning is not a concern of the rich alone. Most people have homes, personal and real property, life insurance, savings, and investments that are subject to distribution at death. It is almost always beneficial to prepare a will specifying the distribution of personal property.

PROPERTY RIGHTS

American rules for the holding of property differ for those states having Community Property Laws (Arizona, California, Idaho, Louisiana, Nevada, New Mexico, Texas, and Washington) and the remainder of the states, which do not have these laws. Basically, whatever the state, property held jointly by both husband and wife need not undergo the estate transmission process. In community-property states only that property acquired during a marriage can be owned by both partners, and on one partner's death the community property automatically reverts to the other partner. All property acquired before the marriage is separate and is subject to the estate transmission process. Noncommunity-property states are those that have passed laws recognizing that *all* assets held by a married couple are owned jointly. When one spouse dies, the other inherits the deceased's share automatically, without the intervention of a will or administrative process.

Forms of Title

Title is an official form of ownership with important implications for taxes and estate planning. Property held in *sole tenancy,* that is, separately, is taxed as the property of the owner and is subject to the estate transmission process. *Community property* and *joint property* present more complex tax situations but may escape estate transmission. Jointly owned property automatically passes to the surviving owner(s) in the event of one owner's death. Property held as *tenancy in common* reverts to the deceased owner's heirs, who may not necessarily be the surviving owners. Only property held as *tenancy by the entirety,* a special form available only to husbands and wives, automatically reverts to the surviving partner.

The Estate Transmission Process

Property that one chooses to include or that is legally included in a transmissible estate must be passed on to interested persons or parties by a court proceeding. If the deceased leaves no will, he or she is considered to have died *intestate,* in which case the court disposes of the property according to the estate descent and distribution laws of the given state, and the inheritors may be persons the deceased may not have wished to inherit the property. For example, if an unmarried man or woman dies intestate, state laws generally require that:

1 The property is to be divided among the parents. If one parent is dead, the surviving parent is to inherit the entire estate.
2 If no parents survive, the property is to be equally divided among the brothers and sisters.
3 If no parents or siblings survive, the property reverts to the nearest relative.
4 If no relatives can be found, the property reverts to the state.

A startling but true fact is that 70% of Americans die intestate.

THE WILL

The person who wishes to have control over his or her property after death must create a will. A male maker of a will is called a *testator;* a female will maker, a *testatrix.* The will appoints heirs and designates the proportion of the estate that each is to receive. A will maker must be 18 or 21, depending on the state, and

"Oh, oh! 'Being of unsound mind' . . . ."

of sufficiently sound mind to understand the contents of the will he or she signs. Most property can be included in a will, but Social Security Survivor Benefits, U.S. Savings Bonds, some life insurance, pension rights and proceeds, and property held in joint-ownership forms are usually excluded from distribution in the will. These special rights and properties are distributed at the owner's death, following specific instructions signed by the will maker in each case, as that no other distribution directions are required in the will itself.

The Components of a Will

It is possible to draft one's own will. Many self-written wills are valid, but many more are not. It is usually best to seek the assistance of a lawyer, an accountant, or a banker before undertaking the estate planning process. The standard will drafted by a lawyer conforms to a plan that has been proved by experience. A will is comprised of words and phrases whose meanings have been established by time and use to be beyond reasonable dispute. A will contains five elements to establish and validate the intentions of the maker:

1 The *opening recitation* describes the maker and the maker's residence, it revokes any previous wills, and establishes the competence of the maker with phrases such as "being of sound mind."
2 The *disposition clauses* indicate the particular portions in which the maker's estate are to be distributed.
3 The *administration clauses* indicate how the maker's plans are to be carried out: who is to inherit what, under what conditions this distribution is to proceed, and so on.

4 The *testamonium clause* bears the will maker's signature of approval, which must appear immediately after the last sentence of the preceding sections.

5 The *attestation* bears the signatures of the witnesses (usually two or more) and describes the place and circumstance of signature. Witnesses should be younger than the will maker so that they can testify to the validity of the will if it should be challenged. Witnesses should not be beneficiaries of the will.

The Letter of Final Instructions

The process of administering an estate begins with locating the will and determining what properties and interests the deceased has left. To assist the person who must begin to administer the will, it is useful if the will maker provides a letter of final instructions containing these six essential items of information:

1 Names and addresses of those persons to be notified at the time of death: relatives, associates, physician, lawyer, and so on.

2 Where the will is located.

3 Instructions for the will maker's burial and funeral.

4 Instructions pertinent to any business enterprises.

5 Location of safe-deposit boxes, stock and bond certificates, insurance policies, pension documents, bank accounts, mortgages, deeds, titles, and other financial interests.

6 Location of vital documents, such as marriage certificate, past tax returns, paid bills, and canceled checks for the past seven years.

The Need for Periodic Review

It is a common but incorrect belief that once a will is made it never needs to be revised. A will should be changed whenever the maker's needs, plans, and/or circumstances change. As major new property is acquired, as the state of residence changes, as new tax obligations accumulate, and as family responsibilities change (additional children, divorce or remarriage, the death of a parent), the will should be modified through *codicils* (amendments) or revoked and remade. A periodic review of the will—say, once a year—helps maintain its relevancy in terms of family conditions and needs. Note that amending a will is a formal process. Amendments cannot simply be noted and initialed; a mere erasure or an improper change can invalidate a will.

PROBATE—EXECUTING THE WILL

When the testator or testatrix dies, the process of executing the will is known as *probate*. Probate has five important stages:

1 Authentication

2 Administration

3 Discharge or claims
4 Tax settlement
5 Distribution to heirs

Authentication   Probate begins when a will is brought into court. The judge or some other probate official examines the will to see that it is prepared according to law and bears the proper signatures, including those of the witnesses. There is a preliminary determination of the size and the liabilities of the estate. The court appoints an executor, usually named in the will, to handle the subsequent stages of execution.

Administration   The executor must appraise and determine the assets of the estate. The executor or the executrix assembles all certificates of ownership, deeds, titles, any other necessary documents. This phase may involve operating or overseeing a business, collecting rents and life insurance proceeds, and/or managing a portfolio of securities.

Discharge of   The executor or the executrix must also assemble a list of liabilities—unpaid
Claims   charge-account bills, business debts, and so forth—within a year, if these claims on the estate are to be valid. This is accomplished by posting a notice of death in newspapers and legal journals.

Tax Settlement   The executor or the executrix is responsible for processing four sets of tax forms:

1 The final federal and state income tax returns of the deceased.
2 The estate's federal income tax return for the period between the time of death and the final distribution of the estate.
3 Federal and state estate taxes, based on the value of the entire estate before its distribution.
4 State inheritance taxes levied on the value of the estate received by each heir.

Distribution   The distribution of the estate according to the directions of the will and the rendering of a final account of this distribution to the probate court is the final responsibility of the executor or the executrix.

CHOOSING AN EXECUTOR OR EXECUTRIX

Estate administration is complex and can consume much time and effort. It may be assigned to a competent friend (who may administer the estate personally or appoint an experienced attorney to perform this job) or to a trust company, or to both a friend and a professional management firm as *coexecutors*. It is advisable to choose a younger person to execute a will, because he or she will be more likely to survive to carry out the duties. In the event of his or her death, an alternative executive or executrix should be named.

Fees for the execution of wills vary from state to state, on a schedule of rates that decline progressively from about 7% of the first $1000, to 4% of the next $9000, down to 1% of estates over $10,000,000.

TRUSTS

A *trust* is a legal entity with a financial life of its own that can be created before or after death. A *living trust* is created during the life of the trust maker and can be revoked after a term of years or at any given time. When the terms of the trust are such that the creator has definitely relinquished control over the assets of the trust for his or her own life or for the term of the trust, income taxes on trust income are paid by the trust or beneficiary, not by the trust creator. But if the creator is able to exercise a good deal of control over the trust's management, then trust income may still be taxable as personal income. In general, trust beneficiaries (those who receive trust incomes) must pay the normal federal income taxes and most of the state income taxes on personal incomes.

Advantages and Disadvantages of Trusts

Trusts are valuable devices for tax planning and also aid the busy investor in managing his or her assets. Trusts can also ensure that a will maker's plans for asset management are carried out long after an executor or an executrix ceases to perform his or her duties. However, trusts can be so inflexible as to retain assets in uncreative or unproductive management. The danger of poor management is greatest for *irrevocable trusts,* in which the beneficiaries and the trust creator permanently lose control over trust assets and management.

Certain trusts can be created to manage the life insurance proceeds or other assets following the death of the trust creator. The advantages of vesting estate assets in a trust is that they can be wisely managed and distributed conservatively; that is, the trust may, for example, survive for the life of a spouse and still preserve some assets for minor children surviving the spouse's subsequent death. The disadvantages of these trusts are that trustees may be legally obliged to follow investment policies that are too conservative. For example, some state laws forbid trustees to hold common stocks and anything except the most secure bonds. Such investments provide relatively little income and may even fail to protect beneficiaries against inflation. Trust management is also quite expensive. State laws governing trustees limit charges to an average of 1% of trust assets per year. But if the trustees invest assets to earn a return of only 6%, then the trustees' fee is $16\frac{2}{3}$%, which is far from inexpensive.

Four Pointers for Trust Makers

1 Trusts should be planned with experienced counsel. Forethought is necessary to ensure that the possible loss of control of the assets is balanced by clear tax advantages.

2 Trust management is complex. Bank trust departments can manage trusts well but tend to administer impersonally. To offset this, family friends may be appointed cotrustees to personalize trust management. Cotrustees' fees should be specified when drafting the *trust instrument* or the *agreement of trust*—the document that creates the trust—to protect beneficiaries from excessive management fees.

3 Irrevocable trusts should contain a clause that permits the beneficiaries or cotrustees (if appointed) to change the trust management when they so desire. A change in professional management under the same trust agreement does not impair the tax status of the trust.

4 Lawsuits suing trustees for poor management are difficult to win. Professional trustees often insert a clause in the trust instrument that permits them to charge the trust any costs incurred defending management in a lawsuit. If possible, a bank or a financial manager should be chosen who will not insist on such a clause.

FEDERAL ESTATE TAXES

The rate of federal taxation on estates ranges up to nearly 77%, so that it is important to understand and to prepare for these taxes. Federal estate tax return Form 706 must be filed within nine months of the death of the trust maker if the gross estate exceeds $60,000.

The Calculation

The federal estate tax is computed by a seven-step process:

1 Calculation of gross estate
2 Deduction of funeral, administration costs, and debts against the estate
3 Deduction of the marital allowance, if married at time of death
4 Deduction of charitable contributions
5 Deduction of a basic $60,000 exemption
6 Calculation of gross estate tax
7 Application of credits to reduce federal estate tax payable

In greater detail, the process of calculating the federal estate tax is:

1 Begin by calculating the *gross estate,* which is comprised of cash, stocks, bonds, real and personal property, gifts made within three years of death, and certain life insurance and annuity interests.

2 From the gross estate, deduct all funeral expenses, probate, execution and administration costs and losses, and debts acquired by the deceased prior to death. This is the adjusted gross estate.

FEDERAL ESTATE-TAX RATES

Taxable estate (after deducting $60,000 exemption)		Tax equals	Plus percent	of excess over
From	To			
$ 0	$ 5,000	$ 0	3	$ 0
5,000	10,000	150	7	5,000
10,000	20,000	500	11	10,000
20,000	30,000	1,600	14	20,000
30,000	40,000	3,000	18	30,000
40,000	50,000	4,800	22	40,000
50,000	60,000	7,000	25	50,000
60,000	100,000	9,500	28	60,000
100,000	250,000	20,700	30	100,000
250,000	500,000	65,700	32	250,000
500,000	750,000	145,500	35	500,000
1,000,000	1,250,000	325,700	39	1,000,000
2,000,000	2,500,000	753,200	49	2,000,000
5,000,000	6,000,000	2,468,200	67	5,000,000
10,000,000		6,088,200	77	10,000,000

3 Deduct one-half of the adjusted gross estate as the *marital deduction,* if married at time of death.
4 Subtract all contributions to charitable or government organizations.
5 Subtract the basic $60,000 exemption available to all U.S. citizens and resident aliens.   Remaining is the taxable estate.
6 Calculate the *gross estate tax.*
7 Subtract credits for state death taxes, prepaid estate taxes, gift taxes, and foreign death taxes.   The remaining figure is the *net federal estate tax payable.*

TAXES ON GIFTS

It is possible to avoid much estate taxation by giving appropriate gifts throughout life.   All gifts of less than $3000 per recipient per year are exempt from the gift tax.   Gifts over this amount must be reported within 45 days of the end of the calendar quarter in which the taxable gift is received.

Both husband and wife may give away $3000 per year to each recipient. Each child may receive this amount.   A couple with four children can therefore

FEDERAL GIFT-TAX RATES

A Total Amount of Taxable Gifts		B Tax on Amount in Column A	C Rate of Tax on Excess Over Amount in Column A
Equal to or More Than	But Less Than		
$ 0	$ 5,000	$ 0	2.25%
5,000	10,000	112.50	5.25
10,000	20,000	375.00	8.25
20,000	30,000	1,200.00	10.50
30,000	40,000	2,250.00	13.50
40,000	50,000	3,600.00	16.50
50,000	60,000	5,250.00	18.75
60,000	100,000	7,125.00	21.00
100,000	250,000	15,525.00	22.50
250,000	500,000	49,275.00	24.00
500,000	750,000	109,275.00	26.25

give away 2 × $3000 × 4, or $24,000 per year tax free.

A person may give up to $30,000 in his or her lifetime without incurring a federal gift-tax liability. This exemption applies to donors, not receivers. A husband and wife may combine their exemptions and give a total of $60,000 tax free. These gifts are in *addition* to the $3000 annual exclusion just discussed.

The federal gift tax is cumulative. If you give $50,000 in one year subject to gift taxation of $5250 and in the following year give another $50,000, the total tax liability is calculated on a gift of $100,000 that has a tax liability of $15,525. But previously paid gift taxes can be credited toward the total cumulative gift liability, so that you pay only $15,525 − $5250 = $10,275.

Federal gift taxes can be deducted from the gross estate-tax liability, so that gift taxes can be considered a form of estate-tax prepayment. But because gift-tax rates are lower per dollar of transmitted assets, they are actually a form of tax discount. Thus, gift giving is valuable in executing estate transmission.

FOUR POINTERS FOR ESTATE PLANNING

1 Estate planning is too complex to be handled by the individual. It is most useful to seek professional assistance from a lawyer, a banker, or an accountant.
2 The creation of trusts and gifts are solutions to some estate-tax problems, but trusts and gifts reduce the individual's personal control over assets. Such steps should be taken only after careful consideration.

3 Federal estate taxes can be prepaid with special Treasury bonds called "flower bonds." These bonds are sold at steep discounts but pay rather low interest rates. For the testator or the testatrix who anticipates an early transfer of the estate, such bonds are useful tax-planning tools.

4 Specific bequests of assets that have paper capital gains circumvents the capital-gains tax, because no sale of assets occurs.

SUMMARY

1 Property may be held in many forms. There is an important distinction in property holding between community-property and noncommunity-property states. Community-property states hold that all property acquired during a marriage is the common property of husband and wife; property acquired prior to a marriage is separate property.

2 The form of title chosen to hold property may include or exclude property from the probate process. Jointly owned property automatically passes to the surviving owner(s) in the event of an owner's death. Property held as tenancy in common reverts to the deceased owner's heirs. Property held in tenancy by the entirety means that the surviving spouse automatically inherits the property of the deceased partner.

3 Persons who leave no valid will are said to have died intestate. Such a person's property is dispersed by the state according to its laws of estate descent and distribution.

4 A will maker must be 18 or 21 years of age, depending on the state of residence, and of sufficiently sound mind to understand the will being signed.

5 A will has five parts:
1 The opening recitation—the testator's name, address, competence to make will, revocation of prior wills, if any
2 The disposition clauses—the property to be distributed
3 The administration clauses—the shares and methods of apportionment
4 The testamonium clause—the testator's signature
5 The attestation—the signature of the witnesses

6 The letter of final instruction should contain six items of information:
1 The people to be notified when death occurs
2 The location of the will
3 Funeral instructions
4 Business instructions
5 The location of financial documents
6 The location of personal documents

7 Wills should be reviewed and changed periodically as circumstances warrant.

8 Probate encompasses five steps:
1 Authentication
2 Administration of assets
3 Discharge of claims

      4 Tax settlement

      5 Distribution

9 Trusts can be created to control assets for tax planning or to relieve the trust creator of administrative burdens. Trusts can be funded from the proceeds of life insurance policies or other assets, and they can be revocable or irrevocable. When the trust creator relinquishes control over trust assets, the trust becomes liable for its own income taxes, thus relieving the creator of tax liabilities on any assets given to the trust.

10 Trusts are tools for conservative asset management. Their advantage is careful professional management, but their cost is excessive conservatism in investment policy in some cases and excessive fees in others. A clause in the trust instrument that permits a change in management is a valuable safeguard against both of these risks.

11 The federal estate tax is sharply progressive, rising from 3% on taxable estates of $5000 to 77% on taxable estates over $10,000,000. However, the calculation of estate taxes permits generous deductions and exemptions for spouses, charitable contributions, and death and estate or gift taxes already paid.

12 The federal gift tax is cumulative; previous gifts always increase the base of the gift-tax schedule. But gift taxes can be credited toward federal estate taxes. Because federal gift-tax rates are lower than real estate taxes per dollar of transferred asset, the federal gift tax can be considered a discount form of estate-tax prepayment.

Suggestions for Further Reading
Blodgett, Richard E. *The New York Times Book of Money*. New York: Quadrangle, 1971, Chapter 16.

Dowd, Merle E. *Estate Planning: A Family's Financial Guide*. Chicago: Henry Regnery, 1971.

The Consumer Workshop

1 Will makers can use many devices to protect their assets from probate and estate taxation: gift giving, trusts, and suitable forms of property holding and title. Yet each of these estate-planning devices causes some change in the individual's present lifestyle. Discuss the appropriateness of each of these forms of defense against estate taxes with respect to a young family's need to retain flexible control over personal property.

2 Sam Lee, a self-made millionaire with extensive real estate holdings, has decided to draft his own will. Sam thinks he can do as well as any tax expert, but he discusses his plans with you, a close business associate. It's up to you to give Sam some directives about the estate transmission process and to demonstrate how assets can be distributed during life as gifts. What will you say?

3 Bill and Marcy Ward are visiting their lawyer to discuss drafting their wills. The lawyer recommends trusts, but both Bill and Marcy are only 25. How could the cost and relative inflexibility of trusts impair their present lifestyle?

"That's just it—if I had any beneficiaries, I wouldn't *be* a hermit."

4 The operation of estate and gift taxation suggests several important political problems for Congress and therefore for Americans in general. Estate taxation prevents a few people from accumulating huge fortunes that could imperil the economic rights of others. But estate taxes are disproportionate. For example, farmers living near cities must bear the brunt of higher estate taxes because their land skyrockets in price as urban development pushes more and more suburbs into the countryside. At a farmer's death, his or her now overpriced land must be sold in part to pay estate taxes, leaving less land for the next generation of farmers. Should more loopholes be created to eliminate these injustices or should estate and gift taxation be reduced or abolished? [For additional information on this subject, *see* John Pierson, "Death and Taxes," *The Wall Street Journal* (April 27, 1976), 1 and 15.]

18 AUTOMOBILE AND HOME INSURANCE

13

> "More than twice the number of American deaths have been due to automobile accidents during the twentieth century than were due to all the U.S. wars since the Declaration of Independence.* "

> "The arson rate in 1974 was at least ten times as high as it was in 1950.† "

In this chapter we develop a method of buying automobile and home insurance. First, the general principles of buying insurance—How much risk to carry and how much to insure—are discussed, and then the different types and costs of automobile and home insurance are examined. In each case we conclude with comparisons and comments on the rate structures of the insurance coverage. Throughout this chapter, we emphasize the ways in which consumers can secure the right amounts of the best insurance for their individual needs.

THE PRINCIPLES OF PROPERTY INSURANCE

Of course, life is full of hazards. Insurance can remove the financial consequences of most the these risks, but insuring every hazard can be prohibitively expensive. To keep insurance costs reasonable, it is best to self-insure the risks that are likely to occur and that are of small monetary value. A cash reserve for such losses is all that is required to maintain this *self-insurance*. On the other hand, *purchased insurance* should be secured for the large and unlikely risks that cannot readily be covered with a cash reserve.

If premium funds are tight, it is usually better to stretch them further by carrying more risks for higher coverage maximums and by extending self-insurance with increased deductibles. (We examine the control of risks and premiums later in this chapter.)

Putting Principles into Practice

Balancing self-insurance with purchased insurance coverage requires that the consumer:

1 Determine the maximum possible money loss
2 Decide what risks and what amounts of these risks to self-insure
3 Decide what risks and what amounts of these risks to transfer to an insurance policy

* C. H. Crainard, *Automobile Insurance* (Homewood, Ill.: Richard D. Irwin, 1961), p. 7.
† *U.S. News & World Report* (September 23, 1974), p. 67.

AUTOMOBILE INSURANCE

Automobile insurance covers five kinds of risks created by or encountered in the operation of a motor vehicle.

Liability insurance covers the risk of injury or death to others and the damage to the other people's property (such as cars, homes, or buildings) that result from the operation of the insured's car. Unlike most property insurance, liability insurance pays the other party—not the insured—for the losses covered. Since this kind of third-party liability is the largest financial risk one encounters in driving, it is the most important type of insurance to own.

Collision insurance covers damage to the insured's car in accidents. This is the most expensive type of automobile insurance and can easily amount to several hundred dollars per year. Most time-payment contracts for the purchase of an automobile require the borrower to carry collision insurance to cover the lender's financial interest in the car. "Deductibles" reduce the cost of this insurance.

Comprehensive insurance coverage provides reimbursement for damage to the insured's car resulting from causes other than collision, such as fire, windstorm, or vandalism.

HOW "DEDUCTIBLES" CAN SAVE YOU MONEY

Most collision coverage policies are worded so that the insured must pay for the first part of the loss claim, or the amount "deductible." A common deductible amount is $50, meaning the collision damages in an accident must exceed $50 before the insured party can collect. A $60 fender dent therefore costs only $50, because $10 is refunded by the insurance firm. To further reduce the cost of collision coverage, motorists can increase the amount of the deductible. If a new car collision policy with a $50 deductible costs $70 per year, then

For a deductible of	*Annual insurance is*
$ 100	$45
250	25
500	20
1000	15

Note that as the amount deductible increases, the premium saved decreases. Large deductibles therefore expose the insured to a loss risk that is of greater potential value than the $5 premium increments saved. Most motorists are content to have deductibles that do not exceed $100 or $200 per accident.

SAMPLE FAMILY COMBINATION AUTOMOBILE POLICY

═══════════════ FAMILY COMBINATION AUTOMOBILE POLICY ═══════════════

No. ACF

RENEWAL OF NUMBER

SPACE FOR COMPANY NAME, INSIGNIA, AND LOCATION

DECLARATIONS

Item 1. Named Insured and Address:　(No., Street, Town or City, County, State)

SPACE FOR
PRODUCER'S NAME AND
MAILING ADDRESS

Item 2. Policy Period:　(Mo. Day Yr.)　(　　Months)

From　　　　　　　　　　to
12:01 A.M., standard time at the address of the named insured as stated herein.

Occupation of the named insured is (IF MARRIED WOMAN, GIVE HUSBAND'S OCCUPATION OR BUSINESS (ENTER BELOW))

Item 3. The insurance afforded is only with respect to such of the following coverages as are indicated by specific premium charge or charges. The limit of the company's liability against each such coverage shall be as stated herein, subject to all the terms of this policy having reference thereto.

CAR 1	PREMIUMS CAR 2	LIMITS OF LIABILITY		COVERAGES
$	$	thousand dollars each person / thousand dollars each occurrence	A	Bodily Injury Liability
$	$	thousand dollars each occurrence	B	Property Damage Liability
$	$	dollars each person	C	Medical Payments
		$ Actual Cash Value*	D	(1) Comprehensive (excluding Collision)
$	$	$ 100		(2) Personal Effects
		Actual Cash Value less		
$	$	$ deductible	E	Collision
$	$	$	F	Fire, Lightning and Transportation
$	$	$	G	Theft
$	$	$	H	Combined Additional Coverage
$	$	$ 25 per disablement	I	Towing and Labor Costs
$	$	thousand dollars each person / thousand dollars each accident	J	Uninsured Motorists
			Form numbers of endorsements attached to policy at issue	
$				
$		Total Car 1 - Car 2		
$	$			
	Total Premium	* STRIKE OUT "ACTUAL CASH VALUE" AND INSERT AMOUNT IF POLICY IS WRITTEN ON STATED AMOUNT BASIS		

Item 4. Description of owned automobile or trailer

Year of Model	Trade Name	Body Type; Model	Identification Number (I) Serial Number (S) Motor Number (M)	F.O.B. List Price or Delivered Price at Factory	Purchased Month, Year　New or Used	Class & Rating Symbol	Sub-Class (if any)
Car 1							
Car 2							

Item 5. Loss Payee: Any loss under Part III is payable as interest may appear to the named insured and (NAME AND ADDRESS—ENTER BELOW)

Item 6. The owned automobile will be principally garaged in the town or city designated in Item 1 above, unless otherwise stated herein: (ENTER BELOW)

Item 7. During the past three years no insurer has canceled insurance, issued to the named insured, similar to that afforded hereunder, unless otherwise stated herein:

Countersigned:

By_____

Authorized Representative

OKP 6013-0-G
(Rev. 1-1-63)

Medical insurance coverage pays for medical services and hospital care for the insured and/or his or her passengers if injuries are sustained in an automobile accident, regardless of fault. These payments are often limited to expenses that arise within one year of the accident. People with nonautomotive medical insurance need not purchase this type of coverage *for themselves;* however, if they do, they can be repaid twice for each medical expense. Since personal medical insurance does not pay for passengers (except family members, in the case of family medical and hospitalization policies), consumers who carry passengers (in car pools, for example) should seriously consider securing medical coverage. Young drivers, who often lack any other medical insurance, are well-advised to purchase medical expense coverage, because automobile accidents are unfortunately a principal cause of injury and disability of the young.

Uninsured motorist coverage pays for injury to any member of the insured's family caused by an uninsured or an insufficiently insured driver. This type of coverage pays for injuries sustained while riding in a car or while walking. It is quite inexpensive, usually amounting to a few dollars per year per $10,000.

How Much Automobile Liability Insurance Do You Need?

Liability insurance is the essential automobile insurance coverage. It is usually described in terms of three numbers. An example is 100/300/25, which means that this particular policy pays a maximum of $100,000 for bodily injury to any one person, up to $300,000 for all personal injuries resulting from the accident, and a maximum of up to $25,000 for all property damages suffered. In theory the wealthy can carry their own risks without insurance, but in practice they do not. As an individual's wealth and earnings increase, his or her financial exposure also becomes greater. A person therefore should buy sufficient bodily injury insurance to cover at least his or her current net worth. A more prudent person would consider carrying insurance in higher amounts to cover future lifetime earnings or, alternatively, in the highest amounts currently awarded by the civil courts to automobile liability cases. Because the odds of causing an accident that necessitates the payment of huge damage awards are quite small, the actual cost of carrying greatly increased liability coverage is relatively slight.

Liability maximums can usually be increased by multiples of $100,000 at a cost of only a few dollars per year, unless the insured is in a high-risk driving category.

The Cost of Automobile Insurance

The cost of automobile insurance depends on the age, sex, and driving record of the insured, on whether the car is to be driven for work or for pleasure, and on the geographical area in which the car is to be driven. Insurance companies attempt to place drivers in appropriate risk categories and then establish rates according to previous experience with clients in each category.

An insurance company seeks to maximize its profits by selecting insurance applicants who probably will not incur unusually high losses. Some people have driving records or exhibit personal characteristics that indicate they are much more likely to be involved in an accident. These high-risk drivers must be insured, however; most states require insurance firms to accept them, but they are subject to suitably higher premiums. At the other end of the scale, individu-

DRIVERS AND POLICY COSTS

Potential Policy-holder*	Home Insurance Company (Gold Key)	St. Paul (Easy Auto)	Fireman's Fund (Economy Plus)	Central Mutual	Safeco Insurance Company	Aetna Casualty & Surety (Auto-Rite)
1	$205.65	$254.80	$228.00	$240.00	$214.60	$226.00
2	205.65	341.80	306.00	324.00	214.60	304.00
3	375.48	461.20	410.00	437.00	323.60	412.00
4	375.48	548.00	494.00	521.00	323.60	490.00
5	169.88	211.40	188.00	202.00	187.00	186.00
6	169.88	298.40	266.00	283.00	187.00	264.00

* KEY:
1. Man and wife, age 45, clean driving record, state job (Tucson, Arizona). Vehicle is a three-year-old, two-door sedan, small engine.
2. Same as 1, except one chargeable accident.
3. Same as 1, except one occasional male operator, age 20.
4. Same as 3, except one chargeable accident.
5. Driver over 65, in good physical condition (as noted on recent physician's report), pleasure use only, clean driving record.
6. Same as 5, except one chargeable accident.

Source: From *Personal Money Management* by Thomas E. Bailard, David L. Biehl, and Ronald W. Kaiser. © 1969, 1973, Science Research Associates, Inc. Reprinted by permission.

DRIVER DISCOUNTS: DO YOU QUALIFY?

Insurance companies employ the following driver and car categories to provide premium reductions of approximately 10%. Firms do not usually allow compound discounts, however, and limit total premium reductions to approximately 25%.

1 "Driver-training" discount, available to those who have completed a recognized course in driver education.
2 "Good driver" discount, available to drivers under 25 who have a good driving record, free of many claims, accidents, and/or tickets.
3 "Good student" discount, available to students with above-average grades.
4 "Nondrinker" discount, available to drivers who abstain from or moderately consume alcoholic beverages.
5 "Limited-use" discount, available to people who rarely drive, including high-risk young drivers who seldom drive.
6 "Multiple-car" discount, available to owners who insure two or more cars with the same company.

A PREMIUM COMPARISON FORM

FIRM

Premium:
   Liability
   Collision
   Comprehensive
   Medical
   Uninsured driver
   Discounts

   Total

als whose driving records and personal characteristics suggest that they will probably not be involved in an accident may be offered special "preferred-risk" premiums at 10–25% below standard rates. When we compare this to the cost for the accident-prone, "assigned-risk" driver, whose premiums may be four to five times the standard rate, we can see that it literally pays to drive safely.

Finding the Right Company. Automobile insurance rates vary widely with risk classification and location. In surveys of automobile insurance costs, *Consumer Reports* has found that different insurance companies charge widely varying rates. The table on page 221 shows this variation.

Discounts Are Available. Many firms have a discount system to attract customers and to reduce premium costs for drivers who are expected to have fewer than the average number of accidents. In comparing insurance rates, it is useful to determine if you qualify for rate reductions.

What Rates Don't Show

Rate comparisons among competing automobile insurance companies do *not* reveal these three important qualities of firm performance:

1 Claim settlement service
2 Policy cancellation rate
3 Financial reliability

Claim Settlement Service. An insurance company should attempt to provide fast and fair claim service. Most do, but some quote low premiums and hold their costs by making inadequate settlements. This unfair practice can put clients who have valid claims in the position of having to sue their own insurance companies to secure settlement. *Consumer Reports* regularly surveys automobile insurance settlement services; check this publication when shopping for automobile insurance.

Policy Cancellation Rate. Some automobile insurance companies cancel policies more frequently than others—for example, when insured customers are in accidents or when they change their occupation or addresses to those the insurance firm deems less desirable. It is a frequent practice in the automobile insurance field to force drivers whose policies have been canceled to purchase high-cost, assigned-risk coverage. Thus if one insurance firm cancels an individual's policy, all other firms will demand higher rates from this driver. Accordingly, consumers should avoid insurance firms that are prone to policy cancellations. *Consumer Reports* also evaluates automobile insurance companies on the basis of number of canceled policies.

WHAT TO DO IN CASE OF AN ACCIDENT

1 Call an ambulance for anyone who is seriously injured, and notify the police if necessary.
2 Record the names and addresses of all occupants in the other vehicle, as well as license numbers.
3 Record the names of witnesses, if any.
4 Take a picture of the accident, if a camera is available. If one is not, record the length of the skid marks.
5 Call your insurance company's claims office.
6 Make no statements about the cause of the accident to anyone except the claims adjuster from your insurance company.
7 File a state accident report, if required.
8 Keep your policy's liability limits confidential.

Financial Responsibility. An unusual problem is presented by small, fly-by-night insurance companies that write low-cost insurance policies, fail to settle claims promptly, exist only for the few years it takes for lawsuits to mature to the point that they must be paid, and then declare bankruptcy, leaving many liabilities unresolved. In the few years that they exist, these firms earn handsome profits. State bonding requirements for such marginal operators are often inadequate. (An insurance company must post a forfeitable bond of $50,000–10,000,000 to ensure good performance.) Consumers should check with the state department of insurance to verify that any unknown firm with whom they intend to conduct business is a bona fide company.

Deficiencies of the Automobile Insurance System

The most troublesome aspect of the automobile insurance system is liability coverage and administration. Assessing blame and determining the correct amount of compensation in practice amounts to a contest between two adversaries: The insurance company defends its assets against the claims of the injured party. The injured victim often claims three times the value of actual losses for "pain and suffering." Discomfort and agony are equally compensable, although they cannot be compared. To make points to the jury, the injured plaintiff's lawyer may bring in gory pictures or have the victim show his or her wounds, in which case the courtroom may be turned into a laboratory or a circus. The victim may be tempted or frightened into settling before a jury determines an award. In many cases these settlements do not adequately compensate the victim for very real losses. In other cases plaintiffs and their lawyers inflate claims to ensure that any settlement will be fair.

Elaborate trial procedures take a great deal of time and money; it is estimated that only 42¢ of each premium dollar is actually paid in claims settlements. Many months may be spent in pretrial investigation and preparation, and years may pass before a case on a crowded court trial schedule is first heard. And after being heard, either side can appeal an unwelcome verdict.

No-fault Insurance

The alternative to the cost and delay of compensating accident victims through court action and assessment of blame is to treat accidents as misfortunes that are similar to illness. Under this so-called *no-fault insurance* system, the victim's own insurance pays for his or her injuries. The injured person simply files a claim with his or her insurance firm without designating who is responsible for the accident. Many court cases can be eliminated by using this approach.

As of February 1976, no-fault insurance has been adopted by 16 states, and a national no-fault insurance bill has been introduced in Congress. In most of its forms, no-fault insurance speeds financial compensation to people who have small claims, say, under $5000, but can make it more difficult for the severely injured victim to acquire adequate amounts of compensation.

No-fault insurance has been heralded as a cost reducer and a premium leveler. Studies indicate that premium reductions of up to 14% can be achieved by employing no-fault insurance.[1] A portion of these reductions would be the $1.4 billion in legal fees included in the $6.6 billion paid in automobile liability insurance premiums in a recent sample one-year period.[2] However, no-fault insurance probably does not level premiums uniformly, because accidents on a per-driver basis tend to occur more often in large cities than in small rural areas.

HOME INSURANCE

Houses and apartments can present many risks to people and property. The owner of a house can be exposed to losses from fire, storm damage, broken windows, and in some cases, crashing cars and airplanes, explosions, and crime. People who live in apartments or in their own houses (rather than rent to others) expose their furnishings to the same dangers. Losses can also be incurred if a guest or a service representative (such as an electrician or a plumber) sustains an injury on an individual's property or premises and a court rules that the owner is negligent or otherwise liable.

Property Insurance

Property insurance policies have several important basic functions, which vary according to the type and extent of risk covered and the amount of the coverage. These functions are designed to compensate the insured financially for any damages and to deal with whatever costs and difficulties arise when other parties sustain personal injuries on the insured's premises.

There are many different kinds of property, and property insurance covers a broad category of perils. There are few restrictions on insuring property. Two primary ones are (1) that land itself cannot be insured (although shrubs, trees, and any other vegetation covering the land are insurable), and (2) that property can be covered only when the insured has a legal interest in it.

What Is Property Worth?

The homeowner and apartment dweller face a common dilemma in estimating insurance needs. Should property be valued at its *market price* or at its *replacement cost*? Market value accounts for depreciation, whereas replacement cost accounts for inflation. Choosing the preferred method is especially difficult in a time of substantial inflation. To clarify this, consider the following example.

A stereo set was purchased in 1971 for $500. According to the insurance company, the set depreciates at a rate of 10% per year. In 1976 the stereo is totally destroyed by fire. After five years of use the stereo lost 50% of its market value *(straight-line depreciation)*, but replacing the set will now cost 50% more.

[1] *U.S. News & World Report* (September 23, 1974), p. 67.
[2] *The New Republic* (May 18, 1974), p. 7.

Does the market value ($240) or the replacement cost ($750) represent the worth of the stereo?

If you wish to buy another stereo in the same used condition, the market value is a reasonable price. If you wish to buy a new unit identical to the one that was destroyed, the replacement cost is the better price. Obviously, the difficulty is that people usually wish to replace goods with new, not used, equipment. If a house is damaged, the owner cannot readily buy used hardware or plumbing. The going price must be paid for repairs, this price is the replacement cost. Yet market value, which is usually lower than replacement cost, is the less expensive form of coverage: You purchase less coverage, and you pay less for it.

How Insurance Companies Value Property

To determine the amount to be paid on a property claim, insurance industry practice is to pay full replacement cost, provided the house or other property is insured for at least 80% of its replacement cost. A property insurance company calculates or estimates the replacement cost of the home by using a rule-of-thumb construction cost (typically $20–40 per square foot of house floorspace × square footage) and pays only the ratio of coverage carried to minimum that should have been carried (80% of the replacement cost).

Here is an example of this important 80% rule. If the replacement cost of Woebegone's house, now burned down, is $50,000 and he carries $30,000 coverage, the insurance company will pay only three-fourths ($\frac{3}{4}$) of the claim. This is because the house should have been insured for 80% of $50,000, or $40,000. Thus

$$\$30,000 \div \$40,000 \times \$30,000 \text{ (loss)} = \$22,500$$

The solution to the dilemma as to whether to use the market value or the replacement cost in determining property insurance is indicated by the 80% rule. To underinsure for less than the appropriate amount can be quite expensive. Premium costs can be saved by insuring for the market value, but a large loss can be incurred in the event of a subsequent claim.

Protect Yourself with an Inventory

Regardless of the type of coverage chosen, property should be reassessed frequently. A list should be made of all items, when and where they were bought, their purchase prices, estimated replacement costs, and current condition. If the insurance company disputes a claim, it may be helpful to have photographs of the lost or damaged articles of property. An inventory should be reassessed at least once a year to determine how inflation has affected the replacement cost of each item. If an inventory is underinsured to save premiums, regular reassessments will provide current estimates of potential losses.

Policy Choices

The homeowner's principal insurance concern is the loss of the house. The basic dwelling insurance policy is the *fire contract,* which covers the main risk to buildings—fire due to lightning, flame, or some form of explosion. The fire con-

PERSONAL PROPERTY DEPRECIATION RATES

Market value may be estimated by the following formula:

$$\frac{\text{Life expectancy} - \text{Age of item}}{\text{Life expectancy}} = \text{Residual value}$$

Example: A refrigerator is 5 years old and has a life expectancy of 15 years, so that

$$\frac{15 - 5}{15} = \tfrac{2}{3} \text{ Residual value}$$

Then *multiply* the residual value *by* the price originally paid to determine the market value. If the refrigerator originally cost $300, then

$$\tfrac{2}{3}(\text{Residual value}) \times \$300 = \$200 \text{ Market value}$$

Life Expectancies

Major Appliances	Years	Furniture	Years	Office Equipment	Years
Air conditioner	10	Card tables	10	Typewriters	10
Dehumidifiers	10	Lamps	15	Furniture	20
Dishwashers	10	Mirrors	20	File cabinets	20
Dryers	12	Upholstered furniture	10	Mimeograph machines	10
Freezers	20	Wood furniture	15		
Stereos	10	Beds	20	**Personal Items**	
Tape recorders	10	Carpets		Wallets	5
Sewing machines	20	under $5/yd	5	Luggage	20
Stoves, ranges	15	$5–10/yd	10	Knives	20
TV sets	10	Over $10/yd	20	Guns	25
Vacuum cleaners	10	Children's furniture	5	Golf clubs	10
Clothes washer	8			Tents	10

tract does not cover personal property and although it is the cheapest form of protection, it offers relatively little protection compared to homeowner's policy insurance.

The *homeowner's policy* includes several types of insurance, covering losses to the home, personal property losses, and personal liability.

The perils coverage extended in homeowner's policies tends to be uniform among all insurance companies in a given locality, although cost and company reputation in claim settlements may vary considerably. Some typical types of homeowner's policy coverage are:

1 Dwelling, outbuildings, unlisted personal property (wherever it is located), landscaping, and living expenses until a damaged or destroyed home can be rebuilt.

2 Personal property while on vacation.

3 Fire department service charges and debris-removal costs resulting from an insured peril.

4 Coverage of stolen money, subject to a limit of $100 per occurrence, a $500 limit for stolen securities and negotiable instruments, and a $1000 limit for jewels and furs.

5 Personal liability for people who are injured on the insured property. Coverage limits are usually set at $25,000, but they can be increased at a cost of $1 per $100,000 of added liability per occurrence. So-called *voluntary medical payments* permit the insured to make small payments of less than $500 to injured persons, thereby avoiding adversary courtroom battles between the insurer and friends or neighbors.

6 Deductibles that vary with the peril and the amount of damage. Small damages are usually subject to $50 or $100 deductibility. When damages exceed $500, the deductible reverts to zero and the insurer pays 100% of the damages.

Policy Forms. The basic features of homeowner's policies appear in five standard policy forms, four for homeowners and one for renters. Naturally, as property and perils coverage increases, premium costs also rise. The five standard policy forms are:

The *basic form:* (Form 1) A basic fire contract that excludes electrical fires, except those caused by lightning. Glass breakage over $50 is not covered. Coverage is void if the residence has been vacant for more than 30 days when damages occur.

The *broad form* (Form 2): Covers fire and explosion damage due to a wide range of causes. Also covers theft and "mysterious disappearance," or the unexplainable absence of the insured property.

The *special form* (Form 3): Expands the coverage of Form 2 to include almost all types of damage to a house and its contents from any source, except earthquake and earth movement. Form 3 offers the broadest coverage at the lowest cost

The *contents broad form* (Form 4): Identical to Form 2, except that Form 4 does not cover the building structure itself. This policy is usually purchased by tenants. Personal property coverage is somewhat broader under Form 4 than under Form 2.

The *comprehensive form* (Form 5): Covers all property against all perils, and extends all perils coverage to personal property. Premiums are twice the cost of any other coverage for this all-inclusive policy.

Floater policies are often appended to homeowner's policies to cover specific personal property against almost all risks except war, radioactivity, vermin, and natural deterioration. Floaters may cover property listed by category or by specific description. Items of substantial value may be included in a floater policy to insure them against any risk. Floater policies are quite expensive.

HOMEOWNER'S POLICIES

Form	Coverage
Basic (No. 1)	Fire, lightning, windstorm, explosion, smoke.
Broad (No. 2)	All perils in Basic Form No. 1 plus falling objects, collapse, water damage, bursting pipes, and freezing.
Special (No. 3)	All risks of physical loss, except those due to flood, earthquake, war, and sewer backup.
Contents Broad (No. 4)	Covers only contents of structure, not building, with coverage of Broad Form No. 2. Typical tenant's policy.
Comprehensive (No. 5)	Covers all risks to structure and contents.

NOTE: All five forms include liability and medical payments coverage.

Getting the Most for Your Premium Dollar. It is necessary to balance insurance needs against the costs of annual premiums. If your money is tight, it's best to cover the big risks that can be devastating and to back up the smaller risks with personal cash reserves. This is accomplished by maximizing the perils covered and taking larger deductibles. Most insurance authorities agree that it is a waste of money to insure against small losses.

Insurance and Your Mortgage. If a house or its contents have been purchased on a mortgage or with other borrowed funds, the lender may insist the house and/or other items to which the loan extended be covered by suitable insurance. The homeowner has no control over this, even though it may cause the property to be overinsured.

Dealing with Rising Insurance Costs

The cost of property insurance has risen drastically in the last ten years due to the increase in fires, crime, and urban strife. For the homeowner, however, the protection offered by Homeowner's Form 3 (Special Form) remains a good value. The risks covered are broad, and the premium payments are relatively small. These special policies are standardized (that is, they are subject to completely variable limits and add-on floaters), but their cost is not. The wise insurance buyer shops carefully to find a low-cost insurer with a good reputation for claims service. Consumers can often obtain rate discounts if they own homes of average cost in low-risk areas—and perhaps even greater discounts if their houses have been constructed with fire-resistant materials. The same discount criteria apply to apartment buildings. Some insurance firms offer special low-rate coverage to homeowners who are nonsmokers and/or whose property is equipped with fire extinguishers and/or fire alarms.

SAMPLE HOMEOWNER'S POLICY

=== HOMEOWNERS POLICY ===

No. H

RENEWAL OF NUMBER

[AUTHENTIC]
UNIFORM PRINTING AND SUPPLY DIVISION

SPACE FOR COMPANY NAME, INSIGNIA, AND LOCATION

DECLARATIONS

Named Insured and P.O. Address   (Number, Street, Town or City, County, State, Zip Code)

SPACE FOR PRODUCER'S NAME AND MAILING ADDRESS

Policy Term:

Years   Inception   Expiration

The described residence premises covered hereunder is located at the above address, unless otherwise stated herein   (No., Street, Town or City, County, State, Zip Code)

Insurance is provided only with respect to the following Coverages for which a limit of liability is specified, subject to all conditions of this policy.

Coverages and Limit of Liability		Section I			Section II		
	A. Dwelling	B. Appurtenant Structures	C. Unscheduled Personal Property	D. Additional Living Expense	E. Personal Liability (Bodily Injury and Property Damage) Each occurrence	F. Medical Payments to Others Each person	Each accident
	$	$	$	$	$	$	$ 25,000

Premium	Basic Policy Premium	Theft Extension	Additional Premiums		Total Prepaid Premium	Premium if paid in installments	At Inception (and)	Payable: At each subsequent anniversary
	$	$	$		$	$	$	$

		Premium for Scheduled Personal Property	$	$	$	$

Form and Endorsements made part of this Policy at time of issue: Insert Number(s) and Edition Date(s)   Form HO-   Endorsement(s) HO-

Combined Premium $ $ $ $

DEDUCTIBLE — SECTION I: Any loss by perils insured against under Section I of this policy is subject to a deductible. Exceptions, if any:

☐ Deductible applicable only to loss caused by the peril of windstorm or hail (Clause No. 1)

☐ Deductible applicable to loss caused by other perils (Clause No. 2)

☐ Deductible not applicable

Special Loss Deductible $
Clause   (Amount)

Special State Provisions: South Carolina: Valuation Clause (Coverage A) $ New York: Coinsurance Clause Applies ☐ Yes   ☐ No

Section II — Additional residence premises, if any, located: (No., Street, Town or City, County, State, Zip Code)

Mortgagee(s)

(NAME AND ADDRESS)

Countersignature Date

Agency at   Agent

RATING INFORMATION	NUMBER OF FAMILIES	Not Townhouse— Number of Families				Townhouse— Families within Fire Div.			HO-4 Self-Rating		If yes, number of apartments				Annual Fire & EC Rate Reference:	Year of Constr.		ZONE
		Code(1) (3) (6) (8)				(2) (4) (9)			Code(9)	No ☐ Yes ☐	1-4 (1)	5-10 (2)	11-40 (3)	over 40 (4)		Year Code		Code
		1 ☐ 2 ☐	3 ☐	4 ☐		3-4 ☐ 5-8 ☐	9-over ☐											

CONSTRUCTION		Brick,Stone or Masonry (1) Frame	Brick,Stone or Masonry Veneer (2)	Brick, Stone or Masonry (3)	Approved Roof	Frame with Aluminum or Plastic Siding (5)	Fire Resistive	Mobile Homes enclosed Foundation (6)	Mobile Homes Not enclosed Foundation (7)	Modular Homes rated as Frame (9)	Specifically Rated—Not Fire Resistive (8)	Unapproved Roof

PROTECTION	Code:	Not more than feet from hydrant	Not more than miles from Fire Dept.	South- ern:	Inside City limits	Inside Protected Suburb	Inside Fire District	Fire District or Town

PREMIUM GR. NO.	DEDUCTIBLE: Type Code Size Code	Disappearing ☐ All Perils ☐	Clause 1 $	Clause 2 $	Other $ ( )

STATISTICAL REPORTING INFORMATION	Codes: No Type Classif. Cov. E Cov. F	Premium: Prepaid; If paid in Installments; Payable at: Inception	Each Anniversary
Snowmobiles	( ) — — ( ) ( )	$ $ $	$
Watercraft	( ) (2) ( ) ( ) ( )	$ $ $	$
Outboard Motor	( ) (3) ( ) ( ) ( )	$ $ $	$
ALL OTHER PREMIUMS (except Scheduled Personal Property)		$ $ $	$

(a) The described dwelling is not seasonal; (b) no business pursuits are conducted on the described premises; (c) the described premises is the only premises where the Named Insured or spouse maintains a residence other than business or farm properties; (d) the Insured has no full time residence employee(s); (e) the Insured has no outboard motor(s) or watercraft otherwise excluded under this policy for which coverage is desired. Exception, if any, to (a), (b), (c), (d) or (e)*.

*Absence of an entry means "no exceptions".

In Consideration of the Provisions and Stipulations Herein or Added Hereto and of the Premium Above Specified (or specified in endorsement(s) made a part hereof), this Company, for the term shown above from inception date shown above at noon (Standard Time) to expiration date shown above at noon (Standard Time) at location of property involved, to an amount not exceeding the limit of liability above specified, does insure **the Insured named in the Declarations above** and legal representatives, to the extent of the actual cash value of the property at the time of loss, but not exceeding the amount which it would cost to repair or replace the property with material of like kind and quality within a reasonable time after such loss, without allowance for any increased cost of repair or reconstruction by reason of any ordinance or law regulating construction or repair, and without compensation for loss resulting from interruption of business or manufacture, nor in any event for more than the interest of the Insured, against all DIRECT LOSS BY FIRE, LIGHTNING AND OTHER PERILS INSURED AGAINST IN THIS POLICY INCLUDING REMOVAL FROM PREMISES ENDANGERED BY THE PERILS INSURED AGAINST IN THIS POLICY, EXCEPT AS HEREINAFTER PROVIDED, to the property described herein while located or contained as described in this policy, or pro rata for five days at each proper place to which any of the property shall necessarily be removed for preservation from the perils insured against in this policy, but not elsewhere.

Assignment of this policy shall not be valid except with the written consent of this Company.

This policy is made and accepted subject to the foregoing provisions and stipulations and those hereinafter stated, which are hereby made a part of this policy, together with such other provisions, stipulations and agreements as may be added hereto, as provided in this policy.

OKP 1001-10 Ed. 10-68 Standard - Rev.

THE NEED FOR SELF-PROTECTION

The common and substantial hazards encountered in owning a home and a car require individuals and families to take steps to protect themselves and others from potential disasters that can be financially devastating.   The person who feels that it's better to save a few dollars in premium costs rather than to carry the appropriate amount of coverage for his or her needs is gambling with quite high stakes.

Although automobile and homeowner's insurance are virtually mandatory, the consumer must approach each industry with a knowledge of its methods and a willingness to shop for a reliable insurance firm with reasonable rates. *Consumer Reports'* surveys have shown that a savings of several hundred dollars per year can be realized on either automobile or homeowner's insurance.

It is impossible to cover all the problems that consumers may encounter in one short chapter on home and automobile insurance. An insurance firm that attempts to make too low a settlement or that appears to be misrepresenting its policies should be promptly reported to the state Commissioner or Superintendent of Insurance.

SUMMARY

1 Insurance should be purchased to cover costly hazards that can endanger personal or family finances. Small hazards should be self-insured via a cash reserve.
2 To balance self-insurance with purchased insurance, the consumer must:
    1 Determine the maximum money loss possible
    2 Decide what risks to self-insure and what amounts of these risks
    3 Decide what risks and what amounts of these risks to transfer to an insurance policy
3 Automobile insurance covers five kinds of risks:
    1 Liability
    2 Collision
    3 Comprehensive
    4 Medical
    5 Uninsured motorist
4 Deductibles reduce the settlement amounts paid by insurance companies and thereby reduce the cost of insurance.
5 Liability insurance should be carried in sufficient amounts to cover: (1) current net worth, (2) total lifetime earnings, or (3) the highest amounts currently awarded in local courts in automobile liability cases. The least expensive and least safe is (1); the most expensive and safest is (3).
6 Automobile insurance costs are based on the driver's characteristics, such as age, sex, driving record, and occupation. One's location and the amount of car use also affect rates. Low-risk drivers may be granted preferred low rates; high-risk drivers must pay high, assigned-risk premiums.
7 Automobile insurance rates are affected by discounts offered by some firms, but rates alone don't reveal an insurance's company claim-settlement service, policy-cancellation rate, or financial reliability.
8 When an insured victim is covered by no-fault automobile insurance, his or her own insurance company covers the insured's injuries. This eliminates some of the cost and delay of settling cases in court.
9 All physical property and real estate, except land, can be insured.
10 Property insurance may cover replacement cost or market value. Replace-

ment accounts for cost inflation, whereas market value accounts for depreciation.

11 The homeowner or apartment dweller should construct and maintain an inventory of insured property.

12 The homeowner's policy in its many forms variously blends coverage for loss of the home, loss of personal property, and personal liability.

13 The typical homeowner's policy covers:
1 Dwelling and other buildings
2 Personal property while on vacation
3 Fire department service charges
4 Stolen property (to specified limits) and deductibles for money and other valuables
5 Personal liability to a common limit of $25,000
6 Small losses subject to $50 or $100 deductibles

14 There are five homeowner's policy forms:
1 Basic form
2 Broad Form
3 Special form
4 Contents Broad Form (for tenants)
5 Comprehensive

15 Floaters cover listed property against all perils except war, radioactivity, vermin, and natural deterioration. Floater policies are quite expensive.

16 To manage insurance costs, it is best to cover more perils for higher limits and to save money by increasing deductibles.

Suggestions for Further Reading

Bailard, Thomas E., Biehl, David I., and Kaiser, Ronald W. *Personal Money Management.* Chicago: Science Research Associates, 1973, Chapters 3, 4, and 5.

Bickelhaupt, David L., and Magee, John H. *General Insurance,* 8th ed. Homewood, Ill.: Richard D. Irwin, 1970.

Magee, John N., and Serbein, Oscar N. *Property and Liability Insurance,* 4th ed. Homewood, Ill.: Richard D. Irwin, 1967.

U.S. Senate, Committee on the Judiciary. *Hearings on No-Fault Insurance.* 93rd Congress, 1st and 2nd Sessions.

The Consumer Workshop

1 Let us say that a person is 20 years old, male, unmarried, a good student, and a careful driver. How will this person's automobile insurance costs compare with those of a 35-year-old married male? Why? Is this rate variance fair to the consumer? How do insurance companies view the problem?

2 As a household expands, its potential liabilities and risks usually grow larger. List and compare the risks a couple with no children faces and the risks a couple with three young children faces. Make assumptions consistent with the example: For example, the childless couple lives in an apartment, where-

as the family of five owns a huge, rambling, old house with many play spaces and toys for the children.

3 How do property insurance rates vary in your area? Call several insurance agents to obtain rate comparisons for renting an apartment versus owning a house in specific locations.

4 Do you have any property insurance coverage yourself or in conjunction with your parents? If so, construct an inventory and calculate the market and replacement values of individual items. Is this coverage adequate, or do you need additional insurance coverage for the risks you face?

5 Much of the difficulty of liability insurance results from the necessity to affix blame in a court proceeding. In *Unsafe At Any Speed,* Ralph Nader argues that cars and roads, not drivers, cause many accidents. What does Nader's argument imply for the conventional third-party liability coverage in which one driver tries to blame the other for an accident neither may have caused? Would it be easier, more socially useful, or less costly to sue state highway authorities or automobile manufacturers in such instances? Explain your answer.

14 TIME AND LEISURE

An individual's work or career can easily become a kind of tunnel in which he or she hides from the larger world outside. In this chapter we discuss the economic and social values of this larger world that includes leisure. Our object is to define leisure, to trace past and present trends in leisure, and to indicate the value of leisure in personal lifestyle.

A PAST WITHOUT LEISURE

Leisure is time that is not committed to basic work or caring for one's physical needs. Widespread leisure is a relatively recent phenomenon. Throughout the history of western civilization, it has been necessary for the vast majority—perhaps 90–95%—of all peoples to devote 12 or more hours a day seven days a week to hard physical labor. In agrarian societies based on farming, work has been especially severe during the summer months of sowing, cultivating, and harvesting; in industrial societies, work has been dispersed fairly evenly throughout the year. In the past, "leisure" under these conditions was usually dictated by famine, expulsion from tillable land, or unemployment. Only the tiny portion of society whose role didn't relate directly to the soil or to the production economy was freed from the need to work constantly. Soldiers, aristocrats, and priests were typically members of this class.

Only during the late nineteenth century did a large part of any country's population have sufficient income and productivity to enjoy a substantial number of leisure hours. By 1900 people living in cities and towns in England, France, Germany, the United States, and Canada could take advantage of weekends, holidays, and most of the other recreation opportunities common today. Generally, as countries industrialize or otherwise achieve affluence, their peoples' opportunities for leisure grow.

THE ADVANTAGES OF LEISURE

Leisure permits us to be ourselves and not simply creatures of the economy. Some people use their leisure to fulfill themselves by renewing their relationship

with the physical world, by studying or acquiring new skills, or simply by having a good time. Yet here, we often face a dilemma of values. Western societies in general, and American society in particular, have rigid notions of time and an acute awareness of it. For many of us, time is the most essential property that belongs to us. As Europeans and North Americans rush about in their pursuit of material gain, they eliminate nearly all pockets of unused time. The need to have a "good time" in one's "spare" time easily becomes an obsession, and people begin to play or relax with the same frenzy with which they work.[1]

The nineteenth century German philosopher Friedrich Nietzsche said that work deprives the mind of concern, meaning that hard work can easily divert our minds from important questions about human and social destiny, world order, and the nature of good and evil. Yet although it is true that work can be an anesthetic that neutralizes physical and moral energies, *leisure acquires its meaning in the context of work.* In other words, leisure is the alternative to work. For many people, a life without productive work would be intolerably boring. Perhaps this is why today we find many housewives entering the labor force after they have raised their families, even when their husbands' incomes adequately meet their families' needs.

[1] Staffan Burenstam Linder, *The Harried Leisure Class* (New York: Columbia University Press, 1970), pp. 22, 23.

The Value of Leisure Pastimes Hobbies, recreational activities, and other leisure pastimes can enhance our lives. In addition to giving us pleasure or helping us to pass idle hours, recreational pursuits can encourage us to develop our personalities. Many of the forces of modern life are narrowing: Our jobs require specialization and concentration on a few tasks; modern life tends to compartmentalize people, restraining their broad development. Sports, hobbies, and other recreations can both broaden and enrich our lives. Repairing old cars as a hobby can give a white-collar worker an opportunity to do something that he or she could not do behind a desk. Fishing can provide a sense of solace, privacy, and tranquillity that harried modern people need.

LEISURE IN CONTEMPORARY LIFE

A person's sense of style and desire can easily be repressed by modern life. The pressures to conform—to observe society's standards—rob many people of their own creative instincts. A hobby can restore the opportunity to be aggressive, to be artistic, to pursue nature, or to meet physical and mental challenges. The mountain climber and the Sunday painter face challenges of their own design. Each can define and achieve goals independently of whatever occupation or role he or she may be committed to in daily life.

A few fortunate people manage to find exactly the kind of work for which they feel they are best suited. Their jobs can be fulfilling, meaningful, and inwardly rewarding. Charles A. Reich terms the kind of work that integrates with one's personality to permit total self-involvement and fulfillment the "non-career."[2] An accountant interested in mountain climbing and jazz could develop a resort in the Rockies and play in his or her own nightclub. An engineer who loves sailing could help design and test sailboats. An economist doesn't have to teach or work out dull business problems; it's possible to be one's own person writing books, producing radio and television shows, and advising governments from time to time.

Leisure and Self-expression Sports and hobbies give people who are narrowed by their work opportunities to express themselves. In this sense of liberating the personality, painting, poetry, boxing, horseback riding, or simple daydreaming are all forms that the expression of ideas and emotions repressed by work can take. A hobby can provide an opportunity for the person who must follow instructions at work without question to achieve a more personal form of self-mastery.

Recently labor economists have noted that many college graduates in the 1970s will not be able to find the work for which their education has prepared them. These BAs, MAs, and PhDs, it is predicted, may wind up driving taxis,

[2] Charles A. Reich, *The Greening of America* (New York: Random House, 1970), p. 368.

"You know the lifestyle so many of us dream about—living in a cabin in the woods, doing some pottery, perhaps weaving a wallhanging and selling it for just enough to buy a week's food, informal meals cooked in a fireplace, no pressure—well, I had enough of that and decided to drop out and become a business executive."

selling real estate, working in part-time jobs, or doing any number of routine industrial tasks. For people such as these, who will have to face years of meaningless, uninteresting, unchallenging work, hobbies and other recreational activities can be important vehicles of self-fulfillment. Even if they get no satisfaction from their work, they still may be able to achieve in their avocations.[3]

The Identity Crisis

Contemporary life is filled with different kinds of conflict that often result in the suppression of individuality. One feels isolated in the midst of society. The larger the society in which we live, the more protective we are of our individuality and the greater our need to have our own "domains."

Associations—clubs, fraternal groups, charitable organizations, churches, political parties—are cores around which people in a mass society gather to find friends who have similar interests. The abundance of such organizations in the United States suggests that this mechanism of using formal frameworks to find and keep friends is our solution to the anonymity many people feel in mass societies.

Any town in America boasts dozens of fraternal orders, such as the Moose, Kiwanis, and Elk. Many college campuses have fraternities and sororities.

[3] *The Wall Street Journal* (June 5, 1974), p. 1.

Grammar and high schools abound with scout troops, clubs, and organizations. Homemakers with some leisure often join charitable organizations or engage in social activities to raise money for worthy causes.

Such clubs and associations provide places where people can meet friends without the inhibitions that business conduct or professional behavior sometimes dictates. Many people promote their business interests by friendly association, but even when social meeting places are used for this purpose they still offer a less formal, more relaxing atmosphere in which to conduct business.

Mobility and Recreation

Americans move their households around the country with great frequency. The average American lives in 14 different places during a lifetime, and about 40 million Americans change their home addresses at least once a year.[4] Careers have become synonymous with mobility. Many young business managers move a few thousand miles and try to establish new personal ties every year or two.[5] In these cases, a hobby or sport that doesn't depend on being in one particular place can serve as an anchor in an ever-changing world. Shriners, stamp collectors, and tennis and chess players, to name only a few examples, all can find immediate associations wherever they move. Their hobbies and recreations partially compensate for their unstable environments and identities in what Vance Packard has so aptly called our "nation of strangers."

TRENDS IN LEISURE

As economies have risen from widespread mere subsistence to general affluence, the range of choices they offer workers has widened. During the nineteenth century, wages in much of Europe, were such that people would have to work 9 hours out of a 12-hour day simply to put bread on the table at home. The worker's economic choice amounted to little more than "work or starve." Today, a loaf of bread can be purchased in the United States for about six minutes worth of labor at the average wage. Household incomes are well above the subsistence level for most of the U.S. population, and workers can often choose between earning more money and having more leisure.

A famous cartoonist whose drawings earn several hundred thousand dollars each year was once asked why he had never taken a vacation since the beginning of his career. He replied that at an average hourly wage of $200, he couldn't afford it: A two-week holiday would cost him at least $16,000 ($200 × 40 hours per week × 2 weeks) in addition to the actual cost of the vacation!

[4] Vance Packard, *A Nation of Strangers* (New York: McKay, 1972), pp. 6, 7.
[5] *Ibid.,* p. 11.

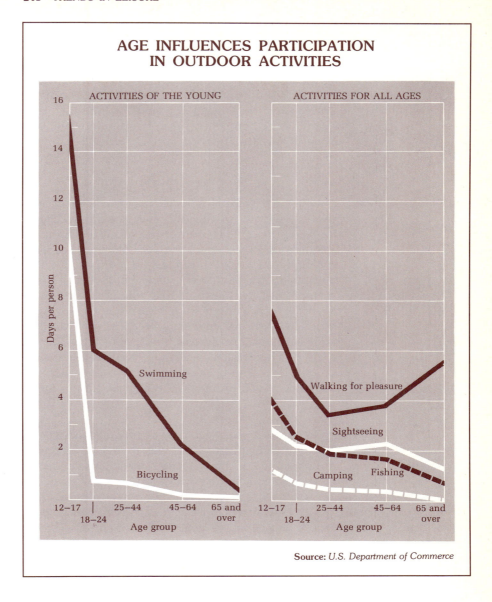

AGE INFLUENCES PARTICIPATION
IN OUTDOOR ACTIVITIES

ACTIVITIES OF THE YOUNG

ACTIVITIES FOR ALL AGES

Swimming

Bicycling

Walking for pleasure

Sightseeing

Camping

Fishing

Days per person

Age group

Age group

Source: *U.S. Department of Commerce*

Money, Work, and Leisure

Why do people work long hours at jobs that presumably will become boring at some point? What are their goals? Do they believe, as our vacationless cartoonist does, that life is at its best on a ration of $200,000 per year and no leisure? But then what's the money for? More cars in an already crowded garage, a yacht that would, paradoxically, take some leisure time to enjoy, a fine painting in the living room to glance at while dashing out the door to work?

It is difficult sometimes to choose between having more money and more leisure. Some people can accommodate their desires for both by compounding their leisure activities and not concentrating on a specific recreation. To take an exaggerated example, at the Houston Astrodome a wealthy sports fan can watch football from a $100,000 dollar suite while sipping 20-year-old whisky, having a haircut and a manicure, and watching yet another football game on television. But is all of this truly more enjoyable and satisfying than walking in the woods or strolling down a pleasant city street? Note that both of these inexpensive alternatives do cost something in terms of foregone earnings and any traveling expenses to reach the woods or a city street that can be safely and pleasurably walked.

The Dependence Effect

John Kenneth Galbraith analyzed the materialism of America in the 1950s in *The Affluent Society,* where he states that people and society work too hard producing the wrong goods. Many consumer goods are not urgently wanted or needed, Galbraith claims, because the public demands them only after heavy doses of advertising convince consumers to purchase products. Arguing that the production of elaborate consumer goods "only fills a void that it has itself created," Galbraith declares that "the notion that wants do not become less urgent the more amply the individual is supplied is broadly repugnant to common sense." [6] This "dependence effect," in Galbraith's words, means that the production process makes people consume too much and perhaps work too hard to do it. Rather than satisfying demands, Galbraith contends, production increases and distorts them. True recreations, according to the dependence-effect thesis, are converted into recreations that are convenient for the economy. [7]

Use of Leisure Time

At this point, let's consider some recent statistical evidence about how Americans make use of their leisure time. In 1870 the average work week was well over 60 hours. In 1950 it was about 40 hours, a reduction of 37%. [8] However, this fairly continuous trend toward a reduced work week seems to have reversed, and no further reduction in the U.S. work week seems to have taken place since 1950. [9] One can find a false indication of a continuing decline in average hours of work per week in the greatly increased participation in the labor force of home-

---

[6] John Kenneth Galbraith, *The Affluent Society* (Boston: Houghton Mifflin, 1960), pp. 152–53.

[7] J.B. Say said much the same thing in the early nineteenth century in his memorable phrase "supply creates its own demand," which was a contribution to a then-raging debate on gluts. Those worried about gluts feared that society would be unable to buy all it produced and that overabundance would eventually lead to depression. Say was telling his followers not to worry, because all money earned would be spent. We can read John Kenneth Galbraith's *The Affluent Society* as a contemporary version of the glut debate, but one that reaches a different conclusion: higher taxes. Galbraith would solve the problem of overprosperity and what he would deem improper wants with higher taxes, so that people could purchase only necessities. Taxes would then be spent on worthier (to Galbraith) things, such as universities.

[8] George Soule, "The Economics of Leisure," *The Annals of the American Academy of Political and Social Science* **CCCXIII** (September 1957), p. 17.

[9] Linder, p. 135.

makers and teenagers, many of whom have part-time jobs so that their below-average work weeks tend to pull down the average for all workers in the labor force. Other workers take second jobs rather than work overtime. Such practices make increases in total work hours appear to be declines in average work hours. Staffan B. Linder has calculated that average weekly hours of full-time, nonfarm work have remained constant at about 45 hours since 1919. The number of people working more than 48 hours a week has nearly doubled, rising from 13% of the U.S. labor force in 1949 to 20% in 1965. About 5% of the U.S. labor force holds more than one job, and some estimates indicate that multiple-job holding has doubled since 1950.[10]

Has Leisure Decreased Recently?

The counterpart of increasing work time is decreasing leisure time. This can be seen in what has happened to reading for pleasure. The number of titles of new books published in the United States in 1950 was 11,000. By 1963 the figure was 19,000, and in 1975 it was 40,000. If we multiply the number of books by an estimated length of reading time, we arrive at impossible figures. So we are forced to Linder's conclusion that "people are buying books as they buy pictures—to glance at."[11]

Linder also has examined sex as a leisure-time activity and has found several meaningful implications. He claims that we are devoting less and less time to it, in spite of the contemporary period's designation as an era of sexual liberation:

> . . . The pleasure achieved by an embrace can hardly be intensified by increasing the number of goods consumed during the period in question. Goods would in fact only be in the way, beyond the minimum requirement in respect of furniture. In this . . . love differs from most other activities, and it is this that has made its status so vulnerable.[12]

The Cost of Leisure

In addition to the opportunity costs of not working, there are direct costs in recreation. Participating in most leisure pastimes involves purchasing equipment or traveling to another place, near or far. Spectator amusements usually require a ticket of admission (even if this is the price of a TV set). The cost of recreation can be borne personally or shared with a group. For example, a swimmer can choose to swim in his or her own pool or use a community pool. With respect to society as well as to the individual, private recreation facilities can be quite expensive. Backyard swimming pools squander concrete and water and are seldom adequate for really serious swimmers. Even if every bowler could afford a personal bowling alley, the demand for such surfaces would devastate the hardwood forests of America.

[10] Linder, p. 136.
[11] Linder, p. 104; *R. R. Bowker Annual of Library and Book Trade Information,* 21st ed. (New York: Bowker Co., 1976), p. 179.
[12] Linder, p. 84.

Clearly, the direct costs of recreation can be reduced if individuals share some facilities, as in the case of apartment-house swimming pools, or use community resources.   Good planning can lower an individual's direct recreation costs as well.   Air travel is often less expensive if you take advantage of pre-arranged charters.   Movies cost less during the daytime; the theater costs less during the week than on the weekend.   Vacations are less expensive if they are taken during off-season, nonpeak times.   Many sports and theatrical events can be attended at a discount by subscribing to a season or a series of events.

Some private interests frequently argue that their preferred recreations should be underwritten by the government; that is, that the costs of participating

SOME TYPES OF RECREATIONS
AND THEIR RELATIVE COSTS

Free:
  Walking
  Mountain climbing
  Jogging
  Practicing yoga
  Reading (by using public and school libraries)
  Visiting museums, parks, zoos (where admission is usually free)
  Charity volunteer work

Low Cost:
  Bowling
  Cycling
  Checkers, chess, card playing
  Skating
  Other sports involving group participation (examples: volleyball, basketball)
  Scrabble
  Gardening
  Club and organization work

Moderate Cost:
  Golf
  Skiing
  Carpentry
  Furniture refinishing
  Listening to records
  Auto mechanics

Spectator Pastimes:
  Football, baseball, basketball, hockey, ballet, theater, movies, opera, musical concerts

High Cost:
  Art collecting, emphasizing established artists
  Traveling (in grand style or for lengthy trips)
  Yachting
  Sports car racing
  Polo
  Breeding race horses

Variable Cost:
  Stamp collecting
  Traveling
  Photography
  Interior decorating
  Home repairs
  Redecorating
  Painting, sculpture
  Music

in the recreation be subsidized by the government and, ultimately, by the tax-payer.   These special-interest groups reason that if the given pastime is extremely popular—say, camping and hiking—then the government will do well to make public lands available for this purpose at reasonable cost.   If, on the other hand, the recreation is not particularly popular—as polo is not in the United States—then the use of public resources for the benefit of only a few people may be improper.   The argument that national or local pride somehow requires excellence in every activity is also an inadequate rationale for the public finance of sport   Games and contests cannot be equated with medical research, and many taxpayers would prefer tax reductions to having their money spent to support obscure sports and hobbies.

LEISURE MUST BE A PERSONAL CHOICE

Defining and selecting a form of recreation must be based on each person's tastes and needs.   For a mountain-climbing guide, a two-week stint on a pro-duction assembly line might be a pleasant relief from the mental and physical stress of regular work.   On the other hand, a bank clerk might seek the total involvement that mountain climbing offers.   Some people may savor the frenzy and exacting challenges of sports car racing; others may want to lie in a field and watch the clouds go by.   The range of recreational opportunities available to people in industrialized countries today is practically infinite, yet solitude—a pre-cious commodity in urban America—is the choice of very few.

Why do people prefer participant and spectator sports that involve compli-cated activities and often crowds?   Why the seeming prejudice against being alone?   Of course, we are social animals, and we need the company and assis-tance of fellow beings.   But few people seem to act on the fact that the pressures of jobs and families can be put into perspective (and not just temporarily forgotten) in moments and activities of solitude, such as hiking or gardening.   Perhaps solitude is rejected by most people because they are afraid to be alone or because they haven't the self-awareness to realize how much there is still to know about the world and themselves.

Recreation is defined rather rigidly by most people as either mass or group events, such as spectator sports and social dancing, or elaborate and expensive rituals, such as boat and car racing, because many physical-education teachers and some sales managers in leisure-product or sporting-goods industries have made a popular success of persuading consumers that their goods are neces-sities.   It's difficult to make much money from people who are content with soli-tude.

Although we can readily identify the business managers' interest promoting sports that use their products, professional educators more subtly influence the public's conception of recreation.   Paul Douglass quotes a U.S. Air Force study of the participation of 5000 pilots in off-duty activities; this study showed that during a two-week period "not a single listed recreational activity attracted, even once, half of the interviewees."[13] Thomas S. Yukic then uses this utterly insignificant fact (does *every* soldier have to play the same game at the same time?) to draw the following false conclusion:

> The fact is that many people lack the ability and skills to enable them to make creative use of their free time. They have not been exposed to leadership which can spark the desire or create and motivate the participation.[14]

Yukic implies that he and his colleagues could be employed to achieve the goal of bringing the populations of cities, schools, or whatever, to enjoy mass recreation together at the same time. Armies of children descending on the same playground or whole labor unions crushing into the same ball park? A remarkable vision. Mass recreation is practiced in China, so it might be possible in North America. But is it desirable in terms of the wisest use of resources, the intelligent construction of recreational facilities, or the role of free choice in a democratic society?

Let's take another example. James C. Charlesworth writes that "Recreation should be compulsorily taught all through the period of school attendance,"[15] ignoring the fact that not everybody wants to play a particular sport or perhaps a sport at all. More importantly, if recreation is required and thus becomes the subject of frequent tests, necessitating practice and homework, can it truly be called recreation?

Adding a political pronouncement to educators' demands for the professionalization of recreation and sports, Charles A. Bucher, in his successful text *Foundations of Physical Education,* adds "[the] cold war has brought about a national emergency and a need for a state of preparedness that warrants a physically fit population at all times.[16] Good health and a fit body are worthy goals in themselves, but it is difficult to perceive how doing pushups relates to foreign defense. If politics can corrupt education, surely it can also pervert recreation.

These examples of misguided intentions simply place in perspective the fact that, to be effective, recreation must be a matter of individual definition and choice. It is useful to have sufficient maturity and perspective to make the decision for oneself. But it is impractical for schools to define recreation arbitrarily, to force students to play their choice of games, and then to expect the students to enjoy them.

[13] Paul Douglass, "Human Wholeness in the Metropolitan Age," *American Recreation Society Bulletin* (July–August 1958), p. 9 (cited in Yukic, footnote 14).

[14] Thomas S. Yukic, *Fundamentals of Recreation,* 2nd ed. (New York: Harper & Row, 1970), p. 10.

[15] James C. Charlesworth, "A Bold Program for Recreation," *The Annals of the American Academy of Political and Social Sciences* **CCCXIII** (September 1957), p. 143.

[16] Charles A. Bucher, *Foundations of Physical Education,* 5th ed. (St. Louis: C. V. Mosby Co., 1968), p. 351.

SUMMARY

1 Leisure is time that is not committed to basic work or caring for one's physical needs

2 Leisure acquires meaning as an alternative to work. The meaningful use of leisure time can rest the mind and body, develop the personality, provide a sense of identity and order, and permit participation in significant and/or creative activity.

3 The amount of leisure time has increased for the population as a whole since 1900. Rising income levels permit basic needs to be satisfied by fewer hours of work.

4 Presently about 5% of the U.S. labor forces holds more than one job. By some estimates, multiple-job holding has doubled since 1950, indicating that some income earners prefer higher incomes to increased amounts of leisure time.

5 The costs of leisure indicate (1) the income sacrificed by not working, and (2) the actual costs of traveling to and participating in chosen recreations.

6 The choice of recreation must be left to the individual. Pressures to "like" certain sports or activities are self-defeating, because people who are so coerced will require recreations from their forced pastimes.

Suggestions for Further Reading

Larrabee, Eric, and Meyerson, Rolf, (eds.). *Mass Leisure.* Glencoe, Ill: The Free Press, 1958.

Neumeyer, Martin H., and Neumeyer, Esther S. *Leisure and Recreation,* 3rd ed. New York: Ronald Press, 1958.

Yukic, Thomas S. *Fundamentals of Recreation,* 2nd ed. New York: Harper & Row, 1970.

The Consumer Workshop

1 The ways an individual spends his or her leisure time express a lifestyle and are in part a response to one's occupation. How is this so?

2 Much work in contemporary society calls for fast and/or mind-dulling activity. How does leisure compensate for these elements in modern life?

3 On occassion, professional recreation personnel advocate that leisure activity should be formalized and taught as a compulsory subject. Can leisure really be taught? If it is treated as a compulsory subject, in what sense is it leisure? In what sense is it not?

4 "Only the prosperous can enjoy leisure time; pity about the poor." Is this statement valid in terms of (1) the number of hours per day that people must work to earn a poverty-level wage, and (2) the meaning of "leisure" as you might define it?

15 FOOD: THE STRUGGLE FOR A SANE DIET

15

> "To shop rationally requires . . . the impulses of a sleuth, the stamina of a weight lifter, and the skill of a certified public accountant."

A.Q. MOWBRAY
*The Thumb on the Scale**

The problem of family nutrition has two components: (1) the medical basis of nutrition, and (2) the economic structure of the industries that grow, process, and sell food. In this chapter, we approach the subject of nutrition by examining the different relationships of diet to income, education, and other population characteristics. We then examine the meaning of good nutrition and comment on some of the noteworthy diet problems that American families face.

In many ways, processed food products are mystery packages. To know what's in the box, the shopper must understand labeling and indentity standards, nutritional labeling practices (or the lack of them), fresh and processed food grading and inspection standards, and food additive characteristics. We briefly discuss the problems and needs in each of these areas. We conclude the chapter with an examination of the structure of the retail grocery market as it affects the consumer and offer guidelines to help the shopper determine the best values among competing stores and selling techniques.

BUYING FOOD IS A COMPLEX AFFAIR

Choosing the right food to buy in contemporary America is no simple matter. In a typical supermarket the retail food industry offers an average of 9000 different products. These products are difficult to assess because they are not labeled as adequately as they could be, and they contain substances that are variously nutritious, harmless, and harmful. Food markets themselves are sales mechanisms, and the items on their shelves must compete among themselves, often by deceptive advertising methods, to attract the consumer's attention. And if this doesn't make food shopping difficult enough, different stores compete for the shoppers' business by using enticing and costly schemes, such as money-losing promotions, contests, cents-off coupons, and trading-stamp offers. If finding the best buys is complicated, getting the most nutrition for the money is even more so. As we'll see, the United States has come a long way in the reform of labeling practices, price disclosure, and the improvement of health standards,

---

* A. Q. Mowbray, *The Thumb on the Scale* (Philadelphia: J. B. Lippincott, 1967), p. 146.

but we still have far to go. Between the food industry and the consumer stands government, which plays an active role in the food market at present and which may have an even more active role in the future.

DIET AND INCOME

Although the United States has a high *average* income per family, the family income range is quite wide. There are more poor people and more wealthy people, as fractions of the population, in the United States than in the Scandinavian countries. In fact, if our average family income is not computed as total incomes divided by total people but as the midpoint of the incomes arranged from lowest to highest, we find that the average family income is higher in some European countries than in the United States. Some Americans who are too poor to eat well suffer from diseases of undernourishment. Does this mean that nutrition varies with income? Yes, somewhat, because if you have more money you *may* eat better. Does nutrition also vary with education? Yes, but education it-self improves with, and improves, income. Does adequacy of diet vary with racial or ethnic background? Not really—bad eating habits are common throughout our population.

Improvements in Food Supply

As nations develop industrially and commercially, their farmers usually become more productive. Farmers who rise above the subsistence level no longer need to raise food to feed their families and begin to specialize in the products that they can grow and sell best. As agricultural productivity increases, more and more farmers leave the land and move into the cities, where they engage in trade, various services (the army, say, or the clergy), or manufacturing. In ancient Egyptian and Babylonian societies (ca. 4500–1200 B.C.), about 95% of the pop-ulation was forced to farm the landlords' great estates. At the height of Roman civilization, about 80% of the population was engaged in farming—a figure com-parable to the percentage of farmers in the United States in 1900. Today, about 5% of the U.S. population grows most of the food that the nation both con-sumes and exports abroad.

From the fall of Rome in the fifth century A.D. until the mid-nineteenth cen-tury, Europe experienced recurrent crop failures and frequent famines. By 1860, transportation and cultivation techniques had improved to the point that death from sheer caloric malnutrition became virtually unknown.

Not only was sufficient food available in Europe by 1900, but the real cost of that food was decreasing. In 1780, the average European family may have spent as much as 70% of its income on food in peacetime; by 1880, that family was spending perhaps 40%. By 1960, the fraction of average European family income spent on food had dropped to 30%. Today, U.S. consumers' outlay for food is the lowest in the world: 15.7% of disposable (after-tax) earnings. But in many developed countries, a family continues to spend a large part of its dis-posable income on food: 37% in Spain; 43% in Ireland.[1]

Demand For Food is Limited by Appetite

There are several important reasons why families in advanced countries spend low fractions of disposable income on food. These societies frown on gluttony and tend to satisfy basic needs in a certain order of importance: food first, clothing second, shelter third. If basic food needs are satisfied, then clothing and shelter become more attractive to most people than the continued con-sumption of food. The tendency for the amount of income spent on food to de-crease as income increases is an important measure of economic progress. Christian Lorenz Engel (not to be confused with Karl Marx's friend Friedrich Engels) identified what today we call *Engel's Law: As income rises, the fraction of income spent on food declines.* Oddly enough, people who earn high in-comes do not necessarily eat nutritiously. For example, a harried business ex-

---

[1] Citibank (First National City Bank), *Monthly Economic Letter* (May 1973), pp. 12–15.

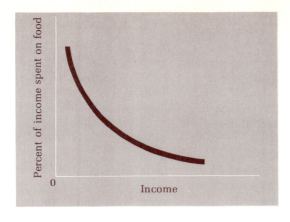

15-1   The Engel Curve

ecutive may just get by with snacks instead of taking the time to eat wholesome meals.

Nonfoods and Services Eat Up the Food Budget

The food processing and selling industries face displacement by prosperity. Engel's law indicates that food-spending tends to lag behind the growth of total family income, so processors and retailers add nonfood ingredients and products to their wares.   Processors add services in the form of convenience; sellers add nonfood items (paper products, household utensils, toys, soaps, pet supplies, and so on) to their shelves and open delicatessen counters that serve and sell prepared food.   Today, nonfood products absorb 23% of all dollars spent in food stores.

Composition of the Food-store Dollar

Nonfoods	23.0%
Meats	23.5%
Produce	9.0%
Dairy	10.0%
Frozen foods	4.0%
Groceries	30.5%

Source: U.S. Department of Agriculture

The severe inflation suffered in America in the 1970s has brought new problems to the supermarket.   In the prosperous 1960s, consumers became accustomed to convenience items.   But recently people have become more price-conscious, exhibiting an observed trend toward more careful and deliberate shopping.   Consumers are returning to basic foods and reducing their purchases of convenience items and nonfoods.[2]   This shopping behavior is contingent on people who are employed having more time to shop.

[2] *The Wall Street Journal* September 9, 1975, p. 32.

THE BASES OF NUTRITION

Every moment we are alive, our bodies are busy converting food into energy. The object of this conversion process is to change the food's energy constituents, measured as calories, into body heat, electrical impulses, and body chemicals. Caloric requirements vary with age, health, and certain inherited characteristics, and increased physical activity demands more energy. The calorie consumption rates given in Figure 15-2 indicate how various activities influence energy requirements.

Calories provide the energy our bodies need at every moment of life, but they offer us nothing else. The nutrients essential to life number over 50 and include three food constituents: proteins, carbohydrates, and fats. Both carbo-

15-2 Energy Cost of Activities Exclusive of Basal Metabolism and Influence of Food

Activity	kcal/kg/hr*	Activity	kcal/kg/hr*
Bicycling (century run)	7.6	Piano playing (Liszt's "Tarantella")	2.0
Bicycling (moderate speed)	2.5	Reading aloud	0.4
Bookbinding	0.8	Rowing in a race	16.0
Boxing	11.4	Running	7.0
Carpentry (heavy)	2.3	Sawing wood	5.7
Cello playing	1.3	Sewing (hand)	0.4
Crocheting	0.4	Sewing (foot-driven machine)	0.6
Dancing (foxtrot)	3.8	Sewing (motor-driven machine)	0.4
Dancing (waltz)	3.0	Shoemaking	1.0
Dishwashing	1.0	Singing in a loud voice	0.8
Dressing and undressing	0.7	Sitting quietly	0.4
Driving automobile	0.9	Skating	3.5
Eating	0.4	Standing (at attention)	0.6
Fencing	7.3	Standing (relaxed)	0.5
Horseback riding (walk)	1.4	Stone masonry	4.7
Horseback riding (trot)	4.3	Sweeping with broom (bare floor)	1.4
Horseback riding (gallop)	6.7	Sweeping with carpet sweeper	1.6
Ironing (5-pound iron)	1.0	Sweeping with vacuum cleaner	2.7
Knitting a sweater	0.7	Swimming (2 mph)	7.9
Laundry (light)	1.3	Tailoring	0.9
Lying still (awake)	0.1	Typewriting rapidly	1.0
Organ playing (30–40% of energy hand work)	1.5	Violin playing	0.6
		Walking (3 mph)	2.0
Painting furniture	1.5	Walking rapidly (4 mph)	3.4
Paring potatoes	0.6	Walking at high speed (5.3 mph)	9.3
Playing ping-pong	4.4	Walking downstairs	†
Piano playing (Mendelssohn)	0.8	Walking upstairs	‡
Piano playing (Beethoven's "Apassionata")	1.4	Washing floors	1.2
		Writing	0.4

* Calories per kilogram of body weight per hour.
† Allow 0.012 kcal/kg for an ordinary staircase with 15 steps without regard to time.
‡ Allow 0.036 kcal/kg for an ordinary staircase with 15 steps without regard to time.

Source: C. M. Taylor and G. McLeod, *Rose's Laboratory Handbook for Dietetics*, 5th ed., p. 18. Copyright © Macmillan Publishing Company, Inc. Used by permission.

hydrates and fats are rich in calories but are poor sources of some essential nutrients. Unfortunately, American diets tend to be overloaded with fats and carbohydrates and deficient in protein.

Social and environmentally acquired eating habits account for the fact that the American nutritional standard is lower than it should be in terms of our level of national income. The acquired taste for sweets that are actually deficient in all nutrients and do little more than provide energy is particularly prevalent in the American diet. And advertisers cultivate the public's acceptance of highly processed, protein-poor foods. Many people eat sweet, greasy foods that do not contain the vitamins and proteins they need to maintain good health. This is especially a problem among teenagers.

VITAMINS

Vitamins produce complex biochemical effects. Although their functions are diverse and not yet completely understood, all vitamins affect body chemistry. With the exception of vitamin D, which the body can manufacture in the presence of sunlight, all vitamins must be consumed.

Since 1943, the Nutrition Board of the National Research Council has issued Recommended Dietary Allowances (RDAs) for good health. RDA labels, in the words of the Board, are "a formulation of nutrient allowances for daily consumption . . . adequate for the maintenance of good nutrition." These levels are used by most nutritionists in planning and evaluating diets. The latest standards, issued in 1974, appear in Figure 15-3.

In recent years, the daily consumption of large amounts of vitamins, often greatly in excess of RDAs, has been advocated. And until recently restrained by the Food and Drug Administration, breakfast-cereal manufacturers and other processors had been adding synthetic vitamins to their products in amounts great enough to be considered drugs. To understand the results of high vitamin intake, we need to know something about the chemistry of vitamins.

Types of Vitamins Vitamins may be classified according to the substances in which they may, in their pure crystalline form, be dissolved. Some will dissolve only in water, others dissolve only in fats or body oils. All vitamins are either fat-soluble or water-soluble. Some examples are:

Fat-soluble Vitamins	Water-soluble Vitamins
A	Ascorbic acid (C)
D	Thiamine (B_1)
E	Riboflavin (B_2)
K	Niacin
	Pyridoxine (B_6)
	Folacin
	Cobalamin (B_{12})
	Pantothenic acid

Fat-soluble Vitamins As their name implies, fat-soluble vitamins in pure form can be dissolved only in fats and related substances. The body readily stores these vitamins in fatty tissues and elsewhere and tends not to excrete them.

Advocates of self-medication with large doses of fat-soluble vitamins ignore the possibility of overdoses and the known poisonous effects of excess intakes. The recommended daily dose of vitamin A promotes dim-light vision, growth, and skin health. But in overdoses of 10–40 times the RDA, vitamin A can cause bone decay in adults, embryonic skeletal deformities, headache,

15-3 U.S. Recommended Daily Allowances (U.S. RDA)*

	Adults and children 4 or more years of age†	Infants	Children under 4 years of age‡	Pregnant or lactating women‡
Protein§	45 g "high-quality protein" 65 g "proteins in general"	—	—	—
Vitamin A	5000 IU	1500 IU	2500 IU	8000 IU
Ascorbic acid (vitamin C)	60 mg	35 mg	40 mg	60 mg
Thiamine (vitamin B_1)	1.5 mg	0.5 mg	0.7 mg	1.7 mg
Riboflavin (vitamin B_2)	1.7 mg	0.6 mg	0.8 mg	2.0 mg
Niacin	20 mg	8 mg	9 mg	20 mg
Calcium	1.0 g	0.6 g	0.8 g	1.3 g
Iron	18 mg	15 mg	10 mg	18 mg
Vitamin D	400 IU	400 IU	400 IU	400 IU
Vitamin E	30 IU	5 IU	10 IU	30 IU
Vitamin B_6	2.0 mg	0.4 mg	0.7 mg	2.5 mg
Folic acid (folacin)	0.4 mg	0.1 mg	0.2 mg	0.8 mg
Vitamin B_{12}	6 μg	2 μg	3 μg	8 μg
Phosphorus	1.0 g	0.5 g	0.8 g	1.3 g
Iodine	150 μg	45 μg	70 μg	150 μg
Magnesium	400 mg	70 mg	200 mg	450 mg
Zinc#	15 mg	5 mg	8 mg	15 mg
Copper#	2 mg	0.5 mg	1 mg	2 mg
Biotin#	0.3 mg	0.15 mg	0.15 mg	0.3 mg
Pantothenic acid#	10 mg	3 mg	5 mg	10 mg

* The term "U.S. RDA" replaces "minimum daily requirement" (MDR). The U.S. RDA values chosen are derived from the highest value for each nutrient given in the NAS-NRC tables, except for calcium and phosphorus.
† For use in labeling conventional foods and "special dietary foods."
‡ For use only with "special dietary foods."
§ "High-quality protein" is defined as having a protein efficiency ratio (PER) equal to or greater than that of casein; "proteins in general" have a PER less than that of casein. Total protein with PER < 20% that of casein are considered "not a significant source of protein" and are not expressed on the label in terms of the U.S. RDA but only in terms of "amount per serving."
# There are no NAS-NRC RDAs for biotin, pantothenic acid, zinc, or copper.

Source: Values are taken from the Recommended Dietary Allowances developed by the Food and Nutrition Board of the National Academy of Sciences, National Research Council, as published by FDA (March 14, 1973).

nausea, drowsiness, and loss of hair. These toxic symptoms disappear shortly after the excess vitamin A is eliminated from the body.

Because the body can manufacture Vitamin D naturally in the presence of sunlight, technically this vitamin is a *hormone*.[3] All animals with backbones (vertebrates) require vitamin D, which is essential for healthy bone formation. Severe deficiencies of vitamin D result in rickets, a bone-formation condition that produces bowlegs and, in infants, improper skull development. On the other hand, overdoses of vitamin D in the range of 2.5–250 times RDA or higher can be toxic.

Vitamin E plays a role in the body's use of sugars and fats and is involved in cell formation. Human beings seldom lack sufficient vitamin E. Vitamin K is involved in blood clotting. Our food has abundant quantities of this vitamin, and its deficiency in adults is virtually unknown.

Water-soluble Vitamins

Water-soluble vitamins dissolve readily in water, are not stored by the body, tend to be fragile and are easily destroyed by cooking, are excreted in urine, and, consequently, should be consumed daily.

Ascorbic acid (vitamin C) is the best known water-soluble vitamin. Low levels of ascorbic acid intake are needed to prevent scurvy, a deficiency disease that produces bleeding gums, tender, weak bones, and other ailments. There is an extensive debate as to whether taking levels of ascorbic acid 20–40 times RDA promotes good health. Nobel prizewinner Linus Pauling and others have reported beneficial effects from taking 1–2 grams of vitamin C per day, but these results have been resisted by many nutritionists and scientists. More research is needed to determine the value and the role of ascorbic acid in the chemistry of the human body.

Thiamine (vitamin B_1) occurs naturally in many plant and animal foods. In areas where cereal grains, such as rice, are polished to remove the coarse outer layer and therefore increase storage life, a thiamine deficiency disease known as beriberi is often widespread. If not quickly treated, beriberi can cause respiratory problems and infant deaths. In adults beriberi can cause abnormalities in the body's retention of water and, on occasion, heart failure.

Riboflavin (vitamin B_2), is found in natural foods. In milk this vitamin can be destroyed by sunlight, but it exists in quantity in meats and vegetables. On the rare occasion when a deficiency occurs, there may be skin disorders and changes in reproductive ability. There is no evidence to date that human beings can suffer from overdoses of riboflavin.

Niacin is an essential element in the body's utilization of carbohydrates, fats, and proteins. A niacin deficiency produces the disease pellagra, which is accompanied by symptoms of skin inflammation, diarrhea, and depression. Severe niacin deficiencies are known to cause headaches, memory loss, hallucinations, and delusions of persecution, followed by death. Broadly based diets furnish adequate amounts of niacin. Overdoses are excreted.

---

[3] H.A. Guthrie, *Introductory Nutrition,* 3rd ed. (St. Louis: C.V. Mosby, 1975), p. 218.

Vitamin A	Thiamine	Riboflavin	Niacin	Ascorbic acid	Vitamin D
Butter	Pork	Milk	Liver	Citrus fruits	Cod and other
Whole milk	Liver	Egg	Chicken breast	Tomato (fresh	fish-liver oils
Cream	Kidney	Liver	Lean meats	or canned)	Body oils of
Egg yolk	Heart	Green leaves	Kidney	Cabbage (raw)	certain fish
Green leaves	Lean meats	Lean meat	Fish	Strawberries	Egg yolk
Other green	Whole-grain	Kidney	Dried yeast	Peas	Irradiated and
vegetables	products	Enriched white	Enriched white	Green leaves (raw)	other fortified
Apricots	Enriched white	cereals	cereals	Broccoli	foods
Yellow vegetables	cereals	Legumes	Peanuts	Green and red	
Tomato	Wheat germ	Buds (broccoli)		peppers	
Liver	Bran (prepared)	Dark poultry		Potato	
Cod, halibut, and	Dried yeast	meat		Cantaloupe	
other fish-liver	Legumes				
oils	Nuts				
	Egg yolk				
	Chard				
	Spinach				

15-4   Important Sources of Vitamins

Pyridoxine (vitamin B_6) occurs naturally in food. Infants whose formulas contain inadequate amounts of B_6 can become highly irritable. Excesses of this vitamin are excreted.

Pantothenic acid occurs in abundance in whole-grain cereals and animal organ meats and, in smaller amounts, in cheeses and vegetables. Deficiency symptoms include distress, fatigue, and poor muscle coordination.

The major sources of six of these important vitamins are given in Figure 15-4.

VITAMIN SUPPLEMENTS

Diet supplements can be of value to a person with a particular vitamin deficiency. If a vitamin deficiency exists, before resorting to pills or tonics, the diet should be improved until it meets RDA nutrient standards. If a vitamin deficiency symptom persists, then it should be brought to the attention of a physician. Self-medication with vitamin compounds may be a waste of money in the case of water-soluble vitamins and may be dangerous in the case of fat-soluble vitamins.

However, it is true that some people have a higher than average need for vitamins. Women in their child-bearing years, for example, have an incidence of certain anemias that can be treated with vitamin preparations. But a physician should be consulted before taking iron pills or tonics, because a low iron level in

the blood may be symptomatic of some other disease. It is always important to investigate any abnormal condition to determine why it exists. [4]

HEALTH AND ORGANIC FOODS

More and more consumers are becoming disturbed about the increasingly common practice of treating foods with chemical preservatives that have little

[4] Maxwell M. Wintrobe, "Iron Fortification of Wheat Products," *Nutrition Today* **VIII** (November/December 1973), pp. 18–20.

Food	kcal	Protein (g)	Calcium (mg)	Iron (mg)	Thiamine (mg)	Riboflavin (mg)	Vitamin C (mg)	Vitamin A (mg)
Brown rice	102	2.1	11	0.6	0.09	0.02	0	0
Sunflower seed	140	6.0	30	2.8	0.5	0.6	0	0
Dried apples	78	0.3	9	0.5	1.0	0.3	trace	*
Soya beans	130	11	73	2.7	0.4	0.2	0	30
Wheat germ	104	7.6	40.5	2.6	0.42	0.2	0	0
Pumpkin seeds	180	9.8	11	3.3	0.13	0.04	0	186
Natural seaweed	104	0.4	252	2.6	0.003	0.07	0	*
Honey	90	trace	2	0.2	trace	trace	0	0
Carob flour	51	1.2	99	*	*	*	*	*
Sesame seeds	140	5.0	290	2.6	0.3	0.08	0	15
Blackstrap molasses	43	*	116	2.3	0.5	0.5	*	*
Soybean sprouts	13	1.7	13.6	0.3	0.06	*	4	22
Desiccated liver	120	28	10	6	0.2	4.4	70	0

* Indicates no data available.

Source: Helen Andrews Guthrie, *Introductory Nutrition,* 3d ed. (St. Louis: The C.V. Mosby Company, 1975), p. 457.

15-5 Nutritive Content of Some Organic Foods (per ounce)

evident nutritional value and that may even be harmful. Meats are colored red to appear more appetizing—and some of these coloring agents have been identified as possible carcinogens. Baby foods are sugared to appeal to mothers, not infants. The sugar used begins the process of tooth decay and cultivates the baby's "sweet tooth"—a problem that may lead to such problems as obesity and diabetes in adult life. The recognition that many food additives are harmful has stimulated the Food and Drug Administration to rule against the routine use of many chemicals in foods.

Consumers have begun to seek out foods that are pesticide- and additive-free. A recent trend among some consumers is a preference for "organic" foods that are grown without the use of synthetic chemical fertilizers, pesticides, or herbicides and that are processed without the use of preservatives and other chemicals. Organic foods, grown near the markets in which they are sold, may be fresher and taste better. But organic food cultivation remains inefficient and requires much more labor than nonorganic cultivation. And because organic foods are not fortified with preservatives, they have a shorter shelf life than standard, processed foods. This may present a problem of bacterial contamination that would not occur in nonorganic products.

Some advocates of health foods urge the consumption of such foods as carob, papaya tea, alfalfa, and wheat germ, all of which provide certain nutrients.   But some of these products are raised and sold only in small amounts, and their cost tends to be relatively high.   Figure 15-5 gives the nutrient values of some of these more unusual foods.

Some stores that claim to sell only organic foods make much higher profits than the 33⅓% average gross markup in chain stores and may even sell many "organic" foods that in fact are grown with synthetic fertilizers and pesticides.[5]

THE FAT OF THE LAND

Americans living in cities tend to lead inactive, sedentary lives.   Heart disease produced by the accumulation of fatty deposits on the principal blood vessels of the heart is a leading cause of death in the United States.   Evidence of such deposits appears regularly, even in American teenagers, as autopsies have shown.   We should therefore adjust our own often rich diets to avoid foods that can in large amounts produce heart disease.

There is, however, much disagreement as to what causes heart disease. Stress, hereditary susceptibility, smoking, diet, and one's occupation are known to play a role.   Fats dissolved in the blood have repeatedly been linked with heart disease, and the recommendation that comes with this finding is to eat fewer heavy animal fats, such as egg yolks, butterfat in milk, ice cream, and butter, as well as the visible fat on meats.   Yet it has been shown that although the traditional diets of Eskimos are comprised of almost nothing but fats and proteins these people have virtually no heart disease.

Recently scientists have found that a sudden ingestion of cane or beet sugar in conjunction with a high fat intake causes the fats in the bloodstream to be deposited on heart's arteries.   When Eskimos eat the American diet of sweetened foods, they also suffer heart attacks, diabetes, and a number of other debilitative conditions common to people in industrial civilization.[6]

Advocates who claim that sugar is the cause of such deterioration in the body urge the elimination of simple sugars from the diet, although they claim that other sweet sugars, including natural fruit sugars, are not harmful.   Heavy fats consumed in reasonable amounts, they say, are not the cause of heart attacks.

Faced with all of these often contradictory statements about health, moderation and compromise in daily diet are perhaps in order.   Fat people are more susceptible to heart attacks and would be wise to reduce their intake of high-calorie, nutritionally weak fats and simple sugars and to avoid eating large amounts of sweets, which are at the least notorious for their effect on teeth. Rich, fried foods, especially such snack foods as potato chips, french fries, and fried bacon rinds, have almost no nutritional value except calories.

---

[5] *Food Processing* (October 1972), pp. 14–15.
[6] Otto Schaefer, "When the Eskimo Comes to Town," *Nutrition Today* **VI** (November/December 1971), pp. 8–15.

Fresh foods are preferable, even for snacks. Generally, the less food is processed or cooked the more vitamins it contains. The most healthful diet is a balanced one that contains a minimum of processed products and of refined sugars and starches.

PACKAGING

When a product is packed in a can or a cardboard box, it's very hard to determine precisely what is inside. Packaging is itself a vast industry, accounting for more than $4.5 billion of grocery industry costs. Of course, foods must be protected in shipment and should be attractively packaged. The packaging industry knows that for the most part the package displayed in the supermarket is the product's only selling point. It must capture the shopper's attention in the few seconds he or she spends scanning the shelf area where the product can be found. In a brief time a package must persuade the potential buyer that *it* is the best product. In 1968 the average family of four spent $357 on packaging alone.[7]

Labels Aren't Clear Federal packaging regulations have been improved and are now more helpful to the consumer. Yet in the view of industry critics these regulations are still tolerant toward food processors. Current federal regulations require that processed foods reveal ingredients by type or category in the order of quantity or meet a specific preset standard of identity. This means that if a food falls under an *identity standard,* its label does not have to reveal the ingredient breakdown by percentage or any other description of the products contents. For example, because frankfurters are covered by an identity standard, the contents of "all meat" franks do not have to be labeled 30% fat, 10% added water, 15% chicken, and up to 2% corn syrup in addition to frankfurter meat.

The Fair Packaging and Labeling Act. The Fair Packaging and Labeling Act (FPLA), passed in 1966, improved a bad situation. Although much weakened to appease industry objections, this legislation requires that all food and many nonfood products sold in interstate commerce bear labels revealing the net contents, the name and address of the manufacturer, the size of servings if the number of servings is stated, and a list of ingredients in order of decreasing weight. Deceptive quantity descriptions are banned, and manufacturers are encouraged to standardize package sizes. One result of this Act is that there are now only five toothpaste sizes instead of the previous 57.

The 1966 Act still leaves much room for reform. The net contents of packages must now be declared, but net contents still include liquid measure.

[7] Jennifer Cross, *The Supermarket Trap* (Bloomington, Ind.: Indiana University Press, 1970), pp. 93, 95.

PACKAGING COSTS AT THE RETAIL LEVEL

Product	Container Cost (cents)	Percent of Retail Price
Canned tomatoes (No. 303)	4.0	25
Canned corn (No. 303)	4.0	21
Canned evaporated milk (14½ oz)	3.0	20.1
Cereal (1 lb box)	4.9	11.8
Ice cream (½ gal)	7.9	9.8
White bread (1 lb)	1.5	7.2
Fresh milk (½ gal)	3.0	6.3
Eggs (1 doz)	3.1	6.0
Processed American cheese (½ lb)	2.1	5.7
Broiler (per lb)	1.5	4.1
Butter (1 lb)	2.3	3.0
Choice beef (1 lb)	1.4	2.0

Source: U.S. National Commission on Food Marketing, *Food from Farmer to Consumer,* pp. 16–17.

Thus canned fruits may be half-filled with water; 8 ounces of canned peaches may contain 4 ounces of packing water and syrup. The FPLA should be amended to specify that *dry weights* be given on product labels. Although the FPLA mandates the disclosure of ingredients by order of weight in the product, it does not require a percentage breakdown or a description of their origin. For example, although vegetable oil must be listed, the percentage of oil and its source (saturated, unsaturated, corn, peanut, or other) is not required to be revealed. Stew must contain specific identity standards regarding the amount of meat contained, but that meat may come from some rather unusual parts of animals.

Unit Pricing

Food manufacturers and processors package foods in a great variety of containers. There are many reasons for the proliferation of packages, including a manufacturer's efforts to place a lower-priced box next to a competitor's product, a desire to reduce the quantity of a product sold while holding the price constant (this produces the same effect as a mark-up), and a sales strategy that is designed to adjust a product's container to match the amount of the weekly food budget that a shopper can spend on the particular item. Faced with so many competing containers, a shopper is hard-pressed to make the best choice.

Unit pricing is a partial solution to the problem of choosing among competing brands and containers of the same product. If one box of cornflakes is 90¢ for

TWO KINDS OF PRODUCT LABELS

Nutrient label showing only mandatory information.

Label providing optional (light type) as well as mandatory (boldface type) information.

Nutrition Information
(per serving)

Serving size = 8 oz

Servings per container = 2

Calories	**560**
Protein	**23 g**
Carbohydrate	**43 g**
Fat	**33 g**
(Percent of calories from fat = 53%)	
Polyunsaturated*	22 g
Saturated	9 g
Cholesterol* (18 mg/100 g)	40 mg
Sodium (365 mg/100 g)	810 mg

Percentage of U.S. Recommended Daily Allowance (U.S. RDA)

Protein	**35**	**Niacin**	**25**
Vitamin A	**35**	**Calcium**	**2**
Vitamin C	**10**	**Iron**	**25**
Thiamine	**15**	Vitamin B$_6$	20
Riboflavin	**15**	Vitamin B$_{12}$	15

* Information of fat and cholesterol content is provided for individuals who, on the advice of a physician, are modifying their total dietary intake of fat and cholesterol.

Nutrition Information
(per Serving)

Serving size: One ounce (1⅓ cup) corn flakes alone and in combination with ½ cup vitamin D fortified whole milk.

Serving per container: 12

	Corn flakes	
	1 oz	*with ½ cup whole milk*
Calories	110	190
Protein	2 g	6 g
Carbohydrates	24 g	30 g
Fat	0 g	4 g

Percentage of U.S. Recommended Daily Allowance (U.S. RDA)

	Corn flakes	
	1 oz	*with ½ cup whole milk*
Protein	2	10
Vitamin A	25	25
Vitamin C	25	25
Thiamine	25	25
Riboflavin	25	35
Niacin	25	25
Calcium	*	15
Iron	10	10

* Contains less than 2% of the U.S. RDA of these nutrients.

Source: Helen Andrews Guthrie, *Introductory Nutrition,* 3rd ed. (St. Louis: The C.V. Mosby Company, 1975), p. 329.

15 ounces and another is 75¢ for 12 ounces, then the unit prices are, respectively, 90/15 = 6 and 75/12 = 6.25 cents per ounce. In this case, the larger package is clearly the better buy.

Unit pricing has voluntarily been adopted by such major chains as A&P, Jewel, and National Tea. And meat, bread, and produce have always been marked with convenient quantity prices (apples at 10¢ per pound, lettuce at 39¢ per head, and so on).

Unit pricing is less helpful in selecting canned and frozen foods measured in net weights. When the product is packed in water and or syrup, the net weight includes the packing fluid. A can of pears weighing 14 net ounces may contain 2–6 or more ounces of syrup. The only way to avoid the dilemma of calculating unit prices and of winding up with expensive water is to know the dry or drained weights of products in their packages and containers. Unfortunately, dry weights are difficult to determine, for products packed in liquids sometimes dissolve partially in their fluids, absorb their fluids, or undergo some other change.

Nutrition Labeling. Although voluntary, nutrition labeling now standardizes disclosures of the percentages of a product's Recommended Dietary Allowances of nutrients in terms of serving size, number of servings, and amounts of protein, fat, carbohydrates, and major vitamins. Food processors and manufacturers must follow this standard form of disclosure when making any statements on the label as to the nutritional value of the product.

Product Dating. Open dating on perishable products is not yet required by federal law, although it is required in some jurisdictions, including New York City. Manufacturers often mark their packages with shelf-life termination dates, but usually in codes recognizable only to store managers and others who have access to the particular store's code book. Open dating with clear descriptions of dates (for example, "Do not sell after January 1978") would be of great help to consumers, although this could mean a higher return of unsold goods to food processors and require a change in inventory control procedures.

Labels and Costs. The problem of labeling is as extensive as is the consumer's need for detailed product information. People who are allergic to specific preservatives or additives need to know if they are present and in what quantities. Vitamin D is actually a group of vitamins. For medical reasons, some people might need to know the vitamin D composition of foods. In many cases manufacturers object to extensive labeling because they feel most consumers don't care about product contents, product labeling can be costly for specialty food processors and can exclude small firms from the market (sellers of farm preserves, for example), or some packages (such as chewing gum packs) are too small to carry labels containing every bit of information that some people might want to know. In the end a price is paid for such labeling, but it is hardly a substantial expense to major food processors who spend far more money on the package as a whole than just the cost of some small print.

FOOD GRADES

Food scandals, particularly meat scandals, have occurred frequently in the United States in the twentieth century. In every case the federal government and/or some state government has responded by imposing additional regulations on food processors. Unfortunately, all too often these rules remain largely unenforced due to the lack of honest and efficient inspectors and inspection methods.

For many years there were loopholes in the meat inspection laws. Poultry was not even partially covered by such a law until 1950, and meat moving intrastate (not crossing state lines) was not required to meet federal standards until 1967. Yet even given new federal inspection standards, the laws governing food inspection are still inadequate in many ways. Here are some of them:

1 There are not enough inspectors to cover all existing processing plants; they are unable to make sufficiently frequent visits or to be in constant attendance where necessary.
2 Inspections are always conducted under the auspices of state and federal agricultural agencies. These bodies are committed to farmer and agricultural business interests and at times in the past have acted in at least partial disregard of consumer interests.
3 Fresh produce is graded on the boxes or crates in which it is shipped, but consumers see produce only on display, out of the boxes. Stores should be required to post notices of each grade standard near the produce on display.
4 Grading standards are voluntary. Although inspection is mandatory in many cases, grading is not. Even if meat is graded "choice," neither the processor nor the vendor is required to reveal this fact (although it would be in the best interests of both to do so).
5 Terminology is inconsistent. Food-grading standards have been adopted by standardizing the *industry's* own terms. Thus "U.S. No. 1" is the highest grade of honeydew melons and radishes but the second grade of brocolli, sweet peppers, and tangerines. "U.S. Grade A" is the highest grade of Swiss cheese but the second grade of butter and cheddar cheese. There is an endless list of terms that are consistent for one product but inconsistent when applied to many products. Grades ought to be standardized to a simple A, B, C, . . . or 1, 2, 3, . . . order.

Meat Grades Meat grades are determined by fat dispersion in muscle tissue and indicate tenderness. Beef grades range downward successively from "U.S. Prime," to "U.S. Choice," "U.S. Good," "U.S. Standard," "U.S. Commercial," "U.S. Utility," and lower grades used only in making sausages. Veal, mutton, and lamb grades include "U.S. Choice," "U.S. Good," "U.S. Standard," "U.S. Utility," and "U.S. Cull."

Processed meats, including the 15 billion hot dogs we consume in the United States annually, are sold without adequate content disclosure standards. Ralph Nader claims that modern sausage processing is largely a misuse of such contemporary chemical techniques as coloring and preservation. Between 1937 and 1967 the fat content of frankfurters increased from 18.6% to 31.2%, and protein content decreased from 19.6% to 11.8%. Hot dogs can also contain up to 10% water. Nader has called these "fatfurters" "some of America's deadliest missles."[8]   Such frankfurter labels as "all beef" or "all meat" are meaningless, because additives in the form of water, fat, chicken, and even goat are permitted under some of these identity standards.

Milk Standards

Milk inspection and grading are based on U.S. government standards in use throughout the country.   Milk grades range from "Certified" through "Grade A," "Grade B," and "Grade C."   The lower the grade, the more bacteria are permitted in a given quantity of milk.   These bacteria are not harmful to human beings but indicate under what conditions and for what length of time the milk has been stored.

Milk prices depend on the amount of butterfat in the milk.   Many dairies sell milk with reduced butterfat content at reduced prices; those that don't are over-charging milk buyers.   Compared to whole milk, which contains 5% butterfat, homogenized milk containing 2% butterfat may cost 5 cents less per quart. When water is extracted from milk, shipping costs decline.   Evaporated milk contains only half the water of whole milk.   Its consistency makes it suitable for cooking, although it has less than perfect flavor when drunk cold from a glass. Dried milks are graded by taste appeal.   They are low in fat and nutritionally comparable to whole milks.   Milks in which part or all of the milk solids have been replaced with soy proteins are available as filled or synthetic milks, respectively.   These milks are less expensive than whole milk and may be desirable for people who are allergic to the various components of cow's milk.

Egg Grades

Eggs are available in sizes ranging from "jumbo" to "peewee."   Retail eggs are graded "U.S. Grade AA" or "Fancy Fresh," "U.S. Grade A," and "U.S. Grade B."   Lower grades of eggs are sold for commercial use.   "Grade AA" and "Grade A" eggs have perfect shells that are free from discoloration, large, round yolks, and firm, stiff whites.   These are eggs best for poaching.   "Grade B" eggs are equally wholesome, but their internal consistency is somewhat thinner. These eggs are best for scrambling and for use in general cooking.   In general, shell color is not related to quality and only reflects the breed of hen.

Egg Minimum Weight per Dozen

USDA Size	Minimum Weight (oz)
Jumbo	30
Extra Large	27
Large	24
Medium	21
Small	18
Peewee	15

[8] U.S. Senate, Hearings: *Nutrition and Human Needs* (90th Congress. 2nd Session, 91st Congress, 1st Session), Pt. 13-A, pp. 3903–904.

Grade Mark

FOOD GRADES

Fresh Fruit and Vegetables

	U.S. Fancy	U.S. Fancy	U.S. No. 1	U.S. No. 1
1st Grade:	U.S. Fancy	U.S. Fancy	U.S. No. 1	U.S. No. 1
2nd Grade:	U.S. No. 1	U.S. Extra No. 1	U.S. No. 2	U.S. Commercial

U.S. Fancy / U.S. No. 1	U.S. Fancy / U.S. Extra No. 1	U.S. No. 1 / U.S. No. 2	U.S. No. 1 / U.S. Commercial
Snap beans	Cucumbers	Apricots	Honeydew melons
Broccoli	European	Artichokes	Kale
Topped	table grapes	Asparagus	Southern peas
carrots	Nectarines	Beets	Radishes
Celery	Peaches	Brussels	Watermelons
Green corn		sprouts	
Greenhouse		Blackberries	
cucumbers		Mushrooms	
Eggplant		Green onions	
Table grapes		Parsnips	
Grapefruit		Parsley (no	
Lettuce		2nd grade)	
Onions (boilers)		Raspberries	
Onions (picklers)		Shallots	
Peas		Squash	
Sweet peppers		Tomatoes	
Pineapples		(2nd grade =	
Plums and prunes		combination)	
Potatoes		Turnips	
Rhubarb		Rutabagas	
Spinach leaves			
Sweet potatoes			
Tangerines			

Apples and summer and fall pears are in a separate category: their 1st grade is U.S. Extra Fancy; 2nd, U.S. Fancy.

Top-grade fresh produce (most supermarkets stock the first or second grades) has the best color, size, shape, and relative freedom from defects.

Processed Fruit and Vegetables

1st Grade: U.S. Grade A or U.S. Fancy; 2nd Grade: U.S. Grade B (or Choice, Standard, Extra Standard Grade C, or Extra Standard).

U.S. Grade A or Fancy processed fruit is the most beautiful in appearance, although lower grades are often riper and excellent for pies and many desserts. The top-grade processed vegetables are again better in appearance and more tender; lower grades are more suitable for stews and casseroles. Most manufacturers' leading brands and top-grade housebrands are Grade A.

Dairy Products

Inspection Mark

Product	1st Grade	2nd Grade
Butter	U.S. Grade AA	U.S. Grade A
Cheddar cheese	U.S. Grade AA	U.S. Grade A
Dry buttermilk	U.S. Extra	U.S. Standard
Dry whole milk	U.S. Premium	U.S. Extra
Nonfat dry milk	U.S. Extra	U.S. Standard
Instant dry milk	U.S. Extra	No 2nd Grade
Swiss cheese	U.S. Grade A	U.S. Grade B

Nuts

Product	1st Grade	2nd Grade
Almonds in the shell	U.S. No. 1	U.S. No. 1 Mixed
Brazil nuts in the shell	U.S. No. 1	No 2nd Grade
Filberts in the shell	U.S. No. 1	No 2nd Grade
Peanuts in the shell or shelled	U.S. No. 1	U.S. No. 2
Pecans	U.S. No. 1	U.S. Commercial
Walnuts	U.S. No. 1	U.S. No. 2

Meat

Product	1st Grade	2nd Grade	3rd Grade	4th Grade	5th Grade
Beef	Prime	Choice	Good	Standard	Commercial
Veal	Prime	Choice	Good	Standard	Utility
Lamb	Prime	Choice	Good	Utility	Cull
Pork	U.S. No. 1	U.S. No. 2	U.S. No. 3	Medium	Cull

Lower grades that do not normally appear at retail, but that turn up in hot dogs or in cans of beef stew or chile con carne are utility (6th), cutter (7th), and canner (8th) for beef, and cull (6th) for veal.

The meat grades identify the main factors responsible for tenderness, juiciness, and tastiness. They are not a guide to food value, which is more or less the same whatever the grade. Prime veal, beef, or lamb are usually snapped up by the hotel and restaurant trade and are rarely found in food stores, except for those that are obviously trying to upgrade their meat departments and that may stock a small quantity of prime meat. Prime meat comes from young, well-fed animals and can be recognized by its top price and by a fair amount of fat, particularly in the marbling (the delicate webbing of fat interspersed with lean).

Poultry is graded A, B, or C, primarily on the basis of a visual judgment of skin color, fat distribution, and visible damage. Chickens are variously sold as "dressed" (organs intact) or "ready-to-cook" (organs removed).

Eggs are a rich source of protein. Even 80 cents per dozen for "Grade A" large eggs represents a good value. This is equivalent to $1\frac{1}{2}$ pounds for 80 cents, or less that 54 cents a pound for an excellent meat substitute.[9]

Fish Grades

In the food industry, the term "fish" refers to seafood that is finned and has scales, backbones, and the other characteristics generally shared by the popular table species. The term "seafood" alone means mollusks, such as oysters and clams, and crustaceans, such as lobsters and shrimp.

Fish processing and packing plants, operating under U.S. Department of the Interior inspection programs, stamp their products with a special shield. Fish quality grades range from "Grade A" through "Grade B" and "Grade C." As usual, the grade indicates appearance and structure, not nutritional value. "Grade A" fish is uniform in size and free from surface defects. "Grade B" fish may not be uniform in quality and may have surface blemishes and bruises. "Grade C" fish may be substantially blemished.

In recent years, there has been widespread concern about marketing fish contaiminated by pollution. In some areas, concern over excess levels of mercury in fish has led to a ban on the sale of swordfish, once a prized and substantial table fish. As a rule, fish on the market is safe for human consumption. Yet a broader problem of sanitation exists throughout the fish industry. Not enough fishing boats have refrigerated holds, and not enough processing installations meet proper standards. Fish and seafood should be carefully inspected before purchase, or bought only from reputable merchants, and properly cooked to ensure wholesomeness.

FOOD ADDITIVES AND FOREIGN MATTER

An *additive* is any substance, apart from a basic foodstuff, that is added to a food in production, packaging, or storage. Additives enter food products either intentionally or incidentally during production, packaging, or storage. Some examples of intentional additives are preservatives, coloring agents, stabilizers, and so on. Incidental additives include herbicide or pesticide residues and filth.

Intentional Additives

Many intentional additives have been proved harmful or judged potentially harmful if ingested in large amounts. Intentional additives give food products a longer shelf life, a better appearance, a more desirable consistency, or, in some cases, a wholesome look when in fact they are not. Safe additives are specified by the "Generally Recognized as Safe" (GRAS) list created by the Food Ad-

---

[9] U.S. Department of Agriculture, *Food for Us All, Yearbook of Agriculture,* 1969, pp. 139–41.

"We'll need a different package. It seems the new preservative dissolves cardboard."

ditives Amendment of 1958. Some of these additives are as common and safe as sugar and salt; the safety of other, usually synthetic additives is increasingly being questioned.

A major problem in testing additives to determine their safety is that the immediate toxicity of any additive can be evaluated but the genetic or other long-term effects of most additives cannot be discerned without years of extensive testing. Dosing rats and other animals with large quantities of chemicals under investigation can be helpful, but the ability of a substance to produce cancer in healthy laboratory rats cannot be equated with the ability of that substance to cause cancer in human beings in varying states of health. A major problem is that it is almost impossible to test each chemical in combination with every other chemical in the varying proportions that it may be ingested. Some food additives may cause a reaction only when ingested by people who live under specific environmental conditions (in high smog areas, for example) or by people who take certain drugs. Some additives are harmful only to fetuses and to future generations. Unfortunately, it will require years of medical research to determine the long-term effects of ingesting chemical additives.

Incidental Additives

Incidental additives are an even more intractable problem for food scientists and legislators. In high-yield American agriculture, large amounts of chemicals are employed to suppress weeds and insects. Some of these chemicals remain with plants after harvesting; others are retained when crops grown for animal feed are ingested by livestock and poultry. In addition, animals themselves store and actually concentrate many metals, herbicides, and insecticides, and the concentrated residues are passed along to the human consumer. The use of all agricultural chemicals could be banned, but this would clearly cause food yields to decline drastically and food prices to rise. This could mean that foods might have to be imported from other countries, and the economic effects of such importation could be substantial (the value of the U.S. dollar could decrease considerably, for example). The alternative of organic farming (the practice of raising food without the use of chemical fertilizers, pesticides, and herbicides) is not yet sufficiently productive to feed Americans by employing the same low proportion of the U S. population (5%) that now produces the food commercially available to nonfarming Americans.

Filth. Some contamination of food from insect parts, rodent hairs and waste, rotten matter of all sorts, bird droppings, and other sources is inevitable, due to the fact that most food is grown outdoors. It is possible to remove almost all filth from food, but this would require additional handling and would increase costs. Of course, some kinds of filth are not "natural" in origin (for example, grease from canning machinery that may fall into canned foods).

Current FDA standards for permissible filth levels in foods are lenient. The FDA allows 300 insect fragments and 8 rat hairs per pound of peanut butter, for example. Under pressure from the Consumers Union and other U.S. consumer-action groups, the FDA recently published its filth standards, which had long been held confidential. It should be noted here that the need to keep filth out of foods conflicts with the need to keep insecticides out of food to the extent that insecticides reduce the number of contaminating vermin present in farm fields.

FOOD MARKETING YESTERDAY

A shopper purchasing a weekly or a monthly supply of groceries 100 years ago could select from several hundred basic staples either at a general store in a rural area or at a specialized butcher, baker, or vegetable dealer in a town of several thousand people or more. Individual families prepared many of their own preserves and such condiments as pickles, relishes, and sauces. In the late 1800s, the family had considerable direct contact with merchants and was familiar with the prices of competing brands of such staples as flour, sugar, corn meal, and bacon.

Food Marketing in 1900

Changes in the way we live have produced vast changes in the structure of the grocery business. At the beginning of the twentieth century, only a small fraction of the North American population of lived in urban centers. Town dwellers knew their merchants and their merchants' products comparatively well. Farms were easily accessible to families who wished to buy fresh produce in season. Farms could be found at the end of big-city trolley lines and were a short walk or ride from the centers of most smaller towns. Numerous independent grocers, well-known to their customers, offered a limited selection of foods, ranging from farmers with a table of fresh vegetables and fruits by the roadside or at a farmers' market to modest general stores boasting barrels of staples and racks of smoked meats.

The Market Becomes More Complex

As more and more Americans moved into the cities, independent grocers found themselves unable to afford high rents in city centers and farmers found it too difficult to spend time commuting to towns with their products. Smaller grocers tended either to go out of business, to combine with other grocers, or to sell their businesses to other grocers who were expanding by *horizontal mergers*. This *chain-store movement* peaked in the 1930s, at which time about one-third of the nation's retail food business were chain-store operations.[10]

The 1930s were a time of great economic hardship. Unemployment rose to 25% of the adult U.S. labor force by 1933. Those still employed suffered wage cuts that averaged 18%. It was hard for stores to sell to customers who had no cash, and harder still for grocers to obtain food from farmers who were dissatisfied with the prevailing low commodity prices. Many independent grocers were forced to close; those that managed to survive did so most often by reducing services and overhead.[11]

The Giants Take Over

By the 1950s, many areas had all the supermarkets and affiliated stores that they could handle. Supermarkets were doing two-thirds of the nation's grocery business. The big chains responded to this market saturation by making *vertical mergers* in which the food retailers absorbed the wholesaling and processing operations preliminary to retail grocery selling. Consumers benefited from this consolidation to the degree that some intermediaries were squeezed out of the food market.[12]

The Situation Today

Today large supermarkets maintain their advantage over smaller food shops by offering customers extensive food selections, abundant free parking, and other amenities. For homemakers who have come to depend on convenience foods in a society in which few people have household servants, centralized shopping is essential. Successful grocery concerns tend to merge into networks of a relatively small number of immense stores, each catering to shoppers who live a considerable distance (perhaps several miles) away from the shopping center.

As long as we continue to want the things supermarkets provide, the pattern of food sales in America will remain much the way it is today. Clearly, many fea-

---

[10] Daniel I. Padberg, *Economics of Food Retailing* (Ithaca, N.Y.: Cornell University Press, 1968), p. 11.

[11] See David A. Shannon (ed.), *The Great Depression* (Englewood Cliffs, N.J.: Prentice-Hall, 1960), pp. 16–34.

[12] Padberg, p. 15.

NUMBER OF GROCERY STORES, 1948–1963

Sales size	Number of establishments			
	1948	**1954**	**1958**	**1963**
All grocery stores	377,939	279,440	259,796	244,838
Grocery stores with sales of less than $100,000	276,511	204,880	175,581	148,714

Source: National Commission on Food Marketing study.

tures of the grocery business are little more than promotional fluff: wide aisles, air conditioning, Muzak. Paradoxically, before the era of the large supermarket, food shopping took less time than it does today.

IS BIGNESS GOOD FOR THE CONSUMER?

Is America better off with its retail grocery business in the hands of large stores? From the grocers' point of view, bigness means the ability to bargain with the large food processors who like to keep wholesale prices up. Large stores reduce shipping and handling costs by buying in carload lots.

From the viewpoint of some articulate consumer groups, however, bigness in the grocery business is bad. Rather than controlling the food prices charged by intermediaries and processors, consumer-action groups argue that large grocery chains happily pass on to consumers the high prices paid for fancy advertising campaigns.

According to the National Commission on Food Marketing:

> High concentration in the food industry is undesirable because it weakens competition as a self-regulating device by which the activities of business firms are directed toward the welfare of the public at large. When large firms dominate a field, they frequently . . . [stop] competing actively by price; competition by advertising, sales promotion, and other selling efforts almost always increases; and the market power inescapably at the disposal of such firms may be used to impose onerous terms on suppliers or customers.[13]

Competitive Tactics

In today's concentrated market, competition takes one of two forms:

1 Intense price competition over products that are familiar to consumers, and sometimes pricing items as *loss leaders* (at less than cost) to attract bargain-minded shoppers.

[13] Cited in James S. Turner, *The Chemical Feast* (New York: Grossman, 1970), p. 83.

THE FIVE LEVELS OF GOOD FOOD MANAGEMENT

1 Plan your food management well by:
   Keeping a file of inexpensive recipes
   Checking weekly food specials in newspapers
   Comparing stores to see how each handles the sales mix
   Planning weekly menus and making use of food specials

   Using leftovers in subsequent meals
   Determining supplies on hand (in cupboards, refrigerator, and freezer)
   Writing out shopping lists and avoiding shopping when hungry
   Choosing foods that are in season and plentiful

2 Buy well by:
   Using unit pricing
   Buying specials in quantity only when they can be used or stored well for long periods
   Sticking to shopping lists, but also looking for good buys of family favorites
   Reading product labels
   Avoiding convenience foods if you don't need the convenience
   Checking package weights and verifying them on store scales
   Avoiding fancy grades unless necessary

   Avoiding impulse buying, crowded stores, shopping with children
   Obtaining service from butchers and store clerks
   Limiting the number of shopping trips, but visiting different stores when economical
   Comparing private-label items to national brands
   Buying meat for lean tissue content, rather than gross package weight
   Watching the cash register window at the checkout counter

3 Store food well by:
   Using stored foods before newly bought foods
   Checking cupboard, freezer, and refrigerator for forgotten items
   Freezing cooked and uncooked foods in convenient quantities for family, guest, and single meals

   Conserving nutrients (for example, store fruit juices in the refrigerator in covered containers to reduce vitamin loss)
   Canning foods to be stored for long periods of time

4 Prepare foods well by:
   Using reliable recipes
   Measuring accurately
   Following directions carefully
   Avoiding unnecessary leftovers and waste

   Conserving nutrients (cook vegetables in a minimum of water and don't overcook; roast meats at low oven temperature—say, 325°; don't drain juices from foods)

5 Serve food well by:
   Making portion sizes to suit individual appetites

   Adding variety to menus without hesitating to repeat family favorites
   Serving hot foods hot; cold foods cold

2 Raising prices on products that are less familiar to shoppers, packaging and designing products to make it harder for consumers to compare them with competing goods, and selling products that have exceptionally high built-in profits (condiments, such as olives; fancy dessert items, such as frozen, frosted layer cakes; ready-made meat products, such as frozen tacos).

This combination of attractive bargains and high-profit items is called the *sales mix*.

Stores and Prices: A Comparison

There are six principal types of food retailers:

1 Chain stores
2 Independent supermarkets
3 Discount stores
4 Independent specialty shops
5 Consumer cooperatives
6 Farmers' markets

Choosing a store is one important way in which consumers can get the most for their food dollar. In a study of price variation by chain and city area in Milwaukee, in any one neighborhood a basket of groceries cost up to 55% less at one chain than at another. Over the entire city, savings of as much as 80% could be realized by picking the lowest priced chain among all the neighborhood supermarkets.[14]

MONEY-SAVING OPPORTUNITIES

Sales

Food sales or "specials" tend to offer shoppers good values. Daniel I. Padberg has found that meat specials reduce *gross profit margins* (the markups between the wholesale and retail price) by 6 percentage points, or 26%. During exceptional price specials on meat, gross margins can be reduced 45% below the margins customarily prevailing when specials are not enforced. Stores may even lose money when gross margins are heavily reduced in the hope that the additional customers the sale or special brings into the store will purchase non-sale items to make up for this loss. When such specials are in effect, other prices, particularly those of items placed near the specials, may be raised to cover any losses that will be incurred by low markups on the sale items.[15] A good principle to follow when shopping is that an item on sale is no bargain unless you really need it.

[14] Gordon E. Bivens, "An Exploration of Food-Price Competition in a Local Market," *Journal of Consumer Affairs* **II** (Summer 1968), pp. 61–73.
[15] Padberg, p. 136.

**Private
Labels**
At chain stores and many large independent or affiliated supermarkets, *private-label* merchandise is available at prices below those of competing items of nationally advertised brands.   Private-label goods are generally of the same quality as the national brands.   Store managers prefer private-label goods because they earn a slightly larger profit than the national brands (about 24.8% and 22.4%, respectively, over the invoice cost of a product).   Most of the distribution and promotion intermediaries are bypassed by private-label sellers, so that the retail prices of private brands are lower than the prices of comparable national brands. Stores that offer private-label goods generally advertise only on the actual sale day.   Typical private-label merchandise studied by the National Commission on Food Marketing sold for 4–35% less than advertised brands.   On the average, according to this study, private-label merchandise retails for 20% less than the national brands.   Thus it pays to shop for these less-promoted goods.[16]

**Bulk
Buying**
It can be worthwhile to buy in bulk.   Large families with the storage space and adequate cash to accumulate an inventory of much used items can save by buying products by the case.   Groups of friends may cooperate to buy whole-

---

[16] Padberg, pp. 85–95. Advertising and sales promotion consume 20 cents of each retail food dollar.   Of this, 12 cents covers television advertising.   Note that the raw materials cost only 21 cents.   The National Commission on Food Marketing, cited in Sidney Margolius, *The Innocent Consumer vs. The Exploiters* (New York: Trident Press, 1967), p. 13.

AVERAGE RETAIL PRICES PER CASE FOR SELECTED PRODUCTS BY TYPE OF LABEL*

Product	Private label†	Advertised brand	Percent difference‡
Frozen orange concentrate (6 oz)	$8.74	$11.84	35
Frozen cut green beans (9 oz)	4.94	6.42	30
Canned cut green beans (No. 303)	4.57	6.09	33
Canned green peas (No. 303)	4.76	5.52	16
Canned sliced cling peaches (No. 2½)	6.24	6.46	4
Canned Bartlett pears (No. 2½)	10.86	12.93	19
Canned applesauce (25-oz glass)	3.29	3.64	11
Catsup (14 oz)	4.46	5.10	14
Tuna fish, light, chunk (6.5 oz)	12.72	15.81	24
Evaporated milk	6.52	7.48	15
AVERAGE	6.71	8.13	20

* Prices are averaged over 12 weeks and include specials.
† Best quality private label compared.
‡ Difference expressed as a percentage of the private-label price.

Source: National Commission on Food Marketing study.

sale lots of fresh produce. But buying by the case or *skid* (as customary lots of cases are known) involves risk and requires expert knowledge. Shoppers must be able to bargain with wholesalers and must know that when buying produce, for example, they are expected to accept some bad produce with the good. Shoppers have no recourse if they fail to inspect their merchandise before buying. To buy fresh produce in bulk requires going to the local wholesale market when it opens (generally at dawn), having a truck or station wagon on hand and perhaps a strong helper to load up, and being prepared to weave through throngs of workers and piles of food. Despite these drawbacks, bulk buying can offer considerable savings to consumers.

Grade Switches   A less risky way to benefit from the price advantage of wholesale buying is to shop for second-grade items. As we have already pointed out, second-grade products are no less wholesome or nutritious than first-grade items; they are simply priced lower due to flaws in their appearance. Chili made with canned tomato chunks, for example, tastes as good as chili that contains costlier, whole, canned tomatoes.

FOOD BUYING TRAPS

Convenience Foods   Many so-called instant foods and convenience foods are less instant and convenient and more expensive than the "real thing," although some convenience foods do save time. For example, a good grade of white rice is available for about 54 cents a pound and takes about 25 minutes to prepare. A package of "instant" rice, on the other hand, can be cooked in 5 minutes, although it costs $1.12 per pound.[17]

Many of the high-priced prepackaged dinners and frozen breakfasts that glut our supermarkets are only noodles or potato starch to which the cook must add meat or milk. Chinese dinners in a can sell for more than $1 per unit, although the instructions require the cook to throw out most of the product's weight in surplus packing liquid.

Sometimes food processors add danger as well as convenience to instant foods. As Sidney Margolius points out, when two convenience foods such as hot dogs and baked beans are combined in a single can, the chance of contamination from factory handling is greatly increased, as is the cost compared to the prices of individual products. Also, in Margolius' eyes, "as real convenience decreases, the price of the product rises."[18]

[17] Sidney Margolius, *The Great American Food Hoax* (New York: Walker & Co., 1971), p. 17.
[18] *Ibid.,* p. 35.

"We better watch out for bait-and-switch."

Freezer Meat Sales The freezer meat sales business is notorious for bait-and-switch selling by firms that offer sides of beef at low prices. A prospective buyer is led into the freezer, past rows of wholesome looking sides of meat to a fatty, tallowy carcass. The salesperson then points out that better meat is available for a higher price, perhaps with a charge for trimming. The customer who decides to buy may then be asked to sign a credit note that is sold to a finance company. Thereafter, under the holder-in-due-course doctrine (see Chapter 10, page 162), the buyer may have no recourse against the seller or the finance company for defects in or misrepresentation of the purchase. For example, in trimming the side of meat, the packer may take off good meat to sell to other buyers. As a result, the buyer may pay more for second-rate meat and overpriced credit than would be paid in cash for smaller amounts of good meat.

FOOD—A PERSONAL PROBLEM

This chapter has been lengthy by necessity. Buying food presents many important and potentially interesting problems in nutrition, economics, and sheer buying strategy. Beyond the basics of preparing a healthful diet for a family or of simply eating well, food shopping offers great opportunities to find imaginative solutions to the problem of obtaining nourishing, healthful food.

At the level of government and law reform, our review of the science and business of food raises important questions as to whether government intervention in the food market helps or hurts the consumer. Food grades are potentially helpful, but the proliferation of inconsistent grade standards (when the mark "Grade A" indicates only the second or third highest grade, for example) under the auspices of the U.S. Department of Agriculture is certainly of little benefit to the food shopper. In the food industry, as much as in any other area of government, consumers should be aware of pertinent developments and should make their interests felt.

SUMMARY

1 Although Americans have a high average level of income, their nutrition is often inadequate.

2 As income rises, the percentage of income spent on food declines. This is known as Engel's Law.

3 Nearly one-fifth of everyone's food budget is spent on nonfood items.

4 There are over 50 essential nutrients, including vitamins, fats, proteins, and carbohydrates.

5 Vitamins can be classified as fat-soluble and water-soluble. Fat-soluble vitamins are stored by and can accumulate in the body. Water-soluble vitamins are fragile, easily destroyed, and excreted daily. Overdoses of fat-soluble vitamins are particularly hazardous.

6 The principal fat-soluble vitamins are A, D, E, and K. Major water-soluble vitamins are ascorbic acid (vitamin C), thiamine (B_1), riboflavin (B_2), niacin, pyridoxine (B_6), folacin, cobalamin (B_{12}), and pantothenic acid.

7 "Organic foods" are grown without the use of synthetic fertilizers, pesticides, or herbicides and are processed without additives. Because organic farming is less efficient than standard commercial farming, organic foods are more costly than nonorganic foods. There is no nutritional difference between the two, but organic foods grown near the markets in which they are sold may be fresher and therefore tastier. Processed organic foods are susceptible to a higher than average risk of spoilage because they contain no chemical preservatives.

8 Packaging is costly to industry and consumers alike. The 1966 Fair Packaging and Labeling Act standardized container sizes and eliminated many deceptions in packaging. Still a problem with packaged foods is the fact that packing liquids are counted in net weight. Labeling in terms of drained or dry weight would be more informative to the consumer.

9 Current law requires that all processed foods either conform to government ingredient standards (the identity standard) or list ingredients in order of decreasing weight. A percentage breakdown of a recipe's contents is not required by law.

10 Unit pricing is not required by federal law, although many large grocery chains and local grocers provide it for their customers. Unit pricing is a great

help to shoppers, but it ceases to be useful when dealing with processed foods that list net weights instead of dry weights.

11 Open dating of all perishable food products is not compulsory, but it would be of great help to consumers.

12 Nutritional labeling is now mandatory on all packaged and processed foods. Food and Drug Administration Rules require processors to disclose the percentages of the Recommended Dietary Allowance (RDA) of major vitamins and protein that their products satisfy.

13 Food inspection is generally mandatory for all products that are moved across state lines. And today, nearly all meat products in intrastate markets as well must satisfy federal standards. Unfortunately, inspection services often have been inadequate and even dishonest. Food-grading standards are provided by the U.S. Department of Agriculture. Although consistent for any one product, these grades are inconsistent when applied to products in general. Consistent standards and simple A, B, C, . . . or 1, 2, 3, . . . grades should be adopted.

14 Additives are classified as intentional or incidental. Intentional additives make food more attractive and/or give it a longer shelf-life. Incidental additives enter food as residues from agricultural chemicals or as filth. Current Food and Drug Administration Standards permit the use of intentional additives that are Generally Recognized as Safe (GRAS) or that are within permissive contamination limits.

15 Retail food selling is dominated by chain stores, which control retail outlets through horizontal mergers and food processors through vertical mergers.

16 Food sales offer reduced prices, but stores adjust their sales mix to compensate for their current price reductions.

17 Private-label goods are less expensive than national brands.

18 Convenience foods bear high markups for conveniences that are often more apparent than real.

Suggestions for Further Reading

Cross, Jennifer. *The Supermarket Trap.* Bloomington, Ind.: Indiana University Press, 1970.

Darrah, L. B. *Food Marketing.* New York: Ronald Press, 1967.

Guthrie, H. A. *Introductory Nutrition,* 3rd ed. St. Louis: C. V. Mosby, 1975.

Hall, Ross H. *Food for Nought: The Decline of Nutrition,* new ed. New York: Harper & Row, 1974.

Hunter, B.T. *Consumer Beware: Your Food and What's Being Done to It.* New York: Macmillan, 1970.

Mowbray, A. Q. *The Thumb on the Scale.* Philadelphia: J. B. Lippincott, 1967.

The Consumer Workshop

1 Suppose that you've been asked to give a 20-minute talk at a local community meeting on the ways in which shoppers can reduce their food bills while

maintaining or even improving the nutrition obtained for the money spent. Prepare an outline of what you will say.

2 Food shopping can be considered an adversary process in which the food shopper confronts the entire food industry on the grocery store battleground. From this point of view, the food sellers' weapons include chemistry (for example making old meat look fresh), packaging (for example, making a few ounces look like a few pounds), psychology (for example, placing "impulse" items at hand or eye level), and store design (for example, forcing the shopper to move in a pattern that is most likely to maximize sales). With what weapons is the shopper equipped to overcome such artful designs of the supermarket and the industries whose products it sells?

3 Why do many people who earn substantial incomes often eat badly and suffer from undernourishment?

4 Food is graded on its texture, color, size, and other asthetic aspects, but food grades do not indicate nutritional value. Examine your own shopping requirements and list any lower-grade substitutions that it would be advantageous for you to make.

5 Packaging is, at present, one of the most important areas of legislative activity in the food industry. Review the section of this chapter that deals with the Fair Packaging and Labeling Act, and the sections dealing with unit pricing, nutritional labeling, product dating, and grading. Each type of labeling is subject to some government control, but these controls are incomplete. How do you think the consumer's needs can be better served by changes in labeling and grading? What information that is not currently available do you and other consumers require to make intelligent and economical food choices?

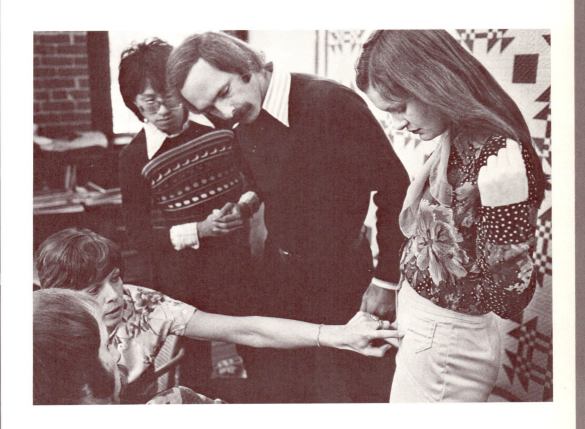

16 CLOTHING AND SELF-EXPRESSION

16 "This year's big fashion is a pronounced chromatic shift from the bright and flashy to the dressier subtle and subdued. . . . Designers . . . sensibly decided that gentlemen should look like gentlemen instead of bougainvilleas."

ESQUIRE MAGAZINE
January 1974

This chapter attempts to make order out of the apparent disorder that confronts the average clothing buyer. We begin with an examination of clothing needs and then we consider the cost and function of an array of clothing, or wardrobe. The function of a piece of clothing depends on its design, manufacture, and material. We analyze each of these factors to determine how the consumer can find good value. Later we examine labels and standards that help the consumer understand the many types of clothing materials. Finally, we examine the various types of clothing vendors to determine the advantages and the disadvantages of the products they offer.

CLOTHING NEEDS AND WARDROBE REQUIREMENTS

Clothing fulfills many needs. It provides basic protection from the elements and special protection when engaging in certain activities, such as sports. Clothing can also confer on the wearer a sense of identity and well-being, or it may merely permit conformance to standards of dress typical of the wearer's group.

A *wardrobe* is the array of clothing a person maintains for various roles and activities in his or her life. More extensive activities usually require more types of clothing. As their incomes rise, people tend to add more variety to their wardrobes. Growing families with extensive wardrobe needs usually endeavor to reuse clothing, handing older children's clothing down to younger children. A young career person may increase wardrobe options by having many accessories to give variety to a basic group of garments, thereby increasing the functions of the wardrobe while keeping clothing costs down.

Value in Clothing: How to Find It

The suitability of any garment to the needs of the wearer depends on:

1 The design of the garment: its external appearance and internal structure
2 Its manufacture: the workmanship and the execution of its design
3 The fiber and fabric of the material used

Design
The design of an item of clothing includes its external lines, the colors used (if they are essential to the design), the amount of body movement that is permitted when the garment fits properly, and the use of internal structural devices such as linings, padding, and sewn-in supporting devices. Some designs allow greater freedom of body movement; others, less movement. Some designs enhance airflow around the body; others restrict it. Designs can make the wearer appear slimmer or heavier, taller or shorter.

A major problem in the sizing of clothing occurs when a manufacturer attempts to make garments fit the entire range of potential customers. Each manufacturer has a concept of, say, a woman's size 10 dress or a man's size 42 suit that depends on what the manufacturer believes is the standard proportion, the most comfortable fit, and the fashion requirements of the garment. This assessment extends beyond the manufacturer's mere estimation of the market, however. Different population subgroups and ethnic groups may vary from the "norm." Fitting everyone with a set range of sizes of women's dresses, for example, may actually require a number of forms in each size. Fitting every man with a size 42 regular suit and 36-inch-waist pants may be impossible. To ensure that their clothes will fit the largest number of customers, manufacturers usually design a line of clothes to accommodate heavier wearers and hope that slimmer wearers will rely on tailoring to take up the slack. Designing for wide tolerances may increase the range of garments, but it may also force consumers to spend more time shopping for clothes that fit really well.

Style changes are an ever-present phenomenon in our society. Clothes that display self-conscious fashion designs become dated more quickly than clothes that exhibit so-called "classic" designs that are less influenced by the current fashion trend. Consumers who wish to avoid rapid obsolescence of style can select garments that flatter them regardless of the moments fashion. Accessories can often make garments appear more up-to-date.

Workmanship

The quality and method of the manufacture of a garment determine its fit, comfort, and durability. Every garment should have regular, close stitching (10–12 stitches per inch), well-formed, clean buttonholes, well-secured fasteners, and evenly matched patterns if a patterned material is used. Trim and cloth parts should be pinked or seamed to reduce fraying. Workmanship is costly but usually is worth paying for because well-made garments last longer and retain a better appearance and shape.

Fabric

The development of synthetic fibers has created many problems for consumers. There are only a few natural fibers—cotton, wool, flax, silk, and jute—and consumers are familiar with their characteristics through much use and experience. Today literally hundreds of new fabrics are produced in chemical plants from such materials as plastics, coal, oil, and sugar. Many of these synthetic fabrics are marketed by manufacturers without adequate testing, and for too long clothing buyers have been forced to conduct product tests at their own expense. Consumers were subjected to unfortunate experiences due to the exaggerated claims of wash-and-wear fabric manufacturers in the late 1950s, and some permanent-press garments today suggest that it is unwise to buy clothes made from fabrics that haven't been on the market for a few years.

Blends of synthetic and natural fibers (usually cotton or wool) increase the thousands of wear-and-care properties that the consumer must understand to make wise clothing selections. Each fiber has particular advantages and disadvantages. Some fibers are blended to improve the usefulness of the resulting fabric. Other blends save the manufacturer or the consumer money. Blending is achieved either by mixing natural fibers, manufactured fibers, or both to make a single yarn or by twisting continuous filaments of synthetic fibers into yarns that can be woven. Pure or blended yarns can also be combined in the process of knitting or weaving the fabric.

GOOD WORKMANSHIP: WHAT TO LOOK FOR

The quality of their construction substantially affects how long most articles of clothing will last. Good fabric suited to the garment's intended use in combination with quality manufacturing tend to assure good value for the consumer's money.

Good stitching is close, uniform, and accurately placed:

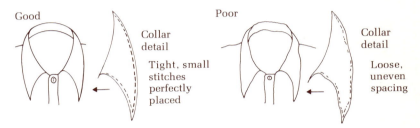

Good

Poor

Collar detail

Tight, small stitches perfectly placed

Collar detail

Loose, uneven spacing

Buttonholes that last are stitched tightly and uniformly around a reinforcing cord at the edge of the buttonhole. On shirts and blouses, very dense, perfect buttonhole sewing replaces reinforcement:

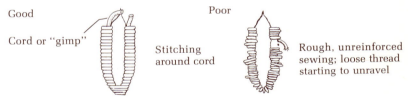

Good

Cord or "gimp"

Poor

Stitching around cord

Rough, unreinforced sewing; loose thread starting to unravel

Hems of all garments should be secured with good, visible stitching or invisible but secure blindstitching. *Pull hem open a bit to check:*

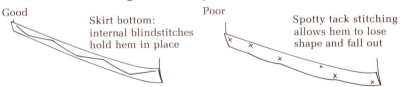

Good

Poor

Skirt bottom: internal blindstitches hold hem in place

Spotty tack stitching allows hem to lose shape and fall out

Plaids and patterns should match on major features of the garment:

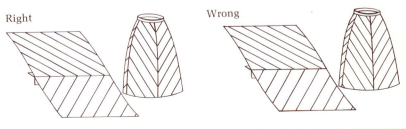

Right

Wrong

> **TYPICAL LABEL REQUIRED BY THE
> TEXTILE FIBER PRODUCTS IDENTIFICATION ACT**
>
> 70% ACRYLIC 30% WOOL
> HAND WASH OR
> MACHINE WASH SEPARATELY
> GENTLE DRY FLAT BLOCK
> TO SIZE DO NOT DRY CLEAN

Fabric Labeling.   Three important federal laws inform consumers about the fabric they buy.   The Wool Products Labeling Act of 1939, the Fur Products Labeling Act of 1951, and the Textile Fiber Products Identification Act, as amended in 1965, broadly require garment manufacturers to state the fiber content of any fabrics used.   These laws protect the consumer against misbranding and false advertising.

The *Textile Fiber Products Identification Act* (TFPIA) is the most important statute to the average garment buyer.   Put into effect in its original form in March 1960, this act requires all textile products to bear a label listing the exact percentage of each fiber in the fabric.   When trademarks and trade names are used, the generic (chemical or scientific name) must also be listed in equally legible print.

Fabric Performance Criteria

The performance of clothing fabrics depends mainly on six critical characteristics: durability, care requirements, color fastness, dimensional stability, finish, and flammability.

Durability.   The durability of any fabric depends on its inherent toughness and its yarn count (the number of threads or yarns per square inch or square centimeter of fabric).   As with a piece of rope, the higher the yarn count and the denser the weave, the longer a piece of fabric will wear generally and the more it will resist abrasion and tearing.   Fabric construction can affect soil holding and soil resistance, creasing, puncture recovery, and odor retention, among other things.

Care Requirements.   Fabrics have different care and cleaning requirements. Not all synthetic fabrics can or should be dry cleaned.   Many synthetics and synthetic blends require special handling to avoid fabric damage.   The care requirements for clothing have been clarified by a Federal Trade Commission Rule that became effective in July 1972. Under federal labeling rules, most items of clothing must bear labels that:

1 Give instructions for regular fabric maintenance
2 Warn against normal care methods that might seem applicable but that are not
3 Remain attached and legible for the life of the garment
4 Are readily accessible within the garment or in its sales package

Care instructions apply to the entire garment, including nondetachable trim and linings. Detachable linings or fittings must be labeled with separate care instructions. Some items of clothing do not need to be labeled. Exempted from Federal Trade Commission care-labeling requirements are some hosiery, headwear, footwear, handwear, fur and leather items, disposable clothing, items that require no maintenance, and completely washable garments intended to retail for $3 or less (and exempted by the Federal Trade Commission on the manufacturer's application).

"For generations we've used wool and grasscloth, but for true colors and durability we now find there's nothing like Acrilan."

FIBER AND FABRIC FACTS

Natural Fibers

Group	Generic name	Trademarks	Characteristics
Vegetable (Cellulose)	Cotton	COMFORTABLE · CAREFREE COTTON	Medium strength, durable, absorbent, easily dyed, excellent launderability. Wrinkles readily unless protected by finish; can be damaged by mildew.
	Linen (flax)		Same as cotton but has superior strength (especially when wet); very absorbent.
Animal (Protein)	Wool and other animal hair fibers. Angora, Alpaca, Camel, Cashmere, Mohair, Vicuna	PURE VIRGIN WOOL	Warm, resilient, medium strength, absorbent, dyes readily, flame resistant, dries slowly, felts in hot water with agitation.
	Silk		Fine, strong fiber with lustrous finish, drapes well, absorbent, dyes readily; damaged by chlorine bleaches, perspiration, and sunlight.
Mineral	Asbestos		Noncombustible; poor conductor of heat and electricity. Can be woven into fabrics for safety purposes.

Synthetic Fibers

Group	Generic name	Trademarks	Characteristics
Cellulose	Rayon (Cupra) (Viscose) (Model)	* Bemberg * Coloray * Evlan * Darelle * Enkrome * Durafil * Fibro * Avril * Zantrel * Vincel	Absorbent, dyes readily, moth resistant; special finishes give properties of crease resistance and water repellency. Yarns can be medium or high strength.
	Acetate	* Celacloud * Celara * Chromspun * Quilticel	Adequate strength, moderate absorbency, good drape, little or no shrinkage, moth resistant; can be solution-dyed; melts at high temperatures.
	Triacetate	* Arnel * Trilan	Higher wet strength than regular acetate (diacetate); withstands higher temperatures, dyes readily; resists shrinkage, moths; takes durable pleats.
Chemical Compounds	Nylon (Polyamide)	* Antron * Nomex * Cadon * Qiana * Cantrece * Unel * Courtauld's * Unel 5 nylon * Union Carbide nylon * Cumuloft * 501/N	Superior strength and abrasion resistance. Lightweight and thermoplastic (yarns can be heat-set for stretch or texture; fabrics for smooth finish resistant to shrinkage). Quick drying fabrics.

Common uses	Care
Most widely used fiber alone or in blends with synthetic fibers for all types of apparel and household fabrics; all weights from sheer to heavy duty; also carpets, sheets, towels, bandages, canvas, and industrial uses.	Usually washable; consult labels for treatment when a special finish is present. Launder or dry clean according to instructions. Iron damp on wrong side with hot iron. Cotton bleaches readily, except some finishes and colorings.
Warm-weather apparel; blends with other fibers; table linens.	Usually washable; consult labels for treatment when a special finish is present. Launder or dry clean according to instructions. Iron damp on wrong side with hot iron. Bleaches readily, except some finishes.
Suitings, coatings, dress fabrics, felts, sweaters, socks, and other woven and knitted cloths of all weights; carpets, blankets, etc. Also important in blends with synthetic fibers.	Dry clean, unless labeled or known to be washable. Hang carefully and "rest" between wearings. Launder sweaters in lukewarm water, with little rubbing or wringing. Lay flat to dry and ease into shape. For sweaters labeled "machine washable," follow label instructions.
Fine fabrics, both woven and knitted, for many types of apparel and household uses. Often blended with other fibers.	Dry clean, unless labeled or known to be washable. Iron on wrong side with press cloth, using a moderately hot iron. Frequent cleaning desirable.
Safety clothing, stage curtains, fire hoses, and many industrial uses.	
Used alone or in blends with natural or other synthetic fibers in all kinds of woven or knitted fabrics for all manner of apparel and household uses. High-strength yarns used for tire cord, other industrial uses.	Dry clean fabrics unless labeled washable. When laundered, can be ironed following instructions for cotton; iron damp on wrong side. Avoid chlorine bleaches.
Used alone or in blends with natural or synthetic fibers in all kinds of woven or knitted fabrics for all manner of apparel and household uses. Acetate tricot is also widely used for bonding to other fabrics.	If washable, launder by hand and do not wring; iron damp on wrong side at low temperature. Avoid chlorine bleaches. Readily dry cleaned.
Used alone or in blends with natural or synthetic fibers in all kinds of woven or knitted fabrics for all manner of apparel and household uses.	Launder by hand or machine in warm (not hot) water; easily ironed (some fabrics need very little ironing). Readily dry cleaned.
Most widely used synthetic fiber, suitable for either sheer hosiery or strongest rope; in fabrics for all kinds of apparel and household use; textured yarns in sweaters, stretch fabrics, carpets; high-strength yarns in fish nets, industrial fabrics, and tire cord.	Washable by hand or machine in soap or detergent. Drip dry when hand washing. If automatic dryer is used, keep temperature low. Little or no ironing needed; iron at low temperature. Wash white items alone and turn knitted garments inside out when laundering.

FIBER AND FABRIC FACTS (*Continued*)

Synthetic Fibers (cont'd)

Group	Generic name	Trademarks	Characteristics
	Polyester	* Terylene * Fortrel * Trevira * Tergal * Dacron * Tetoron * Kodel * Crimplene	Shares strength, light weight, and abrasion resistance with other thermoplastic fibers. Resilient and versatile in blending with natural and other synthetic fibers.
	Acrylic	* Orlon * Acrilan * Courtelle * Creslan * Zefran	Also thermoplastic, with all quick drying, easy-care properties. Also has great bulking power for soft, warm, and light weight fabrics; takes brilliant, fast colors.
	Modacrylic	* Dynel * Verel * Kanekalon * Teklan	Resilient and resistant to chemicals. Lightweight, soft and wrinkle resistant.
	Chlorofibres (Saran)	* Rovana * Velon	Naturally water repellent, abrasion resistant, strong. Resists sunlight, moths, and mildew. Colorfast.
	(Vinyon)	* Rhovyl	High resistance to chemicals; flameproof, but melts at low temperatures.
	Vinal (Vinylal)	* Kuvalon * Mewlon	Strong and resists abrasion; soft, warm feel; flame resistant.
	Olefin (Polypropylene)	* Celaspun * Protel * Herculon	Lightweight, strong, thermoplastic, and resilient. Resists sunlight and chemical deterioration. Can be solution dyed.
	(Polyethylene)	* Pex * Voplex	As above except difficult to dye and melts at low temperatures; important plastic.
	Nytril	* Darvan	Soft and resilient, but melts at low temperatures. Good wrinkle resistance.
Protein	Azlon	* Fibrolane	Warm, resilient, soft; keeps whiteness, dyes readily. Low strength; felts in hot water with agitation.
Polymer	Rubber (Lastrile)	* Lastex	Will stretch to many times its original length, whether manufactured from natural or synthetic rubber. Damaged by light, heat, and bleach.
	Spandex (Thanelast)	* Lycra * Vyrene * Unel	Exceptionally strong, durable, excellent restraining power, yet lightweight; high elasticity and recovery ability. Can be readily dyed.
	Anidex	* ANIM/8	Elastic fiber with superior resistance to heat, sunlight, and chemicals, but with less elasticity.

Common uses	Care
Widely used in blends with natural fibers in all kinds of fabrics, particularly those given durable press finishes. Also used alone in such apparel and household fabrics as curtains, drapes, or carpets and in such industrial uses as tires, firehoses.	Washable by hand or machine in soap or detergent. Drip dry when hand washing. If automatic dryer is used, keep temperature low. Little or no ironing needed; iron at low temperature. Wash white items alone and turn knitted garments inside out when laundering.
Knits of all types, sweaters, half hose, dresses; also wool-like woven fabrics, deep-pile fabrics, and carpets.	Same easy care washability as above, except for deep pile fabrics or artificial fur fabrics which should be cleaned by fur cleaning processes, unless labelled washable.
Mainly used in carpets, synthetic furs, and chemically resistant work clothing; also in wigs and artificial "hairpieces.	Same easy-care washability as above, except use only cool iron. Deep-pile fabrics or artificial fur fabrics should be cleaned by a fur-cleaning process, unless labeled washable.
Auto seat covers, outdoor furniture upholstery, webbing.	Wash off with soap and water. Do not iron.
Draperies, knitwear, pile fabrics, and industrial uses.	Launder in lukewarm water, drip dry, and use only cool iron; deep-pile fabrics should be dry cleaned.
Primarily industrial uses, but also used in blends with cotton and rayon for apparel.	Easy-care, quick drying material, but iron only dry on warm setting. Fabric will stiffen if it is ironed damp.
Carpeting, sweaters, hosiery, knitting yarns, cordage, and upholstery.	Care instructions as for other thermoplastic wash-and-wear fibers. Do not dry clean. If ironing is required, keep temperature low.
Limited use in textiles; some outdoor furniture and auto fabrics.	Wash off with soap and water. Do not iron.
Used in blends with wool, in knitwear, and in pile fabrics.	Washable by hand in warm (not hot) water; if ironing is required, keep temperature low.
Used primarily in blends with wool; sometimes with rayon.	Launder by hand, with care, following instructions for wool.
Used mainly as the core around which yarns of other fibers are spun for foundation garments, surgical supports, and elastic webbing.	Launder by hand in warm water, drip dry; iron at low temperature. Avoid caustic soda and chlorine bleaches.
Foundation garments, swimsuit fabrics, support hoisery, and all kinds of core-spun knits, stretch fabrics, and apparel.	Wash in warm water by hand and drip dry. Can be machine dried, but only at low temperature. Iron at low temperature . Avoid chlorine bleaches.
Used to provide stretch qualities for fabrics and apparel.	Launder following instructions for Spandex (above).

Synthetic Fibers (cont'd)

Group	Generic name	Trademarks	Characteristics
Glass	Glass	* Fiberglas * Vitron	Good tensile strength; unaffected by moisture and sunlight; excellent chemical resistance and insulating properties; noninflammable.
Metallic	Metallic	* Lamé * Lurex * Mylar	Nontarnishable, washable when protected by film. Can be produced in colors as well as silver, gold.

Federal Trade Commission care-labeling rules inform the consumer of how costly it will be to care for otherwise comparable items of clothing. If one garment must be dry cleaned and another can be hand- or machine-washed, or if one garment must be ironed and another is permanent press, the care requirements in terms of money and time differ appreciably for the two items. The choice then depends on the time and funds the consumer has available compared to his or her estimates of the different values of the two garments. The consumer who reads the labels will make an informed choice.

Colorfastness. Fabrics retain colors in varying degrees when they are washed or dry cleaned. There is no uniform industry standard for fading, yellowing, or bleaching. The American National Standards Institute (ANSI) has established a standard, known as L-22, that specifies colorfastness expectations for several dozen apparel uses, but this standard has not been adopted by all clothing manufacturers. When buying saturated colors and pastels, it is important to determine and to evaluate claims about the color durability of the fabric. If a garment is colorfast in the presence of sunlight and/or perspiration, for example, this fact will probably be listed on a hangtag or a label. Most colors are fairly durable. If they are not, the consumer should return the article to the place of purchase, because some mistake may have been made in the dyeing process. Many bright- or dark-colored fabrics contain extra amounts of dye that must be washed or bled out. Such bleeding usually does not change the original shade of the fabric.

Dimensional Stability. Dimensional stability is a continuing problem in fabric design. There are no industry-wide standards for shrinking or stretching. Some size-stabilizing processes, such as Sanforizing, are fairly reliable; others are not. The exact meaning of "preshrunk" is unknown and can vary among textile mills and garment manufacturers. There is a need to define the many terms manufacturers use to infer that the sizes or shapes of garments won't alter after they are worn. Appreciable shrinking usually indicates inferior manufacturing. If a garment does shrink appreciably, it should be returned to the place of purchase.

Common uses	Care
Draperies, sheer curtains, and industrial fabrics.	Launder in warm water with mild soap or detergent. Drip dry without wringing or flexing. No ironing needed.
Decorative fabrics and trimmings; solid lamé or glitter effects added to other fabrics.	When used in fabrics that are washable, these yarns need no special care. Can be dry cleaned.

Source: Canadian Textiles Institute, Montreal.

Finish. When shopping for clothes it is important to check the finish of the items under consideration.   Finishes are treatments applied to a fabric, once it has been woven or knitted, to obtain a particular appearance or to make the material perform in a certain way.   Finishes that can change the surface quality of fabrics include *napping,* a process that raises the fiber ends on the surface of a fabric, and embossing, a process that changes the surface texture of the cloth. Other finishes can make the product resistant to stains (Scotchgarding is a well-known example), moths and mildew, water, static, flames, or creasing.   Some finishes are available for home use; these include water repellents, fabric softeners, and antistatic products.

Flammability. Flammability is an important aspect of clothing manufacture, especially in garments worn by children and the elderly.   All natural fibers are flammable unless they are specially treated.   Most synthetic fabrics will also burn under certain conditions.   (Some manufactured fibers have been marketed that are even explosive!) How easily a material will catch fire depends on its fiber, its weight, its weave or knit (the flame will burn faster if air can circulate within the weave), its surface (fluffy surfaces burn faster than plain or level surfaces), and its design and trim.   Moisture content is an important determinant of flammability in all fabrics, because the dryer the cloth, the faster it will burn.   Of course, a fabric's susceptibility to fire depends largely on the care with which it is worn near a flame!

The likelihood of clothing catching fire is a factor that consumers rarely consider when shopping.   Lives can be saved and major injuries minimized if fire and electrical burns cannot be spread by clothing.   Electricians who touch high-voltage lines may suffer second-degree burns on their hands if they are properly clothed; wearing garments that ignite, they can and do often incur third-degree burns over 85% or more of their bodies.   Children playing with matches may suffer only slight burns if they are wearing flame-retardant clothing; if they are wearing clothes that burn rapidly, they may be badly injured.

The problem of flammability is as diverse as the range of garments and fabrics that must be treated or modified to reduce their susceptibility to fire.   As we noted earlier, each cloth and garment must meet many different wear needs.

We want our clothes to be durable, to be warm in winter and cool in summer, to resist spotting and creasing, to be inexpensive, colorful, and so forth. Each of these requirements is of more immediate concern to the consumer than fire resistance, for the chances are that fire will not strike. Yet the factor of flammability must be considered.

Some Fabrics Are Naturally Flammable

If all fabrics were required to be highly flame-retardant, fewer textiles and garments would be available to consumers. Many natural fibers, such as cotton, are quite flammable. For example, consumers prefer bedclothes and blankets that are fluffy and hold air. Rigid and severe fire-resistance standards would compromise these and similar fabric and clothing characteristics. However, three areas of clothing production can be identified in which the variability of standards can be reduced and in which flame-retardance is extremely important:

1 Special work clothes for hazardous occupations or activities
2 Clothes for the elderly
3 Children's clothing

Workers who are subject to fire exposure simply require outerwear that offers protection from the machines and processes involved in their jobs. Special-protection clothing can readily meet flammability requirements because it must satisfy few other needs. The elderly and infirm face substantial hazards from careless smoking and even from movement near, say, hot stoves or radiators. And children are naturally careless, tend to have poor judgment, and can't really evaluate their clothing needs. Flammability standards for these consumers can be usefully and wisely imposed on manufacturers as a public safety measure.

Yet it is important to point out that almost any fabric will burn if it is exposed to flame long enough. Reducing flammability standards to total flame and fire resistance would prove quite expensive for the clothing industry and for consumers. On the other hand, industry improvements have been made; today some fabrics exist that only char slowly in direct flame, with their fire dying out immediately after the open-flame sources are removed.

The Flammable Fabrics Act of 1953. The U.S. Flammable Fabrics Act of 1953, amended in 1967, removed many of the most flammable fabrics from the market. Garments that would burst into flame when exposed to a small, relatively cold flame for one-tenth of a second have been excluded from retail sale. As a result, children's clothing is now more flame-retardant.

Consumers should understand that flame retardance, which has its costs both in cash and choice, is a performance improvement. Having to pay more for a somewhat smaller selection of safer clothing can be considered an insurance charge. Paying a few dollars more per year for fire protection in clothing is not unlike buying fire insurance for a house.

SHOPPING SOURCES

Clothing can be purchased at retail from a variety of sources, including department stores, mail-order and catalog firms, variety, chain, and specialty clothing shops, and boutiques, to name only a few. Discriminating buyers can have most garments tailor-made and thereby closely control the fabrics and the colors of their clothes. Retailers' profit markups range from comparatively low markups at discount stores, to "standard" markups at department stores, to large profit margins at some "exclusive" stores and boutiques.

Speciality stores tend to cater to a certain type of customer and may therefore stock a better selection of merchandise for a particular need or taste than a department store would. *Discount stores* offer lower prices but tend to carry goods that turn over fast. Discount-store merchandise is often lower in quality than what can be purchased at better department stores.

In general, *department stores* employ a standard markup on clothing of about 50% of the retail price, or twice what the store paid for the goods. *Discount stores* may reduce their markup by 10–15%, but they may also sell cheaper goods at regular prices. Some discounting is sham, and customers actually find themselves paying regular prices for less convenience and less service. Boutiques and specialty shops often vary their markups to match market prices. If a specialty store can sell a garment for more than a 50% markup, it may price the item at the highest amount that the market will bear. Department stores and major chain catalog firms don't usually have the time or the desire to do this.

Why Do Costs Vary? Overhead is important in determining what the markup must be to yield an expected return on sales for the firm. Department stores that offer a reliable "money back if not satisfied" policy, 30-day charge accounts without interest, free delivery, gift wrapping, lavish advertising, wide selections of merchandise, and expensive decor can incur service costs that equal as much as 28% of their retail gross sales. Transportation and delivery can add an average of 14–16% to the prices the stores themselves pay for their goods, in which case a 50% department-store markup may be reduced to only 6–8% profits after costs. As a rule, discount stores offer fewer services, so their goods are worthwhile only if they are comparable in quality to those found in department stores.

A Strategy for Saving Money What can consumers do to make the best use of their clothing budgets in the next few years? First, it is wise to avoid fashion extremes or fads. Well-made garments from good, durable materials may be relatively expensive, but when they are cut to the basic proportions of the body and properly fitted, they can be in style for several years. It's possible to accent the part of a garment that is currently in style with a piece of jewelry, a belt, a scarf, or some other accessory. Men's clothes that are cut to body proportions and are not exaggerated in style—the middle ground of width and length—can wear well over the years. Colors should be selected on the basis of their fashionable and functional durability. Expensive basics in loud colors are vulnerable to early fashion death.

It pays to visit sales and to be informed about current prices. In 1975 retail market analysts found that clothing budget expenses reflected an average increase of about 20%. Many consumers may begin to purchase cheaper clothing made from poorer fabrics to stabilize their clothing expenses; others may reason that if good garments are too expensive, they may as well spend a little more money to buy fine garments. Many people can still remember when a full-sized Ford cost $2000. Today a family-size Ford with power options may cost $5000. Many buyers feel that if they must spend that much money, they may as well spend a few hundred dollars more and buy a Buick. This curious behavior is one response that today's consumers are making to increased inflation. It is difficult to determine whether it's better to choose cheaper clothing or expensive clothing rather than garments of medium quality and durability, because such decisions are based on individual preferences. But we can point out the buying patterns of families in the 1974–1975 food-price escalation. As many foods increased in price during this period, consumers rushed to buy them, assuming—sometimes accurately, sometimes inaccurately—that further price increases were inevitable. Some people hoarded beef and pork; others went without these meats. However no one can give up all foods, and it's hard to avoid buying clothes for a growing family.

THE CLOTHES-WISE CONSUMER: POINTS TO REMEMBER

Know Your Clothing Needs. Select clothes that you can wear often. Buy outfits that will complement your wardrobe. Avoid multipiece garments if you already have several of the complementary items in sufficient quantities and colors. Don't stock up on special formal apparel or sportswear if your opportunities to use them are limited.

Plan Your Wardrobe. Try to spread your clothing expenses over an extended period of time. It's harder to cope with your budget when you have to buy or replace 50% of your clothes at one time. Instead, try to maintain a clothing fund for special buys and sales. You can buy winter clothes in spring, summer wear in the fall, and make the most of your money if you always have a reserve clothing budget on hand.

Allocate a Portion of Your Budget for Clothes. If you are a student and your college expenditures are paid by your parents, you can spend a substantial portion of your discretionary income or funds on clothes (say, 30%). However, if

you have other major expenses—a car, perhaps, or a family with growing needs—you may wish to reduce the amount of money you spend on clothes.

Resist Fashion Extremes or Fads. Garments that emphasize the most radical features of current design or that are made from fabrics dyed in the latest, most unusual colors are the clothes most likely to go out of style quickly. Build a wardrobe of basic outfits of durable cut and color. Styles that conform to the geometry of the body and colors that don't glare are serviceable for many years. For example, it's always possible to give a garment a "high-waisted" look by wearing a belt conspicuously above the waist.

Select Medium-priced, Serviceable Garments. In the long run, the best clothing values are garments made from durable fabrics rather than cheap clothes. For lasting wear, seams should be tightly and evenly stitched (at least 10–12 stitches per inch). Look inside the garment to determine if it is well made: are there even runs of uniform stitching, neatly cut or pinked trimmings and cloth parts, securely fastened buttons with thread that doesn't fray when it is rubbed slightly? Check the fabric itself for flaws. You can usually find

good clothing values in the medium-price range—garments that are priced above the cheap fabrics but well below clothes bearing the labels of expensive and famous designers and manufacturers.

Buy Clothes That Flatter *You*. Many of the more durable fashions are proportioned to the body. The middle ground of proportion lasts. Dresses should not make the waist appear too far from where it really is. Men's suit lapels should not cover the entire chest and seem to extend beyond it or peep out from the collar like a bit of trim. Pant cuffs and flares should be of a comfortable size: those that seem to devour the wearer's feet are a waste of cloth and can be hazardous. Tight pant legs that don't leave room for socks are restrictive and inconvenient.

Check Fiber Content and Washing Instructions. Consider expense when buying fabrics that require frequent and expensive dry cleaning. As beautiful as they are, white silk suits are clearly not within the confines of the average student's budget, either in terms of purchase price or maintenance expenditure. Wool wears well, but it must often be specially laundered or dry cleaned. Some manufactured fibers can be washed easily by hand but may not wear well.

Ensure Proper Fit. A bargain is not a bargain if it isn't your size. Children's clothes should either be slightly large when purchased to permit growth or encompass growth features in their design. Inspecting clothing labels before purchase may indicate if an additional allowance should be made for shrinkage (except in the case of most denim clothes).

Compare Prices Among Different Stores. Try to determine if a bargain sale represents a true saving or if it is just a promotional gimmick. If you do not have a variety of stores to choose from, try to find a comparable garment in the catalogs of major mail-order firms.

Shop at End-of-Season Sales. Merchants frequently reduce prices to their own wholesale costs to free valuable shelf and storage space and to avoid retaining out-of-date goods. Careful shopping at such sales can result in substantial savings.

Consider Making Your Own Clothes. Many garments can be made inexpensively on a sewing machine. Accessories can be knitted with low-cost yarn in a few hours. Family members and/or friends may enjoy sewing for you if needlework isn't your specialty. Making your own clothes offers you a greater choice of fabrics and colors and better control of size and fit. Sewing can be a way to show your individuality. As a hobby, sewing can provide a sense of fulfillment and the satisfaction of doing something well. New sewing machines can be purchased for $50–$300, or more. The price reflects variety of the stitches that the machine can produce. Good used machines, particularly basic industrial models, may cost as little as $25.

Avoid Children's Clothes That Will Be Quickly Outgrown. Much of the infantwear industry operates on the assumption that parents, relatives, and friends adore children and will purchase large quantities of lavish children's wear. Clearly, it is unwise to buy clothes for anyone on an inefficient, wasteful, "the sky's the limit" basis.

SUMMARY

1 Clothing can confer on the wearer a sense of identity and well-being, match standards of dress, or merely provide protection from the elements.
2 A wardrobe is a person's total array of clothing.
3 The value of clothing depends on design, manufacture, and fabric and fiber.
4 Design consists of lines, colors, fit, and internal structure of the garment.
5 Size standards are not uniform. One manufacturer's size may fit well; another's may not. Each manufacturer has its own standard of fit.
6 Stitching, detail and pattern matching are three ways to determine if a garment is well made.
7 Fabrics can be made of natural or synthetic fibers, or blends of the two.
8 The fiber composition of any fabric must be disclosed under the Wool Products Labeling Act, the Fur Products Labeling Act, or the Textile Fiber Products Labeling Act.

9 Fabric performance depends on:
    1 Durability
    2 Care requirements
    3 Colorfastness
    4 Dimensional stability
    5 Finish
    6 Flammability.

10 Durability depends on the inherent toughness of the yarn and the yarn count (number of threads or yarns in any square measure of fabric).

11 Care requirements can be determined by examining fabric tags for care and cleaning instructions. These tags are required by Federal Trade Commission rules effective since July 1972.

12 Colorfastness can often be determined from the fabric label or hangtag. Most dyes in current use are colorfast when the garment is properly cleaned.

13 Dimensional stability is an inexact term; uniform shrinkage standards have not yet been established.

14 Finishes may be soft, hard, spot-resistant, or flame-retardant, among others.

15 Flammability is determined by fabric weave or knit, surface, garment design, and trim. Flammability is a particular concern in the manufacture of special work clothes, garments for the elderly, and children's clothing. In making garments, other qualities should be sacrificed to achieve flame-retardant finishes. The U.S. Flammable Fabrics Act sets flame-retardance standards for clothing.

16 Clothes stores vary in service, variety, price, and markup.

17 The rules of good clothes management are:
    1 Know your clothing needs
    2 Plan your wardrobe
    3 Allocate a portion of your budget for clothes
    4 Resist fashion extremes or fads
    5 Select medium-priced, serviceable garments
    6 Buy clothes that flatter you
    7 Check fiber content and washing instructions
    8 Ensure proper fit
    9 Compare prices among different stores
    10 Shop at end-of-season sales
    11 Consider making your own clothes
    12 Avoid children's clothes that will be quickly outgrown

Suggestions for Further Reading

American Fabrics, "Make No Mistake About It, Consumerism is a Live Issue." Spring–Summer 1971, pp. 43–48.

Davies, Jessica. *Ready-made Miracle.* New York: Putnam, 1967.

Horn, Marilyn J. *The Second Skin.* Boston: Houghton Mifflin, 1975.

Jarnow, Jeanette, and Judelle, Beatrice. *Inside the Fashion Business.* New York: Wiley, 1965.

Roach, M.E., and Eicher, J. *The Visible Self: Perspectives on Dress.* Englewood Cliffs, N.J.: Prentice-Hall, 1973.

Ryan, Mary S. *Clothing: A Study in Human Behavior.* New York: Holt Rinehart & Winston, 1966.

Tate, Mildred, and Glisson, Oris. *Family Clothing.* New York: Wiley, 1961.

The Consumer Workshop

1 Compare the desire to be *unique* (dressing differently than your friends do) with the desire to be *similar* (staying in style and dressing as your friends do). Which desire predominates in your circle of friends? Which desire, if either, influences your wardrobe selection?

2 "Infatuation with one's own body is an infantile trait that . . . persists in many an adult's subconscious . . . The ethics of exploiting it . . . to sell goods . . . are something else." (*Fortune* as cited by Vance Packard in *The Hidden Persuaders,* forepiece to Ch. 8). Is this a sufficient explanation for clothing design and style? Or do other forces affect how and why we buy clothing and build wardrobes?

3 You have $500 with which you plan to buy a new winter wardrobe containing about 20 garments. You'll need special clothes for skiing and for formal dress, as well as school and/or work clothes for class and for your part-time job as a salesclerk. You want to get the most for your money. What clothes should you buy and what characteristics should you consider in terms of design, manufacture, and fabric?

4 How can consumers with limited budgets get the most immediate and long-run value for their money when shopping for clothes?

5 "You can't tell about clothes. A store's reputation is the only guide," Rachel claims. "No," responds her friend Claudia, "you can check the cloth, quality, and label of any garment and get a pretty fair idea of what you're buying." Comment on each point of view. Where do you stand on this question?

17
A HOME OF YOUR OWN:
RENTING AND SHARING

" Miserable and disreputable housing conditions may do more than spread disease and crime and immorality. They may also suffocate the spirit by reducing the people who live there to the status of cattle. They may make living an almost insufferable burden. They may also be an ugly sore, a blight on the community which robs it of charm, which makes it a place from which men turn. The misery of housing may despoil a community as an open sewer may ruin a river. "

WILLIAM O. DOUGLAS
Associate Justice
United States Supreme Court, 1939–1975

Establishing an independent residence is a part of almost everyone's experience as a young adult. In this chapter, we discuss the social problems involved in renting and sharing dwellings. We examine the effects of living in groups and the relationships between landlords and tenants; we also investigate the landlord and tenant laws in North America and then suggest some directions for current and future housing reform.

REASONS TO RENT

There are many reasons for renting instead of buying living space. Some people simply need less space than even a small house offers. Others find that they haven't the cash to make down payments on or purchase a home or a cooperative apartment. In a few highly developed areas, there are simply no more houses or apartments for sale, and would-be homeowners must settle for long-term leases. Young people often prefer rentals because they are temporary commitments. The city apartment has a mystique of independence and style that is highly appealing to men and women who have recently launched careers or marriages and have not yet acquired family responsibilities. Older persons at the other end of the family life cycle may prefer to be free from certain responsibilities of maintenance that are associated with ownership.

Sharing with Care

Living with others requires some adjustment, but with care and patience, compatible people and situations can usually be found, even in the largest of cities. A renter may share some facilities—and perhaps grocery bills—with others, so it's essential that people who live together share at least some of the same tastes and values. Of course, this doesn't mean that everyone must be the same in

every respect; different people lend variety to a neighborhood and can also contribute special abilities, permitting tasks to be divided among those who share a single apartment or house.

Successfully adjusting to the needs of life within a community makes it possible to enjoy the economic benefits of being a tenant. Renters who share utilities and land—and perhaps duties and food—save time and money, at least in the short run. Savings can then be spent on other things, such as education, a car, clothes, or entertainment (a pet, a health club, a crafts class). People who live together can become companions, and personal enrichment can result from cooperative living.

THE TENANT AND THE LANDLORD

Relationships between landlord and tenant are as varied as types of people. A landlord may be an elderly person eager to rent a single room to a student; a dentist who owns entire blocks of apartments as a tax-deferral device; or a corporation that rents some of the tens of thousands of apartments that surround major cities.

The Role of the Law   The laws that pertain to landlords and tenants in the United States and Canada were originally modeled after English farm leases in the fourteenth century. From this common point in history stem at least 60 different interpretations of landlord and tenant law in North America, for each of the 50 states and the 10 Canadian provinces. Courts and governments have applied English law in various local situations, thereby producing laws that represent different compromises of interest, politics, local conditions, and legal precedent. Like other laws, landlord and tenant laws are always being readjusted to meet changing social situations. Yet there are many contemporary social situations in which landlord and tenant law doesn't function well (for example, the rights of administrators to enter and inspect rooms and occupants in college dormitories).

THE CURRENT MARKET

Federal, state, and local laws are designed to regulate economic forces in the rentable housing market. Landlords want to maximize their profits by keeping maintenance costs as low as possible so that they won't suffer undue depreciation and lose tenants to competing landlords. Tenants want the best facilities and maintenance possible for their money.

When the landlord and the tenant bargain with relatively equal knowledge and resources, an equally beneficial agreement can result. Such an equality of bargaining power between landlord and tenant exists in industrial leasing and in some types of agricultural land leasing. Businesspeople know the costs of various sites for manufacturing, wholesale, or retail trade. Farmers who live in a specific region are familiar with the soil quality, drainage, and crop-risk factors of various fields. The reputation and experience of each group in land dealings may be known to the other group.

Of course, there are exceptions to these equitable customs. For example, on many occasions poor sharecropping farmers have been forced by circumstance to work inferior fields that yield poor returns. In the nineteenth century, vast tracts of land were given to the railroads to induce their expansion across North America, but these very railroads often used their total ownership of town sites to force small business owners to pay excessive rents. These exceptions show that inequality of bargaining knowledge and power can produce unfair results; where economic equality and good information are absent, injustice often prevails.

Tenants Lack Bargaining Strength   In the residential rental of houses, apartments, and rooms one party, the landlord, usually has much more knowledge, experience, and power than the other party, the tenant. Rooming-house and dormitory tenants are not wealthy, and apartment tenants are almost always less affluent than their landlords. To purchase a house in North America, a potential homeowner must normally make a

THE ORIGINS OF LANDLORD AND TENANT LAW

The United States modeled its forms of representative government after British rule, and the interpretation of landlord–tenant relations was no exception. From 1350 to 1450 England underwent rather rapid social change. Many prices rose dramatically, impoverishing people with fixed incomes. During the preceding parts of the Middle Ages, landlords had fixed the rents that tenants owed them in physical terms (so many bushels of grain; the milk of so many cows). But agricultural productivity outpaced productivity in other sectors of the British economy, and the prices of agricultural commodities did not rise as fast as the prices of other goods. The purchasing power of bushels of grain decreased, and as a result the real incomes of those who received these products in fixed amounts also decreased.

Commerce had redeveloped in towns, and the fortunes of the town merchants' grew. The cities gained wealth as kings and rural knights squandered their fortunes on endless feudal wars. To obtain more money, rural landlords had to find tenants with cash. Rich town merchants, who sought the prestige and benefits of farming, were natural tenants for the landlords. But at this point a problem developed. Land was still the principal capital asset. Most of the townspeople who rented farms did not maintain agricultural productivity. To make a quick profit, they overlooked good farming practices, sacrificing crop rotation and the wise use of pasture and animals. Thus, the townspeople often ruined the fields and let buildings decay. The comparatively poor landlords requested help from the courts.

Our earliest landlord and tenant regulations state that the tenant is obliged to pay rent and to maintain the rented property. A tenant who rents dilapidated property must not allow it to deteriorate significantly. Every promise or agreement (the law calls them "covenants") is independent of every other promise in a lease agreement, so that tenants cannot say that the landlord has broken any minor promise. This law was necessary when landlords were poor and had to be protected by law. But today such regulations should be reversed, because most tenants are not as rich as their landlords. However, courts must obey the law and follow its precedents. Where old, unreformed landlord and tenant law exists, the courts are necessarily prejudiced toward the landlord. Fortunately, the law of landlord and tenant in most parts of North America is now changing in favor of the tenant.

down payment of at least 20–25% of the purchase price and earn a stable income over $8000 per year. People who rent houses often do so because they cannot meet these purchase requirements. Students and other young people are seldom affluent and are usually not experienced in landlord and tenant relations.

The Landlord Has Bargaining Power   The landlord is a property owner. Although he or she may be stuck with declining tenement property and faced with high taxes, the landlord does have assets. A landlord usually can afford to wait for a certain period of time before renting to an individual or a family. Landlords who have been active in the market for a few years know what lease conditions they can require. They also recognize that most tenants are inexperienced in writing leases and have the added advantage of being able to investigate prospective tenants through credit bureaus. An inexperienced landlord can easily obtain the services of a property management firm. In many cities, most dwellings are controlled by these professional managers, and tenants often don't even know *who* their individual landlords are!

In some cities, vacancy rates are very low, because there are more people seeking apartments than there are apartments available. A *seller's market* is then said to exist, where landlords can reject tenants who even dare to try to assert their rights. In such situations, landlords often demand and receive security deposits of more than two months' rent and impose the most rigorous rules and conditions on their tenants.[1] Tenants who object to these market realities have only two alternatives: to stifle their protests, or to move to another city. Yet the housing market in almost every city and town in North America is segregated by type of tenant (single, married, or family), by wealth or income, by social status, and—despite a decade of civil rights legislation—by religious, ethnic, and racial background. Landlords are reluctant to rent to tenants whom they believe are not as desirable as their customary tenants. In many cases, landlords charge working people fairly reasonable rents and students much higher rents.

Not All Landlords Are Unfair. The foregoing analysis of the economics of the rental market describes landlords on a broad scale. Fortunately, not all landlords are that authoritarian. The landlord behavior just described is more typical of property management firms and corporate landlords; some property owners—particularly individuals who are more likely to deal with their tenants on a person-to-person basis—are reasonable and understanding people. Vacationers who rent their homes for several months, although justifiably concerned for the security of their homes, are seldom experienced landlords. People who rent and manage only a few apartment units themselves are usually quite fair in landlord–tenant dealings. A little old lady who rents out a room may have a few eccentricities, but it is unlikely that she would abuse her market power.

LEASES

When one person pays for the use of living space or land that belongs to another person, a tenant–landlord relationship is said to exist. The law tends to recognize the relationship as such, but exceptions occur when this relationship is considered *contractual* (as between innkeeper and guest), *custodial* (as between hospital and patient), or one of *wardship* (preparatory school officials in charge of minors living in dormitories).

A *lease* is a formal, usually written agreement in which a landlord agrees to rent some space, with or without buildings and other improvements, to a desig-

---

[1] Associated Students, University of Oregon, *A Report on Student Housing Problems* (Eugene, Ore.: ASUO, 1973), p. 4.

"It's right here in your lease—after 10 P.M. you may play only Debussy or Andrés Segovia."

nated tenant.   There are many types of leases, not all of which are recorded in writing.   Country landowners frequently rent fields to neighboring farmers merely by making an oral agreement concerning rent, duration, landlord and tenant rights, and other factors.   Oral understandings are workable between parties who know one another, the value of what is to be rented, and the system in which they are operating.   Corporations, on the other hand, tend to issue formal leases for many pieces of property.   Corporate leases may be 100 or more pages long and discuss every imaginable development in detail.

**What
A Lease
Contains** Leases for houses and apartments that are individually rented are usually written and are a few pages long (perhaps 5000 words).   These leases are written in legal language that is designed for precise specification of the property being leased, its condition at the time of leasing, the duration of the lease, the amount the tenant must pay, and the actions the landlord intends to take in the event the tenant fails to pay rent, damages the rented structure or its equipment, or uses the property in a way the landlord does not permit.   Beyond these standard provisions, leases drafted by landlords may give the landlord or the landlord's agent the right to inspect the property under certain conditions; to raise rent without

notice; to obtain large security deposits against the risk of tenant abuse of the property or the tenant's failure to pay rent; to require that the tenant admit that he or she is guilty of any breaches of the lease, should they be committed; to prevent the tenant from subleasing the premises to a third party who then becomes the tenant's tenant; to pass on to the tenant tax and other cost increases; and sometimes even to allow rents to change in line with international currency movements that are irrelevant to the rented premises.

Legal Limits on Lease Conditions

Courts have not always permitted landlords to impose arbitrary conditions and duties on tenants, but the concept of freedom of contract has given rather broad powers to landlords and tenants to enter into various types of agreements, many of which are unfair to the tenants. Courts all too often fail to ask why a tenant has signed a contract in tiny print that is barely legible and that gives away most of his or her rights. Obviously, people need shelter, and when apartments are hard to find or are too expensive for their budgets, they may agree to some difficult conditions simply to have a roof over their heads. When landlords force people to adhere to unjust terms, the American courts generally disregard the unfair aspects of the leases the tenants have signed and help tenants instead on the basis that they signed these "contracts of adhesion" under duress. Canadian legislatures have created standard leases that limit the conditions landlords can demand in tenant leases. Some U.S. state legislatures are now considering the Uniform Residential Landlord and Tenant Act, a statute designed to balance existing laws and to reduce the frequently excessive powers of landlords.

Tenants Can Write Their Own Lease

A tenant may prepare his or her own rental agreement, and if the landlord accepts and signs this agreement, it is binding on both parties. A simple lease can be only a few sentences clearly stating what premises are to be occupied, by whom, for what duration, for what rent, and what the landlord is required to do in terms of maintenance, utilities, services, and so on. This type of lease holds rent constant for as long as it applies. (Some landlords offer lower rents if a long-term lease is signed.) Such an agreement should be dated and then signed by both parties. Certain states and provinces require these agreements to be signed in the presence of a notary public or with a legal seal. The required notary authorization or seal can be obtained for less than a dollar in most of these localities.

Signing the Standard Lease

Although tenants can be assured of fair treatment by writing their own leases, landlords prefer their tenants to sign standard leasing agreements that usually favor the owners and their agents. Before signing a standard lease, a tenant should read the agreement carefully, line by line and page by page. The landlord or the agent should explain any unclear words or passages in plain language. If the landlord is unable to do so, it should be noted that neither party understands the document and both should initial this comment.

Everything that is promised, suggested, or alluded to in the leasing agreement should be in writing. A tenant is not legally entitled to any rights that are not incorporated in the written lease. Landlords in large housing developments often promote apartments by promising "planned" swimming pools, boat docks, community clubs, or other recreational facilities. Yet they don't include these commitments in their written leases, and tenants are often lured into renting small, badly built apartments on the unenforceable oral assurance that fancy facilities are to be constructed. Many leases contain clauses waiving the landlord's responsibility for anything that is not in writing. Such deceptions are actually criminally fraudulent if, for example, they are designed to hustle resort homes in large interstate development promotions.

Lease Terminology

The terms of a lease, such as the length of a tenant's occupancy, may be changed if the tenant bargains determinedly and if the dwelling's vacancy rate is high enough to make the landlord competitive. But to bargain in this way, a tenant must understand legal language.

Security Deposits. Landlords often require *security deposits* of up to several months' rent to protect themselves in case a tenant damages the apartment or house or fails to pay the last month's rent. Many landlords feel that because such events occur infrequently, security deposits are preferable to raising rents to cover their occasional losses. Tenant damage severe enough to require the use of these generally large deposits is actually quite rare. Yet most landlords continue to hold security deposits without paying interest and may even confiscate these deposits to supplement their income.

Statistics show that 30% of all small-claims court cases in the United States involve wrongful retention of security deposits by landlords after tenants have vacated their premises. This is the most frequent type of complaint that is heard in these courts.[2] Many states and provinces have reduced the landlord's power to abuse security deposits. Today, this area of landlord and tenant law is undergoing radical change. In some jurisdictions at present, security deposits of no more than one-half of one month's rent can be requested by the landlord. Other jurisdictions award tenants triple damages (three times as much as the landlord wrongfully kept) if they can prove in small-claims court that the landlord did not have sufficient cause to retain the deposit. A few states require landlords who intend to keep security deposits to state their reasons in court. Some Canadian provinces no longer require tenants to appear in court to receive their deposit refunds; instead a simple administrative process is employed in which a civil servant returns the deposit to the tenant. Most reforming states and provinces require landlords to pay an interest rate of 4–5% on tenant security deposits.

Many security-deposit problems can be avoided if the tenant and the landlord inspect the rented premises when the lease is signed. If the landlord won't

[2] *Consumer Reports* (November 1971), p. 627.

agree to inspect the premises or if the landlord's and the tenant's assessments of the condition of the premises differ, the tenant should make a full inventory of each wall, appliance, carpet, ceiling, window, door, cabinet, venetian blind or shade, and all other contents of the dwelling place and send it to the landlord via registered or certified mail. When the tenant moves out, this inventory should be repeated, so that the landlord cannot claim that the tenant has abused the premises, estimate high repair costs and then pocket the difference between the estimate and the actual maintenance charges incurred. Tenants who find themselves in such a situation should demand to see the actual receipts for repairs that the landlord claims to have made. Tenants can dispute such claims in small-claims court for amounts ranging from $5 to a typical limit of about $300. Small-claims courts offer help to consumers, and the filing fee is only a few dollars. Receiving a summons to appear in court often encourages a guilty landlord to return the tenant's money.

"Wear and Tear." Most leases and laws vaguely define "wear and tear." Leases usually state that ordinary wear and tear cannot be charged to the tenant and that willful or gross neglect (often called "waste") can be charged to the tenant and deducted from his or her security deposit. Landlords tend to abuse this concept of measurable damage by claiming that every dent in a floor or smudge on a wall is the result of tenant neglect. Yet landlords who accept tenants who have pets and/or children are aware that a certain amount of accelerated wear and tear is to be expected. Of course, some tenants are clearly careless or even intentionally negligent. Perhaps the fairest practice is for tenants to modify the "wear and tear" clause in a lease, if possible, to state that only unforseeable damages resulting from gross negligence or willful destruction can be deducted from their security deposits.

Entry. The landlord is permitted to enter the rented premises to examine and repair them or to exhibit them to prospective tenants if the present tenant has given notice of intention to move. In many states entry is also permitted by law when the landlord has begun proper eviction proceedings. Many leases assert that the landlord can have access to a tenant's premises for any purpose at any time of the day or night. Courts are usually reasonable about this clause, however, stating that a landlord cannot go in and out of a tenant's apartment indiscriminately. Such practices deny the "quiet enjoyment" to which all tenants are entitled and may be grounds for terminating a lease. If a landlord does appear at an unreasonable hour with no sound and urgent purpose, such as fire, flood, or leaking gas, the tenant can request the landlord to leave. Tenants who are subjected to such harrassment regularly should consult a lawyer or a legal-aid service. Landlords often behave lawfully when they know that their tenants understand their rights and know how to enforce them.

Acceleration. If a tenant fails to pay one month's rent on time, all the remainder of the rent can be demanded immediately. Called *acceleration,* this practice makes it worthwhile for the landlord to take the tenant to court. Instead of paying a lawyer simply to collect a single month's rent, the landlord can legally demand the maximum rent due on a one-year lease. Some Canadian provinces (Manitoba and Ontario) no longer regard acceleration as legal and enforceable in court, but landlords can still take such action in U.S. courts. Deleting this lease provision is recommended if the landlord agrees to the modification.

Tort Liability. *Tort liability* is the responsibility for personal injury. The word "tort" is derived from a Norman French verb meaning "to twist." Landlords try to eliminate tort liability by asking tenants to disclaim their right to recover damages for any kind of negligence on the part of the landlord, no matter how severe. Most tenant and landlord law states that the tenant is responsible for his or her own property and actions. If a tenant breaks a foot tripping over a rug that he or she should have secured, it's not the landlord's fault. But if the landlord fails to repair a gas leak after being informed of it and an explosion occurs, the landlord is responsible for gross negligence. Of course, the most common landlord/tenant problems result from ordinary rather than gross negligence. Clauses waiving the right to sue the landlord for ordinary negligence actually can prevent a tenant from making successful recovery from the landlord. But clause or no clause, juries in gross negligence cases aren't easily swayed by a landlord's lawyers.

Confession of Judgment. If a tenant doesn't pay rent on time, the landlord can secure a statement before appearing in court that the tenant is in the wrong. This is called a *confession of judgment.* Long leases usually contain this clause, although courts and legislatures are rapidly making them illegal and unenforceable. A confession of judgment generally includes the landlord's rights to appoint an attorney to appear in court and to confess judgment by the tenant. Most of these clauses also require the tenant to pay the appointed lawyer's fees. If possible, these landlord rights should be eliminated from a lease, because they actually reduce a tenant's power to regulate the behavior of a bad landlord. (It should be noted that when a clause is deleted from a lease, both the landlord and the tenant must initial or sign the deletion.)

Joint and Several Liability. *Joint and several liability* applies to a multiple-tenant lease and to a lease signed by a single tenant, usually a minor or a dependent, who must provide cosigners who agree to share the financial responsibilities of the lease. In the typical case of two people sharing an apartment and a lease, *each* occupant is liable for his or her individual portion of the rent due and, with the other occupant, is also jointly responsible for the total rent due. This kind of clause usually presents no difficulty when a tenant rents an apartment with a friend. But when joint and several liability is used to lock students into leases in apartments rented by corporations in college towns, it can be quite unfair.

In the last ten years, developers have built modern apartments around many colleges and universities, and their rental agents have put students together who didn't even know one another previously. College authorities frequently welcome the private development of these "quasi-dormitories," because they reduce the university's heavy capital expenditure budgets, eliminate administrative troubles, and insulate the college from parental concern about current changes in sexual mores. When educators relinquish their responsibilities in these areas, students become the pawns of apartment developers, locked into incredibly mismatched living arrangements and then forced by a joint and several liability clause to assume the collective responsibility for people they barely know. Some courts have already ruled that joint and several liability is improper in such college quasi-dormitory situations. Generally, students should be reluctant to sign leases that require joint responsibility.

Independent Covenants. Lawyers who draft leases often include a statement to the effect that each clause is independent of *every* other clause in the lease. This *independent covenants* item, which appears near the end of many leases, means that if a court finds that one clause is illegal, the lease is not broken but only reduced by one clause. Similarly, the landlord's breach of one written promise doesn't cancel the lease, and tenants will still have to pay rent until the lease expires. Courts permit independent covenants to stand if the breach of promise by the landlord isn't too serious, but courts tend not to sustain leases if the landlord is grossly in violation of his or her own lease.

THE LIMITS OF LEGALITY

In the last decade tenant unions have developed in college towns and some large cities. Collective action will be discussed later in this chapter, but we should note here that some landlords write standard leases that allow them to evict tenants who organize or who join tenant unions. In labor law it is illegal to fire a worker for joining a union. In landlord and tenant law there is a need for similar statutes to protect tenants who are involved in union activities from retaliatory eviction. Courts tend not to allow such evictions, but landlords who are armed with long, complex leases can usually find an obscure reason to force tenants they consider undesirable to vacate the rented premises. An example of a trivial basis for eviction is the requirement that all garbage be "securely wrapped and tied and deposited in such containers as the landlord may designate."

The Law Today:
A Right to
Decent Housing?

From the tenant's viewpoint, the most essential issue in landlord and tenant law is whether a tenant is entitled to a decent place to live. In the United States and Canada the answer is a qualified "perhaps," depending on where you live.

The United States Supreme Court decided an important landlord and tenant case in February 1972. In *Lindsey v. Normet,*[3] the court majority ruled that an

---

[3] 405 U.S. 55 (1972).

Oregon law requiring tenants to pay rent regardless of the bad state of repair of the rented dwelling (a house) was valid and more important than any claimed right to decent housing.

In the case, Lindsey rented a house from Normet. Lindsey asked Normet to repair broken windows, rusted gutters, broken plaster, missing steps, and improper sanitation, but Normet refused to make these repairs. Fearing eviction, Lindsey sought a court judgment declaring Oregon's eviction procedure unconstitutional because it was so heavily prejudiced in favor of the landlord. The Oregon law known as the Forcible Entry and Detainer Statute permits a landlord to begin eviction proceedings ten days after a tenant's nonpayment of rent. The case can be tried before a jury, but the tenant must be formally notified of the trial not less than two or more than four days before it is to be held. To be entitled to repossession, the landlord is only required to describe the rented premises, and to prove that the tenant occupies these premises and hasn't paid the rent. Any tenant who is inexperienced in legal matters would have a difficult time finding a lawyer and arranging a defense in the two to four days that Oregon law allows.

The U.S. Supreme Court's Answer. In the case of *Lindsey v. Normet,* the high court ruled that the Oregon eviction procedure central to the case was technically lawful. The court was not necessarily indicating its approval of the Oregon statute; it simply ruled that the Constitution does not require different procedures. The decision reasoned that tenants and landlords are equally capable of reading leases (assumed by the court to be signed without coercion) and of understanding their content. It said that the Constitution does not guarantee "access to dwellings of a particular quality." However, the Supreme Court did deem illegal an Oregon procedure that required a tenant to post a bond of double the monthly rent to appeal an eviction notice. In a vigorous dissent, Associate Justice Douglas stated that the one-third of the American population occupying rented dwellings is entitled to decent living quarters.

Laws such as the Oregon statute that view a lease merely as the right to occupy space and that assert that the right to occupy rented premises is not diminished by the condition of the living quarters are historical relics that can only harm contemporary city dwellers. Although in *Lindsey v. Normet* the U.S. Supreme Court did adhere to the old view that a lease is merely a right to occupy space—a right that is not impaired by any defects in the space leased—a number of U.S. states, counties, and cities have ruled that a tenant is entitled to decent living quarters.

State and Local Law

Some courts hold that a landlord who allows premises to become so dilapidated or dangerous that safe human habitation is impossible has *constructively evicted* the tenant. A constructive eviction can follow a landlord's failure to provide heat, to eliminate vermin, to eradicate offensive odors, or to stop dampness and leakage. Unfortunately, most courts require the tenant to abandon the premises before they sustain the claim of constructive eviction. Moreover, low-income tenants are faced with other obstacles: Even if they are able to find other homes and to pay the security deposits, these tenants may not be able to afford to move. [4]

Housing Codes.   By 1971, more than 1000 American communities had enacted *housing codes* to comply with and to benefit from the Federal Housing Act of 1954.   However, the majority of these codes have not been enforced, because community officials have not had the resources or felt the urgency to deal firmly with slumlords.   Prior to 1900, housing authorities were empowered to order tenants to vacate condemned and substandard buildings.   But from time to time, this procedure fell into disuse, for housing shortages made it impossible to relocate tenants forced to leave condemned buildings.   When enforced, however, such orders to vacate did require landlords to make the necessary repairs or to be deprived of rent.   Courts usually have been reluctant to levy jail sentences on middle-class slumlords.   Most of these slumlords know that they face only minimal fines that are normally less than the cost of the necessary repairs.

Repair and Deduct—Legal Self-help.   More recent laws utilize procedures that reduce the rent a landlord receives.   A popular device among state legislatures is the *repair and deduct statute,* which allows a tenant to make any repairs to the rented premises that the landlord refuses to make and to deduct the cost of these repairs from the rent due.   California, Louisiana, Montana, Massachusetts, North Dakota, Oklahoma, and South Dakota presently permit this kind of tenant self-help.   But California and Montana limit the amount of deductible repairs to one month's rent, which is hardly sufficient to rehabilitate, say, a tenement. And most of these states allow a landlord to block this statute by requiring tenants to sign away their rights to such self-help in the original lease.

Rent Reduction.   Several states permit tenants or public authorities to reduce the rents in substandard dwellings, including New York, New Jersey, Massachusetts, Pennsylvania, Michigan, and Missouri.   But a landlord in Michigan can demand that all back rent be paid once repairs begin, whereas a landlord in Missouri must complete repairs to collect back rent.   Some states, including New York, Massachusetts, and Delaware, also appoint public administrators to manage the repair of dilapidated buildings.   But public administrators are reluctant to be held responsible for the improvement of vast slum tracts.

A Warranty of Habitability.   A new trend in court decisions with respect to housing has recently emerged.   A number of courts now recognize the existence of an *implied warranty of habitability* in residential leases.   These courts think that no tenant leases a dwelling for any purpose except to live in it.   Accordingly, they hold that the concept of leasing is itself assurance that the dwelling is fit for habitation and thus rule that no tenant is required to pay for an unfit dwelling. Courts that apply this theory of the implied warranty of habitability discard the

---

[4] 40 Fordham L. Rev. 123 (1971).

outmoded practice of independent covenants discussed earlier and instead view the lease as a contract. Critical cases in Hawaii, New Jersey, and the District of Columbia in 1969 and 1970 may, if other courts subsequently support these rulings, provide the basis for making leases a part of contract law rather than real estate law. If this happens—in other words, if courts regard *Lindsey v. Normet* as a decision limited to Oregon eviction procedures—the resultant judicial revolution would provide every tenant with the right to a decent place to live.

ALTERNATIVE I: A UNIFORM LANDLORD AND TENANT ACT

A novel and important approach to the modernization of landlord and tenant law is contained in the *Uniform Residential Landlord and Tenant Act.* Other fields of law, notably contracts and negotiable instruments such as bank checks have been modernized and standardized on a nationwide basis by the adoption of similar laws by legislatures. After three years of research and hearings, the National Conference of Commissioners on Uniform State Laws, based in Chicago, released the final draft of the Uniform Act in August 1972. The proposed statute essentially brings landlord and tenant relations out of the historical backwaters of real estate law and into the twentieth century. The Uniform Act is designed to make landlord and tenant relations a variety of contract law, discarding the old view that each obligation of landlords to tenants is independent of every other obligation. The Uniform Act recognizes that a residential lease represents much more than the right to occupy space; it requires that decent living quarters be provided for all tenants.

Repairs The Uniform Act allows a tenant to make essential repairs to a dwelling if the landlord refuses to make them. The tenant may deduct the cost of the repairs up to $100 or half of one month's rent, whichever is greater. Tenants are permitted to break their leases if landlords do not perform necessary major repairs that materially affect health and safety. Tenants may also recover damages if the landlord does not fulfill the required duties detailed in the lease or if the landlord interrupts essential utility services. A tenant can obtain an *injunction* (a court order requiring the landlord to obey the law and to fulfill obligations to tenants) against the landlord's misconduct. If the dwelling is damaged by fire or some other cause to the extent that the use of the premises is substantially impaired, the tenant may terminate the lease or reduce rent payments.

Leases Must Be Reasonable Landlords cannot impose unreasonable conditions on tenants or construct leases that are unconscionable. Courts can disregard leases that have unconscionable clauses. Landlords are forbidden to evict tenants in retaliation for complaints under the Uniform Act or for union activities. The Uniform Act pre-

sumes that any eviction within one year of a tenant complaint is retaliatory. The Act requires landlords to disclose to tenants the names and addresses of the managers and owners of rented dwellings.

Security Deposits

The Act limits security deposits to one month's rent and requires the landlord to present an itemized bill to the tenant for any deductions from this deposit within 14 days after the tenant vacates the premises. If the landlord doesn't return the security deposit or deducts an excessive amount from it, the tenant can take the landlord to court and obtain twice the amount of the deposit that was wrongly withheld.

The Uniform Act: An Appraisal

The Uniform Act is a valuable piece of legislation that hopefully will be accepted by all states. (One criticism to be noted here is that the Act does not adequately prevent landlords from harassing tenants by entering their premises at odd hours.) The provision that awards tenants double damages for the wrongful withholding of security deposits after the tenants have vacated their dwellings may be amended to provide even larger amounts. Tenants who lose only a small sum (say, less than $25) or who move far away need an adequate incentive to take the trouble to file a suit to recover their deposits; obviously, triple damages would provide a greater incentive than double damages.

ALTERNATIVE II: TENANT UNIONS

Tenant unions represent an alternative to the modification of landlord and tenant law with new statutes. A tenant union is an organization of tenants formed to bargain collectively with their landlord(s) to secure an agreement that defines the parties' mutual obligation.[5] Studies prepared by the American Arbitration Association for the Office of Economic Opportunity indicate that tenant unions are currently being formed throughout the United States.[6] The common incentive for tenants to unite is the greater bargaining power gained in negotiating rents and lease conditions and in improving building maintenance and neighborhood safety and cleanliness. The potential success of tenant unions is great; their common problem is the isolation and apathy of tenants in slums and high-rise apartments.

Tenant Unions in the Past
The concept of the tenant union goes back at least to the 1890s. Recurrent housing shortages, particularly acute in some areas during World War I, gave rise to numerous tenant organizations, and the Depression fostered a number of tenant unions with specific grievances and rather short life spans. More recently, massive rent strikes led by Jesse Gray, in New York City in the winter of 1963, may be considered the end of the single-issue concept of the tenant union and the beginning of a stable, continuing, tenant union organization.[7]

Ways to Organize
There are currently two principal forms of tenant union organization: the unincorporated association (an informal group that does not have standing in law), and the chartered, legally recognized union group. Informal tenant unions are unincorporated associations. Most tenant groups begin this way, although in states such as New York and Ohio even unincorporated groups can represent their members.[8] An unincorporated group may not be able to bargain collectively as efficiently as an incorporated union group, but an unincorporated tenant union may be even more of a threat to the landlord. An unincorporated

---

[5] H. Edward Hales, Jr., and Charles H. Livingston, "Tenant Unions: Their Law and Operation in the State and Nation," *University of Florida Law Review* **XXIII** (1970), p. 85.

[6] Ibid., p. 85.

[7] Ibid., pp. 85–86.

[8] Ibid., p. 87.

association can publicize unfair living conditions, appeal to legislatures, advise tenants of their rights, and remain relatively immune to legal efforts by the landlord to stop its work. Should the landlord attempt to sue the association or to serve it with a court order (perhaps to stop the picketing of a building), the unincorporated association can quickly dissolve. The landlord is then faced with the prospect of having to take elaborate legal actions against dozens, hundreds, even thousands of tenants.[9]

**Landlords
React to
Tenant Unions**

Landlords have developed a predictably negative attitude toward tenant unions, although these unions can actually be of help to landlords. For example, a tenant group that draws up a comprehensive list of tenant demands ranked in order of urgency or importance is relieving the landlord of some management problems. When organized, tenants may take better care of their premises[10] and be more vigilant with respect to crime, less destructive of their dwellings, and more responsive to legitimate complaints from the landlord. But in most cases landlords attempt to disband tenant associations by retaliatory eviction, intimidating tenants, and making sufficient repairs to convince tenants for the moment that their problems have been solved.

**Tenant Union
Weapons**

Incorporated or unincorporated, tenant groups have a large number of weapons that they can use against landlords. The first is the withholding of rent, subject to the laws of the state or province in which the withholding action is organized. Picketing and other forms of adverse publicity, entering briefs in court, taking legal action against landlords, assisting management to obtain help from tenants in solving such problems as proper garbage and litter disposal, and publishing ratings of landlords and their buildings are other useful procedures that can be undertaken by tenant associations. The National Tenants Organization (NTO) in Washington, D.C., is currently organized somewhat loosely as a federation of tenant groups with ten or more active members. The NTO, still in its infancy, one day may be able to lobby Congress and state legislatures to modify landlord and tenant laws into forms that are more applicable to contemporary urban life.

ALTERNATIVE III: CANADIAN INNOVATIONS

American approaches to landlord and tenant law reform have concentrated on converting landlord and tenant relations from real estate law to contract law, assuring that dwellings are fit for habitation, and improving tenants' chances of receiving security-deposit refunds when their leases expire. Most measures

[9] Ibid., pp. 86–88.
[10] Liz R. Galese, "Light in the Hallway," *The Wall Street Journal* (April 18, 1973). p. 1.

taken by various states have been piecemeal and cannot be considered part of a comprehensive effort to create modern landlord and tenant law. The only American statutory innovation that is comprehensive in character is embodied in the Uniform Act discussed earlier.

The U.S. Constitution Protects Everyone

There are several reasons why state legislatures cannot easily dispense with the basic right of landlords to construct leases primarily as they wish. The Bill of Rights of the U.S. Constitution makes all parties equal before the law. All parties are said to be entitled to due process of and equal protection under the law. This means that a state legislature cannot impose standard leases on all landlords and tenants even if it wishes to do so, thereby eliminating a great load of court cases concerned with the fairness of irregular leases. Similarly, no state legislature can compel landlords and tenants to settle their disputes by arbitration or by turning to state-appointed administrators. Yet an out-of-court approach of this kind would have desirable features. Investigative officers could eliminate the time-consuming adversary process of presenting evidence in court, and they could have more expertise than most courts.

Courts Are Not a Perfect Answer for All Purposes

People who are afraid of courts or who have moved far away from previously rented dwellings may not be able to obtain security deposits that have been wrongfully withheld. The American judicial approach to the return of security deposits (one party goes to court; the other must respond) is most difficult for people who are far from their old dwellings and who must either travel or hire an attorney to collect the few hundred dollars that their landlord owes them. These tenants may decide that getting their money back isn't worth the expense or the effort.

Canadian Provinces Change the Law

Several provinces in Canada, led by Manitoba and Ontario, have approached landlord and tenant law reform by creating standard leases that apply to all rented dwellings and by taking landlord and tenant disputes out of the courts. Canadian legislatures are not bound by the equal protection of laws and due process concepts in the Bill of Rights of the U.S. Constitution and therefore can take greater liberties with contractual agreements. Although much Canadian reform legislation is not applicable to American landlord and tenant problems for this reason and would probably be considered unconstitutional if used, other aspects of the Canadian approach to landlord and tenant law reform could provide helpful models for U.S. state legislatures.

Manitoba's Model Law

The Province of Manitoba's Landlord and Tenant Act, as amended in 1970, is a good example of the Canadian approach to landlord and tenant law reform. The Manitoba Act recognizes the existence of a warranty of habitability and regards any significant deficiency in a rented dwelling as reason for the tenant to reduce rent payments or to terminate the lease. Manitoba has created a standard lease that is binding on all residential dwelling-unit rentals. Any landlord—tenant disputes are resolved by an administrative officer, called a *rentalsman,* who investigates all issues pertinent to the lease and serves as a mediator between the two parties who are in disagreement. If a landlord imposes a special lease on a tenant and if some part of that lease is then disputed, the rentalsman only extends to the landlord the rights that he or she would have had under the relevant clause of the standard lease.

If a landlord refuses to make repairs or permits a building to become so rundown that safe and healthy living is not possible there, the rentalsman may either rule that the lease is *frustrated* (terminated) or may charge the landlord twice the amount of the estimated repairs or one month's rent, whichever is greater, and then arrange to have the repairs made.

When security-deposit disputes arise, the deposit, together with 4% interest per year compounded annually, is forwarded to the rentalsman subject to the disposition of the case. No security deposit can exceed one-half of one month's rent. Landlords may not enter a rented dwelling, except in case of fire, flood, or some other emergency, without giving 24 hours notice of the intent to enter. And such entry must be during daylight hours. Landlords are required to install reliable locks on the entry doors to rented premises. Landlords are not permitted to prevent tenant entry by changing locks while tenants are away from home. If the landlord violates any one of these rules, the lease is considered broken. The landlord's remedies for nonpayment of rent, such as *acceleration* (in which all future rent is due if one monthly rental payment is not made on time) and *distraint* (seizing a tenant's personal possessions) have been abolished. Rent increases can no longer be charged unless 90 days notice is given to the tenants who are to be affected.

The effect of the Manitoba legislation and of quite similar legislation in Ontario and British Columbia has been to make the lease an ordinary contract with completely interdependent parts. The tenant must pay rent, and the landlord must do everything he or she promises to do. The contract can be settled out of court by the rentalsman, who investigates all complaints. The terms of the contract are defined by the standard lease, the provisions of which are binding when any clause in a nonstandard lease signed by a tenant is disputed. Clearly, the Manitoba, Ontario, and British Columbia acts defend the tenant against the excess bargaining power of the landlord and give the tenant a kind of "bill of tenant rights" that can be enforced by the use of simple administrative machinery.

SLUMS

Slums are a problem that is still unresolved in landlord and tenant law. Some landlords create slums by their greed and viciousness toward tenants. Other

"A slumlord has to eat, too, you know."

slumlords are entirely passive in their management of dilapidated buildings. It is true that there is little any single landlord can do to prevent the decline of an entire neighborhood. As a building deteriorates, it suffers vandalism and a decreasing occupancy rate; a landlord may have less income with which to meet increased maintenance costs. If the building is located in a neighborhood that is in a state of transition from residential use to business use, the landlord's property taxes may be increasing at the same time that the building is being devastated by forces that are beyond any one person's control. So a landlord may easily find it cheaper to pay fines than to rebuild and fight a losing battle against vandals and rising tax assessment.

Most of the landlord and tenant law reforms discussed in this chapter punish the landlord. Economic sanctions imposed on landlords who can afford them may be workable. But as many as one-third of the slum owners surveyed by George Sternlieb[11] in Newark in the mid-1960s lived in their own buildings—they were poor people, too. Yet Sternlieb found that the worst

---

[11] George Sternlieb, *The Tenement Landlord* (New Brunswick, N.J.: Rutgers University Press, 1966), p. xviii.

slums were owned by the wealthy or by firms that specialize in slum properties. Each of these slum specialists controlled or owned a large number of slum properties.

Some useful reforms include property tax reductions for resident slum owners, who could use the money saved in the tax reduction for building improvements. Owners of many slum properties have easy access to credit; resident owners must often pay 50–100% more than the normal purchase price to obtain credit. Clearly, better credit could help resident slum owners to improve their buildings. But tax reductions and better credit should not be extended to the owners of multiple-building slums.

Stanley Lebergott[12] suggests that public housing authorities could reduce the enormous amount of deliberate damage to public housing projects by offering rent rebates or reductions to tenants. Lebergott's rent reductions would reflect the amount by which each tenant could reduce the individual apartment's monthly maintenance cost below the normal level. The Lebergott plan would enable tenants to benefit from helping their landlord by paying lower rent—a benefit currently absent in public housing administration.

IMPLICATIONS

A tenant's life is in part a matter of his or her own making and in part a matter of the legal circumstances that pertain to the place of residence. Many problems that tenants encounter in rented dwellings could be anticipated and prevented by making the right choices of neighbors and friends. But the law of landlord and tenant in any one state or jurisdiction is not easy to change. Persuading courts and legislatures to update their laws is an extremely slow process. In a sense, it is also an inevitable one: Some of the most progressive jurisdictions in landlord and tenant law reform are also the most urbanized.

Consumers and tenants who wish to change landlord and tenant laws must face some important political issues. How deeply, for example, do we want governments to interfere with the construction of private contracts? If we believe that landlords have excessive bargaining power, we may be willing to allow the state to put its power behind the tenant. Do we prefer to use courts or bureaucracies to help tenants resolve their landlord problems? How could the cost of these bureaucracies be financed? From general taxes or special taxes levied on landlords and/or tenants? What role should the courts play in the wrongful confiscation of tenant security deposits by landlords? Should landlords be forced to prove in court that tenants are responsible for the damages claimed? Or should the tenant be allowed to go to court with the added incentive of double or triple damages if he or she is proved right? What is a good

[12] Stanley Lebergott, "Slum Housing: A Proposal," *Journal of Political Economy* **LXX** (1970), pp. 1362–66.

upper limit on security deposits—one-half of a month's rent, a week's rent, two months' rent, or three months' rent? Tenants can improve their situations in some ways without the prolonged court battles essential to law reform, primarily by organizing tenant associations.

SUMMARY

1 When sharing living space with others in apartments or houses, many savings accrue and the monies saved may be put to other uses.

2 Unreformed American and Canadian landlord and tenant law is a relic of fourteenth century English farm lease law. Landlords no longer require this kind of judicial protection.

3 Landlords usually have greater bargaining power than tenants, which makes it possible for them to impose unfair leases on tenants.

4 Unless landlords operate in a jurisdiction that has recently reformed its land-lord–tenant laws, the quarters they provide are not required to be decent, safe, or sanitary to be considered legally acceptable. This independence of landlord and tenant obligations is known as the theory of independent covenants.

5 Leases must be read with great care before they are signed. It is vital to understand relevant clauses on entry, security deposits, wear and tear, confession of judgment, tort liability, acceleration, and joint and several liability.

6 When tenants are confronted by landlords who refuse to provide maintenance or essential services, it may be possible to terminate the lease or to reduce rent payments by use of the theories of constructive eviction and implied warranty of habitability or by way of rent reduction and repair and deduct procedures.

7 The Uniform Residential Landlord and Tenant Act is a comprehensive modernization package that recognizes an implicit warranty of habitability. The Act makes landlord and tenant relations a type of contract law, ending the concept of independent covenants, and permits lease revocation or rent reduction if the landlord fails to make repairs. It also limits security deposits and forbids retaliatory eviction.

8 Tenant unions offer an important and an immediate solution to groups of tenants who have similar landlord problems and who wish to help themselves.

9 Canadian solutions to landlord and tenant law reform substitute administrative officers for courtroom proceedings. Much of Canadian reform legislation would not apply in the United States, due to the Bill of Rights' guarantees of due process and equal protection of laws.

10 Both tenants and landlords must be given incentives to improve slums. Slum owners who live in their own slum buildings should receive tax reductions and improved channels of credit. But such incentives should not be extended to wealthy, absentee, or specialist slumlords who own many slum buildings.

The details of landlord and tenant law vary so widely that no single source can readily explain it all. It may be helpful to check the law pertinent to your own state or province at a law library. Many campus and community legal aid services offer concise summaries of local laws. In addition to the authoritative sources given in the footnotes in this chapter, the following should be of interest:

Suggestions for Further Reading

Consumer Reports (October, November 1974; January 1975).

Goodman, Emily J. *The Tenant Survival Book.* Indianapolis, Inc.: Bobbs-Merrill, 1972.

Rejnis, Ruth. *Everything Tenants Need to Know . . . .* New York: McKay, 1974.

Time-Life Books. *The Family Legal Guide.* Boston: Little Brown, 1971, Chapter 4.

The Consumer Workshop

1 Compare the bargaining abilities of landlords and tenants in terms of economic power and experience in the rental housing market. In what specific parts of a lease do the different bargaining abilities of landlord and tenant manifest themselves?

2 Write a "bill of tenant rights" that equalizes the legal duties and economic powers of tenants and landlords.

3 Assume that you and a dozen friends living in a medium-size apartment building are organizing a tenant union to bargain with building management. You want to make the common terms of a lease as favorable as possible to the building's tenants. List the important points in the lease that you would discuss with management. Beside each point, list the landlord's probable position and compare it with your own best interests.

4 Part of the cost of any house or apartment rental is the amount the landlord charges for anticipated maintenance and management chores and tenant damage. Tenants who are noisy and destructive cost management additional time and expense and raise the average rent that the landlord must collect. What can peaceful, orderly tenants do to separate themselves from destructive and disorderly tenants? Consider:

1 Writing a refund clause into the lease to compensate tenants who are orderly

2 A system of references for good tenants

3 A tenant union to discipline unruly members.

Evaluate each of these alternatives in terms of its advantages and disadvantages to both landlords and tenants.

5 What is the landlord and tenant law in the state in which you live or study? Consult a local law library, legal-aid office, or consumer-assistance office, or ask a local lawyer if he or she would address your class. Once you are acquainted with landlord and tenant law and its problems, recommend any changes you would make in these laws in your state.

18 BUYING AND OWNING A HOME

18

> " Ya gotta house like the sample house. Of course, ya didn't getta house exactly like the sample house, but where in ya contract does it say ya should? Nowhere, is where. If it said in the contract an exact facsimile, that's something else again. But it don't say that inna contract. Ya read ya contract, bub? "

> JOHN KEATS
> *The Crack in the Picture Window**

Owning a home is the cherished desire of many: Nearly two-thirds of all Americans live in their own houses.[1] This chapter explores the reasons why so many people find the ownership of a home both a satisfying and a practical investment. Here we will examine the market for owner-occupied housing to understand why the costs of housing are high. We will survey the different forms of ownership and what to consider when deciding whether to rent or to buy a house in terms of personal and household goals. Then we look at the process of purchasing a home—from the first encounters with real estate brokers and house checklists to the technicalities of deeds, titles, and mortgages. Finally, we will discuss the special kinds of problems that the mobile home and household movers might present, and identify some current changes in law that benefit the home buyer.

THE DEMAND FOR HOUSING

The demand for housing depends on both (1) people's need for physical space, and (2) their desire to have special types of and locations for that physical space. Changes in the population of the nation as a whole, as well as population variations in given areas, affect the adequacy of existing housing and the consequent demand for additional housing. For example, an increase in the rate of marriages can stimulate a demand for new suburban housing. The American Public Health Association estimates that each member of a household of one to six people needs 300–400 square feet of personal living space. It is also estimated that 40% of all American families want to move to obtain better homes or homes in better neighborhoods.[2]

---

* John Keats, *The Crack in the Picture Window* (Boston: Houghton Mifflin, 1956), p. 28.
[1] *The Statistical Abstract of the United States 1972*, Table 1159, p. 690.
[2] E.B. Phillips and S. Lane, *Personal Finance* (New York: Wiley, 1963), pp. 222–24.

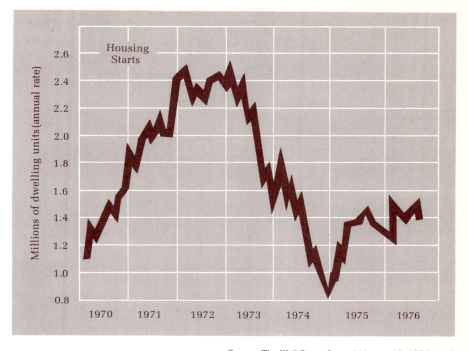

Source: *The Wall Street Journal* (August 19, 1974), p. 1.

18-1   Recent Housing Starts

The Supply of Housing

About two million new housing units are started in the United States each year (see Figure 18-1). They are erected by tens of thousands of contractors, most with very small companies, each of whom may build only a dozen houses annually. Within the industry, however, several large firms operate from coast to coast, constructing significant amounts of the total national housing market. One large builder of tract homes, Kaufman & Broad, has a capital base of about $200 million and is traded on the New York Stock Exchange.

The large number of small companies in the industry precludes the economies that would be possible in large-scale production that could be passed on to home buyers. The small contractor is usually unable to employ mass-production techniques or to obtain quantity discounts for purchased materials or for trade specialty services, such as electrical wiring and plumbing, and must hire subcontractors to do this work instead.

Construction Codes Are Not Uniform

Each city and county has its own housing construction code. These codes are designed to protect the buyer by ensuring that houses meet adequate structural and architectural standards. But all too often they merely serve to protect industry or construction trade-union interests by permitting the use of cheap

materials or requiring expensive building methods, thereby assuring contractors of high profits. More importantly, the existence of literally thousands of different construction codes means that a standardized product cannot be built or sold across the country. There are tens of thousands of different requirements for wiring, plumbing, insulation, wall thickness, roof construction, nail spacing, drain placement, many other construction features. The Federal Housing Administration and The Veterans Administration also require certain construction standards to be met before they will approve mortgages and loan guarantees. Various levels of regulation do protect the buyer from many of the abuses of dishonest contractors, but such requirements also make it difficult to achieve economies when using new construction methods.

Moreover, the factory construction of major house components has not created the savings that mass production has made possible in the manufacture of other consumer goods. Factory assembly costs are considerably lower than on-site construction costs, but the high cost of transportation limits the market area to within 500 truck miles of the assembly plant.[3] Furthermore, buyer and market preferences for style variations limit the quantity of any one house model a factory can sell.

Availability of Land

The cost of suburban land throughout North America is soaring as people abandon declining neighborhoods and move to new suburban areas that are temporarily free of core-city crime and decay. The market's incessant demand for free-standing, single-family homes uses a great amount of land in basically low-density formations. Given average families of four persons and five houses to the acre, suburban housing density accommodates only 20 people per acre.

The cost of land and the price of a finished house are considerably reduced if buyers purchase row houses, town houses, or some other kind of semidetached construction. Much land has been by-passed or left in a state of decay in the cities, and this land can be purchased for reasonable prices if developers are willing to commit themselves to urban redevelopment. Core cities also contain much architecturally sound construction that can be renovated to compete with new homes in the market.

FORMS OF OWNERSHIP

There are several kinds of home ownership. The traditional and the most common form of ownership is the detached, single-family dwelling on its own ground space: The entire lot and the structure are owned fully by the family that resides there. The owner can do virtually anything he or she desires with the house and land: repaint, build additions, rent out a room—anything that does not violate local building codes or zoning ordinances. And interest payments and real estate taxes can be deducted from the owner's taxable income, thereby providing a significant tax saving.

Cooperatives and Condominiums

Soaring land costs and the desire of many homeowners to avoid continuous maintenance costs have produced two new and important varieties of detached home ownership: the cooperative and the condominium.

Cooperatives. *Cooperative housing* is based on the joint ownership of all property within a housing development. An apartment building or a series of semi-

---

[3] L.J. Gordon and S.M. Lee, *Economics for Consumers,* 5th ed. (New York: Van Nostrand, 1967), p. 403.

detached town houses together with all common grounds and passageways is owned by a corporation. Each apartment or town house owner purchases a share in the corporation and signs an occupancy agreement (usually for three years), which is automatically renewed if the member does not violate the rules of the cooperative. The cooperative itself obtains any needed financing and charges members interest expenses, maintenance costs for common areas, and real estate taxes. The advantage of cooperative living is that members can deduct their shares of real estate taxes and mortgage interest from their taxable income and realize the same tax advantages that traditional homeowners enjoy. The cooperative member can sell his or her share of the corporation and apartment in accordance with any rules the cooperative may devise. Cooperative apartment buildings have flourished in New York City and a few other major cities but have not yet developed into a major alternative to traditional home ownership.

Condominiums. This newest form of home ownership results from a real estate law that permits individual dwelling-unit estates to be established within a larger total property. Common grounds, recreational facilities, passageways, and utility plants are all part of the common estate in which condominium owners have a joint, undivided interest. The condominium owner obtains financing and can sell the unit at will, always accompanied by a share in the total common property of the development. The condominium owner must obtain personal financing but can deduct mortgage interest costs and real estate taxes from taxable income.

Advantages and Disadvantages

Cooperatives and condominiums share several advantages and disadvantages. The advantages lie in a more efficient use of land, structures, and common facilities. The disadvantages are some loss of privacy and control. Both the cooperative and the condominium relieve members of the burden of the maintenance of grounds and usually of the obligation to repaint outside building surfaces. But members remain responsible for the interiors of their own town houses or apartments. The members of a cooperative or condominium development elect a board of directors to manage or hire others to manage the estate as a whole. Majority rule normally prevails, and from time to time the corporation may elect to spend funds for projects that do not interest particular members. If a majority of the members wants tennis courts, the board can erect them and even charge nonplayers their proportion of the cost.

Efficient Use Of Land. Cooperatives and condominiums are usually more densely arranged on the given land space than private, detached houses would be. This naturally reduces land costs, and some of this saving can be invested in recreational facilities. Community properties can be and often are developed to include such features as swimming pools, saunas, clubhouses, boat marinas, and private beaches. If the dwelling units are attached to one another—and they normally are—more efficient heating and cooling is possible, because fewer walls are exposed to weathering and also because the necessarily large machinery can provide economies that are impossible in detached housing.

Community Living. Owners living in a shared community must follow the dictates of majority rule. The board of directors of the development can establish parking regulations and pool rules, draw up contracts for expensive landscaping, or ignore what one owner feels is a glaring fault—and all members must abide by the board's decision. Owner's who do not agree with the board's decisions can vote to dismiss the directors (if the majority of the members agree); otherwise, they must put up with the decisions or move out.

Cooperatives and condominiums attempt to combine the freedom from responsibility that a tenant has with the tax and investment advantages that the homeowner has. The record of cooperatives is largely free from incidents of developer abuse, but this is not true of condominiums. The last ten years has seen a great surge in condominium construction. Many apartment buildings have been converted to condominiums, thereby forcing the tenants either to accept the obligations of ownership or to move out when their leases expire.

Condominium Costs Can Be Unpredictable

Condominium owners often fail to estimate the correct costs of ownership. Annual joint reassessments of tax, utility, and maintenance rates for condominium owners increase with inflation just as these costs increase for private homeowners. Some condominium developers deliberately conceal these true costs from buyers or build exorbitant management fees or facility rental charges into their sales agreements.

Abusive Contracts. Developers often retain ownership of recreational facilities and rent them to condominium owners on a long-term contract basis. The buyer must agree to such an arrangement at the time of the purchase. This is a widespread practice in Florida, where an attorney has charged one developer with soaking condominium members for $250,000 a year on a 99-year lease for a small swimming pool.[4]

New Laws Protect Condominium Buyers. The abuse of consumers by condominium developers is being exposed and controlled by disclosure statutes and investigations. In 1964, New York State passed strict condominium laws that forbid developers to retain control of condominium facilities. The New York statute also compels developers to publish prior to sale extensive, detailed statements disclosing the method of financing, the developer's background, the details of the project and estimated operating budgets. Illinois requires developers to present prospective buyers with condominium bylaws, regulations, budgets, and floor plans.[5] Overseeing the sales techniques of the entire industry, the

[4] *The Wall Street Journal* (March 29, 1974), p. 1.
[5] *Ibid.*, p. 1.

Federal Trade Commission has begun to examine condominium sales to determine the extent of unfair and deceptive sales practices in this field.[6]

TO RENT OR TO BUY?

The choice of whether to rent or to buy a house or an apartment is a difficult one. In some cases, the advantages and disadvantages of home rental or ownership are hard to measure. A homeowner has privacy, the pride of ownership, a sense of place and security, and the pleasure (and cost) of being able to improve the property. A renter is not required to outlay major capital, is free from the homeowner's chores, and is more mobile in terms of changing residences. Yet the advantages and the disadvantages of renting versus buying a home are not beyond measurement.

Comparing Costs: An Example

Most people approach a rent-or-buy decision in terms of direct, out-of-pocket costs. Although the same house or apartment is seldom available for rent *or* purchase, we will assume for the purpose of comparison that a $36,000 new house can be acquired either way. Moreover, we will assume that the house is priced fairly and, although it has been efficiently built and sold for only a small profit, that it requires $600 per year in maintenance (for repainting, for reserves set aside to replace appliances, rugs, and so on). If the prevailing interest-rate level is 6%, then this $36,000 house must rent for at least $36,000 × .06, or $2160 per year. If it does not, the landlord will sell it and deposit the money in a bank, where it will earn that 6% interest rate. Adding the maintenance charge gives us a minimum acceptable rent per year of $2160 + $600, or $2760, which amounts to a monthly rent of $230.

If the house is to be purchased outright, then the monthly cost of ownership apart from utility costs and taxes is also $230, because this is the amount of interest that the owner loses by *not* depositing the price of the house in the bank where it would draw 6% interest. If the owner wants or needs to borrow some of the purchase price by means of a mortgage and if the owner makes a down payment of $6000 on the house, then the monthly cost of paying off a 30-year mortgage at 6% on the balance of $30,000 is $178.45 Adding the 6% interest loss that the $6000 down payment could earn in a savings account ($360 per year, or $30 per month), the total monthly cost of a mortgaged ownership becomes $208.45, a smaller amount than the minimum monthly rental on the same house. (For the purposes of comparison, the monthly costs of repaying $30,000 on 7% and 8% mortgages are $197.59 and $217.42, respectively, to which the interest loss on the down payment must be added.)

[6] *The Wall Street Journal* (July 5, 1974), p. 15.

Our example appears to show that it costs less per month to buy than to rent a house. But there are many hidden costs and gains in both home ownership and rental. A homeowner must pay title examination and insurance fees, legal fees, appraisal fees, termite inspection fees, and more. For a house in the $36,000 price range, a recent Housing and Urban Development (HUD) survey indicates that total purchase-related costs were $3148.[7] Rounding off this figure to $3000 and assuming that the homeowner retains the house for the full 30 years of the mortgage, these costs add another $100 to annual ownership costs.

Maintenance

Maintenance costs are included in a tenant's rent but in large part are drawn directly out of a homeowner's pocket. The homeowner who can or who is willing to learn to make repairs can take care of much of the necessary maintenance and home improvements. A homeowner can undertake a professional exterior paint job estimated at $1000 with $100 of paint, $30 of tools, and a great many hours of labor. Some people find home maintenance a rewarding and a pleasurable pastime, and because the equipment used in home repair is constantly being improved, the task is becoming ever easier.

A tenant relies on the landlord for routine and emergency repairs. But many landlords try to do as little as possible, because every repair they must make eats away at profits. There are conscientious landlords, but many deliberately shirk their responsibilities. A tenant faced with a landlord who refuses to make needed repairs can accept the bad situation, sue, harass, or otherwise persuade the landlord to repair, or move out (see the discussion of the case of *Lindsey v. Normet*, pages 316–17).

Property Taxes

Property taxes are levied on virtually all residential property to cover the cost of local government and education. Property taxes are paid by a landlord out of rent payments or are paid once a year by the homeowner. Unlike income taxes, property taxes have no relation to the current ability to pay but are calculated at a rate based on the appraised value of the house or apartment building. Appraisals are prepared by an artificial and sometimes corrupt process in which a house is assigned a value based on estimates of its market value, and the value of its furnishings, the land the house occupies, and so on. If an owner is unable to pay the property taxes, the local government has the power to seize the house or building and to resell it. In such cases, ownership is virtually a kind of rental in that the local government can evict the owner for nonpayment of annual land "rent."

When inflation sends house prices soaring, tax increases tend to lag behind prices. This advantage is offset during depressions when house prices decrease

---

[7] U.S. Senate Committee on Banking, Housing, and Urban Affairs, *Mortgage Settlement Costs: Report of the Department of Housing and Urban Development,* 92nd Congress, 2nd Session (March 1972), p. 36.

but taxes remain fixed. Yet it is important to be aware that the current trend in house prices, taxes, and the business cycle is definitely inflationary. As government costs rise, property taxes increase. A homeowner who pays reasonable taxes of $500 per year when a house is first purchased may be paying annual taxes of $2000 10–15 years later. If the amount of the homeowner's disposable income that is available for property taxes doesn't increase in proportion to these taxes, a family can be forced to move to less highly taxed quarters just as a tenant who can't meet increased rent payments must find a less expensive apartment. Thus the best counsel for house buyers is modesty: A house whose taxes are low may at least be affordable ten years later; a house whose taxes are just bearable at the start may be too costly to maintain after a decade of inflation and increases in property taxes.

The homeowner has some tax advantages that the renter doesn't share. An owner can deduct local property taxes and mortgage interest from the adjusted gross income to reduce taxable income for U.S. federal income tax purposes. The higher the owner's income, the greater the tax savings. The owner who is in the 50% bracket (that is, whose income is taxed at a rate of 50%) and whose house taxes are $2000 per year can deduct $2000 from income, thereby saving $1000 in income taxes. This tax-reduction advantage is most effective for owners who earn $20,000 or more in gross income. Beneath this level, taking the standard tax deduction of 15% usually results in savings that are as good or better. But renters in certain states may deduct 10–25% of rent paid as an equivalent measure of taxes paid. These "homestead" tax credits can reduce taxable income or payable taxes, depending on the state of residence.

Forces Beyond Personal Control

Property values are always changing. Neighborhoods grow better or worse. Rezoning can permit a factory to open in a residential neighborhood, severely reducing the value of any adjacent property. Uninsurable "acts of God" may devastate homes. Hurricanes on the Atlantic and Gulf shores, tornadoes in the Midwest, mud slides in the Appalachians, earthquakes in California, and beach erosion in vulnerable areas are all disasters that local insurance companies normally refuse to cover at affordable rates. When threatened or affected by any of these calamities, renters can gather up their possessions and move elsewhere. Individual homeowners, on the other hand, can only bear the burdens. They may be able to salvage the bulk of their property and rebuild or to sell at lower market prices, but they cannot easily escape losses.

Assets and Inflation

Inflation is a dominant force in the economy today, forcing rents, house prices, taxes, and mortgage interest rates upward. But the homeowner's mortgage costs and the resultant monthly housing costs are fixed, at least until the end of the mortgage term. The homeowner has a growing capital asset in a house or an apartment. The sale of such property can represent a capital gain, although the homeowner would probably pay a similarly inflated price for equivalent accommodations elsewhere.

It has been said that the renter has an advantage over the homeowner in that the renter can invest the amount of the unnecessary mortgage down payment in the stock market (perhaps in a "growth stock") and make more money than the person who invests in a house. However, the validity of this statement depends on the state of the stock market and since 1970 the stock market has behaved erratically. As we observed in Chapter 8, truly reliable stocks are few and far between, and mutual funds as a whole have performed poorly. Not only have stocks frequently failed to keep abreast of inflation, but many have decreased in value due to investor jitters over the energy crisis, inflation, wars, and Presidents. These concerns have collapsed the prices of good and bad stocks alike. Since 1970, real estate investment has definitely outperformed the stock market, as have investments in many basic commodities.

Nevertheless the renter is in a more flexible position in the long run. Because his or her income isn't tied up in a 20- or a 30-year obligation to make fixed monthly payments, the renter is free to take advantage of good investment opportunities. But the homeowner has excellent collateral with which to obtain loans. A house can be remortgaged or used as collateral for other types of loans. A past record of regular mortgage payments can improve the owner's credit rating, which may result in more favorable loan rates.

Personal Factors The choice of whether to rent or to buy depends in an important way on a person's situation in life. Someone who will probably remain in the same community for at least five years can spread out the fixed initial cost of buying a home. But someone without a secure or permanent position might wish to avoid being saddled with an immovable object and a major debt. It can take several months to sell a home at a desirable price, and such a delay can force a homeowner to forego a job offer in another community.

BUDGETING FOR OWNERSHIP

Different lifestyles require different budgets, so that normative rules about how much to spend are not necessarily meaningful to every homeowner. A bachelor homeowner with a given income obviously can more freely allocate income to housing than the head of a large family who earns an equal income can. Nevertheless, average family spending patterns can provide an insight into budget norms. According to U.S. Department of Labor data for 1972, an urban family consisting of an employed husband, age 38, a wife who is not employed outside the home, and two children, ages 8 and 13, has the average income and housing budgets shown in the following table:[8]

[8] U.S. Department of Labor, Bureau of Labor Statistics, *Handbook of Labor Statistics, 1974,* Bulletin 1825, Tables 135–137, pp. 340–45.

	Low Budget	Intermediate Budget	Higher Budget
Total Budget	$7,386	$11,446	$16,558
Housing Outlay	$1,554	$ 2,810	$ 4,234
Housing as % of Total	21.0%	24.5%	25.5%

Housing tends to cost more in large cities than in small towns and more in the Northeast than in other parts of the United States.[9] These data show that families tend to spend an upper limit of about 25% of their after-tax income on housing. A frequently applied rule is that the annual cost of home ownership, including mortgage payments, maintenance, insurance, and other factors is 10% of the purchase price of a house. For the intermediate-budget family, a housing expenditure of $2810 suggests a house with a purchase price of about $28,000, which in this case represents approximately $2\frac{1}{2}$ times the annual after-tax income. The rule that housing outlays should not exceed $2\frac{1}{2}$ times after-tax income is a common benchmark. It is a useful guide, but it need not be an inflexible rule. Each family can adjust its expenditures to more or less than this amount.

The initial costs of home ownership must be taken into account. Total purchase-related costs, including lawyers' fees, title insurance, and land transfer charges, on a $25,000 house averaged $2609 in 1971.[10] To this must be added the down payment required if the prospective owner mortgages the house. More than 90% of all home purchases are financed by loans, and the down payment is a significant cost. Depending on the interest-rate level and on the condition of the money market in general, down payments required by lenders may range from 5–50%. Insured mortgages (in which an insurer, usually the Federal Housing Administration, guarantees the lender repayment if the borrower defaults) permit down payments as low as 5% of the purchase price. The minimum down payment for a $25,000 house is $1250. Including the other purchase-related costs of $2609 increases the initial and immediate cash expense of purchasing a $25,000 house to at least $3859.

The Current Cost of Ownership

The price of housing has climbed dramatically throughout North America since the late 1960s. U.S. Department of Commerce data indicate that home-ownership costs were 57.2% higher in March 1974 than they were in 1967. The average cost of a new home in April 1974 was $38,400, and an existing home cost $32,200. The mortgage loans on these houses were $29,400 and $23,500, respectively, with down payments remaining fairly constant at about $9000.[11]

[9] *Ibid.,* Tables 129–131, pp. 293–95.
[10] *Mortgage Settlement Costs,* p. 36.
[11] *Federal Reserve Bulletin* (May 1974), p. A–31.

There are many reasons why housing prices have risen so rapidly. The costs of land, interest, construction materials, labor, and transportation have all climbed steeply. Shortages of basic materials such as steel, plasterboard, cement, and flooring can force builders to buy supplies at retail rather than factory prices.[12] At 10% or more, mortgage rates are substantially higher in 1976 than they have been in the previous few years. But less mortgage money is available for loans due to the massive withdrawals of funds by savers from savings and loan associations which are the main source of lending available to potential home buyers.[13]

As long as interest costs and the prices of materials remain at currently high levels, buyers in search of detached, single-family housing will be forced to consider less expensive, semidetached housing, mobile homes, or renting. So great is the pressure to find alternatives to detached dwellings that single-family homes

[12] *The Wall Street Journal* (May 23, 1974), p. 1.
[13] *The Wall Street Journal* (August 19, 1974), p. 5.

constituted only 50% of all housing starts in 1974, down from 78% in the early 1960s.[14]

Although the prices of new homes are unlikely to decline, the prices of existing, older houses do decline from time to time. Resale housing prices fluctuate with consumer confidence in the future (including the willingness of home buyers to incur mortgage debts), the interest rates charged on mortgages, the relative cost of comparable new housing, and other factors. A combination of uncertainty about the future, the business cycle of prosperity and recession, and fluctuating interest rates can and often does cause housing prices to decrease as much as 10%.

CHOOSING A HOUSE

Househunting A search of the house market can be either personal (checking newspaper ads, driving through desirable neighborhoods, asking friends if they know of any houses for sale) or professional (consulting and relying on a real estate broker). Do-it-yourself househunting can be exhausting, yet a thorough personal search of the market results in a valuable understanding of the worth of houses.

Real Estate Brokers Real estate brokers charge commissions that average 6% of the sale price of the house. An honest, energetic broker will direct a buyer to the half dozen houses that are most suitable to the buyer's needs. Of course, the prospective buyer must candidly inform the broker about price range and lifestyle. A good broker can save a buyer the time, the exhaustion, and the difficulties of choice that inevitably arise after several dozen houses have been visited.

Finding a reliable broker can be difficult. In too many communities, brokers include scores of part-time salespeople with little knowledge of housing construction and community development. Even those with the best intentions can do little more than pass on their own sparse knowledge of house buying to the customer. The meaning of licenses and association memberships varies locally, because they are ruled by local rather than national standards. In any event, brokers who use high-pressure sales tactics should be avoided.

Choosing a Location The location of a house is a critical factor in determining its value. The quality and convenience of the neighborhood have a substantial impact on a house's purchase and resale price. Accordingly, it is necessary to consider seven neighborhood characteristics when evaluating the market.

1 *Character and stability of the neighborhood:* Deteriorating neighborhoods are marked by houses in poor repair, single-family dwellings that are being con-

[14] *The Wall Street Journal* (September 3, 1974), p. 1.

verted to apartments and rooming houses, and an increase in commercial property. No house can command a premium price if it is surrounded by slumlike conditions. Because neighborhoods that are in a state of transition tend to decline rather than to improve, it is essential to realize that a good house in a slightly rundown, "bargain" area could be practically worthless after a decade of neighborhood decline.

2 *Zoning:* A neighborhood that has stable house values must be protected from the invasion of undesirable industries, businesses, rooming houses, and over-building. Consulting the local government, usually the city or the township, should reveal what local zoning regulations are and whether they may be changed in an unfavorable way. For example, will future urban development or road construction affect the neighborhood adversely?

3 *Taxes:* What are the annual local property taxes? This information can be provided by the current owner of an existing house in the form of the house's tax bills or by a real estate agent when a new home is purchased. Then the local tax authorities can be consulted to determine the current tax assessment. What municipal services—schools, sewers, roads, lighting—are taxed? Is it necessary to pay supplemental charges or private maintenence workers to obtain such services as trash collection and snow removal?

4 *Utilities and services:* How adequate are police and fire protection, road main-tenance, and community recreational and cultural facilities?

5 *Schools:* If the family has children of school age, are the local schools supe-rior, adequate, or inferior? Is the school board responsive to local interests?

6 *Commuting and shopping:* Is it necessary to travel great distances to stores, schools, and places of employment? Is convenient public transportation available at a reasonable price? Is the nearest airport accessible, and is air-plane noise a problem in the area?

7 *Traffic patterns:* Is it necessary to spend hours each week crawling through traffic simply to get to work and back? Does traffic snarl local streets and blanket the neighborhood with fumes, vibrations, and noise? Are local railroad tracks and truck routes a problem?

The House Itself

The quest for the right house can be long and difficult, but it can be a methodical process if the following criteria are kept in mind.

Size. A house should contain at least 1000 square feet and an adequate number of bedrooms and bathrooms for family members and expected guests.

Design. The interior and exterior design features of the home should be both pleasing and functional. Bedrooms should be removed from immediate living areas for sufficient privacy and quiet. The kitchen should be efficiently arranged and designed and should contain enough power and electrical outlets for appliances.

Lot Size and Landscaping. Single-family, detached dwellings should be sepa-rated by 10 feet or more to assure privacy. Yards should be large enough to

accommodate family activities. The lot should be graded to ensure runoff of rain water. Shade trees are desirable for moderating summer temperatures.

Construction. Are there cracks or signs of seepage in the foundation? Are structure members free of termites and wood rot? (Consult a specialist if in doubt.) Are sloping roofs and exterior walls straight? (If not, the frame of the house may be sagging.) Is masonry free of major cracks? (This can be quite serious in an all-brick house.) Is wiring adequate for contemporary living? (A minimum requirement for major appliances in use is 100 amperes.) Is the heating system in good working order? If not, what kind of repairs does it need? Is plumbing in good repair? (Connection with a municipal sewer system is preferable to a septic tank or a cesspool.) Is the roof sound? (Check the attic for water stains and rot.) The insulation? (In areas with wide temperature variations, good insulation is essential, particularly with the present soaring rates for gas and electricity. Past utility bills should be inspected to ensure that these costs are affordable.)

No house is perfect, and almost any house can be brought up to high standards for a price. Hot-water heaters, furnaces, attic insulation, and roofing can all be repaired at prices of $300–1000, for average homes. A defect in almost any feature of the house, *except foundation and main structural members,* should be deducted from the asking price rather than considered a disqualification.

Few home buyers are expert judges of house quality and condition. Before buying a house, it is wise to have a professional appraiser or another realtor estimate its worth. Such an appraisal usually costs $25–50 and is well worth this amount. When in doubt about utility systems or other housing features, seek the advice of qualified professionals. But check their reputation with previous customers first; some may give inflated estimates of required work to drum up essentially unnecessary business.

Considering a New House

Although two out of three people who buy homes purchase "used" houses, a new house may be better suited to some homeowners' needs. It is essential to choose a reliable builder. Check with previous customers and inspect the builder's past work. Above all, don't take anything for granted. A model home that contains expensive furniture means nothing if sales agreements do not specify that the purchased house is *identical* to it. Every detail of construction must be specified in the contract. Who is to pay for the installation of sewer and water lines, sidewalks, driveways, streets, gas and electrical connections? Who is responsible for landscaping? Is the sales price specified initially, or is the builder permitted to increase costs when necessary? Is the construction completion date firm?

PURCHASING A HOUSE

Much of the ceremony and formality of medieval English land transaction has survived in American real estate law, which accounts for its intricacy and for local variations. In spite of the complexity of real estate law, many common processes can be employed to acquire land and houses.

Bargaining

Both the buyer and the seller bargain over price and terms of purchase. Using the recent sale prices of similar houses in the area and current appraisals as points of reference, the buyer offers somewhat less and the seller asks somewhat more than the market price. The buyer must be aware of any necessary repairs and should request that the market price be reduced accordingly. (If buyer and seller cannot agree on a satisfactory price, they part company here.)

If an understanding is reached that establishes the price, the date of occupancy, and the date of the final transaction (the "closing"), these terms and

"Houses used to be cheaper far from the city, but now, in what we call the pollution-free zone. . . "

some others are normally incorporated in a *purchase agreement.* The buyer deposits a required sum of money to ensure that the purchase will be made. If the buyer does change his or her mind, the seller retains this deposit. Some additional important points that the purchase agreement cover are:

1 A precise description of the property to be sold
2 The appliances and fixtures included in the sale
3 A disclosure of zoning regulations and easements (the rights of others to enter and perhaps to use the property)
4 An agreement as to who is to pay certain legal costs involved in checking the title to the property

The purchase agreement is the first of several critical documents to record the sale. Its terms control later aspects of the transaction. Errors and omissions here can be expensive and troublesome to correct later. It is wise for the buyer to consult an attorney before signing the purchase agreement to ensure that his or her rights and interests are completely protected.

Deeds and Titles

The most important document of the sale is the *deed,* the instrument that transfers *title* (formal ownership) from the seller, who is known as the *grantor,* to the buyer, who is known as the *grantee.* The process of transfer is quite strict to insure that the grantee receives only as good a title as the grantor has to offer. For example, if a grantor only partially owns the property, the grantee should receive the same partial ownership.

There are several forms of deeds to indicate the quality of the title that the grantor transfers. The *quitclaim deed* certifies only that the grantor intends to "quit the claim" and make no future claim to ownership of the property. However, the quitclaim deed doesn't indicate the extent of the grantor's title. Accordingly, quitclaim deeds are often considered inadequate; they are shabby merchandise as far as deeds are concerned. On the other hand, *warranty deeds* assure the grantee that the land and property being transferred are not encumbered by other claims of ownership or any restrictions (apart from zoning) regarding what the grantee can do to the property. A buyer who receives a warranty deed and later finds that the title is defective can sue for breach of the promise in the warranty, reclaim the purchase price, and recover damages as well.

Because there is always a risk that another claimant may appear to contest a title, buyers often take additional steps to protect their newly purchased titles. The principal device that assures buyers that their property won't be snatched away due to a footnote in a lawbook is *title insurance*. A number of insurance companies specialize in title insurance in each state, using a number of attorneys who concentrate on land transactions and who (in their opinion) are sufficiently knowledgeable in real estate law to make reliable judgments on the quality of titles. These lawyers search land-office records to ascertain whether clear titles are being transferred. If a buyer's title is challenged, the insurance company will defend the buyer in court and pay the defense expenses. Mortgage loans usually require that the buyer obtain title insurance to protect the lender's interests. But wise buyers also obtain insurance to protect their own interests in the property.

Mortgages

Over 90% of all home buyers either don't have the ready cash or have the money but lack the willingness to use it to purchase a home outright. A mortgage enables a buyer to purchase a house with a loan from a bank or some other lender. The mortgage is an instrument that conditionally permits the lender to repossess the mortgaged house or property if the borrower fails to meet the mortgage repayments. The process of seizing the mortgaged property is called *foreclosure* and usually entails the resale of the property. The specific conditions of the loan—the amount borrowed, the amount to be paid, the schedule of repayments, the penalties for variations from this schedule—are contained in a mortgage note. When the note is repaid, the mortgage is released. The person who mortgages the property is called the *mortgagor,* and the person who lends the money for the purchase of the property is called the *mortgagee.*

The length of a mortgage on a residential property is typically 5–35 years and is negotiated by the mortgagor and the mortgagee. The cost of the mortgage in terms of charged and repayable interest depends on four major factors:

1 The down payment
2 The prevailing interest rate at the time the loan is extended
3 The repayment period
4 The surcharges attached to the loan

The Down Payment. Lenders require a down payment from the borrower to ensure that the buyer has a financial interest in the house. Committing some of the buyer's money to the property should persuade the buyer to take good care of the house and, more importantly, not to abandon the investment by defaulting on the mortgage. Down payments of 5–50% are common. The higher amounts are required when mortgage money is difficult to obtain or when there is a question as to the financial responsibility of the borrower. Higher down payments reduce monthly repayment costs, but they also decrease the liquid cash reserves that the borrower maintains for emergencies and other purposes.

The Prevailing Interest Rate. At the present time, interest rates of $9–10\frac{1}{2}\%$ are charged on home mortgages in the United States. Inflation has driven interest rates higher than the partially controlled mortgage-funds market can afford to pay. Lenders therefore prefer to obtain higher rates from nonmortgage loans that can be extended at noncontrolled rates. The structure of interest rates has steadily risen throughout the United Sates and much of the western world since the beginning of the twentieth century. Mortgage rates of 3–4% and 6–7% prevailed in the 1950s and the 1960s, respectively. We can anticipate a return to interest rates of $7\frac{1}{2}–8\%$ in the late 1970s *if* the double-digit (10% or higher) inflationary rates prevailing in the mid-1970s abate.

The Repayment Period. The period during which a loan is repaid is called the *period of amortization*. A 20-year mortgage is amortized (that is, paid off) in 20 years. The longer the period of amortization, the longer interest must be paid to maintain it. Thus although extending the repayment period of a loan does reduce the required monthly payments, such an extension substantially increases the total amount of interest charged over the life of the loan.

Most borrowers prefer to have low monthly payments and therefore select fairly long amortization periods of 20–30 years. If mortgage insurance is available, the amortization period may sometimes be extended to 35 years.

Residential mortgage interest rates are limited by state and federal laws and by government actions in the markets for loanable funds. At times over the past few decades, home-mortgage rates have fallen below the interest rates charged for similar loans and financing for ordinary business purposes.

The Surcharges. To compensate for lending money at submarket rates, mortgage lenders add various fees to the regular mortgage interest rate. The

MONTHLY AMORTIZATION AND TOTAL COST OF INTEREST ON A $20,000 HOUSE

Interest Rate per Annum

Time to Amortize	6%	8%	10%	12%
5 years	$475/ $3,740*	$501/ $5,046	$528/ $6,380	$555/ $7,741
10 years	$272/ $7,174	$298/ $9,806	$325/$12,549	$354/$15,397
20 years	$174/$14,874	$204/$20,741	$235/$26,984	$268/$33,552
30 years	$145/$23,589	$178/$33,296	$212/$43,648	$248/$54,486
40 years	$133/$51,169	$168/$47,088	$205/$61,807	$243/$77,043

* Monthly payment/Total loan interest

most prominent of these surcharges are *points*—a lump-sum fee that the lender requires the borrower to pay when the mortgage is approved. One point is 1% of the amount borrowed. As a rule, 2 points are charged for each $\frac{1}{4}$% difference between the commercial mortgage rate and the maximum rate that can be charged on government-controlled mortgages. For example, if the commercial mortgage rate is 10% and the government-controlled rate is 8%, then a 2% spread exists that represents 16 points. One point on a $40,000 house is $400, and 16 points are charged for a total surcharge of 16 × $400, or $6400. Sometimes lenders add loan origination fees as well, which are also expressed in terms of a surcharge of a few points.

Sources. Mortgage loans can be obtained from a variety of commercial lenders. The terms of most of these mortgages extend 20 years or more. The amount of the loan is usually 60–90% of the appraised property value. If the appraiser estimates that the value of the property is 75% of the market value, then a loan at 60–90% of the appraised value represents 45–67$\frac{1}{2}$% of the market value. In this case, a sizeable down payment would be required.

Several U.S. government agencies enable borrowers to obtain mortgages with lower down payments than would otherwise be possible. Although the Federal Housing Administration—a part of the Department of Housing and Urban Development—does not extend loans, it does insure them. With the purchase of such FHA–HUD insurance, a 3% down payment is acceptable on a house that costs up to $15,000. To cover risks and operating costs, FHA–HUD charges the borrower an annual premium of $\frac{1}{2}$% per year on the unpaid principal balance of the mortgage. In evaluating a house and its potential buyer, FHA–HUD employs all standard credit checks. The agency also inspects the property to verify that it is insurable. But a potential buyer should not consider a FHA–HUD inspection a warranty that the house is perfect or entirely satisfactory in all details. HUD also insures mobile-home loans up to a limit of $15,000 and 12 years, allowing a reduced down payment of as little as 5%. But the mobile home must be located on a site approved by HUD, be at least 10 feet wide and 40 feet long, and meet HUD construction standards.

Similarly, the Veterans Administration insures loans, although it does not usually extend loans itself. The VA currently guarantees lender investments up to a maximum of 60% of the appraised value of the home to a limit of $12,500. In addition, the loan cannot carry an interest rate greater than the VA limit, and the buyer must have served at least 90 days of active duty in the armed forces. In October 1970, VA procedures were modified by the GI Home Loan Law. Among the features of this law is a new statute that extends the expiring VA loan privilege for World War II and Korean War veterans and that permits VA financing to be applied to mobile homes (up to a maximum interest rate of $10\frac{3}{4}\%$ to a limit of 12 years and $10,000 coverage, or 15 years and $17,000 coverage for a developed lot). Congress also requires that the VA extend loans of the full purchase price directly to veterans who are severely disabled and require a specially modified home to accommodate their disabilities.

MOBILE HOMES

The mobile-home market has flourished in America's transient society. Mobile homes reduce housing costs because they are produced on factory assembly lines and then transported to their installation sites. However, it is a misconception to stress mobility when referring to these houses, because mobile homes that truly compete with houses and apartments as permanent residences are too clumsy and often too poorly constructed to permit frequent or long moves.

Because mobile homes compete with less expensive homes in the marketplace, mobile builders find it profitable to cut corners. Many consumer complaints about mobile homes stem from shoddy construction practices. To correct such abuses, both the FHA–HUD and the VA have established manufacturing standards in cooperation with the American National Standards Institute (ANSI). To date, over 35 states have also adopted the ANSI Standard Number A119.1. ANSI covers the mobile home's body and frame, plumbing system, heating system, and electrical circuits. Where ANSI standards apply, a manufacturer must certify that its product complies with these standards, must provide a diagram indicating the tie–down points for the houses attachment to the ground, and most significantly, must disclose the geographical area for which the trailer has been built to be certain that it can stand the prevailing winds, snow loads, and temperatures.[15]

Mobile homes are usually located on rented sites in trailer parks. The management of these parks is often quite arbitrary. Fees have been imposed on overnight guests, unexpected charges have been made for routine maintenance,

[15] *Building and Financing a Mobile Home* (HUD-243-F(3)) (September 1973).

and residents have been evicted in retaliation for voicing their objections. Many states are now in the process of protecting mobile-home residents by passing statutes that forbid such practices.[16]

The major advantage of owning a mobile home is that its purchase price and down payment requirements are less than the requirements for the purchase of conventional housing. The disadvantages of mobile homes are that they tend to depreciate rather than to appreciate in price (as conventional houses do), are built to less than "permanent" standards, and if located in a trailer park, can expose their occupants to obnoxious and harassing management.

MOVING

Vance Packard estimates that at least 40 million Americans, or one-fifth of the U.S. population, move at least once a year. People who have college educations and/or who earn above-average incomes are more likely to move across county lines. Three-quarters of these Americans work for large corporate or government organizations and are moved by long-distance movers. These people are primarily managers, professionals, or technical personnel. People who are unemployed also move with above-average frequency, but they tend to move shorter distances.[17]

Regulation

There are over 12,000 movers, but less than 3000 of them are certified by the Interstate Commerce Commission (ICC) to operate on an interstate basis. The ICC's regulation of the moving industry has been of the greatest benefit to the firms in this industry—not to the consumers. As in most of its operations, the ICC has converted its historic mandate to control monopoly into a legalistic procedure guaranteeing that firms can operate as if they are part of a great monopoly whose rates and practices are not subject to competition.

Quality of Service

Some houshold movers are scrupulous, honest, and careful in their work. But most movers—including the franchised national moving firms that maintain coast-to-coast offices and warehouses—tend not to be. Moving suffers from a lack of mechanization, the excessive handling of merchandise as it is shifted about in vans during reloadings (this happens when a customer's load doesn't fill a van and additional merchandise is taken aboard), and the division of responsibility between sales offices, van drivers, and the owners and operators of the

---

[16] *The Detroit Free Press* (January 9, 1973), p. 10A; U.S. Office of Consumer Affairs, *State Consumer Action: Summary '71*, p. 81; *Summary '72*, p. 179.

[17] Vance Packard, *A Nation of Strangers* (New York: McKay, 1972), pp. 7–12.

trailers they pull. Often all three entities are separately owned and separately financed, although they may operate with identical trademarks. Such a division of ownership requires extra profits and is therefore more expensive for the consumer. Finally, employees in the moving industry tend to be people who can't find better-paying or easier jobs in other fields. The backbreaking work of moving is left to the mover's helpers, whose tenure in the industry is brief and whose sense of responsibility is hardly encouraged by the minimum wages they receive.

The Consumer's Situation

Household moving is perhaps the only industry in which customers must pay for a service before they can evaluate it. ICC procedures and industry practice require that the moving-van driver be paid for goods on delivery before they are unloaded and inspected. If the customer cannot pay for the goods or wishes to protest their condition, the mover is instructed to return them to the warehouse—inevitably at the expense of the customer. Moving charges are based on shipment weight and distance traveled, although piece rates are charged for special services such as packing and appliance removal and installation. ICC practice permits movers to accept only cash, certified checks, money orders, or traveler's checks. The customer who does not have the amount of the estimated cost of the move plus 10% readily available faces the prospect that his or her goods will be placed in storage. If the moving charges exceed the original estimate by more than 10%, however, the customer is required to pay only estimate plus 10% when the move is completed and can take up to 15 business days to pay the balance.

Loss and Damage

The American Movers Conference reports that 25% of all moves involve some damage claims and that these claims average $42. This doesn't seem like a large claim to incur when moving the entire contents of a house, until we consider two facts:

1 The standard insurance charge for household effects is a rate of 60¢ per pound or the actual value of the goods, whichever amount is smaller. How many possessions are worth only 60¢ a pound?
2 Some unscrupulous movers use the inventory condition list required by the ICC to record that goods are in worse condition than they actually are. This practice protects movers from some damage claims, because they can refuse a claim on the grounds that a piece of furniture that was really in good condition was already damaged before it was loaded in the van.

Greater insurance coverage is available at a premium of 50¢ per $100 of declared value for the entire shipment, and this insurance offers valuable protection at a modest cost.

Self-protection

What can consumers do to avoid being ripped-off by a mover? Not much, really, because most large movers charge standard ICC rates and perform similar services. But these 11 preventive steps can be taken:

1 Check with friends and associates to see who has had the least disappointing experience with movers.
2 Consider renting a truck and moving smaller and more precious possessions.
3 Check to see if some merchandise can be shipped more economically by United Parcel (which has an excellent record for promptness and care) or, if items are not breakable, by straight rail freight.
4 Obtain a copy of the ICC "Summary of Information for Shippers of Household Goods," Form BOp 103, from the ICC or the mover. Interstate movers are required to provide this summary to customers.
5 Throw out useless junk and consider selling goods, particularly those that can be easily replaced or that are heavy and/or worn out.
6 Request pickup and delivery dates from the mover. ICC procedures permit movers to charge for "expedited service," so that a mover can levy a surcharge if goods arrive at the destination on time or no charge if they are late.
7 Obtain enough insurance from the shipper or from a private source to cover possible losses.
8 Prepare an inventory and check the mover's list of goods to verify that it is complete and that the condition of any item is not incorrectly recorded to compensate for possible damage during the move.
9 Accompany the mover to the public weight scales, where the shipment is weighed and where part of the moving bill is computed. Be sure that the van driver doesn't add his or her own weight, the weights of the helpers, or any other weights to the load to increase profits.
10 At the destination, record any damage or lost articles. It may be helpful to write over the acceptance signature the phrase "accepted subject to concealed loss or damage," which will faciliate any later claims that may be necessary. Claim the original value of any item, because the company will depreciate damaged goods before compensation. Anyone who is not reimbursed for losses should contact the Interstate Commerce Commission or a lawyer.
11 Maintain records of all moving costs, including house-hunting trips, meals, gas and mileage, temporary living expenses, and fees incurred in buying, leasing, or renting a residence. These costs are tax deductible, as are any articles that are donated to charity.

REFORMS

The current market for residential housing and real estate is adversely affected in three important ways:

1 Deceptive sales
2 Discriminatory sales practices
3 Unwieldy mortgage interest rates

We'll discuss each briefly.

Sales Deceptions

The ancient rule of the market is *caveat emptor* "may the buyer beware." When looking for a house, it is wise to keep this phrase in mind. Buyers should exercise extreme caution in choosing a house that will cost a few times their annual income and that they may own for years or even decades.

Houses are complicated propositions. Important defects can be concealed within walls and foundations. Most consumers are inexperienced in evaluating houses; usually only the builder or the previous owner knows the true condition of the property being sold. Accordingly, several states explicitly limit the rule of *caveat emptor* as it applies to new housing that is sold by a builder to a first owner. An Alabama appelate court held in *Cochran v. Keeton* that a *warranty of implied fitness for habitation* exists in such cases.[18] Canadian officials are currently proposing that sellers of all houses, old and new, be held liable for 10 years for any hidden defects that they fail to disclose at the time of the sale. Of course, the willful concealment of serious flaws in property or title has always been considered fraudulent and subject to civil and criminal prosecution.

Land-sales promotions in which lots or houses in another state are offered as resort or vacation homes have especially abused the buyer's right to an honest pitch and a square deal. As is true in any transaction, it is unwise to buy before seeing *exactly* what is being sold. In the past, some more accomplished promoters have sold lots at the bottom of swamps, perched on cliffs, or located miles from roads and electricity. Since 1969 interstate sales of building sites of less than 5 acres each that are part of a development of 50 or more lots have been subject to HUD antifraud reporting requirements. Developers of these sites must file a *property report* with the HUD Office of Interstate Land Sales and provide copies to all buyers more than 48 hours before the contracts are to be signed. Failure to provide such a report is grounds for canceling the sale. Interested parties can obtain these reports from HUD for a small fee.

The property report, which some states require for all developments, discloses the builder's experience, assets, and plans. Any alleged "plan" to build recreational facilities must be fully detailed, and the builder must specifically state whether these facilities will or will not actually be constructed. The plan to finance the development must be fully outlined. When financing is conducted by *land-sales contracts,* buyers should be especially wary. Unlike a mortgage, during which the buyer accumulates some equity as he or she makes payments, a land-sales contract does not grant the buyer ownership until the last payment is made on a contract that can extend as long as 20 years. However, if an owner fails to meet payments on a 20-year mortgage, after 15 years, the owner would be awarded the principal less foreclosure costs in any legal proceeding. In such a case, the owner might receive a reimbursement of 50% or more of the original purchase price. But if this owner had signed a land-sales contract, there would be no reimbursement, because no ownership interest would be conveyed until the last payment was made on time.

Discriminatory Sales Practices

In the Civil Rights Act of 1866, Congress ruled that "All citizens of the United States shall have the same right, in every State and Territory, as is enjoyed by

[18] 252 So. 2d 307.

white citizens thereof to inherit, purchase, lease, sell, hold, and convey real and personal property.'' However, this legislation was not effective or really enforced until the recent Johnson administration began its civil rights activities in the Congress and the courts. Throughout the twentieth century, landlords and real estate agents had a place to put everyone: one area or building for the white Protestants, another for the Jews, areas for more recent immigrants, and, last of all, whatever was left for blacks, Puerto Ricans, Chicanos, and anyone else who wasn't sufficiently white.

The Civil Rights Act of 1968, Title VIII, forbade racial, religious, or any other form of discrimination on the part of a seller or a lessor employed in the business of selling or leasing housing. Essentially, any refusal to sell a house or to negotiate with a potential buyer, or any imposition of discriminatory practices on the buying process (for instance, making favorable mortgage rates available only to racially or otherwise preferred buyers) now is illegal. The 1968 statute applies to any case involving discrimination in advertising or on the part of a real estate broker. But the law contains one glaring loophole: Homeowners who do not employ brokers can sell only to chosen buyers if they do so infrequently (no more than once every two years if the seller has not been the most recent occupant of the dwelling). In other words, the loophole probably allows 95% of all owner-occupants of single-family dwellings to sell selectively, as long as they don't use brokers or obviously discriminatory advertising. Landlords who live in their own two, three, or four family dwellings may lawfully discriminate, too, as may religious organizations that wish to admit coreligionists and exclude others and private clubs that operate for noncommercial purposes. An important aspect of the 1968 statute is that it illegalizes the practice of ''block-busting'' —persuading owners to sell or rent at bargain prices by alleging that minority groups are moving into the neighborhood and then reselling or rerenting the same properties at higher prices.

Although the Civil Rights Act of 1968 may be functionally inoperative in smaller towns where homes can be sold informally and quietly, it is potentially powerful in cities where the housing market is in the hands of the large corporations. Such firms risk federal civil and criminal prosecution if they violate this Act. Unfortunately, the enforcing agency, HUD, may merely employ informal conciliation or recommend that the aggrieved person sue in federal court in such cases. The standard penalty fee for discrimination in housing is $1000, which is a small price for a big firm to pay. Criminal penalties are imposed only if the discriminating seller or lessor threatens to interfere violently with or intimidate a person who wishes to exercise his or her rights under the Act. This type of prosecution would be comparable to police officials negotiating with a burglar to stop stealing, and if the burglar won't stop, telling the people who've been robbed to sue the burglar themselves. If they win, they are awarded $1000 (no matter what the value of the stolen goods). The burglar risks jail only if he or she threatens the victims or the police with violence.

Mortgages and Inflation Mortgage interest rates have risen dramatically from a level of 5–6% in the mid-1960s to 10–12% today. The payments required to amortize these mortgages (remember the escalation of house prices in the same period, too) have risen even more rapidly. Many families of moderate means have been excluded from the market for owner-occupied housing. From 1965 to 1973 the wage and salary income of the average employed civilian rose 57% (12% in real terms), but the monthly payment required to amortize a standard term mortgage on an average new house rose 85%. Therefore, the average U.S. family can afford less housing now than it could 10 years ago.

As Donald P. Tucker pointed out in a perceptive article in *The Wall Street Journal:*

> . . . the basic defect with standard mortgage loans is their rigid adherence to a level repayment schedule. . . . The burden is heaviest in the first year, and it declines each year thereafter as inflation continually raises the borrower's income and the real value of his house and reduces the real value of the level mortgage payments.[19]

Tucker recommends that the first-year impact of high mortgage costs can be eased by adopting a graduated repayment schedule, in which subnormal interest payments are made in the early life of the mortgage and larger-than-present payments are made toward the end of the mortgage. Such a repayment method would be advantageous to the borrower as long as inflation rates do not decrease significantly. But adopting this mortgage plan would require the amendment of federal and state regulations that specifically prohibit mortgages whose payments and interest rates increase over time.

SUMMARY

1 Home ownership fulfills the personal goals of independence and security and offers some protection against the rising cost of shelter.

2 The demand for housing depends on people's absolute physical requirements for space and their preferences for types and locations of housing.

3 The supply of housing increases by about two million units annually. House production is characteristically inefficient because small-scale contractors are unable to operate at an efficient level of output.

4 In cooperative development each member purchases a share in a jointly owned corporation and signs an occupancy agreement for a private dwelling space. In a condominium development each member owns one dwelling unit outright and has a voting share in the development's operations and common properties. Both cooperatives and condominiums offer their owners tax advantages (property tax and mortgage interest deductions) that are not available to renters.

5 The rent-or-buy decision is analyzed financially by comparing rent and mortgage amortization payments for equivalent property. Taxes and maintenance are assumed constant and are charged either directly to the owner or indirectly to the renter. Any savings account or other investment interest that the owner loses on the down payment must be included in the calculation. Initial purchase-related costs should be amortized over the buyer's ex-

[19] *The Wall Street Journal* (June 12, 1974), p. 38.

pected period of occupancy. Inflation and forces beyond the personal control of the buyer can be estimated. During an inflationary period, the buyer benefits in that the value of the house increases.

6 In 1974 home ownership costs were about 60% higher than they were in 1967. The average homeowner spends about 25% of after-tax income on housing. Mortgage interest rates have approximately doubled since 1967, and the required monthly mortgage payments have also doubled. This means that homeowners in 1976 could afford less housing than they could in 1967.

7 The selection of a house should be determined by the qualities of the neighborhood (character, stability, zoning, land taxes, utilities and services, schools, commuting and shopping, traffic patterns, noise) and by the house's structure (size, design, lot size and landscaping, construction). Expert appraisals are worth their cost.

8 The process of buying a house consists of the initial bargaining, the preparation of a purchase agreement, and the closing of a transfer of title. The deed of sale may vary from a quitclaim (a limited offer by the seller not to challenge the deed) to superior guarantees of good title that are contained in warranty deeds. Possible flaws in a title can result in the loss of the house; accordingly, buyers should purchase title insurance to protect their interests.

9 Over 90% of all house buyers have mortgages. Down payments range from 50% when money is tight to as little as 3% on government-insured mortgages. Monthly repayment charges depend on the down payment, interest rate, repayment period, and surcharges.

10 Mobile homes cost less to purchase initially, but their mortgages extend for shorter terms. Mobile homes depreciate, in contrast to the customary appreciation of houses. Shoddy construction and trailer park mismanagement are two current problems that mobile home buyers must face.

11 When household goods are moved, the consumer has a government-guaranteed disadvantage. One-fifth of the U.S. population moves at least once each year. Consumers can protect themselves somewhat by moving as few of their goods as possible, renting a truck and moving themselves, carefully checking the mover's charges and furniture condition reports, and reading the ICC "Summary of Information for Shippers of Household Goods."

12 Current reform activity in the housing industry includes legislation in three important areas:

   1 Deceptive sales (governments should require land-sales disclosure statements and force house sellers to provide warranties against hidden defects)

   2 Discriminatory sales practices (racial, ethnic, and religious discrimination is illegal under the Civil Rights Acts of 1866 and 1968, subject to enormous loopholes)

   3 Recommendations for a graduated mortgage repayment schedule that begins with subnormal interest payments, thereby permitting homeowners to escape some of the large initial impact of inflation on their budgets.

Suggestions for Further Reading

". . . Closing Costs," *Consumer Reports,* August 1975, pp. 482–88.

Keats, John. *The Crack in the Picture Window.* Boston: Houghton Mifflin, 1956.

Shafer, Ronald G. *"A Fading Dream," The Wall Street Journal* (September 3, 1974), pp. 1, 21.

United States Savings and Loan League, *What You Should Know Before Buying a Home* (1972).

U.S. Department of Housing and Urban Development, *Wise Home Buying,* HUD Publication HUD-321-F(3) (July 1973).

U.S. Interstate Commerce Commission, *Summary of Information for Shippers of Household Goods,* ICC Form BOp 103, revised (1974).

U.S. Veterans Administration, *Home-Buying Veteran,* VA Pamphlet 26—6, revised (June 1973).

U.S. Senate Committee on Banking and Currency, Subcommittee on Housing and Urban Affairs, *A Study of Mortgage Credit,* 90th Congress, 1st Session (May 22, 1967).

U.S. Department of Housing and Urban Development, *Questions About Condominiums,* HUD Publication HUD-365-F (June 1974).

U.S. Senate Committee on Banking, Housing, and Urban Affairs, *Mortgage Settlement Costs: Reports of the Department of Housing and Urban Development,* 92nd Congress, 2nd Session (March 1972).

The Consumer Workshop

1 Examine your current family living situation. How many people are in your household, what sorts of things do you do at home, what budget needs and financial resources do you have? For your lifestyle, is owner-occupied housing better than rental housing?

2 You are moving to New York City to work for a major bank at a salary of $30,000 a year. You have ample choice of housing at this income level, but you want to stay in the city rather than live in the suburbs. You can choose a detached house, a cooperative, or a condominium. What are the advantages and the disadvantages of each choice in terms of your own needs and the alternative of a rented apartment?

3 Suppose that you intend to purchase a detached house for $40,000. What would you require in a house? List your needs in order of their importance. Among other design and location features, evaluate house design, structure, land size, location, utility/service, schools, and area of the country.

4 You are employed by a large firm that requires you to move every year or two. Your spouse and children are unhappy with these frequent moves, but you have no choice in the matter. Should you:
    1 Rent a home in each location?
    2 Buy and sell houses when necessary?
    3 Live in a mobile location?

Consider cost, other financial factors, and the personal satisfaction provided by each solution.

5 You are renting a house now but you wish to buy a house in the near future. You expect inflation to average 10% per year for several decades. How does the level of inflation affect your rent-or-buy decision?

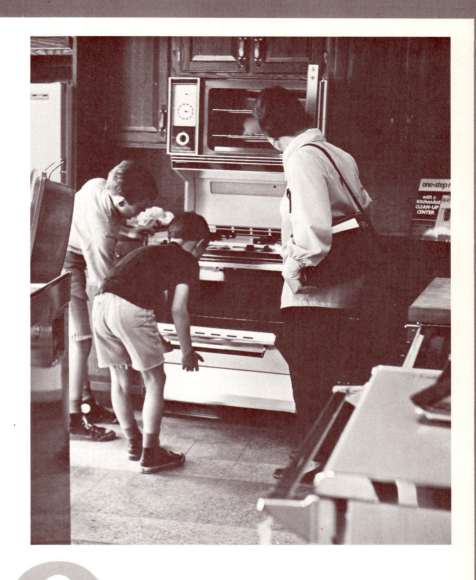

19
FURNISHING YOUR HOME

19 "Once in my life I would like to own something outright before it's broken! I'm always in a race with the junk-yard! I just finish paying for the car and it's on its last legs. The refrigerator consumes belts like a goddamn maniac. They time those things. They time them so when you've finally paid for them, they're used up."

WILLY LOMAN IN ARTHUR MILLER'S
Death of a Salesman

Buying and owning furniture and appliances is a complex matter that can involve sorting through the vast range of home furnishings and home equipment that the market offers. In this chapter we attempt to simplify that task by examining the manufacturing, marketing, and servicing of furniture and appliances. With such information, the consumer can make more intelligent and therefore more accurate market choices.

HOME FURNISHINGS AND THE CONSUMER

In furnishing a home, the consumer must solve a series of interrelated problems in planning, budgeting, design, and product evaluation. Because a significant amount of current and future budgets are allocated to furniture, appliances, and other home furnishings, it is imperative that consumers know their present and future needs and resources. When choosing furniture that is to be serviceable for years, it is best to purchase products whose materials, finishes, styles, and other characteristics will not become outmoded in style and will wear well over the period of expected use. To do this, the consumer must have at least an elementary knowledge of how furniture is made. Home appliances vary greatly in price and quality. Comparing their values and relative qualities often requires an understanding of basic appliance design and may necessitate some specific research in terms of the type of appliance being considered. Energy costs are now substantial budget costs for most homeowners; the purchase price of an appliance must therefore be available in terms of the estimated gas or electricity consumption during the appliance's expected lifetime.

Most manufactured goods have a limited life. Eventually, they deteriorate; in the meantime, they require service, parts, and other maintenance. Product warranties enable the consumer to predict and control service and parts costs. Although warranty service has often posed a problem for consumers in the past, important legislation has recently been passed in this area. We review this legislation here in the context of describing the consumer's new legal rights when dealing with appliance and other product manufacturers and dealers.

THE HOME FURNISHING BUDGET

Many people feel they must buy an entire array of home furnishings as soon as they move into a new house. But this practice requires more cash than most of us have readily available and can cause consumers to incur large and costly (high-interest) debts that can carry interest charges as high as or in excess of the purchase price of the items. A less costly approach is to furnish a home using the method of *planned acquisition*.

Planned Acquisition

Planned acquisition means furnishing the home in keeping with the family's or the individual's changing lifestyle. For example, most young families earning average incomes do not need elaborate entertainment facilities for, say, formal parties. As their means and responsibilities increase, a greater portion of their budget can be allotted to home entertainment. Another example of planned acquisition is a family with young children that postpones buying fine furniture until the children are old enough to treat it with care.

FURNITURE

Furniture should be selected that is consistent with the quality, durability, style, and cost of the family's or the individual's acquisition plan. Consumers need guidelines to recognize good values in the furniture market, and we provide some overall rules in the following sections. But remember that, like most generalizations, these rules have their exceptions. Only careful shopping can be the final guide.

Some Furniture Is Built to Last

Major furniture manufacturers usually recognize their responsibilities to build good products. The record of consumer advocates who have publicized the shoddy work of some furniture manufacturers in the past has encouraged other companies to attempt to achieve quality control and to provide a good standard of expected performance. Many firms now engineer products to weather average family use and abuse, including anticipated wear and tear by children. Furniture fabrics, frames, and finishes are now available in attractive and durable materials. Of course, consumers who buy "childproof" furniture but have no children receive that much more performance life for their money.

"You can have either comfort or style or durability, but not all three."

Upholstered Furniture

The quality of upholstered furniture is often difficult to judge, because the cover and styling of a sofa, for example, do not affect its durability as much as the quality of the frame and its supporting padding and springs do (see Figure 19-1). Upholstered furniture of good quality (well-made but not handcrafted) varies greatly in price. Six-foot long sofas can cost as little as $200 or more than $1000. Stuffing and covering are two important determinants of price. A sturdy, serviceable dining or recreational chair can be purchased for $25; imported chairs featuring expensive woods and finishes or leather coverings can cost $250 or more. Thinly padded lounge chairs that are covered with inexpensive materials start at $100; chairs with thicker padding that are covered in leather or some other fine fabric can range as high as $500.

Construction Materials. Good chair and sofa frames are made of kiln-dried hardwood. Woods that aren't dried or that are improperly dried can warp easily. The supporting structure of the seats should resemble bedsprings: separate drop-in coils connected by cords of rugged fiber. Cushions can be filled with a variety of materials, but their contents are required by law to be listed on attached tags. The down of any domestic bird retains its resilience for an average of 25 years; it is the most durable and most expensive filling. A medium-cost alternative is natural foam rubber, which lasts an average of 15 years. The least expensive filling, polyester (synthetic) foam, usually lasts about 5 years. But compare prices to personal need to determine the best value: If a polyester-filled sofa costs $300, one with natural foam will cost about $350. The same sofa with down-filled cushions will cost about $400. Pick the item and the price that best fit the need. Quality can't be considered an absolute, because it's related to price and intended use.

Hard Unupholstered Furniture When buying wooden dining tables and occasional tables, as well as desks, vanities, chests of drawers, and other pieces of wooden furniture, look for signs of quality manufacture. Tabletops should be resistant to warping. Solid tops of fine hardwoods are seldom found in today's tables, because the costs of these woods are high and they tend to warp. Most modern tabletops are made of plywood or of a sawdust–woodchip–glue concoction, both of which offer good warp resistance. Fine veneers are often matched so that grains seem to form a repeated pattern. This type of matching is attractive, but it is also expensive because many pieces of veneer may be discarded before a set of well-matched pieces can be found and assembled.

Good tables should have aprons under the tops. Aprons provide a rigid base and anchor for the table legs and enable a table to stand years of hard wear

19-1 Structure of a Chair

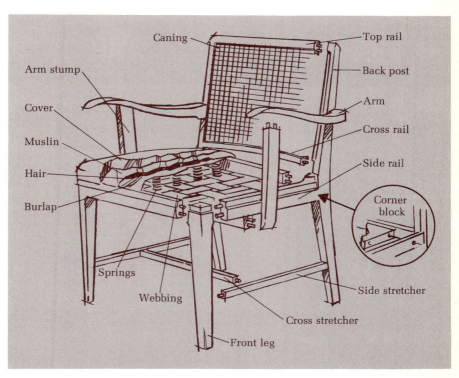

without becoming wobbly. Furniture joints should be made with interlocking and reinforcing features to maintain shape and rigidity (see Figure 19-2). Dining tables with teak veneers are priced as low as $100; a finely finished hardwood table can cost as much as $2000.

Desks and chests with drawers should be constructed so that drawers will open and close easily for years. Good drawers have dovetail joints and center and side glides (see Figure 19-3). Drawer supports on better chests are made of birch—a wood preferred by cabinetmakers because it is resistant to wear, warping, and swelling. Drawer bottoms should be made of mahogany plywood; this material is highly resistant to breaking and bulging, has a pleasant smell, and is odor resistant. Drawers should be separated by dustproof liners. Good chests and desks range in price from $100 to $1000, or higher.

Types of Furniture Sellers

Furniture can be purchased in department stores, specialty shops, decorator shops, and discount houses. Most department stores offer extensive services at no additional charge; they usually deliver and repair furniture and, when necessary, grant refunds on the merchandise they sell. Department stores mark up their furniture prices 40–50% over the original purchase costs, but these stores tend to represent their merchandise honestly. Their profits are substantially reduced by high service costs that often amount to half of the wholesale prices they pay.

A greater selection of special or unusual merchandise may be found at decorator stores, but their prices are often marked up to match the look of the furniture on display and do not necessarily reflect the standard markups found in the furniture departments of larger stores. A piece of furniture that retails for $100 in a department store may be marked up to $200 at a specialty store if its appearance can justify the higher price tag. Specialty furniture stores usually avoid the standard, major-brand, middle-priced lines carried by large department stores, because these smaller stores don't buy in volume and can't obtain the discounts granted to larger stores that buy millions of dollars of inventory

19-2 Well-Made Furniture Joints

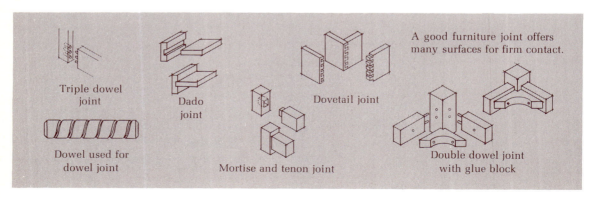

Triple dowel joint

Dowel used for dowel joint

Dado joint

Dovetail joint

Mortise and tenon joint

A good furniture joint offers many surfaces for firm contact.

Double dowel joint with glue block

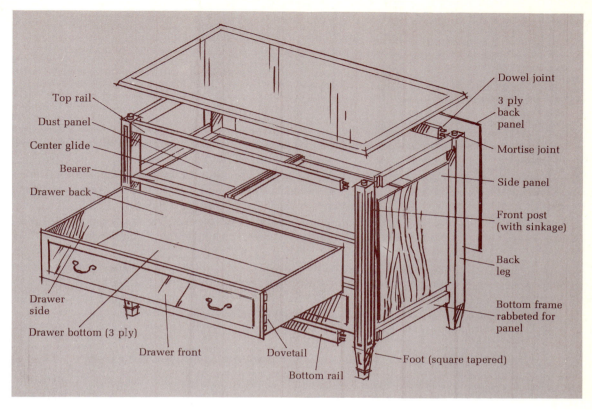

Top rail

Dust panel

Center glide

Bearer

Drawer back

Drawer side

Drawer bottom (3 ply)

Drawer front

Dovetail

Bottom rail

Dowel joint

3 ply back panel

Mortise joint

Side panel

Front post (with sinkage)

Back leg

Bottom frame rabbeted for panel

Foot (square tapered)

19-3   Structure of a Chest with Drawers

every year.   Their position in the market requires specialty furniture stores to carry the types of odd styles that department stores and other major distributors prefer not to inventory for many months or even years.   It is important to be aware that the higher the turnover in merchandise is, the lower the prices for a given profit level are.   In other words, the rarer the goods, the slower they sell; the slower goods sell, the higher they must be priced to cover interest and warehousing costs.

Furniture discount stores often charge lower prices than other retailers, but the quality and selection of their merchandise may be poorer.   Some discount-house merchandise may appear to be similar to articles that are sold in department stores but may actually be quite different in construction and in upholstering.   For example, vinyl-covered kitchen chairs that appear to be identical may last for months or for years, depending on their construction: to last many years, the vinyl covering must have a cloth backing.   When buying discount-store furniture, consumers must be sure that the quality of construction is worth the discount price.

Shopping for furniture requires care and patience.   It is profitable to spend a few days checking several sources for a desired item.   Study the market to become acquainted with variations in price, brand, construction, and many other determinants of quality and value in furniture.

APPLIANCES

The household appliance market offers a fascinating variety of both useful and practically useless products. Some of these appliances, such as stoves and refrigerators, are essential for any lifestyle. Others, such as electric knives, power toothbrushes, and electric can openers, are time-saving but unnecessary devices primarily purchased as gifts or by people without the agility to use basic tools properly. In this section we draw substantially on the findings of the Massachusetts Institute of Technology's National Science Foundation study *Consumer Appliances: The Real Cost,* concentrating on two types of major appliances: white goods and brown goods. *White goods* are the basic kitchen appliances, so named in the days when white was the only color they were painted. *Brown goods* are household electronic appliances, such as televisions, stereo phonographs, and air conditioners.

Total Lifetime Cost

There are three elements in the total cost of any power appliance:

1 Its purchase price
2 Its service and warranty costs
3 The electricity or gas required to operate it.

Although the purchase price is known at the beginning of the life of an appliance, its service and power costs can only be estimated over the *useful life span* of the device. Refrigerators have an average useful life span of 14 years, color televisions sets, of 10. The life span of washing machines and dryers depends on the intensity of their use, but their average is just over 7 years. The purchase price of a refrigerator is only 36% of its total cost in terms of service and power over its life span. The purchase price of a color television set is half its total life cost.

Purchase Price

The purchase price of major appliances has actually declined over the last 20 years. Since the beginning of World War II, the consumer price level has more than tripled but the prices of basic appliances have decreased. In 1950 an automatic washer cost $300; a 12-inch black and white television and a 12-cubic-foot refrigerator with incessant frost, about the same. A dryer then cost well over $200, as did a decent gas or electric range or a monaural console phonograph. Today, $300 buys a 16- or 17-cubic-foot, two-door, frost-free refrigerator, or an electric range with a self-cleaning oven, or a portable 18-inch color tele-

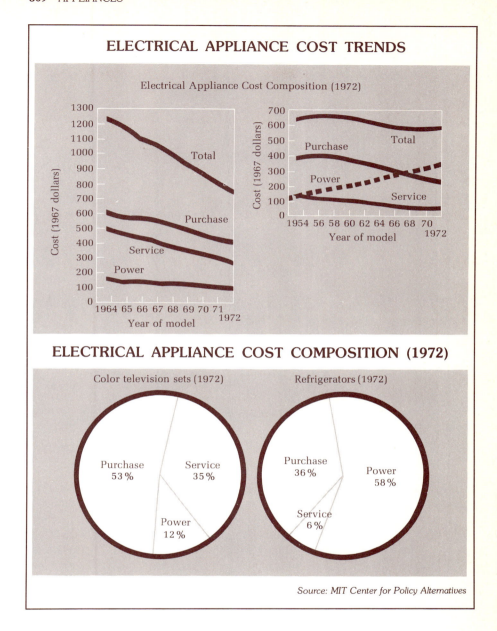

ELECTRICAL APPLIANCE COST TRENDS

Electrical Appliance Cost Composition (1972)

ELECTRICAL APPLIANCE COST COMPOSITION (1972)

Color television sets (1972)

Purchase 53%
Service 35%
Power 12%

Refrigerators (1972)

Purchase 36%
Power 58%
Service 6%

Source: MIT Center for Policy Alternatives

vision, or three 12-inch black-and-white televisions. A good two-speed automatic washer costs less than $200; a good dryer, about $150. These and other substantial price reductions have resulted from more efficient designs, cheaper materials, production shortcuts, automation, and more efficient management. Intense product competition ensures that technological improvements are at least partially passed on to the consumer.

Competition   Appliance manufacturers have long faced a difficult profit situation: The field is saturated with firms that manufacture or sell appliances either under their own names or on private labels for large retailers.   To increase profits, new business must be found either from customers who are dissatisfied with their old but functional machines, from the sale of new kinds of appliances (such as electric combs and electric knives), or from customers who have recently become members of the servantless affluent class.   Significantly, the least saturated markets are located in foreign countries, which have not yet been glutted with American-style gadgets.

The competitive responses of manufacturers to the problems of earning a profit in the appliance market often produce wasteful results.   One example is the appliance that is designed to wear out after a short time so that it will have to be replaced.   Author Vance Packard has called this practice of engineering early death "planned obsolescence."   North America is deluged, usually around the Christmas season, with rather useless minor appliances that are designed to be unique for a short time.   Recently, such items have been gadgets to enhance personal appearance: machines that dispense hot shaving foam, that spray steam on the face, or that wiggle away hair knots are some examples. A few years ago it was the electric can opener, and earlier, the electric knife sharpener. Many of these products are more troublesome than useful. Their construction is often so flimsy that they cannot be repaired, only replaced, which accounts for the profusion of the so-called "replacement-only" warranty. Each year the previous year's gimmicks are copied by competitors, who may reduce the price up to 50% or more as dozens of firms struggle to squeeze the few last dollars out of people who are trying to buy a gift for "someone who has everything."

Price and Construction

The price of a major appliance is directly related to the complexity of its construction. As the price rises, the number of knobs and buttons goes up. A plain 30-inch electric range may cost $150, but timers and an accessory plug can raise the price to $200. More heavily insulated ranges with self-cleaning ovens are priced above $200. A $500 range is self-cleaning and replete with thermostatic cooking elements, timers, an extra warming oven, a rotisserie motor, fans, and several florescent lights.

Small-model refrigerators are priced as low as $200; large refrigerators can cost $1000 if they contain lights, fancy doors, automatic defrosting devices, cheese and butter thermostats, and soda dispensers. An automatic ice maker costs an extra $150 on expensive models.

A basic washer and dryer combination may cost $300, but for $800 special buttons and valves preset water and air temperatures for a variety of fabrics. For $300, the consumer must twist the dials to obtain these settings.

"This set is an excellent buy. The picture is sharp, the colors distinct, the radiation emission minimal, and this model hardly ever catches fire."

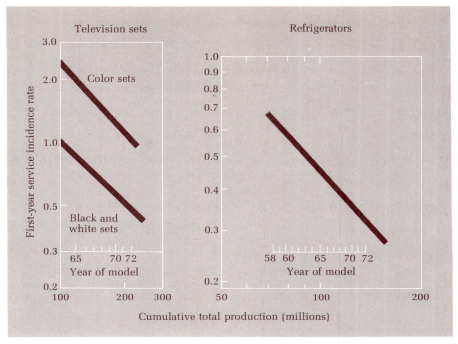

Source: MIT Center for Policy Alternatives

19-4   First-Year Service Incidence Rates

SERVICE COSTS

The reliability of major appliance has improved considerably over the past 20 years.   A typical color television failed six times a year when it was first introduced to the American market in 1954.   By 1960 new color televisions on the average failed only three times a year.   But the need for service grows over the 10-year life span of a color television.   By the time its useful life ends, service accounts for 35% of the average color TV's lifetime total cost.   Although the service charges for major appliance repair rose 50% from 1965 to 1972, the need to service these appliances declined by slightly more than this amount during the same period, producing a slightly declining trend in total service cost (see Figure 19-4).

Home Service   Major appliances must be serviced in the home.   This is inefficient, because the technician must spend about half the total work time traveling from home to home.   This limits productivity to 5–7 service calls in a given day.   At present, the best opportunities to reduce service costs do not lie in directly increasing the technician's productivity, but in improving appliance reliability, lowering the fraction of unnecessary service calls that, for example, require only plugging an appliance wire into a socket (this now comprises 30% of all warranty service claims), and prosecuting appliance service fraud vigorously at both the criminal and the civil level.

Warranty Costs

Warranty costs increase as manufacturers assume greater post-sale responsibility for their products. (Warranties are discussed in greater detail later in this chapter.) We already noted that the average color television failed six times per year when it was first introduced. Manufacturers "protected" customers who purchased these sets with 90-day, parts-only warranties, thereby effectively placing the burden of product reliability directly on the consumer. Since the 1960s, the one-year, parts-and-labor warranty has become nearly uniform for both brown and white goods throughout the industry. Some components of major pieces of equipment are covered by extended parts warranties. Refrigerator and air-conditioner compressors are often backed by five-year parts warranties; color television picture tubes carry two-year parts warranties.

Consumers' insistence on better warranties has increased the warranty expense that is built into a product's purchase price. A 90-day, parts-only warranty adds $3 to the average established price of an item. A one-year, parts-and-labor warranty adds $25 to the purchase price, but the extended period of responsibility is a strong incentive for manufacturers to improve product reliability to reduce the service costs they must absorb.

Energy Costs

Electrical power constitutes 58% of the total lifetime cost of a refrigerator and 12% of the total lifetime cost of a color television. The power consumption of refrigerators has risen over the last two decades as automatic-defrosting models have become increasingly popular. The power consumption of color television sets has declined about 50% due to design improvements.

Energy costs are rising quite rapidly today. During 1974 gas and electrical utility charges increased 30–300%, depending on the location and the utility involved. In 1971 the residential sector used 32.7% of all the electrical energy sold in the United States (see Figure 19-5). On the average, residential electrical power use increased 8.9% per year from 1960 to 1971, representing the fastest growing component of energy use. Because energy costs are currently the largest part of the total cost of a refrigerator and promise to represent a significant portion of the cost of many other appliances, it is important for consumers to know the cost of using each appliance. Manufacturers and retailers must provide meaningful disclosures of energy costs to enable consumers to make rational and efficient choices among competing products. Such disclosures will also provide manufacturers with an incentive to improve the energy efficiency of their products.

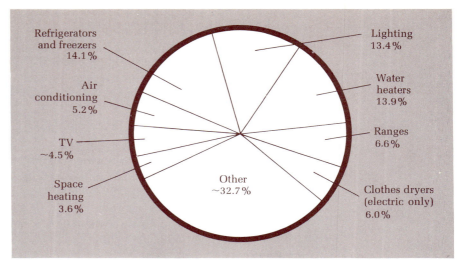

Refrigerators
and freezers
14.1%

Lighting
13.4%

Air
conditioning
5.2%

Water
heaters
13.9%

TV
~4.5%

Ranges
6.6%

Space
heating
3.6%

Other
~32.7%

Clothes dryers
(electric only)
6.0%

Source: MIT Center for Policy Alternatives

**19-5   Residential Electrical Energy Use in the United States (esti-
mated for 1967)**

BUYING WHITE AND BROWN GOODS

When considering buying household gadgets, common sense indicates that
complexity decreases durability. Elaborate controls often mean trouble: Service
costs will be much higher and the product may actually prove to be less flexible
in use, because preset controls cannot be amended. Refrigerators with automatic defrosting devices consume much more power than refrigerators that are
defrosted manually. Built-in beverage dispensers require constant cleaning and
reduce the overall efficiency of the refrigerator. For dependable appliances,
buy the best and the least complicated models available. Examine the results
of the tests published annually by *Consumer Reports*. For even greater reliability, buy restaurant models of ranges and refrigerators and laundromat models or
commercial versions of washers and dryers. Commercial equipment costs more
and has fewer extras, but it lasts longer. Some restaurant and commercial
laundry supply firms may not sell directly to the public; check the Yellow Pages
of the telephone directory to determine those that will.

Consumers should also consider buying used major appliances. Refrigerators last a long time and, like most white goods, have exhibited few basic
improvements over the last few decades. In most areas, a good used refrigerator can be purchased for less than $100. Check the classified ads in a local
newspaper. An excellent, used restaurant range can be purchased for less than

the price of a new residential model—and restaurant ranges are becoming fashionable.

In terms of minor appliances, some industrial wet-and-dry vacuum cleaners are available for as little as $20. These vacuums are easy to repair, wear well, have much better suction than domestic models, and can easily pick up large amounts of dirt and sludge without clogging.

WARRANTIES

A *warranty* is a legally binding promise that a product or a service will do the job for which it is purchased. "Warranty" is often used interchangeably with "guarantee," but warranty is the more correct legal term. Consumers encounter warranties in shopping for appliances, furniture, cars, floor polishers, and numerous other goods that carry a statement by the manufacturer to the effect that the product should do its job and that if it fails, it will be replaced or repaired or its purchase price will be refunded under given conditions.

By law *all* goods and services carry implicit warranties. An *implicit warranty* exists in the common law because judges recognize that no one will buy something without a reasonable expectation that it will serve its purpose. As an extension of the notion of a contract (an exchange of money for something of value, or of value for value), implicit or implied warranties exist for fitness (stating that a product will do the job it is intended to do) and merchantability (stating that the particular item is worthy of sale).

A Long History of Abuse Warranties have long been abused by the retail industry. They are recognized as a necessary sales tool but in many cases have been pared down until they are almost worthless. It is common practice for a manufacturer or a seller to issue a *limited warranty* that cancels all implied warranties and replaces them with a restrictive warranty that lasts for only a short time, requires the owner to pay all shipping or service costs, and covers only those parts found defective on receipt by the manufacturer. In other words, the manufacturer becomes the sole judge of all warranty claims. These limited warranties are usually accompanied by small cards that are to be signed and returned within ten days of purchasing the item, giving the date of purchase and other marketing information.

A major problem in warranty administration is that some manufacturers have established a policy of paying only a small fraction of the claims. To keep costs down, some manufacturers pay small fees to a service establishment that may not be competently trained to repair the appliances. Manufacturers may even refuse to pay repair claims. Indeed, this evasion of warranties becomes a profitable sideline if meaningless warranties mislead consumers into buying appliances. Common law warranties can be canceled, and a much more restrictive warranty issued—possibly embellished with advertising jargon such as "fully guaranteed!'' to convince the buyer that the warranty is valuable—although the manufacturer actually administers the warranties in a manner that is prejudiced against the buyer. The Major Appliance Consumer Action Panel actually discovered that warranties often do not even contain the name and address of the issuing firm!

New Legislation: Consumer Warranty Rights

The rising outcry over warranty deceptions produced the Magnuson–Moss Warranty Act, which became effective in 1975. This Act does not force any manufacturer or seller to provide warranties for products, but it does clarify the law and terminology of any warranty that is issued. A warranty can no longer be a fancy wrapping for empty promises.

Full and Limited Warranties

If a firm chooses to issue a warranty for a product that costs more than $5 retail, the warranty can be designated ''full'' only if it meets broad and inclusive federal standards. Otherwise, it must be designated ''limited,'' and the limitations of coverage must be described in clear language that the Federal Trade Commission is empowered to approve or to disapprove.

Under a *full warranty,* a consumer is only required to advise the issuing firm that the product is defective or that it otherwise fails to comply with the warranty to institute claim proceedings. The *warrantor* (the firm issuing the warranty) must then repair or replace the product within a reasonable period of time. The warrantor cannot charge the consumer for any service, labor, or parts costs incurred in fulfilling the warranty. The warrantor must compensate the consumer if he or she suffers incidental expenses during any unreasonable delay in honoring the warranty. If a product is still defective (as defined by the Federal Trade Commission) after a number of unsuccessful attempts to repair it, the warrantor is then obliged to refund the purchase price, less any charge for useful product life already served.

The Magnuson–Moss Warranty Act makes the practice of requiring consumers to use factory-specified parts (''use only genuine Blasto parts in your Polluto outboard engine'') illegal when any competing brand of parts, fuel, or lubricant is just as effective. Finally, the Act establishes regulations for settling disputes between manufacturer and consumer. Claims procedures can no longer be merely another obstacle to consumer redress. The FTC can review any firm's warranty claim and compliance records. If several consumers find themselves victimized by warranty evasion or misrepresentation on the part of a single manufacturer, they can institute a federal class-action suit for redress of grievances.

SUMMARY

1 Furnishing a home involves:
    1 Budgeting
    2 Design
    3 Planning

4 Product evaluation

5 Long-term cost control

2 The planned acquisition method of home furnishing permits a household to pace its purchases to meet the demands of its changing lifestyle.

3 The details of furniture construction are important determinants of durability.

4 Price markups among furniture retailers range from low markups in discount stores to mid-level markups in department stores to high markups in specialty shops.

5 The total lifetime cost of an appliance is comprised of:

1 Purchase price

2 Service and warranty costs

3 Energy operation costs

6 The purchase and service costs of major appliances have declined over the last 20 years, but energy costs have risen sharply. Competition has been the major factor in lowering appliance purchase prices. Technological improvement has increased appliance reliability.

7 Some appliances are purposely designed to wear out or to become obsolete in a relatively short time so that they will have to be replaced.

8 As the complexity of an appliance increases, it becomes more expensive and less reliable.

9 A warranty is a legally binding promise that a product or a service will do the job for which it is purchased.

10 The common law provides implicit product warranties of fitness and merchantability, but some manufacturers and retailers have reduced implicit warranties by issuing limited and deceptive written warranties that are designed to attract rather than to serve customers.

11 The Magnuson–Moss Warranty Act became effective in 1975. This Act establishes the clear terms of full or limited warranty coverage for firms that issue warranties on retail products selling for more than $5; it also ends replacement parts abuses and defines claims settlement procedures.

Suggestions for Further Reading

"Product Warranties." *Consumer Reports,* March 1975, pp. 164–65.

Ray Faulkner and Sarah Faulkner. *Inside Today's Home,* 3rd ed. New York: Holt, Rinehart & Winston, 1968.

Charles F. Klamkin. *If It Doesn't Work, Read the Instructions.* New York: Stein and Day, 1970.

Massachusetts Institute of Technology, Center for Policy Alternatives. *Consumer Appliances: The Real Cost.* Washington, D.C.: National Science Foundation, 1973.

The Consumer Workshop

1 What types of furniture and appliances should a couple or an individual buy who is establishing a first long-term (5–10 year) home? In one case, assume

that the first dwelling is an apartment; in another, assume that it is a small house.

2 Visit several furniture and appliance stores in your area to determine how great the price variation is on comparable items, such as stuffed chairs or kitchen tables. Question salespeople about the performance warranties offered on furniture and appliances.

3 Visit a furniture store in your area to check manufacturing details (joints, finishes, materials) to determine the quality of the furniture construction. Compare these details with those of older pieces you may have in your home. If possible, discuss your findings with a cabinetmaker or a carpenter and report any conclusions you may draw to the class.

4 "In our energy-conscious era, it pays to save money on appliances." Discuss this statement in terms of the determinants of the total lifetime costs for appliances.

5 "A buyer is always fortunate to get a warranty." Is this true? Discuss implicit versus limited warranties. How does the Magnuson–Moss Warranty Act of 1975 aid consumers?

20

PUBLIC AND PRIVATE TRANSPORTATION

Although Julius Caesar had to ban chariots and carts from the streets of Rome during the daylight hours so that pedestrians could walk in safety, managing traffic did not become a critical problem until man and beast began to move at speeds greater than a brisk walk or an occasional gallop. Marco Polo encountered many problems on his walk to China, but collision wasn't one of them.

Today, however, transportation has become a fierce game with millions of players, most of whom don't know the rules, and with costs hidden behind scores of laws and regulations. A transportation firm can win not only by being fastest or cheapest but by making another firm or industry pay more for its facilities and thereby charge more to its customers. In this morass of conflicting interests and rules, the voices of the consumer and the traveler are those heard least.

In this chapter we examine the broad problem of transportation directly, from the traveler's point of view, and indirectly, from the point of view of the consumer who buys commercially transported goods. We discuss the structure of competing transportation industries and their relationships to the goals of efficient transportation and wise resource use. We examine the process of creating transportation regulations and show that the regulators all too often favor industries rather than consumers. Then we investigate the public and private costs of automobile ownership and operation and train and airline services, to answer the essential questions of who pays and what does each cost. Finally, we discuss the basis for a national transportation policy.

MODES OF TRANSPORTATION

The would-be mover of people or products must be aware of the different modes of transport available. Physical commodities can be transported on sur-

* John Keats, *The Insolent Chariots* (Philadelphia: Lippincott, 1958), p. 59.

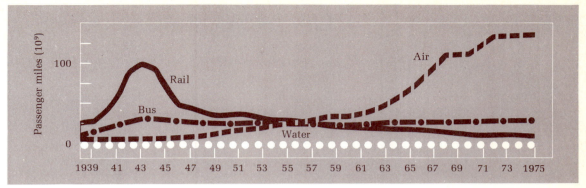

Source: Transportation Association of America, Transportation Facts and Trends (July 1970). p. 16.

20-1 Growth and Decline in Intercity Mass Travel Modes

face routes by ships, barges, trains, trucks, or automobiles, or on air routes by scheduled or private airline carriers. Some forms of transport such as water-borne carriers are intrinsically the lowest-cost transportation mode, because they require the least energy per ton-mile (one ton moved one mile) of movement and because they can travel routes that have been created by nature. Airplanes, on the other hand, are highest-cost transportation mode per ton-mile, but they can be the least expensive when time is a factor in transportation costs.

TRANSPORTATION POLICIES AND INTERESTS

All physical forms of transport consume the environment. Iron and aluminum must be mined to make cars and planes; oil must be pumped from the earth to fuel them. Every vehicle takes up a certain amount of space, and some—the jet and the ubiquitous automobile—require some prodigious amounts of it. Our culture is wasteful of the environment. Suburban subdivisions of look-alike homes spill across the land in endless rings surrounding the decaying cores of large inner cities throughout the United States. As new communities sprout up, highways must be created or extended to link them to the growing transportation maze. Airports must often be enlarged or relocated after they have eaten their way into once-distant suburbs or the suburbs have encroached on them.

From the viewpoint of the individual traveler, the decision as to how to transport a trunk full of clothes should be made on the basis of cost and how long the trunk will take to arrive at its destination by different transportation modes. But transportation costs can be obscure. It's easy to pick the mode of transport with the lowest out-of-pocket cost. For trips of less than 300 miles, travelers

ENERGY AND TRANSPORTATION

Automobile and truck transport are relatively inefficient in terms of energy use.:

Mode Energy Efficiency

Intercity Freight Transport (ton-miles per gallon)		Intercity Passenger Transport (passenger-miles per gallon)	
Pipeline	300	Bus	125
Waterway	250	Railroad	80
Railroad	200	Automobile	32
Truck	58	Airplane	14
Airplane	3.7		

But highway transport comprises more than 75% of all energy consumption in the United States:

Energy Consumption

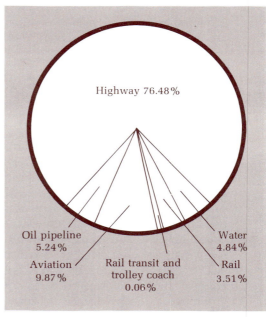

Highway 76.48%

Oil pipeline 5.24%

Aviation 9.87%

Rail transit and trolley coach 0.06%

Water 4.84%

Rail 3.51%

Source: U.S. Department of Transportation, *Summary of National Transportation Statistics* (November 1972).

will probably drive a car if they have one. But a car rides on highways that have been built with gasoline taxes and general tax revenues. And traveling in private automobiles means that a railroad built 100 years ago from enormous public subsidies will probably be underused. If problems such as these appear to be only academic ones for the individual traveler, they are substantial from a national standpoint, because the misuse of resources is the cause of most of today's great problems in transportation.

Why There's No National Policy

As this chapter will indicate, the United States has no national transportation policy. There are many reasons for this. Congress had not had the funds or the staff to prepare a U.S. transportation policy. Federal government agencies established to regulate the transportation industry for the benefit of the public more often than not manipulate consumers to benefit the industry. The electorate —the ultimate consumers of all transportation services—at present does not have a staff of lobbyists and thus cannot compete on Capitol Hill with the "reasoned" persuasion of the transportation industry's public relations representatives.

Private Interests

Every substantial private interest is represented in Washington. The truckers and the teamsters have buildings full of lobbyists, arguing for ever more highways to be financed largely with nontrucking money and for an ever more drastic leveling of the landscape, for every higher road they climb costs them more money in fuel, parts, wear, and time. That trucks are far less energy-efficient than trains and barges is never mentioned. Railroads, claiming poverty, beg to be relieved of their passenger-carrying responsibilities, while they invest their profits in nonrailroad enterprises. Airlines demand more and larger airports, although passengers who travel less than 300 miles can be transported faster and cheaper by bus or train from city center to city center. And on and on it goes. The public's voice is seldom heard in the conference rooms of these planners and regulators.

A fundamental point in our economic theory is that efficiency depends on competition among producers, on free choice based on adequate information provided to consumers, and on the free movement of resources within the economy. The transportation industry, however, reflects the antitheses of these requirements. The Interstate Commerce Commission (ICC) does not permit transportation companies and industries that provide transport service across state lines to engage in price competition. If one transport firm wishes to carry a commodity between two points for a lower rate, the Commission normally disallows the reduction as "unfair" to other carriers. The Civil Aeronautics Board forbids airlines to compete by lowering fares and instead forces them to solicit business by using such nonprice tactics as serving better desserts or showing more recent movies.

Regulations:
A Mixed Blessing

The regulatory process has been corrupted, and the prevention of monopoly pricing it was meant to enforce has come full circle. In the 1880s, when the Interstate Commerce Commission began operations, railroads charged as much as the traffic would bear. Congress established the ICC to force the railroads to charge more reasonable fares, but over the decades the ICC became peopled with the only available experts on trains—the railroad workers themselves. Today, the ICC prices railroad services in a monopolistic way, again based on what the traffic will bear, so that in effect every railroad can offer the least service and make the most money possible. The railroads could not have invented a better railroad monopolist than the ICC itself. And the ICC is only a model of how the public interest is "served" by the Highway Trust Fund (the planner of interstate roads), the Civil Aeronautics Board, the Army Corps of Engineers (to which barge operators are beholden for *free* canals),[1] and the Federal Communications Commission (the regulator of nonphysical transport services—radio, TV, telephone, and telegraph—that cross state lines).

There is no agency in Washington that truly considers the social and economic consequences of having toll roads, interstate highways, railroads, and airplane routes all running absolutely parallel between cities that may be only 200 miles apart. Excess capacity is designed into *inter*urban transport, whereas *intra*city public transportation is nearly nonexistent in many large cities. While a railroad goes bankrupt as a result of its own inefficiency and the ICC's inability to do anything more than increase the fares, an eight-lane interstate highway may be built next to it, thereby guaranteeing that the railroad will fail. The Army Corps of Engineers can change the course of a river, fatally alter the ecology of a wilderness, and ensure that the railroads serving cities along a navigable waterway lose some of their most valuable freight business. Such examples are endless, because the transportation network is overbuilt, uncoordinated, and, in an overall sense, totally unorganized.

THE PRIVATE AUTOMOBILE

The private automobile is the preferred and dominant choice of transport in America. By choice and for lack of a better alternative, North Americans take the vast majority of their trips in the 100 million cars they have at their disposal.[2] The automobile is a symbol of twentieth-century life; the industries that manufacture and market it are fundamental to the contemporary economy. One out

---

[1] Barge lines repay none of the $500 million that the Corps of Engineers spends each year on canals and rivers. See John Burby, *The Great American Motion Sickness* (Boston: Little, Brown, 1971), p. 286.

[2] *Statistical Abstract of the United States,* 1971, p. 534, Table 847.

AUTOMOBILE OPERATING COSTS

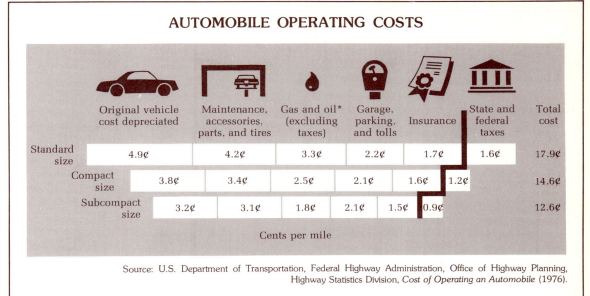

	Original vehicle cost depreciated	Maintenance, accessories, parts, and tires	Gas and oil* (excluding taxes)	Garage, parking, and tolls	Insurance	State and federal taxes	Total cost
Standard size	4.9¢	4.2¢	3.3¢	2.2¢	1.7¢	1.6¢	17.9¢
Compact size	3.8¢	3.4¢	2.5¢	2.1¢	1.6¢	1.2¢	14.6¢
Subcompact size	3.2¢	3.1¢	1.8¢	2.1¢	1.5¢	0.9¢	12.6¢

Cents per mile

Source: U.S. Department of Transportation, Federal Highway Administration, Office of Highway Planning, Highway Statistics Division, *Cost of Operating an Automobile* (1976).

* Add 100% after 1973 to compensate for increased petroleum prices.

of every six jobs in the United States is directly related to vehicle production, automobile suppliers or dealers, or vehicle repair.[3]

Relative Costs of Automobile Travel

U.S. motorists spent more than $25 billion on new automobiles in 1974.[4] An automobile is the second most expensive purchase the majority of Americans make during a lifetime; their most expensive purchase is the owner-occupied home. The average U.S. car has a life of ten years and 100,000 miles before it reaches the junkyard. During this period the owner of a standard-size car would pay $6000 for 7350 gallons of gasoline, $2500 for maintenance and repair, $1500 for insurance, more than $2000 for garages, other parking, and tolls, and $1700 for federal and state taxes.[5]

The U.S. Department of Transportation indicates that the average standard-size U.S. automobile costs 13.6¢ per mile to operate. For a trip from New York to Chicago, a distance of approximately 730 air miles, a coach seat on a sche-

[3] Tabor R. Stone, *Beyond the Automobile* (Englewood Cliffs, N.J.: Prentice-Hall, 1971), p. 117n.

[4] *Statistical Abstract of the United States,* 1975, p. 571, Table 953.

[5] U.S. Department of Transportation, Federal Highway Administration, Office of Highway Planning, Highway Statistics Division, *Cost of Operating an Automobile* (1976).

"Miles per gallon? That's another thing that's new. It gets 1,500 *yards* per gallon."

duled airline in June 1976 cost $78, or 9.75¢ per mile. Because the highway route is not as direct as the air route, the actual road distance is almost 800 miles, requiring the motorist to stop for meals and perhaps to sleep one or more nights on the trip. For the single traveler, then, the automobile is hardly the most economical choice of travel when alternate public transportation is available.

**Model
Changes**   Many factors contribute to the present high costs of purchasing and operating an automobile. Simplicity and reliability are the primary design requirements of few automobile models. Car manufacturers know that a good design is what sells an automobile and all that Detroit has wrought has suited the American public's taste.

In an important study published in the *American Economic Review* in May 1962, Franklin Fisher, Zvi Grilliches, and Carl Kaysen examined the cost of annual car model changes and its impact on the gross national product.[6] They found that the cost of model changes amounted to about $700 per car (over 25% of the purchase price) during 1949–1956, or to about $3.9 billion annually during 1956–1960. This study essentially excludes the cost and value of technological improvements, because it assumed that the 1949 automobile was produced under continuously improving levels of technology and performance. In addition to the direct costs of annual car model changes, other costs were imposed on the economy in the form of the accelerated obsolescence of repair parts, higher costs for retraining mechanics, stocking parts, and repairing models

[6] Franklin Fisher, Zvi Grilliches, and Carl Kaysen, "Costs of Automobile Model Changes Since 1949," *Journal of Political Economy* **LXX** (October 1962), 433–51; abstracted in *American Economic Review, Papers and Proceedings* **LII** (May 1962), 259–61.

as they became more "stylish," and increased gasoline consumption. Concentrating on the last of these cost increases, Fisher, Grilliches, and Kaysen concluded:

> Whereas actual gasoline mileage fell from 16.4 miles per gallon in 1949 to 14.3 miles per gallon ten years later, then rising to about 15.3 in 1960 and 1961, the gasoline mileage of the average 1949 car would have risen to 18.0 miles per gallon in 1959 and 18.5 in 1961. This meant that the owner of the average 1956–1960 car was paying about $40 more per 10,000 miles of driving (about 20% of his total gasoline costs) than would have been the case had 1949 models been continued.

The additional gasoline consumption resulting from model changes was estimated to be about $968 million per year during the 1956–1960 period. Summing up their results, Fisher, Grilliches, and Kaysen "estimated costs of model changes since 1949 to run about $5 billion per year over the 1956–1960 period with a present value of future gasoline consumption of $7.1 billion." Commenting on these findings, Baran and Sweezy estimated that annual car model changes in the late 1950s cost the United States about 2.5% of its gross national product.[7]

Opportunity Costs

In addition to these direct, out-of-pocket costs, there are indirect and opportunity costs of automobile production and operation. It is important to understand that choosing any good or service provided by an individual or by society involves giving up some alternative good or service. If the alternative choice would have produced greater profit, value, or happiness, then the person, firm, or group making the decision pays what is called an *opportunity cost* for selecting less than the best alternative. Only when the opportunity costs are zero has the best choice been made. As we will learn later in this chapter, available data indicate that America's choice of and dependence on the automobile as the principal means of personal transportation inflicts high opportunity costs on society and on the economy.

Environmental Costs

Some 40,000 square miles of North America—an area about the size of New England—was paved with roads by the late 1950s.[8] It would be hard to calculate how much more land has been covered over with parking lots, car junkyards, gas stations, and other facilities to accommodate our automobile-centered culture. That so much land has been devoted to the needs of cars is not in itself evidence that the land has been misused, but in conjunction with substantial evidence that the automobile is an *inefficient* mover of people, this fact does indicate the scope of this waste of land. Railroads use less fuel and less land to carry more people than cars do. In explaining why New York state paid

---

[7] Paul Baran and Paul Sweezy, "The Real Cost of Producing an Automobile," in *Monopoly Capital* (New York: Monthly Review Press, 1966), pp. 131–38.

[8] John Keats, *The Insolent Chariots* (Philadelphia: Lippincott, 1958), p. 14.

TOTAL MILEAGE OF U.S. RURAL ROADS AND MUNICIPAL STREETS

Year	1935	1945	1955	1965	1972
Miles	3050	3319	3418	3690	3787

Source: U.S. Department of Commerce, Bureau of the Census, 1974

$65 million for the decrepit Long Island Railroad and another $250 million to put it in good running order, then Governor Nelson Rockefeller stated, "We made a survey and found that we would have had to build 24 lanes of highway through New York City to handle the commuters who depended on the railroad."[9]

The automobile has had an obvious effect on the quality of breathable air available in major cities. Before Los Angeles initiated automobile exhaust controls, cars dumped 13,000 tons of lethal wastes such as carbon monoxide, sulfuric acid, nitrous oxide, and lead residues into the air every day.[10] California's crop losses from air pollution alone average $45 million a year.[11] Exhaust pollution is the responsibility of automobile manufacturers. Although car buyers may know what they want in terms of flashy styling, they are rarely well enough acquainted with chemical engineering and hydrocarbon reduction processes to make significant suggestions related to engine design. Just as airplane manufacturers should assume that passengers expect to ride in safe planes, so automobile manufacturers should assume that buyers prefer to drive cars with clean engines. Yet until prodded by the Environmental Protection Act and other related legislation, Detroit automobile manufacturers did little if anything to ensure that their engines were clean. During 1967–1969, General Motors spent $250 million to change its slogan on billboards, dealers' signs, and other promotional material to read "GM Mark of Excellence." Ralph Nader has estimated that these funds alone could have been successfully used to develop a cleaner automobile engine.[12]

Social and Economic Impact of the Automobile

At all levels of government, the resources for dealing with many societal problems tend to be concentrated on the automobile. It has been found that 70% of the activities of state and local law enforcement agencies, for example, are committed to traffic management and attendant parking and driving of-

[9] *Great American Motion Sickness,* p. 153.
[10] *Beyond the Automobile,* p. 24.
[11] Ralph Nader, "A Citizen's Guide to the American Economy," *The New York Review of Books* (September 2, 1971), p. 17.
[12] Ibid, p. 17.

fenses.[13]   Interstate auto theft and vehicle recovery has become a preoccupation of the Federal Bureau of Investigation.

Given that the private automobile is usually not the most efficient way to achieve mobility, there is enormous economic waste in maintaining the industry in its present size.   The automobile industry consumes 61% of all the rubber, 20% of all the steel, and 10% of all the aluminum currently used in the United States.[14]   If some of these resources were available for housing, school, or hospital construction, the crises in these economic sectors could be minimized.

A GREAT CONSUMER PROBLEM—SAFETY

A deadly combination of the consumers' ignorance of automotive mechanics and the manufacturers' disdain for all areas of design except that of style operate to make contemporary automobiles little more than frailties in search of disasters.   As Ralph Nader pointed out in his important book *Unsafe At Any Speed,* "Nearly one-half of all the automobiles on the road today will eventually be involved in an injury-producing accident. . . . At present rates, one of every two Americans will be injured or killed in an automobile accident."[15]

A car may be bought for many reasons, almost all of which are wrong.   It is said that men often choose cars with such features as speedometers that read far higher than the car can or should be used, rakish styling and paint stripes that suggest the autoracer's dash and speed, or instrument panels decorated with lights so that they look like jet cockpits.   Women are said to look for signs of comfort and security in a car, such as a carpet on the floor, a vanity mirror on the visor, fancy upholstery, and plenty of arm rests.

At the same time, few car buyers know or insist on reliability, simplicity, and safety—qualities incorporated in the products produced by almost all engineers and product designers except those in the automotive industry.   Yet the best car for most people is the one that will run for the longest period of time for the least maintenance effort and cost and that will afford its occupants the greatest chance of surviving a crash.

Safety Is Not Always the Highest Priority   Knowing that automobile buyers often select cars for reasons that are only remotely connected to transportation, manufacturers do not hesitate to conserve design resources in fundamental engineering and to squander them in styling. Manufacturers tend to make car owners and drivers do their own product testing, often with tragic results.

The basic design of the early model Corvair has been a source of controversy.   Preproduction designs purportedly contained a suspension element nec-

---

[13] *Beyond the Automobile,* p. 34.
[14] Ibid., pp. 117–18.
[15] Ralph Nader, *Unsafe At Any Speed* (New York: Pocket Books, 1966), p. 129.

essary for good handling. This design feature, not present in the early model, was subsequently added. It would seem that the GM product-development staff's main consideration was not total engineering but rather styling and cost. In *Unsafe at Any Speed,* Ralph Nader criticized GM for failing to stabilize Corvair handling by instituting a few design changes that in his opinion would have cost a little more and produced only a slightly rougher ride.[16] The Corvair controversy is still alive, although it should be pointed out here that General Motors did not lose its court suits. GM no longer manufactures this model, but many Corvair loyalists still drive older models, some of which have recently begun to sprout "Recall Ralph Nader" and "I Love My Corvair" bumper stickers.

Recalls   Statistics in the mid-1970s indicate that more cars have been recalled during the late 1960s and early 1970s than were *built* during the same period. Many of the defects in these recalled cars, such as exhaust pipes burning through the brake-fluid hoses they touched, could have been eliminated by more thorough design analysis, better testing, and the willingness to spend more money on engineering fundamentals and less on style. It should, however, be noted that the heyday of bizarre styling is largely past. Detroit no longer molds glitter into its steering wheels and is currently as safety conscious as the law requires. Yet product testing is still left to the millions of drivers who are brave or foolish enough to buy the early products of each year's new automobile production runs.

   Most cars that are placed on the market are practically untested and are engineered to sell rather than to last. Automobile manufacturers must demonstrate durability, so they issue warranties that they often have little intention of honoring. With flotillas of junk crumbling in their driveways, garages and service stations can easily exploit befuddled car owners. And the manufacturers stand ever-ready to provide the numerous parts necessary for repairs at enormous profit.

WARRANTIES

The consumer's first line of defense against any domestic or imported automotive failure is the warranty. Issued with new cars and covering variable periods of time and miles driven (usually between one and two years and up to 24,000 miles for some parts), the warranty is a written statement of what the manufacturer, through the dealer, will do and will not do when the car is in need of repair. Such warranties are more remarkable in what they say they will not cover than in what they claim they will cover.

[16] Ibid., pp. 16–18.

We learned in Chapter 19 that according to the common law—the legal tradition of the nation expressed by the opinions of judicial rulings in courts—a vendor is bound by warranties of fitness and marketability that are implied in the act of sale. Implied warranties hold a person or a firm responsible for what is offered to the public as fit merchandise for use and sale. If the merchandise proves to be unfit, the customer is entitled to cancel the contract, to obtain damages for the immediate value of the deficiency in the goods sold, and to sue for consequential damages. If the steering wheel of a car falls off due to improper manufacture just as the car is turning a curve on a mountain road, the implied warranty would entitle the owner or the owner's estate to direct replacement of the vehicle or full repair and damages in the amount of the value of lives lost, personal injury, and any other adverse results of the accident.

Written automobile warranties do nothing to enhance these common-law protections; instead, these warranties actually limit the law. For example, the manufacturer may state in the written warranty that a new master brake cylinder will be provided if the original cylinder fails during the warranty period but at the same time may disclaim responsibility for any accident that occurs as a result of the cylinder's failure. Even when part failures don't wreck the vehicle, most warranties leave the expense of obtaining a substitute vehicle while repairs are being made up to the owner.

It is interesting to compare the conventional automobile warranty with the stated policy of such major retailers as Sears Roebuck and J. C. Penney. These giant merchandisers squarely offer the customer satisfaction or their money back. Some of their products have limited warranties that disclaim consequential damages, but many do not. Isn't it ironic that if a new pair of socks turns out to be just so much lint after one correct washing, you can get your money back, but if your new car is a lemon you can't? (See Chapter 19 for a detailed discussion of warranties in general and the Magnuson–Moss Warranty Act of 1975 on pages 375–76.)

Automobile manufacturers are understandably reluctant to offer broad warranties indicating that they stand honorably behind their merchandise. The average new car examined by *Consumer Reports* each year has about three dozen defects, ranging from minor to serious. Some vehicles are so crippled by their defects that they can hardly be driven. Others are filled with hidden risks waiting to turn into disasters. In a study from September 1966 to December 1969, Nader, Dodge, and Hotchkiss found that 38% of all domestic vehicles built were recalled due to safety-related defects.[17] It should be noted that recall campaigns are purely voluntary; the 1966 National Traffic and Motor Vehicle Safety Act does not allow the federal government to require manufacturers to initiate them. Recalls tend to be instituted when defects are present in a large number of vehicles but not in a large percentage of a particular type of vehicle. For this reason, a Chevrolet has a much greater chance of being recalled than a low-volume import, even though the import may be much more unsafe.

---

[17] Ralph Nader, Lowell Dodge, and Ralf Hotchkiss, *What To Do With Your Bad Car: An Action Manual for Lemon Owners* (New York: Grossman, 1971), p. 116.

Warranties May Boost Sales

Manufacturers offer warranties because they are under competitive pressure to do so. The warranty is both a pre-sale selling feature and a post-sale device that can make the owner a captive of the dealer's service department. From 1931 to 1960 the typical automobile warranty was valid for 90 days or 4000 miles, whichever came first. In 1960 all car manufacturers switched to a one-year or 12,000-mile warranty. During the 1961 and 1962 model years, the market share held by Chrysler dropped from 14% to 10%. New Chrysler management launched the 1963 models with a five-year, 50,000-mile warranty on the "power train" (the main moving parts in the engine, transmission, drive shaft, and rear end). By 1966 Chrysler's share of the market had increased to 15.4%, and sales volume doubled that of 1963. In 1967 Ford and General Motors also switched to the five-year, 50,000-mile warranty. But the long-term warranty was doomed. Manufacturers found the headaches of the continuing responsibility for their products too great to bear. The cost of correcting their mistakes was enormous, and they did not employ enough trained mechanics to make the repairs required by their warranties. During the 1970s warranties were reduced to the one-year, 12,000-mile form again. Owners can now buy extended warranty coverage from some automobile dealers, notably American Motors.[18] These service insurance policies shift product reliability problems back to the consumer, but at least they standardize maintenance and repair prices.

Solving Warranty Problems

When a problem arises that a dealer will not or cannot manage, the automobile owner can follow one or both of the following two courses:

1 Address complaints directly or indirectly to the manufacturer or the dealer
2 Take legal action to force the manufacturer or the dealer to stand behind the warranty

It may even be possible to charge the dealer with criminal fraud if the deceptions are blatant enough and can be proved beyond a reasonable doubt.

Letters of Complaint. Persuasion through letter writing can be a lengthy process which merely incites the manufacturer or dealer to respond with threats of a lawsuit for damaging its pristine reputation. Yet such lawsuits are not likely to be initiated. The first letter of complaint of inadequate performance or poor dealer treatment should include the customer's name, address, and telephone number, the selling dealer's name and location, the vehicle make, model, year, and serial number, the date of purchase, a description of what actions the dealer has taken thus far, the mileage at present as well as at the time the problem arose, and an indication of any financial loss suffered due to the problem. The letter should be written on one page, if possible, and should be accompanied by photocopies of supporting documents such as repair orders.

Nader, Dodge, and Hotchkiss recommend that copies of the first letter of complaint be sent to the manufacturer's regional headquarters or to the distributor, as well as to the president and the chairman of the board. Manufacturers

---

[18] Ibid., pp. 126–27.

tend to evade responsibility at the district level, and including top officials on the mailing list at this initial stage may discourage routine, form-letter snubs from customer relations departments. If prompt action is not forthcoming from the manufacturer's regional headquarters, the dissatisfied consumer should begin a protest campaign by contacting all consumer-action groups and other people who receive consumer protests. Photocopies of the initial letter of protest and of all supporting documents, including repair orders, should be made and a covering letter describing the inaction to date should be composed. This will require several dozen sets of letters and documents initially and perhaps as many again later in the campaign.

Stronger Steps. The strategy of protest can escalate from direct correspondence by letter with the manufacturer or the dealer to advising responsible government officials of the problem. You can also enlist the aid of consumer-action groups in picketing the dealer. At every stage, it's useful to have the next plan of action in mind. Pacing the escalating protest stages at two-week intervals should give both the dealer and the manufacturer time to respond.

If necessary, the protest campaign can be extended to include state and U.S. Senators and congressional representatives. A letter to the President of the United States can be directed to the Special Assistant for Consumer Affairs. Additional copies can be sent to the National Highway Safety Bureau (Washington, D.C. 20591), the agency that initiates safety design changes in automobiles. Warranty evasion and deceptive sales techniques can be brought to the attention of the Federal Trade Commission in Washington or to any of its regional offices. The Subcommittee on Antitrust and Monopoly, U.S. Senate Committee on the Judiciary (Washington, D.C. 20510) has a strong interest in automobile repair problems. In local jurisdications, outright fraud can be brought to the attention of the state attorney general or the district attorney. In fact, it is theoretically possible to have an automobile dealer's license revoked for fraud, but the likelihood of this is remote. However, it never hurts to try; a rash of complaints could be troublesome for the offending dealer.

Other consumers should be informed of the protest campaign as it progresses. Copies of the initial letter of protest and subsequent documentation can be sent to the Center for Auto Safety (P.O. Box 7250, Ben Franklin Station, Washington, D.C. 20044), and to the Consumers Union of the United States (256 Washington Street, Mt. Vernon, New York 10550), in addition to local consumer-action groups in your area. A word of caution here about Better Business Bureaus: They are financed by local businesses, whose interests they serve. These Bureaus offer to arbitrate or to intervene only in cases where the consumer has suffered such obvious wrong that a lawyer could win the consumer's case with ease. They do not assist consumers once legal action has been initiated. Thus, in most cases, the local Better Business Bureau is not an essential ally.

Legal Action. If mere protest is ineffective or inappropriate, legal action via an attorney can be instituted. Local lawyers' arguments vary with their particular jurisdictions, so we cannot usefully discuss legal strategies in detail. However, certain legal procedures that are the same in any area can be stated here.

The basic appeal for redress in the case of a severe car problem will focus on the sales contract. A legal argument to secure a new replacement car for or the return of money paid by the buyer will center on the theory that an inferior car does not satisfy the owner's need for a safe and reliable vehicle. A suit can be brought to compel the manufacturer to honor the warranty and/or to accept additional damage liabilities that are actually canceled in the express warranty. Using this legal approach, the general theory of redress is that in the interests of the public good manufacturers must accept the responsibility for products that they manufacture or that they know are dangerous, regardless of the reductions in their liabilities that they can force customers to accept through greater bargaining power.

Car owners can handle the fairly simple problems of dealer nonperformance (such as repairs charged and paid but not made) in local small-claims courts. There consumers can represent themselves and the defendant (the dealer) is often not permitted representation by an attorney. Small-claims courts offer quick and effective resolution of automobile complaints that involve amounts of only a few hundred dollars, but these courts are an ineffective means of recourse for the true owner of a true lemon.

It is beyond the scope of this chapter to provide a detailed list of all the government officials and consumer groups that represent and all the legal strategies that apply to automobile owners who have problems. For the troubled owner, a superb consumer-action manual called *What To Do With Your Bad Car: An Action Manual For Lemon Owners,* has been written by Ralph Nader, Lowell Dodge, and Ralf Hotchkiss (New York: Grossman, 1971), which is available in a paperback edition. This consumer's manual about cars and their troubles is worthwhile reading even for nonlemon owners.

REPAIRS

Routine repairs are necessary even when a car doesn't suffer from grave design or manufacturing faults. All machinery requires maintenance, its parts eventually wear out and must be replaced. In the automobile industry however, some features of the parts repair and replacement business can be detrimental to consumers.

Labor Costs

Suprisingly, automobile mechanics are often underpaid. A skilled mechanic's wages in the automobile repair industry tend to be lower than the wages earned by an unskilled laborer on a Detroit production line. This is because the productivity of assembly-line workers tends to be greater than that of repair mechanics, and unions are far better organized at the assembly-plant level than they are at the repair-shop level. Both independent and dealer-operated repair garages have trouble attracting and keeping skilled mechanics when equal skill can earn them higher wages on the assembly line or in some similar line of work (diesel service or aircraft engine maintenance, for example). Semiskilled labor, on the other hand, is abundant in the automobile-repair industry: Literally millions of people who tinker with their own cars or who acquire more useful skills in the military have a smattering of automotive knowledge and ability.

Equipment Costs

A fairly substantial amount of money is required to equip a full-service garage which must contain tools, hydraulic lifts, electronic diagnostic equipment, and parts inventories, among other pieces of automobile repair equipment. Because these funds are not available to individual mechanics themselves, businesspeople who have the needed funds often operate the garages in which mechanics work. Garage owners must earn a profit above the cost of their equipment, and mechanics must be paid reasonably well if they are to be dissuaded from taking better-paying jobs. Having enough work to keep the mechanics busy, to pay capital and overhead costs, and to make a profit for the garage owner, combined with the great mechanical ignorance of most automobile owners, encourages the unnecessary work that is often fraudulently performed by service stations and dealer service departments.

Rate Books

Even when outright deception isn't involved, auto-repair firms tend to overcharge their customers. Most garages have large sets of flat-rate books indicating the time required to do a given repair job on a given car. These books tend to overestimate the time required, so that a garage that "goes by the book" is essentially overcharging its customers for time that it does not need or use to complete repair jobs. Each of these flat-rate manuals includes a charge for "set-up time"—the time required to jack up the car or to remove obstructions in the engine—for each repair job. The owner who has two repairs made at one time may actually be paying for the same set-up work *twice*. Automobile manufacturers are aware of this and provide their own repair-time guides to reduce the overcharges in the regular flat-rate manuals. But garage owners feel that they can't make enough money on factory-timed work and tend to overcharge customers for nonwarranty work or invent unnecessary repairs to compensate themselves. Garages may even keep a third set of internal accounting books. The wary customer can only demand to see a garage's rate books, refuse to pay for multiple setup time, and insist on paying the lesser cost in terms of actual job time versus book time.

Parts Are Costly

Automobile replacement parts represent yet another problem area for consumers. Although engine parts are fairly standardized and don't vary widely among various car manufacturers, body parts proliferate as models multiply through style changes and as Cougars, Impalas, Marlins, and Barracudas spawn offspring. The cost of carrying vast inventories of parts is enormous. The markup on parts carried by dealers averages 100% and even larger markups are common on rare or less frequently used items. The rarer the car, the higher the markup, so that parts for foreign cars cost more per part, per pound of part, or per size of part, than parts of domestic automobiles.

The owner in search of an automotive part is often a captive of the dealer. Independent manufacturers do sell some of the more common replacement parts for comparatively reasonable prices. But the thousands of special fittings that each car model may require can usually only be obtained from dealers—or junkyards (a low-cost alternative for those who have the time to search). Knowing that their customers have few alternatives, manufacturers build huge profits into the wholesale prices of automotive parts. Some of this high-cost base is used to maintain regional parts warehouses and nightly air-freight parts deliveries to local dealers, but much of it is sheer markup.

An important consideration for owners who intend to keep their cars until they wear out is the cost of engine replacement or overhaul. Rebuilt engines and rebuilt engine components cost much less than equivalent new materials and can work just as well. Rebuilt engines often carry their own 12-month, 12,000-mile warranties. Rebuilt engines and parts for the popular models of Fords, Chevrolets, and Plymouths are most readily available. They are scarce for "luxury" domestic cars and for all imports except the Volkswagen "beetle." The rarer the car, the higher its cost—now and later.

FOREIGN CARS

Cars that are manufactured abroad may exhibit design qualities that cannot be found in American-made cars. People often express their personalities or show others how they wish to be regarded by the type of car they purchase. For such reasons, some stress their individuality by buying rare foreign cars: tiny imports like the Austin Mini and the Honda Civic with golf-cart sized engines, elegant but delicate cars like the Lotus, and Alfa-Romeos slung so low that they have been officially certified unsafe to drive over the gaping potholes in New York City streets.

Granted, a foreign car gives its driver a "different" look, but usually at an enormous price. Some imported cars are not powerful enough to handle normal freeway driving. Many can only be serviced knowledgeably in the suburbs of a few large cities. And finding parts and special tools to make repairs on a foreign car can be an endless quest. Still other problems arise when imports cease to be imported. In the past Ford, General Motors, and Chrysler, in addition to foreign manufacturers, have marketed small cars produced by European and Japanese subsidiaries and, after finding that these "imports" were poor sellers, simply dropped them.[19] The resale value of an automobile that is

[19] *The Wall Street Journal* (August 22, 1973), p. 1.

no longer marketed declines drastically, repair parts are no longer stocked, and owners become victims of mechanics who make these special replacement parts in their spare time.

Foreign Car Recalls

Foreign cars are recalled less frequently and usually in much smaller numbers than domestic cars. That 3000 Volvos are recalled is much less notable than the recall of 1.2 million Chevrolets. Both the public and the goverment tend to underestimate the defects of foreign cars. The Department of Transportation recalls imports on the basis of gross complaints rather than on the basis of the percentage of the model that exhibits a particular problem on the road. Thus some foreign cars have never been recalled, although they are dangerous to their occupants as well as the other vehicles and pedestrians they may strike.

It is also difficult to judge the age of some foreign cars. Both the United States and Canada have birthday-tag laws, effective since 1966 and 1971, respectively, which require manufacturers to attach a plate or a strip giving the date of the car's manufacture on the left-hand (the driver's) door or doorpost. American cars change enough in appearance each year to make birthday confusion a minor problem. But many foreign cars are redesigned only once in every five to eight years. They arrive in large quantities and may remain on the importer's lot for several years before they are sold. A car that has not been driven for a few years requires maintenance work and the replacement of hundreds of vital seals, gaskets, bearings, and possibly some major components. The customer eventually pays for all this. The importer who has an overload of aging cars may sell them to dealers at year-end discounts, as domestic manufacturers do, thereby permitting the dealers to discount the cars heavily when they are received. The low-priced merchandise sells quickly and the stock is cleared. Or the importer can load the cars back on the boat and send them back to the factory. But to increase their profits, many importers allow the cars to rot on the lot until a hapless buyer can be persuaded to buy a car without a date tag. Dealers have been known to attach a 1974 tag to a 1971 car, assuming customers are too stupid to know the difference.[20]

Self-help

Given such varied types of deception, how do consumers avoid being robbed? There's no simple, single answer to this question, but a few things can be done to improve the odds. Don't put much faith in the "quality by association" advertisements with which many promote their products. Ignore "best car of the year" prizes: So many prizes are awarded in different categories that *every* car model can win several prizes and medals. To obtain reliable information concerning car performance, read *Consumer Reports*. Most issues examine and rank a few cars, and comprehensive reports on all but the rarest automobiles are published each year in the April and December issues. *Consumer Reports* is the best available source of detailed owner-satisfaction data and automotive performance and repair information regarding such subsystems as engine, suspen-

---

[20] *Toronto Globe and Mail* (June 8, 1974), p. 1.

sion, and electrical assemblages. Few sports-car or hot-rod magazines can match CR for honesty, because CR *buys* the cars that it tests. Commercial magazine representatives are invited to resort areas on free automobile inspection trips sponsored by the producers of the cars that these magazines are supposedly evaluating. CR also tells consumers how to buy used cars, lists used-car prices, and discusses the latest deceptive practices in the automobile industry.

PUBLIC TRANSPORTATION

A system of public transportation in which people provide other people with modes of transportation for hire has distinct economic advantages. Such a system distributes the high capital cost of mechanical means of transport and route construction over many users and gives millions of shippers and travelers the technical advantages of such complex transportation vehicles as airplanes that they could never afford individually. The cost and administrative difficulties of maintaining such transportation networks as telephones and telegraphs is distributed among all potential users, each of whom bears a small and readily supportable part of the total cost. Most transportation systems pass costs directly on to their users; those systems that do not pay their full costs are given outright subsidies (as are airlines that fly unprofitable routes) or hidden subsidies (free canals for barge operators or roads built to truckers' specifications but largely paid for by individual motorists).

Transportation has always been a big business. The very history of the New World began with the formation of great merchant transportation and production companies in the seventeenth century. The leading industries of the nineteenth were, successively, canals and trains. In the twentieth century, the automobile industry is the leader.

Railroads Railroads consisting of cars pulled by horse or steam that traversed short tracks from mines to dump sites were employed in the English coal mines in the late eighteenth century. Engine efficiency improvements permitted locomotives to pull more than just their own weight, and by the 1830s steamdrawn railroad cars were hauling passengers and cargo over a spreading network of tracks throughout the industrialized regions of Europe and North America.

Private Enterprise and Public Finance. Railroad finance posed many problems. Enormous amounts of capital were required to construct rail networks. Shippers and passengers in the eastern United States were fairly close together geographically, but in the West they were comparatively far apart. Congress was aware of the advantages of establishing a national transport network that offered the relative speed and convenience (compared to the horse) of

"Just what we need—mass transit."

the railroads, and between 1850 and 1971 that body granted more than 130 million acres of land—an area as large as the New England states, New York, and Pennsylvania combined—to the railroads and their builders. State and local governments were in effect blackmailed ("pay us or we'll skip your state/county/town") into authorizing another 49 million acres for railroad construction. At the end of the railroad building boom the railroads had been granted one-fourth of the entire area of both Minnesota and Washington, one-fifth of Wisconsin, Iowa, Kansas, North Dakota, and Montana, one-seventh of Nebraska, one-eighth of California, and one-ninth of Louisiana. In 1882 Texas discovered that its donations of railroad land had exceeded the amount remaining in the public domain by 8 million acres.[21]

Local governments approved additional railroad cash grants, loans, and subsidies worth $500 million (or approximately $2½ billion today). By 1870 public contributions comprised about 60% of all railroad construction costs. To this figure must be added the incalculable price of stock frauds—the standard technique that railroad builders employed to obtain private capital. The railroads are now America's largest landowners, deriving billions of dollars in rent annually from their holdings.

Railroad Rate Policies. Once they began operating, the railroads charged the highest prices their traffic could bear. When only one railroad line ran through an area, it charged very high prices; when competing lines ran through the same area, each tried to drive the other out of business by lowering prices. Competing railroad lines tried to bankrupt one another, because bankrupt railroads

[21] Louis B. Wright et al., *The Democratic Experience* (Chicago: Scott, Foresman, 1963), p. 242.

could be bought cheaply and absorbed by the conquering railroad or left to rot. The victorious railroad could then raise its rates drastically to recover the costs of the price war. This brief history shows that the real railroad financiers were not the multimillionaires who milked the farmers and shopkeepers of America, but these people themselves, who poured their money into the coffers of the railroad barons in exchange for the right to be overcharged. Under the guise of private property, railroads were established as a system of "socialism" for the rich and "capitalism" for the poor.

Origins of Regulation: The ICC

Thus railroading in the late nineteenth century was little more than extortion masquerading as legitimate business. In response to public demands for protection from the thumbscrew-style pricing policies of the railroads, but motivated by unclear and contradictory goals, Congress summoned enough public spirit in 1887 to pass the Interstate Commerce Act. Section 3 of this Act stated that a railroad could not maintain a price policy that proved detrimental to its customers. A series of ten amendments to this Act extended the authority of the Interstate Commerce Commission. In 1920 the ICC gained the power to establish minimum as well as maximum rates, to prevent new railroads from taking business from established lines, and to update and otherwise improve nineteenth-century style railroad operating procedures in general.[22] As Congress's oldest regulatory agency, the ICC was already displaying an inevitable trait of all regulators: fatherly protection rather than careful observation. The ICC inevitably granted the railroads the very powers of monopolization that the rail barons could not completely achieve themselves, while ignoring the public interest that the Interstate Commerce Act instructed the ICC to protect.

The Nader Study

In a well-executed 1969 study, a Nader Study Group concluded that the ICC had corrupted its original mission to the point that it was in fact operating *against* the public interest. The ICC had become "an elephant's graveyard for political hacks," a repository for transportation-industry executives who protected their own, and a rest home for old bureaucrats. ICC regulations served the public interest only occasionally, and then by sheer coincidence. The economic framework envisaged by top ICC staff members had prevailed in the 1930s, and ICC rulings were 40 years out of date at best.[23]

ICC loyalties still lie with the transportation industry; the public and consumers in general rarely attend agency proceedings. Top ICC personnel and staff are an extension of the transportation industry in that they attend its social functions, have free use of its private railroad cars and jets, and waste untold sums of public money delivering mindless speeches "in the surface transportation meccas of Puerto Rico, Hawaii, and the Bahamas."[24] If they behave,

[22] *Great American Motion Sickness*, p. 277.
[23] Robert C. Fellmeth, *The Interstate Commerce Omission* (New York: Grossman, 1970), pp. 311–25.
[24] Ibid., p. 312.

ICC staff members have good jobs paying high salaries waiting for them in the industries they "regulate." Accordingly, the ICC considers its primary functions to be to maintain the health of the firms it regulates. It seldom exercises its sanctions, does not investigate firms before approving their rate increases, and does not even know who owns the most influential railroads. Far from doing the specific job for which it was established in 1887, the ICC actually impedes the ability of farmers, for example, to obtain boxcars to transport their produce and shoehorns passenger operations into the "death" that railroad management craves.[25]

Regulation, Decay, and Collapse

The past and present errors of the ICC are tragedies masked as broad farce. On the eve of the biggest financial bankruptcy in American history involving the largest transportation company in the United States—the Penn Central Railroad—the ICC proclaimed, "On the whole, applicant [the Penn Central] is in a strong financial condition."[26] In fact, the Penn Central's accounting had suffered from questionable practices, and its management had not been successful.

Although U.S. railroads have been largely financed with public money, today the railroads are in a state of advanced decay. The ICC permits passenger trains to go out of business when they become less profitable than freight trains—which is often. Many passenger trains lose money, but such losses are easily recovered in the form of real estate profits from the land originally given to the railroads in the nineteenth century.

In freight operations the railroads also cry poor. They claim to be so impoverished that they cannot pay track maintenance fees. But only their deceptive form of railroad accounting makes them seem poor; the real estate profits of

[25] Ibid., pp. 322–24.
[26] Joseph R. Daughen and Peter Binzen, *The Wreck of the Penn Central* (Boston: Little, Brown, 1971), p. 253.

OTHER INCOME OF SELECTED CARRIERS COMPARED WITH PRETAX RAILWAY OPERATING INCOME, 1968
(millions)

Railroad	Pretax Net Railway Operating Loss*	Net Other Income*
Penn-Central	$45.4	$119.6
Chicago & NW	2.3	13.4
Rock Island	7.3	3.0
Chicago & Eastern Ill.	1.2	1.4

* In millions of dollars.

Source: Robert C. Fellmeth, *The Interstate Commerce Omission* (New York: Grossman, 1970), p. 410.

most railroads are ample enough to cover their repairs. But instead railroad tracks are abandoned and grow dangerous. Rather than order the railroads to improve these tracks, the ICC orders the trains to slow down. So passengers and freight move over dangerous tracks at slow speeds, and their trips consume increasing amounts of time and fuel.

The ICC and the Public Interest

So remote from serving the public interest is the ICC that the agency itself can be regarded as the largest single problem in the entire American transportation industry. If the ICC were abolished, competitive transportation could be restored and all the advantages of competition could be passed on to the public. Transportation rates could be restructured, and the industry could be massively reorganized. Obviously, this would cause the industry considerable inconvenience, but it would be of enormous benefit to the public. Railways could specialize in relatively swift passenger travel over distances of less than 200 miles—speeds at which airplanes are neither efficient nor economical—and in the transportation of those manufactured goods in which they have a natural cost advantage. Any instances of price-fixing or collusion by railroad managements that might arise could be regulated by existing antitrust laws. In any case, no collusion by industry can match the ludicrous obstruction perpetrated each day by the ICC in the name of "regulation."

AIRLINES

The airline industry in the United States suffers from an abundance of riches and an inability to control them. New planes with higher and higher price tags arrive before old equipment has been paid for. In an effort to increase its market share, each airline attempts to offer "discounted" fares that are identical to the rates of competing airlines that would fly the same passenger to the same destination via the identical route. The airline fare structure is more gibberish than logic, and passengers who try to fly for the least expense pay the lowest applicable price only by a combination of skill, effort, and luck.

Aircraft Technology Can Outrun Economics

Much of the critical airframe, engine, and control system research essential to any new generation of airplanes is conducted free of charge as part of U.S. defense efforts. Many new aircraft are therefore underpriced. Boeing readily adapted designs of the military's B-52 bomber and the KC-135 tanker to make the commercial 707. A generation earlier, Douglas used its World War II design experience to build the DC-4, DC-6, and DC-7 planes. Advancing technology is irresistible. The prospects of moving more passengers greater distances at ever-decreasing operating costs inevitably produces a commercial design incorporating the latest design concepts. New generations of planes are built because they are technically possible, not because they are economically feasible under existing market conditions. And here yet another transportation problem begins.

A new plane arrives and the manufacturer proudly displays it to an admiring world using millions of dollars allotted in the advertising budget. A prosperous airline or two may order several new planes, hoping that offering something new will attract more passengers. Afraid of being left behind, the remainder of the industry follows, herdlike. The airlines run up huge bills for new planes, new starting equipment, new luggage and boarding facilities, and new "persuasions" to the public and the politicians to build additional airports to accommodate these new behemoths and their legions of passengers. The old equipment, with a remaining flight life of ten or more years, is sold on an already glutted after-market, and the ground equipment for these older planes becomes just so much scrap metal.

The Load Factor

Airlines use a measure of aircraft capacity called the "load factor" to estimate their market and profit potential. The *load factor* is the percentage of plane seats that must be filled for an airline to break even on a given route or on all its routes. As expenses increase, the load factor rises. Because landings and take-offs are costly in terms of fuel used and airport fees charged, the load factor is higher for short hauls than it is for long-distance operations. Such nonsensical frills as pianos in 747 "astrolounges," conceived by marketing staffs in the hope of attracting more passengers, simply increase costs, reduce seating space, and raise the load factor.

Air Travel Markets

The market for airplane seats is usually divided into *discretionary travel,* such as vacationers and people visiting relatives, and *nondiscretionary travel,* mainly businesspeople for whom travel by air is necessary to their work. Discretionary travelers can choose from a variety of flights and departure dates and may decide to travel by car or even train instead of by plane due to cost considerations or personal preference. When they must fly, businesspeople are less concerned with cost and more concerned with the factors of time and convenience. So commercial airlines usually have two different rate levels: lower prices to attract tourists, and higher prices for businesspeople who must travel at specific times on specific routes. Extending this multiprice marketing strategy, airlines offer even lower fares to passengers who can't pay tourist fares. Students, ministers, and soldiers often fly for a lower than tourist rate.

The effort to match airline fares to passengers' ability to pay produces rates that vary by day of the week and hour of the day, by days elapsed since the passenger left the first airport on the trip, and by any other direct or indirect measure of ability to pay that the airlines can persuade the Civil Aeronautics Board (CAB)—similar in function and prejudice to the ICC—to adopt. But eroding their fare base, the airlines endanger the revenues they must earn to pay for their 747s and 1011s. Ticket prices are no longer based on the cost of getting from one place to another: One passenger subsidizes another, one route pays for another, and the financial structure of the entire industry grows ever weaker.

Charters

As major commercial airlines attempted to cope with their runaway technology, they were faced with yet another burden: chartered airlines and nonscheduled carriers. These airlines buy the serviceable aircraft discarded by the larger airlines, offer lower rates than these commercial giants, and take valuable passenger traffic away from them. The CAB allows private groups to charter planes and to divide the cost of the trip among their members. If a group fills a chartered plane, the cost of the trip may be one-third the regular tourist fare.

Charter flights primarily appeal to vacationers who plan expensive trips far in advance. Enormous amounts of the North Atlantic market between New York, Montreal, and European destinations has been captured by charter operations. Charters are presently organized under Advanced Booking Charter (ABC) rules. ABC regulations establish low passenger fares that are equal to about one-third of the regular economy fares on commercial airlines. Charter passengers must make predeparture deposits at specified intervals up to 30 days before the flight. A passenger who cancels a reservation or misses a flight for any reason other than demonstrable ill health can lose up to one-half the deposited fare.

Charter Problems: A Warning. Charter operations have not entirely benefitted air travelers. A dishonest charter operator can easily advertise a list of inexpensive flights, request large deposits with no intention of refunding them, and then abscond with the money. In other cases, honest, well-intentioned charter airlines advertise a shopping list of flights for which they will hire planes if they can recruit enough passengers. If not enough passengers sign up for a specific charter, these airlines may return the deposits, but they are entitled to and usually do deduct a large fee for the service of having tried to organize the charter flight. Many passengers have actually been stranded in remote countries with no money to return home when their charter organizers or aircraft failed to appear. To guard against such dangers, a would-be charter passenger should read the charter contract carefully, investigate the charterer (worthwhile here are long-distance calls to police, consumer groups, and even the Better Business Bureau in the charter airline's city) and check with the carrier to see if the charter group has actually arranged to transport passengers to the advertised destinations. The deposit check should also be marked "refundable in full" on its face and back and sent by certified or registered mail with a covering letter stating exactly what is expected in return. A refund can even be extracted from a tough, fraudulent charter operator if victimized passengers are well-prepared to prosecute.

Airports

Perhaps the greatest airlines problem and the most glaring example of economics and technology at odds with one another is evidenced by the design and location of airports. Airports by definition consume vast amounts of land. Ide-

ally, an airport should be located far enough from human habitation to reduce noise and danger factors for adjoining residents but close enough to the city it serves to be reached quickly via highway. The present situation at almost every airport in the United States is precisely the opposite: Suburban housing crowds near the runways, making their extension to accommodate ever larger planes expensive or impossible and increasing noise and danger levels for adjoining residents. Where the airport has grown to meet the suburbs, land values have been drastically reduced, thereby undermining the tax base that supports the airport.

Poor Airport Planning. The people who plan airports are not city planners (if indeed anyone can be said to plan either cities or airports). Local zoning boards permit high-rise residential apartments to be built in the paths of descending aircraft, which endanger building occupants and airplane passengers equally. Ideal airport remotely located from cities and served by exclusive-use expressways are corrupted by local highway boards that agree to let developers build along the airport access road. Soon city suburb or town meets airport, danger looms, and future airport expansion becomes impossible or quite costly. Once again, the trip to airport or city is then a lengthy process that can often consume as much time as the flight itself.

Today's aircraft are rigorously tested before they are approved for passenger transport, but airports are built and operated as mere afterthoughts to the planes and passengers they serve. New generations of larger and still larger planes confront airport managers with volumes of passengers and luggage that were probably inconceivable when the airport was originally planned. The inefficiency of ground movement within airports tests passengers' strength and endurance, as anyone who has ever tried to traverse Chicago's O'Hare or New York's Kennedy airport can attest.

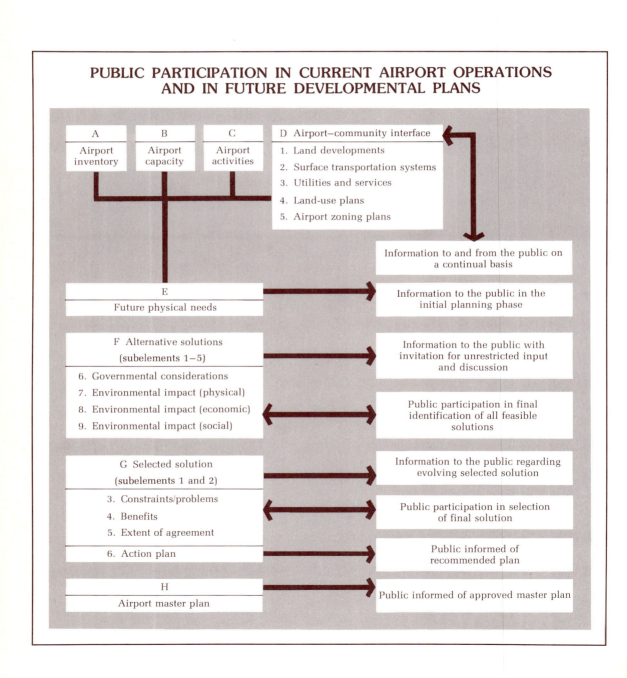

PUBLIC PARTICIPATION IN CURRENT AIRPORT OPERATIONS AND IN FUTURE DEVELOPMENTAL PLANS

A	B	C	D Airport–community interface
Airport inventory	Airport capacity	Airport activities	1. Land developments
			2. Surface transportation systems
			3. Utilities and services
			4. Land-use plans
			5. Airport zoning plans

Information to and from the public on a continual basis

E
Future physical needs

Information to the public in the initial planning phase

F Alternative solutions
(subelements 1–5)

6. Governmental considerations
7. Environmental impact (physical)
8. Environmental impact (economic)
9. Environmental impact (social)

Information to the public with invitation for unrestricted input and discussion

Public participation in final identification of all feasible solutions

G Selected solution
(subelements 1 and 2)

3. Constraints/problems
4. Benefits
5. Extent of agreement

6. Action plan

Information to the public regarding evolving selected solution

Public participation in selection of final solution

Public informed of recommended plan

H
Airport master plan

Public informed of approved master plan

To all airport design problems there can be only one solution—comprehensive and inclusive planning for every aspect of commercial flight from city to city and from luggage drop to luggage pick-up.   Getting from one airport to another is only one part of the air-travel system; airport planners must solve city-to-airport and airport-to-city problems as well.   To do this, zoning authority must be reassigned from local boards to airport planners, with the special condition that airports are not to interfere with the rights of nearby residents to the safety and sanity that thundering jets make impossible.

A PLANNED TRANSPORTATION SYSTEM

In this chapter we have examined the American transportation system and have answered the essential questions of who pays and at what cost.   Through neglect and conspiratorial practices, both business and government have failed to protect the consumer from bearing a disproportionately large share of the costs of public transportation while deriving less than a proportional share of benefits.   We also saw how automobile manufacturers pass along the costs of product testing to car owners and drivers and how many of these manufacturers fail to correct product defects when accidents due to negligent design maim or even kill.   The American people bought and built the railroads with their taxes and savings, but the railroad authorities constantly cry poor as they place their operating funds in nonrailroad investments.   Airlines and their finances are victims of technology and passengers often are victims of the airlines.

Excess Investment in Transportation

America has overinvested in transportation.   City trolley lines, if they were still running, would be faster than many automobile or bus trips on today's congested freeways.   The U.S. railroads could be resurrected to provide energy-efficient, safe, and comfortable transport for far less than the cost of driving.   More than 100 million American-owned cars represent a monstrous overinvestment in personal transit, a small portion of which could easily be spent to bring back low-cost public transportation.   The total cost of public transportation in the United States is comprised of more than merely the factor of private cost.   The public costs of the air pollution from 100 million automobile engines, of neighborhoods torn apart by freeways, and of legal systems devoted entirely to the automobile are perhaps incalculable.

A National Policy Is Necessary

The high personal and public costs of moving from place to place in America can only be reduced by forming and implementing a national transportation policy.   This policy must be democratic in its appeal if it is to serve the nation for many decades.   What fragments of transportation policy the United States now has in the forms of the ICC, the CAB, the Maritime Administration, and other agencies are no more than a mockery of a well-conceived transportation policy. Collusion between industry and government cannot be equated with intelligent cooperation.

Public transportation costs should be shared by business, government, and consumers, and a good transportation policy must cope with public as well as private costs. Those who benefit from this policy could be required to pay in proportion to the advantages they derive from an improved transportation system. Transportation pricing without subsidies or public gifts to private-interest groups could be the first step toward a rational system. But transportation could be subsidized on the basis of public rather than private interests.

The private car is an inefficient transportation investment because it is idle most of the time. Reducing the total social cost of transportation would serve to deemphasize the central role that the private automobile plays in the system. The private capital saved in this way could then be used to provide more and better public transportation and a greater choice of transportation modes and to reduce damage to the environment.

The Transition Period

The transition to a planned transportation system may be difficult. Should the system be planned by a central authority, such as the Department of Transportation or Congress? Or should the government simply restore the existing transportation system to free competition and let the economy take care of the rest? The problem of free-market solution versus central-planning solution is beyond answering in this book, yet we can make one suggestion based on historical experience: Big plans produce big mistakes. Therefore, it seems wise to favor a free-market solution with a minimum of government restraints. The degree to which government intervenes should be based on the public interest and an attempt to lower social costs. In the short run, the nation should rebuild the true backbone of the economy—the railroads. Forcing railroad authorities to use their real estate profits to maintain passenger and freight operations and an overhaul of the Interstate Commerce Commission could and probably should be the first two steps toward establishing a planned public transportation system.

SUMMARY

1 The United States has no public transportation policy. Regulatory agencies oversee the welfare of various modes of transportation such as automobiles, trains, and airplanes, but there is no policy for the transportation system as a whole.

2 The private automobile is the dominant type of transport in America. Automobile manufacturers and related industries are central to the economy. But car transport is expensive compared to such alternatives as the train, bus, or plane.

3 The private costs of automobile travel are further increased by the tendency for manufacturers to design what sells rather than what runs dependably and inexpensively.

4 Car travel is relatively costly in terms of both private and environmental costs.

5 Manufacturers' warranties help to sell cars and limit the warranties implied by common law. It is possible to force car manufacturers to honor their warranties or even to provide a new or adequate vehicle by waging an aggressive letter-writing and publicity campaign or by taking direct legal action. Some courts ignore limited express warranties if they are convinced that the public good requires car manufacturers to be responsible for their products regardless of what liability limitations these companies can obtain by greater bargaining power.

6 Automobile mechanics are underpaid because their productivity is lower than that of assembly-line workers. Automobile repair work is expensive due to the high overhead of operating a full-service garage and the high costs of parts.

7 Repair work is priced on the basis of rate tables in job-time manuals, many of which overcharge in terms of actual repair time required.

8 Automobile manufacturers or garages can charge more for parts because the customers are their captives. The rarer the car, the harder it will be to find a particular part and the more the part will probably cost.

9 Foreign cars that don't change in appearance every year may be sold at current prices but be from old stock. Laws that require a birthday tag to appear on the driver's car door are frequently ignored by dishonest dealers.

10 Public money rather than private funds has financed a large share of the U.S. railroad system. Public lands originally given to the railroads have been retained and rented or sold for huge profits. Extortion of and by state and local governments and fraud involving private investors was present in much early railroad financing.

11 Created in 1887 to prevent railroads from charging whatever rates the traffic would bear, the Interstate Commerce Commission quickly became a monopolistic maintainer of high railroad fares. The ICC now seems to be too concerned with protecting the transportation industry.

12 Claims of poverty made by the railroads should be examined in light of the revenues the roads derive from their nonrailroad operations.

13 Airlines buy new planes when they appear on the market rather than when they are needed. New airplanes are underpriced because they have been researched free of charge by the government in its defense program.

14 The load factor is the number of seats on an aircraft that must be filled for an airline to break even on a given route or on all its routes. High aircraft purchase prices and short-distance flights tend to increase the load factor.

15 Airlines try to charge fares that are based on what passengers can afford to pay. Accordingly, they establish a high fare for people who are on short business trips, a lower fare for tourists who can plan their trips further in advance and thereby benefit from reduced rates, and an even lower rate for passengers who cannot afford tourist fares. These differential fares may help to spread air traffic more evenly over the hours in a day or the days in a week, but they can also erode the airlines' revenue base.

16 Any comprehensive transportation policy should emphasize public transport and deemphasize the private automobile. An important political issue is whether such a policy should operate in a free market or be centrally planned.

Suggestions for Further Reading

Burby, John. *The Great American Motion Sickness.* Boston: Little, Brown, 1971.

Chandler, Alfred D., Jr. *The Railroads.* New York: Harcourt Brace Jovanovich, Inc., 1965.

Daughen, Joseph R., and Binzen, Peter. *The Wreck of the Penn Central.* Boston: Little, Brown, 1971.

Fellmeth, Robert C. *The Interstate Commerce Omission.* New York: Grossman, 1970.

Keats, John. *The Insolent Chariots.* Philadelphia: J.B. Lippincott, 1958.

Locklin, D. Phillip. *Economics of Transportation,* 7th ed. Homewood, Ill.: Richard D. Irwin, 1972.

Nader, Ralph. *Unsafe At Any Speed.* New York: Simon and Schuster, 1966.

Nader, Ralph, Dodge, Lowell, and Hotchkiss, Ralf. *What To Do With Your Bad Car: An Action Manual for Lemon Owners.* New York: Grossman, 1971.

Stone, Tabor R. *Beyond the Automobile.* Englewood Cliffs, N.J.: Prentice-Hall, 1971.

Consumer Reports. Published monthly; especially see each year's April and December issues.

The Consumer Workshop

1 List the different ways in which travel is important to your lifestyle.
2 Is the private automobile vital to your way of life? Even if a car is important to you, what could you do with the funds required to operate a car if you didn't have to meet these expenses?
3 We can view alternate forms of transportation in terms of several criteria:
  1 Cost
  2 Speed versus maintenance required
  3 Ease of access
  Discuss the value of the private automobile versus public transit for:
  1 A student who has an income of $3000 per year
  2 A business executive who has an income of $20,000 per year, a suburban home, and three children
  3 A retired husband and wife who have a combined income of $6000 per year
4 Suppose that your new car has a severe mechanical problem and that the dealer refuses to honor the warranty. With one or more classmates, map out your strategy to force the dealer to uphold the warranty.
5 Why are automobile repairs so costly? What can car owners do to reduce their repair and maintenance bills?

21

THE HEALTH-CARE
INDUSTRY AND
THE CONSUMER

“ The Ill: . . . This silent minority is indeed silent! They have no organization and exert no pressure. No more quiet nor submissive lot exists. And yet, in their number, they have carried the economic burden of supporting the professions and sustaining the profits of an aggressive, sophisticated industry. ”

THE ADVISORY COMMITTEE ON DRUG PURCHASING, 1972*

It is paradoxical but true that modern medicine is curing the patient's body and killing the patient's budget. This chapter focuses on the efficiency and the expense of the health-care industry in the United States, and examines specific areas in which medical-care facilities can be improved. We begin by identifying the reasons for the soaring costs of medical and dental care and prescription and nonprescription drugs. We then briefly examine the conditions and problems in nursing homes. Because 85% of all medical services performed in the United States are prepaid, we investigate the field of health insurance. Finally, we discuss the vested interests of medicine, weighing the somewhat selfish concerns of physicians and hospital administrators against the consumer's interests and needs.

THE COST OF MEDICAL CARE

In 1970, U.S. consumers spent approximately $67 billion on health care, about 7% of the gross national product (see Figure 21-1). This figure represents an increase of 1.1% in health-care expenditures in five years—a substantial reallocation of national resources. During the 1960s, medical-care costs rose almost twice as fast as the prices of all consumer goods combined. This trend is not unique in the United States; in recent years, it has been paralleled in most industrialized western countries.[1]

* The Advisory Committee on Central Drug Purchasing and Distribution (Manitoba), *Report* (April 1972), p. 19. Hereafter cited as *CDP*.

[1] Walter J. McNerney, "Why Does Medical Care Cost So Much?", *New England Journal of Medicine* CCLXXXII (June 25, 1970), p. 1460; Odin, W. Anderson and Duncan Neuhauser, "Rising Costs . . . In Health-Care Systems," *Hospitals* (February 16, 1969), pp. 50–53; *Canadian Medical Association Journal* CIII (September 12, 1970), p. 562; U.S. Department of Health, Education and Welfare, Social Security Administration, Office of Research and Statistics, *The Size and Shape of the Medical-Care Dollar* (Washington, D.C.: 1971), pp. 5, 13. Hereafter cited as *MCD*.

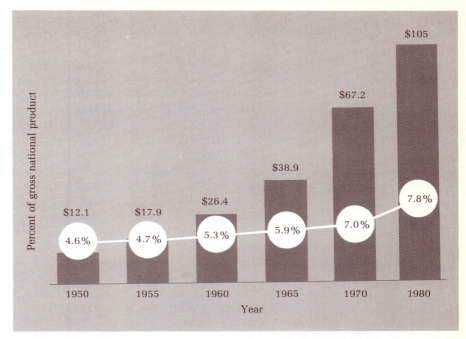

Source: U.S. Dept. of Health, Education and Welfare

21-1   U.S. Health-Care Expenditures (in billions of dollars)

It is not our purpose here to determine the correct proportion of resources that any country should devote to health care.   Instead, we simply intend to inquire into the efficiency of such spending.   The basic question underlying this discussion will be "What are we getting for our money?"

We can point to three overall reasons for the soaring cost of medical care in the United States:

1 Misallocation of physicians
2 An increasingly expensive medical technology
3 Lack of competition in the health-care services market

Misallocation of Physicians   It has often been said that medicine is expensive because there are not enough doctors, but this statement is not altogether true.   Of course, physicians have more than enough patients, as anyone who has waited three hours in a doctor's outer office knows.   However, the trend toward medical specialization has caused many physicians to forsake direct doctor–patient practice in favor of research, administration, and such no-contact fields as pathology.   Some physicians leave therapeutic medicine to work for insurance companies or for the government.   Others leave the medical field altogether to become corporate heads or politicians.   It is therefore naive to believe that simply increasing the number of doctors will increase the supply of general medical practitioners. Merely funneling money into the construction of medical schools will produce more practicing physicians, but it will also produce more specialists in fields that may already be adequately filled, thereby indirectly spawning more insurance company doctors and more bureaucrats.

It takes 10–12 years before a commitment to build a new medical school yields a flock of new doctors who are trained to practice medicine. It has been estimated that it would take 30 years to double the total number of physicians in this country, even if the output of U.S. medical schools could be instantaneously doubled.[2] This solution to excess medical costs and the inadequate number of physicians is therefore a distant and expensive option at best. Short-range, immediate solutions offer more immediate hope for improvement.

The High Cost of Medical Technology

There is a promising trend of increasing productivity in both the medical and dental services. From 1961 through the end of 1965, for example, physicians and dentists increased their productivity by about 2.5% through the use of better equipment and substitute health technicians. But compelling evidence exists that what is basically wrong with the health-delivery system is the misallocation of existing resources. In 1973 in Mississippi there were 94 physicians for every 100,000 persons; in New York there were 240 per 100,000. Cities are gaining physicians; rural areas are losing them. Some common surgical procedures are performed four times as often in some areas as they are in others, not only due to variations in the disease or condition treated, but also due to differences in the specialists, surgeons, and hospital facilities available. Whites live about 10% longer than nonwhites and have one-fourth the rate of maternal mortality, half

[2] McNerney, "Why Does Medical Care Cost So Much?", p. 1459.

21-2 The Cost of Medical Care

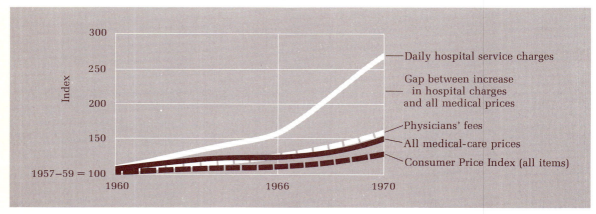

Source: U.S. Department of Health, Education and Welfare

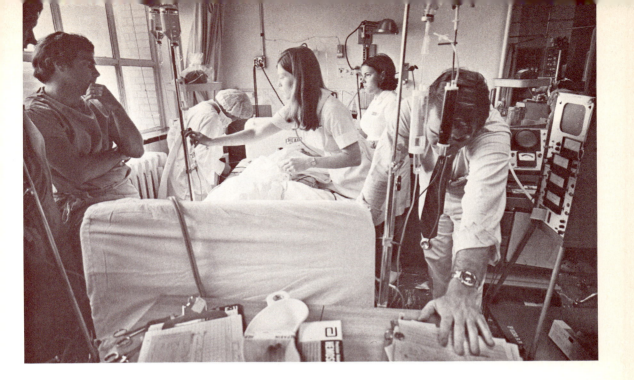

the rate of infant mortality, and one-fourth the rate of mortality from such treatable diseases as tuberculosis and pneumonia. When we look at variations in the ratios of such discretionary medical services as psychoanalysis for mild neurosis, soft-tissue plastic surgery, and such no-result procedures as cold and flu therapy and teenage dermatology, we find even more grotesque variations.[3]

Hospital Care. The fastest rising component of medical costs is hospital care. Between 1965 and 1970, daily hospital service charges increased more than twice as fast as the average of all medical-care prices. Hospital costs dramatically reflect the costs of advancing technology. For example, a $500 microscope used to be used for blood-cell counts. However, since 1960 most hospitals have employed electronic cell counters that operate much faster and more accurately than optical counters but cost $5000 or more. Diagnostic x-ray machines that once cost $10,000 now cost $100,000 or more. Although every new medical device is greatly improved in terms of speed, accuracy, and safety compared to its predecessors, it substantially increases medical technology costs (see Figure 21-2). Improved technology shortens patient stays in hospitals, but exposure to hospital routine is something over which patients have little or no control. For its purpose to be justified, elaborate diagnostic machinery must be used. Just as pilots log in flight time to improve their abilities, doctors endeavor

[3] Ibid., pp. 1459–60; *Statistical Abstract of the United States,* 96th ed. (Washington, D.C.: 1975), Table 111, p. 74.

to maintain their skills and to acquire new ones. To become familiar with new equipment is to advance in competence, so that new technology justifies its own use. A doctor with elaborate and advanced equipment achieves greater esteem and importance in a specialty and in a particular hospital. For pathologists and other specialists working on commission, each laboratory test provides more income. Considering that pathologists earn an average annual income of $100,000, making them both the most mechanized and highest paid specialists, the influence of money cannot be entirely disregarded.

Lack of Competition

Faced with illness, we have a desperate desire to be well, but most of us have neither knowledge nor the emotional independence and security to shop around the medical market searching for alternative treatments and lower prices. We have already said that physicians tend to prescribe the latest and the best treatment, even when an equally good result can be obtained at a lower cost by using an alternative approach.

Obviously, an ill person is in no condition to comparison-shop for a doctor the way a consumer might select a new kitchen appliance. The seriously ill are rarely ambulatory and may even be unable to think clearly. Patients with less debilitating conditions who are able to research the medical market often find major obstacles to rational choice. Medical ethics prevent physicians from advertising their services or prices. The most physicians are permitted to do is to list their medical specialties; tables of their success and failure rates are not available to patients. The alternatives to a treatment recommended by one physician can only be learned from another specialist. Direct questions about other doctors' surgical techniques, for example, are answered reluctantly, if at all, by most physicians.

DRUG PRICES

In the area of prescription drugs, most consumers have little or no objective knowledge of the effectiveness or the comparative cost of the medicines they must purchase. When buying patent nonprescription medicines and other products, consumers rely primarily on the advertising claims of manufacturers who make essentially similar products. Let's examine the structure of the drug market to determine why medicines are so expensive and then discuss what can be done to reduce the high cost of medication.

Prescription Drugs

Prescription medicines are called *ethical drugs* because they can be dispensed only by pharmacists who are supposedly bound by a professional ethic. These compounds cannot be purchased without a physician's prescription. There are two structural elements in the price of ethical drugs: the wholesale price that is

DRUG COST COMPONENTS

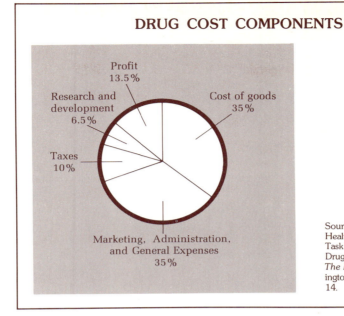

Profit
13.5%

Research and
development
6.5%

Cost of goods
35%

Taxes
10%

Marketing, Administration,
and General Expenses
35%

Source: U.S. Department of
Health, Education and Welfare,
Task Force on Prescription
Drugs, *The Drug Makers and
The Drug Distributors* (Washington, December 1968), p.
14.

determined by the manufacturer, and the local retail price that is established by the dispensing pharmicist.

The major drug companies defend present wholesale drug prices on the grounds of increased drug effectiveness, more elaborate research and development efforts, and quality control improvements in the manufacturing process. In truth, these claims are not entirely valid. Another cause—lack of competition—better explains the level of high wholesale ethical drug prices.

Drug Companies Are Interlocked. Almost any major ethical drug—cortisone, steroids, tranquilizers, antibiotic subgroups—is produced by only one, two or three manufacturers, although as many as 12 drug packagers may be licensed to sell the drug. A major drug firm may manufacture a compound that has only limited competitive potential and then license its use or inclusion in many different compounds to other drug manufacturers. The original manufacturer of the compound then becomes a licensee of a limited number of competing drug firms that produce ethical drugs containing this compound.

In essence, each ethical drug is made by a few firms and sold by a few others. Manufacturers of certain drugs do not sell them to pharmacists but license the entire sale and distribution of the drug to another firm or to a few firms. A few firms do not make any drugs but sell only drugs made by other manufacturers. In this context, a firm that wishes to be price competitive may find that the drug firms it undercuts will refuse to renew sales licenses or to market their other drug lines. It is therefore hardly surprising that the average return on each dollar invested in the drug industry is much higher than the dollar return in any other U.S. industry.

Research Claims. The concentration of both the manufacturing and distribution structure of ethical drugs in the United States provides a more reasonable explanation for wholesale drug price levels than claims of high research costs and drug uniqueness. Most of the major drug companies channel large portions of their research and development budgets into the salaries of sales representatives who visit physicians and druggists and into the tons of promotional toys and literature with which physicians are deluged each year.

In recent years drug firms have spent an annual average of more than $3000 in advertising and selling costs per U.S. physician.[4] The most important basic research in ethical drugs is conducted essentially free of direct charge by universities and government laboratories that are subsidized by federal tax dollars and tax-deductible contributions. The results of such drug research are usually published and made available to drug firms at no charge.

Although drug manufacturers often claim that new compounds are unique, most of them are really only new combinations of old drugs designed to minimize side effects. Unfortunately, some of these new compounds eliminate *all* effect:[5] A classic example of this is a tranquilizer–stimulant compound, the elements of which cancel out one another and thus have absolutely no effect on the patient. The cost of these new compounds is often far greater than the cost of the constituent drugs if bought separately. If a tablet of Miltown (meprobamate)—the first great tranquilizer in the late 1950s—which may cost 1¢ in wholesale lots of 1000 is mixed with a layer of amphetamine stimulant at the same wholesale price, the new compound will probably carry a wholesale price of 10¢ rather than 2¢. Many of these compounds are not only overpriced but are meaningless mixtures concocted to justify a new, marketable brand name for a product that other drug manufacturers are already marketing.

Quality. The number of cases in the courts pertaining to the premature sale and incompetent manufacture of drugs suggests that the level of quality control in the drug industry could be markedly improved. The perilous effects of Thalidomide, a tranquilizer that seriously deformed the unborn children of the pregnant women who used it, or injectable solutions that contained fatal organisms, or the all too frequent drug recalls are only the most blatant examples of profit motive interfering with public safety.

Retail Costs. The price of a drugstore prescription includes an average 86% markup on wholesale cost plus a "dispensing fee" for pouring pills from a big bottle to a smaller one.[6] Sometimes this fee also includes typing and affixing a numbered prescription label to the smaller bottle. The dispensing fee is normally a fixed amount of approximately $2. This means that the greatest portion

---

[4] U.S. Department of Health, Education and Welfare, Task Force on Prescription Drugs, *Second Interim Report and Recommendations* (Washington, D.C.: August 30, 1968), p. 14.

[5] *CDP*, p. 8.

[6] U.S. Department of Health, Education and Welfare, Task Force on Prescription Drugs, *The Drug Makers and the Drug Distributors* (Washington, D.C.: December 1968), p. 63; *Final Report* (Washington, D.C.: February 7, 1969), p. 16.

of the cost of a prescription with a low price of, say, $2.25 is the dispensing fee, whereas the dispensing fee on a high-price prescription of, say, $20 is only a small portion of the total retail price.

Proprietary Drugs

Now let's examine patent medicines, drugs whose brand names are the property of their manufacturers. Proprietary drugs carry trademarks or copyrighted names and are sold over the counter. Most of these drugs are backed by huge and expensive promotional campaigns. Geritol, Anacin, Preparation H, and Bayer Aspirin are among the proprietaries.

Safety. Proprietary medicines tend to be safe when used as their labels direct. This also means that they do not contain particularly powerful drugs; if they did, they couldn't be sold across the counter without a prescription. Most proprietary drugs do have a psychological healing effect; if you expect to feel better when you take two aspirins and your headache goes away after you swallow the pills, the healing effect may be due as much to the hope for a cure as to the acetylsalicyclic acid the aspirin contains. However, most proprietary drugs can be habit-forming, either physically or psychologically; cough-medicine and aspirin addicts are not rare in our society.

Profit. Most proprietary drug compounds are meaningless, overpriced, false differentiations of a few useful ingredients. Aspirin does work, but no particular compound works better or faster than any other—despite the advertising claims. In analgesic aspirins such as Bayer and Anacin, most of the difference in products is the advertising. A manufacturer can't make much selling 200 tablets of 5-grain brandless aspirin for 25¢ but can earn a good profit by adding some caffein and anti-nausea powder and selling 12 tablets of the same aspirin for 89¢. If you have a headache, buy the cheapest aspirin you can find.

Advertising. Over the last two decades, the federal courts have been filled with prosecutions instituted by the U.S. Food and Drug Administration in an attempt to force proprietary drug companies to stop claiming that their compounds can do amazing things. It took the federal government 13 years to get the Carter Company to admit that its little "liver" pills had no special effects on the human liver. Now the FDA is moving against the headache-pill industry and is meeting strong resistance. Proprietary pill advertising costs are quite high; the strongest active ingredient in most of these compounds is their advertising.

What Can the Consumer Do?

Now let's examine what actions the consumer can take. Consumers can respond to high drug prices both personally and politically.

Personal Preventive Action. When buying proprietary or ethical drugs, always try to buy the basic chemical compounds, called *generic drugs* from the Latin *genus,* meaning "type" or "category". A generic drug is an unadvertised chemical compound without a brand name. Generic aspirin USP or BP (the letters mean that the pills conform to accepted professional and national standards in the United States and the British Commonwealth) have the same effect as any brand-name aspirin. Ask your physician to prescribe the lowest cost generic drug available, and request generic proprietaries at the drugstore. Compare prices whenever possible. When buying a particular compound in quantity, try to buy it in large lots. Pharmaceutical lots of 1000 tablets can cost only 5% of the price of the same product purchased in smaller quantities.

The best way to save money on nonprescription drugs is to avoid taking needless remedies and using counterproductive drugs (for example, Nytol and No-Doz—a sleeping pill and a pep pill, respectively) in quick succession.[7] And do not self-medicate serious physical problems; when really ill, see a doctor.

Legislation. At the level of political change, consumers should demand that legislators follow the Canadian example of compulsory generic substitution laws. Pharmacists in Manitoba, Ontario, and Saskatchewan are required by law to substitute equivalent generics for brand-name ethical drugs when a physician has not prescribed the least expensive type of a particular drug that is available. Many U.S. states, institutions, and federal government agencies buy in quantity from drug companies through competitive bidding.[8] Drug chains may also do this, but they rarely pass such savings on to the consumer.

Consumers should also demand that pharmacists be allowed to advertise prescription prices. The Osco drug chain in Illinois has taken a lead in posting the prices of its most frequently prescribed drugs. Other Illinois pharmacists have objected strongly, claiming that drug advertising is unethical and insisting on professional confidentiality about drug prices. But concealing drug price information can hide only the profits that these manufacturers earn.

NURSING HOMES AND THE AGED

Approximately 20 million Americans, or 10% of the U.S. population, are over 65 years of age. For many of these people illness is a permanent way of life. One survey indicates that 97% of the aged couples interviewed incurred some medical expenses during the survey year. On the average, the person over 65 spends more than twice as much as the person under 65 for medical care but earns only half the income. Compared to the younger population, noninstitutionalized aged persons are twice as likely to have a chronic illness and almost

[7] See Consumers Union, *The Medicine Show* (New York: Simon and Schuster, 1961).

[8] Under a November 15, 1974, HEW proposal (*Federal Register,* 11/15/74), HEW and state drug costs in Medicare and Medicaid programs could be cut by $89 million a year by (1) limiting reimbursement to pharmacists for prescriptions to wholesale cost plus dispensing fee, (2) limiting reimbursement to the price of the lowest-cost generic equivalent, and (3) publishing a comprehensive list of all drug prices.

MORE THAN ONE-QUARTER OF EACH PERSONAL HEALTH-CARE DOLLAR IS SPENT ON THE AGED, WHO COMPRISE 10% OF THE POPULATION

$103,200,000

19-64 years

65years and over

under 19 years

$216,624,000

19-64 years

65 and over

under 19 years

Source: Division of Health Insurance Studies, Office of Research and Statistics, Social Security Administration, U.S. Department of Health, Education and Welfare (fiscal year 1975).

three times as likely to have days when their activity must be restricted due to illness.[9]

In 1970, per-capita hospital-care expenditures for an aged person ($372) were more than 11 times greater than those for a young person ($33) and more than $2\frac{1}{2}$ times greater than those for a person in the intermediate age group. The average aged person's expenditures for physicians' services ($136) was 3 times greater than that for a youth ($41) and more than 2 times greater than for a person in the intermediate age group ($64).[10]

Illness and Age   Illness and age are closely related.   In the United States, approximately 80% of the elderly suffer from one or more chronic illnesses or conditions compared to

[9] Claire Townsend, *Old Age: The Last Segregation* (New York: Grossman, 1971), pp. 25–26; *MCD*, pp. 28, 30.
[10] *MCD*, p. 31.

40% of those under 65.[11]   As the Task Force on Prescription Drugs wrote in 1968:

> For many elderly people, illness serves as a major cause of their poverty by reducing their incomes, while poverty serves as a major contributory cause of illness by making it impossible for them to obtain adequate health care.[12]

Americans tend to allocate more of their resources to the concerns of the young and less to the often much more substantial problems of the old.   As families redefine themselves in the process of urbanization, they draw inward and do not include the old.   The typical pattern of North American family life today excludes aged parents, forcing them into nursing homes or—if they are unavailable or too costly—often into hospitals or mental institutions.

Retirement   Social progress for the young has often been made at the expense of social regression for the old.   The availability of pensions now dictates compulsory retirement at the age of 65.   The very structure of Social Security regulations force older workers to leave the workforce even when they and society can mutually benefit from their continued employment.   Pensioners who do manage to earn a decent living must give up their Social Security allowances.   However, if a wealthy elderly person receives $100,000 in investment income each year, the Social Security check still comes regularly.   According to Ralph Nader's Study Group Report on Nursing Homes:

> The practical alternatives for an aged person in need of limited care are a paltry three: hospitalization, institutionalization in a nursing home, or life with younger, more capable relatives.   Life at home, except for the few lucky or rich enough to snare one of the few available nurses or homemakers, is impossible.   Medicare will pay for 100 visits a year by home health aides, but only one of seven Medicare recipients lives in an area where such services can be obtained.[13]

Too many elderly persons are forced to pass their remaining years in cheap, crime-ridden hotels, in nursing homes, or in poverty concealed behind the walls of homes and apartments they desperately strive to maintain.   Those consigned by relatives or by lack of another alternative to nursing homes perhaps face the worst predicament.   As Congressman David Pryor of Arkansas said in 1970, "We have turned over the sickest, the most helpless, and the most vulnerable patient group in the medical-care system to the most loosely controlled and least responsible [part] of that system.[14]

Nursing Homes   The guiding princples behind the operation of many nursing homes could be defined as incompetence and greed.   State regulations for nursing-home administrators are extremely lax.   A Massachusetts study has revealed that among

[11] Task Force on Prescription Drugs, *Final Report,* p. 12.
[12] *Task Force on Prescription Drugs, Second Interim Report,* p. 4.
[13] Townsend, *Old Age,* p. 134.
[14] Ibid., p. 21.

nursing-home administrators in that state, "only 18% had completed college, 29% were high-school dropouts, 1% had no formal education at all; and of these administrators, 85% supervised all personnel and 56% supervised nursing care directly.[15]

Federal law now requires nursing-home administrators to be licensed. But nursing-home owners, who are often remote from public view, are not licensed and many control their nursing facilities via interconnecting corporations. Since federal funds began to be channeled into nursing homes, an aggressive industry has sprung up to build and operate them. Led by firms that often later become involved in stock-market scandals, the nursing-home industry seems to have been more closely modeled after a fast-food franchise than after a medical-care and rehabilitation center.

Entrance Contracts. Nursing homes with religious affiliations often require patients to sign an entrance contract on admission that to varying degrees makes the home the trustees of the patient's assets or the recipient of the patient's assets when he or she dies. Such contracts can be justified on some kind of insurance or cost-sharing basis. For example, if all the patients in a nursing home sign their total personal assets over to the home, a wealthy patient who dies soon after admission will actually finance the costs of caring for poorer patients who live longer. But this theoretical point cannot mask the fraudulent tactics of nursing homes that hold patients' personal assets even after they have been released to their families. No entrance contract should be signed without the approval of the patient's lawyer. Even if the home is entirely reputable and the contract is more or less a legitimate device to finance medical-care operations, before admission patients can place many of their assets beyond the reach of nursing-home owners by sale, conversion, transfer, or trusteeship. There is, after all, no need to overpay—even for well-rendered services.

Staff. Nursing-home personnel are often undertrained and/or uncaring. Nursing aides have the most direct and frequent contact with patients. They handle the major workload of daily patient care, which includes washing, dressing, changing beds, cleaning rooms, feeding the patient if necessary, doing laundry, and scrubbing floors. For this demanding and not entirely pleasant work, nursing aides usually receive a minimum wage.

Because their work is hard and their pay is quite low, there is a high rate of job turnover among nursing aides. Data from the U.S. Department of Labor indicate that the annual turnover rate for all nursing-home personnel is about 60%, but the turnover rate for aids and orderlies approaches 75%. Obviously, low pay and unpleasant work do not attract the most conscientious personnel. Jim Treolar, a reporter for the Detroit *News,* posed as a mentally unstable person with a criminal record when he applied for a job at a nursing home; he was hired immediately.[16]

[15] Ibid., p. 82.
[16] Ibid., p. 100.

Nurses. The active administration of nursing homes is in the charge of registered nurses. Federal law requires that at least one R.N., or in his or her absence one licensed practical nurse (L.P.N.) be on duty at all times. Because only R.N.s are qualified to maintain clinical records of patient care and to administer medicine, extensive amounts of their time must be devoted to these meticulous routines. Good nursing homes have several R.N.s, but there is little profit in this practice because R.N.s cost more than nursing aides or L.P.N.s. And the good nurses tend to avoid unpleasant homes in which their duties are confined to the dull work of record keeping and administering pills.

A Pennsylvania study comparing nonprofit nursing homes with proprietary homes run for profit found employee turnover to be reduced and employee pay and facilities for patient care to be clearly superior in nonprofit nursing homes. High staff turnover rates in this study were found to be characteristic of proprietary homes.[17]

The problem of improving nursing homes and making life more livable for the elderly is not an easy one to solve. Good nursing care is expensive, and we have already noted that age and poverty are closely related. Forcing workers to leave the labor force at the age of 65 does not necessarily benefit society or the retirees. Many people have a considerable capacity for continued work and may actually have reached the peak of their productivity at 65. Mandatory retirement forces them to become inactive, and aging often becomes more rapid and severe when the incentive to remain in the world of the active is removed.

Government Control. Many well-intentioned proponents of the nursing-home industry have suggested that new federal government offices be added to the

[17] Robert Pecarchik and Bardin H. Nelson, Jr., "Employee Turnover in Nursing Homes," *American Journal of Nursing* **LXXIII** (February 1973), pp. 289–90.

21-3 Age and Health Care Costs (fiscal year 1970)

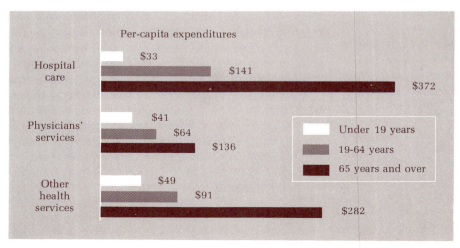

Source: U.S. Department of Health, Education and Welfare

bureaucracy to command the diverse federal offices now involved in nursing-home operations. But ample evidence already indicates that federal regulators recognize nursing-home owners and operators—not the elderly and the ill—as their clients. Efforts to require nursing homes to disclose comparative costs to consumers have been blocked by the Social Security Administration in response to the preference for anonymity by the individual member homes in the American Nursing Home Association.[18]

It is doubtful that more bureaucracy will upgrade nursing-home conditions. Existing federal standards should be vigorously enforced, and setting hospital standards for nursing homes would in itself be a major improvement.[19] In addition, license standards should be backed by training programs for nursing-home personnel, and entrance contracts should be tightly controlled. The ultimate concern of applicable laws should be the welfare of the patient, not the financial well-being of the nursing home and its operators.

HEALTH INSURANCE

Costs   The average American's health bill in 1971 was $358, which represents a 10% increase over 1970 and 10 times as much as the amount spent at the end of World War II.[20] Average health-care expenditures per capita in 1976 are estimated to exceed $550. Hospitals and medical costs for older persons are three to four times greater than they are for the young[21] (see Figure 21-3). In some respects, these increased costs are misleading. Health care has become much more expensive, but by some indexes it has also become much better in terms of quality. Physician productivity increased by about 2.5 percent between 1959 and 1965.[22] The 14 years following 1951 showed a steady decrease in the average number of days a patient remained hospitalized. Some hospital charges rose in the 1951–1965 period by large amounts (for example, the cost of treating breast cancer), but major reductions in the mortality rate were achieved in conjunction with these large cost increases.[23]

To summarize, hospital and other health-care costs are rising substantially, not only due to inflation but also due to qualitative improvements in therapy. However, this does not mean that abundant waste does not occur in the health-care system. Laboratories run by pathologists on a fee-sharing basis undoubtedly add appreciably to patient fees and to the wasteful use of computers, costly nursing education programs, and the lack of competition that we have already indicated is characteristic of the entire health-care system.[24]

---

[18] Ronald Schwartz, "New Help for the Consumer," *Modern Healthcare* **II** (July 1974), p. 58.
[19] Ibid., p. 43.
[20] *Hospitals* **XLVI** (February 1, 1972), p. 29.
[21] *Statistical Abstract of the United States,* 96th ed. (Washington, D.C.: 1975), Table 102, p. 71; *MCD*, p. 31.
[22] McNerney, "Why Does Medical Care Cost So Much?", p. 1459.
[23] *Modern Hospital* (March 1973), p. 55.
[24] *The Wall Street Journal* (December 10, 1974), p. 40.

DRUG USE BY AGE AND INCOME

Selected Characteristics	Number of Acquisitions per Capita			Cost per Acquisition		
	All Ages	65 or Over	Under 65	All Ages	65 or Over	Under 65
Family income						
Under $2,000	6.4	12.2	4.1	$3.50	$3.60	$3.38
$2,000–$3,999	5.0	11.8	3.7	3.60	3.90	3.42
$4,000–$6,999	4.2	10.7	3.8	3.70	4.50	3.58
$7,000–$9,999	4.4	11.6	4.2	3.50	4.20	3.43
$10,000 or over	4.6	9.9	4.4	3.90	4.50	3.84

Source: U.S. Public Health Service, National Center for Health Statistics, *Cost and Acquisition of Prescribed and Nonprescribed Medicines, United States, July 1964–June 1965,* Series 10, No. 33 (Washington, D.C.: U.S. Government Printing Office, 1966).

Distribution of Costs. The average cost per patient per day for hospital services exceeded $100 in 1975. The average number of hospital days per stay was five, so we may estimate average hospitalization costs to be about $500. We have already noted that the average costs of health care per person exceeded $400 in 1975. What these figures do not reveal, however, is the *distribution* of these medical costs, or in other words, who pays what.

It is obvious that older people pay more for health services, and we have already noted the intimate connection between poverty, old age, and illness. This connection is dramatically illustrated by the fact that the old and the poor use more drugs than the young and the affluent.

The Role of Insurance

Insurance itself does not change the fact that medical and related costs average over $400 per person per year in the United States. But although this bill for health services cannot be canceled, it can be deferred until the individual is better able to pay or absorbed by society if the individual cannot afford to pay. In other words, health insurance can spread existing costs among insurance-plan participants and minimize the financial effect of illness on any one person or family.

Minor illnesses and accidents are predictable events that most people expect to encounter. Colds, flus, and occasional scrapes and bruises are all accepted as a part of living. Financial reserves can be set aside to pay for routine medical care and checkups, thereby avoiding the nuisance and expense of insurance administration. Insurance should be reserved for truly unpredictable medical expenses that can devastate personal and family finances. Health insurance policies with large portions of deductible coverage (those that require the insured patient to pay charges up to a predetermined limit of $100, $250, $500, or some higher amount) in effect achieve the goal of self-insurance. And because these policies exclude many aspects of routine health care, they are much less expensive.

Goals and Controls

Health insurance is designed to provide health care for its participants at reasonable prices that they can afford. Basically, health insurance is a prepayment program for future health services. Unfortunately, medical costs have a tendency to skyrocket. What the insured patient can afford is a crude but effective limit on what is charged. Without this limitation, doctors could prescribe innumerable tests and/or checkup visits and patients could run to their doctors with the smallest ailment. Removing cost controls can increase health insurance costs, so that it is useful to maintain some disincentives for excess medical charges. *Deductible* portions of health insurance policies force patients to pay for a defined first portion of their personal health-care costs. *Coinsurance* can also be combined with the deductibility features in health insurance policies. Coinsurance requires the patient to pay for a given percentage of his or her medical costs. A policy with a good chance of forcing patients to question charges and to control costs would offer $100 or $250 deductible and 20% coinsurance. But as cost-control incentives increase, the effectiveness of insurance decreases. Forcing the poor patient to accept a limited amount of health care is the antithesis of providing health-care insurance. Similarly, excluding coverage for diseases or conditions of choice that can be prudently avoided (for example, pregnancy tests and maternity costs) saves money but denies medical benefits to people who may need them the most desperately.

Types of Medical Expense Coverage

Hospital Expense Coverage. The most popular type of health insurance coverage is hospital expense coverage, which is written as a renewable one-year policy because its rates increase with the age of the insured. Hospital expense coverage often extends to any dependents designated by the insured. Subject to deductibility and coinsurance terms, the hospital expenses covered can include room-and-board charges to a predetermined limit, hospital services (laboratory tests, x-rays, physical therapy, drugs), maternity charges, and nursing costs. There are several types of hospital expense policies, and each treats hospital costs in a different way. For example, hospital room-and-board may simply be refunded up to the daily policy allotment or it may be reimbursed on a policy-valued basis so that a fixed payment of, say, $100 (no more, no less) is made to the patient for each day spent in the hospital. Maternity benefits are often not extended in individual policies until 9–12 months after a policy has been written. Maternity benefits are a costly portion of hospital expense policies, because maternity is usually a condition of choice.

Surgical Expense Insurance. This insurance reimburses surgical expenses up to predetermined limits. The policies usually stipulate that reimbursement will be more only for legal operations performed by qualified surgeons. Most surgical expense insurance policies exclude such procedures as plastic surgery that is nonrestorative or noncorrective of congenital defects.

General Medical Expense Insurance.   This insurance reimburses nonroutine visits to physicians.   It excludes physical checkups, eye examinations, maternity costs, x-rays, and prescribed drugs.   The benefits of a general medical expense insurance policy are slight, and the insured can readily achieve the same protection via self-insurance or holding financial reserves.

Major Medical Insurance.   This is a package approach to large and burdensome medical expenses.   Major medical policies cover all expenditures related to a serious illness or disorder: hospital room and board, surgery, physicians' and nurses' fees, anesthesia, x-rays, physiotherapy, drugs, blood work, prosthetic devices, wheelchairs, respirators, defibrillators, and so on.   The upper limits of this policy coverage are quite high, but these policies also contain substantial deductibles of $500 or more to exclude minor claims and thereby keep costs down.

Disability Coverage.   This coverage replaces income lost due to a disabling injury or illness.   Disability contracts usually establish a waiting period for reimbursable loss of from one week to several months after the accident or the onset of a disabling disease.   Compensation can continue for as long a period as the insured's lifetime.

Dread Disease Policies.   These policies are frequently issued in combination with disability policies by mail-order firms, but their exclusions are so broad that they are practically worthless.   When marketed through large newspaper and direct-mail campaigns, this coverage often boasts $50,000 disability for terrible but obscure diseases.   The probability of collecting anything close to this amount is so slight that some of these firms have never even paid their announced coverage limit.

Types of Insurers

There are several types of insurers in the health insurance market.   Private firms operate for profit by selling all lines of insurance from property coverage to life and health.   Nonprofit firms, notably Blue Cross and Blue Shield, cover hospital and medical bills in addition to their other activities.

The ratio of premium income to income paid to policyholders is an important measure of the efficiency of the performance of health insurers.   Blue Cross and Blue Shield, administered by the American Hospital Association, pay out more than 95% of their premium income in claims.   In comparison, private insurers pay about 80% of their premium income.   Superficially, Blue Cross, which covers hospital expenses, and Blue Shield, which covers physicians' services, appear to be best suited to people who want coverage for a reasonable price.   However, this is not wholly accurate.   Blue Cross and Blue Shield do have lower management fees and selling costs because they concentrate on group coverage, do not maintain a vast, aggressive sales staff, and do not have to pay dividends to stockholders. On the other hand, Blue Cross and Blue Shield do not provide the custom-tailored policy service that can be obtained from private firms at higher costs.

Health Maintenance Organizations

Health maintenance organizations (HMOs) are a new approach to health-care delivery. Members of an HMO prepay for health services and, if necessary, receive actual medical treatment rather than financial compensation. The Kaiser Permanente Medical Care Program in California is an early example of a voluntary program of prepaid health care. Presently enrolling over 2 million Californians and 2000 physicians, this program offers specialized medical treatment and consultation, low-cost drugs, and hospitalization at moderate fees. A disincentive fee of $1 per visit is paid to a Permanente doctor; the first $60 of maternity costs are deductible.

The U.S. Department of Health, Education and Welfare is encouraging the growth of HMOs to improve health care. Unfortunately, federal incursions into the private sector, however well-intentioned, are not always successful. At present, HEW's concepts of health prevention are sheer lip service, because HEW prefers to exclude meaningful health maintenance from its policy administration.[25] The pattern of HMO growth also poses a threat to the individual that ordinary insurance does not. HMOs tend to balance their budgets by controlling the amount of medical services they extend, which can reduce the degree of required services provided to patients who endanger the HMO budget.

Medicare

An important amendment to the Social Security Act, Medicare became law on July 30, 1965 and began to operate one year later. In its two main sections, known as parts A and B, Medicare provides hospitalization and medical-fee insurance for persons 65 years of age and older. Like many other government programs, Medicare is exceedingly complicated, and we cannot do justice to its complexity in our brief coverage here. But we can summarize its chief features and further advise applicants and others who wish to understand it in greater depth to make use of the published literature on Medicare.

Medicare: Part A. Part A of Medicare covers hospital or nursing-home services. All Social Security or railroad retirement beneficiaries who are 65 or older are automaticaly entitled to Part A coverage. Others must apply for Part A coverage at a local Social Security System Office.

Hospital benefits are derived from the Social Security contributions of both employees, which are matched dollar for dollar by their employers, and self-employed persons. The contribution rate for the hospital insurance program was 0.9% of the first $16,500 of earnings in 1976. After incurring hospital or Christian Science sanitorium expenses in any given benefit period of 60 days,

[25] D.F. Davies, Comment, *New England Journal of Medicine* (August 8, 1974), p. 312.

the insured is required to pay the first $124 of the cost. Part A medicare benefits also cover the cost of all skilled nursing facilities for the first 20 days of the benefit periods and all but $15.50 per day up to 80 additional days in the same period, if the condition treated in the facility originates in or is connected with hospital-ization that terminates within 14 days of admission to the facility.

Part A Medicare benefits also covers home health-care services for as many as 100 home visits during a benefit period. These visits must be in connection with hospital treatments furnished within 14 days of discharge from the hospital. Of course, all skilled nursing facility treatments and home health-care services must be ordered and approved by a physician.

Medicare: Part B. Part B of Medicare furnishes medical services insurance for a charge of $7.20 per month. It covers physicians' services, outpatient hospital services, home health services, and outpatient physical therapy, among other things. All medical services covered are subject to a deductible cost of $60 per year and to the exclusion of routine physical checkups, routine foot care and the treatment of flat feet, eye examinations and prescriptions, and routine immuni-zations. Limited coverage extends to dental work resulting from facial surgery and to ambulance service to the nearest available hospital, between hospitals, and from a hospital or a skilled nursing facility to the patient's home. Outpatient hospital benefits are also covered by Part B, excluding the annual $60 deduc-tible.

Medicaid   Blue Cross, Blue Shield, and other health insurance firms in the private sector have developed supplemental policies to cover some of the medical expenses not covered by Medicare. Medicaid, a supplement to Medicare, requires indi-vidual states to share the costs of a number of medical and hospital services with the federal government. Medicaid legislation, under Title XIX of the Social Security Act, permits the federal government to share 50% of allowable costs in states with higher per-capita average incomes (such as New York) and 83% of these costs in states with low average per-capita incomes (such as Alabama). Eligibility for Medicaid coverage is limited to persons who can meet rather low means and assets tests. Most of the middle class is therefore excluded from Med-icaid programs.

Dental Insurance   People tend to neglect their teeth—a fact that should be considered when dis-cussing dental care and insurance. Although preventive and tooth-saving thera-peutic dental facilities have expanded greatly since 1959, there is still a great de-mand for restorative dentistry, much of which could be avoided by proper oral hygiene.

Dental Hygiene. The United States does not hold the worst dental hygiene record among industrialized nations; that distinction belongs to the United Kingdom. The health of teeth and gums is directly related to the amount of

---

CHANGES IN DENTAL PRACTICES, 1959–1969

Total estimated increase in dental treatment for the U.S. civilian population:

Flouride treatments	454.5%
Orthodontic treatments	127.3%
Root-canal treatments	124.4%

Total estimated decrease in extractions (despite an increase of 13.9% in the civilian population): 6.7%

Source: *Journal of the American Dental Association* **LXXXI** (July 1970), p. 26.

---

candy and other sweets consumed and to societal and personal attitudes regarding cavity prevention versus extraction. In addition to eating 50% more sweets per capita than Americans, many Britishers, astonishingly enough, prefer to have their teeth extracted rather than treated.

It can be said with statistical certainty that persons who see their dentist regularly, refrain from eating sweets, brush properly and frequently, and use dental floss have a far better chance of avoiding decay and gum disease—the major causes of tooth loss—than those who eat sweets, brush infrequently, and do not use floss.

Cost. Dental-care statistics indicate that Americans spent an average of $23.55 for dental care in 1973,[26] but this figure does not reflect the "need" for dental care. We know that many people do not properly care for their teeth, and such a low figure simply reflects dental neglect.

The greatest drawback of dental insurance is its potentially high cost. If dental work were insured for all Americans, it is doubtful that enough dentists could be found to handle all the patients. And if this dental insurance were to include orthodontics (braces), peridontics (gum work), and such cosmetic work as capping, the total U.S. dental bill would be enormous. Manageable dental insurance can only be successful if insured individuals practice prevention. But the federal government cannot force people to brush their teeth. However, any government or business firm that provides dental insurance without taking steps to encourage prevention will surely encounter budget difficulties.

A dental program instituted in the Netherlands may offer a solution. Holland provides insurance that covers all dental costs under the stipulation that patients visit their dentists for routine checkups and cleanings with clockwork regularity. Anyone who misses a designated semiannual dental appointment loses

[26] *Journal of the American Dental Association* **LXXXIX** (December 1974), p. 1383.

coverage and must pay all personal dental bills thereafter. This approach encourages prevention and participation.

Drug Insurance

The U.S. Department of Commerce has estimated that the average per-capita drug expenditure in the United States in 1973 was about $41. However, the costs that comprise this average range from very low to very high. A person can be stricken with a condition that requires large amounts of costly drugs. One solution to the problem of potentially prohibitive medical costs is drug insurance. Individual health insurance policies may include drug insurance, but such coverage is seldom comprehensive.

Drug insurance poses some unique problems; the most particular is the question of definition. What precisely is a drug? A prescription drug? But what about prescribed aspirin? Prescribed foods? Prescribed vitamins? Prescribed air conditioning? Self-medication and patent medicines?

If drug insurance coverage were confined to prescription drugs, physicians could prescribe aspirin for their patients so that they could obtain coverage. Pharmacists would happily fill such prescriptions; after adding their dispensing fees, a bottle of aspirin costing 25¢ could wind up costing $2.25.

The Canadian province of Manitoba began an interesting experiment in drug insurance on January 1, 1975. Under its "Pharmacare"[27] program, all Manitoba residents are entitled to coverage of 80% of all drug costs in excess of $50 in any given year, and no family is required to pay more than $100 for drugs per year. The deductibility and coinsurance features of the "Pharmacare" plan are good disincentives to drug overuse, although they can be burdensome to the poor. However, the poor in Manitoba can rely on ample alternatives in the form of existing social assistance programs, which provide coverage for the deductible portion and coinsurance share of the plan. The "Pharmacare" plan only extends to prescription drugs; it excludes all patent medicines, vitamins, contraceptive compounds and devices, and surgical supplies. "Pharmacare" costs—as well as virtually all medical expenses in Manitoba—are funded by a charge built into provincial and federal income taxes. As we learned in Chapter 6, this form of funding is subject to criticism, but it is equitable in the sense that in a progressive tax system those who are most able to pay compensate for those who are least able to pay.

HEALTH-CARE DELIVERY: EFFICIENCY AND COMPETITION

The traditional concept of health insurance is fundamentally inefficient. Most individual and group policies do not cover routine health-care expenses such as

[27] The term "Pharmacare" is a copyrighted word used by the Manitoba Department of Health and Social Development courtesy of the Canadian Pharmaceutical Association.

annual checkups. The incentive to join any health insurance plan is greatest for the old and the ill—precisely the people that private, profit-making insurers wish to exclude from coverage to maintain high profits and low costs. Insurance arrangements provide few financial incentives for the insured individual or family to live in the best health. The health-care industry is still in the rudimentary stage in that the entire health-delivery system still revolves around the patient's initiative to seek help in instances of illness.[28] Insurance plans in the United States actually discriminate against preventive action, because they prefer to hold costs down by having the insured pay (or avoid) routine bills. But the high incidence of heart attacks, cancer, and strokes—which can often be successfully treated or prevented in their early stages—indicates the irresponsibility with which the majority of the population views good health.

It would be foolish and improper to try to compel people to live healthy lives. Society implicitly allows people to live as they please, as long as they do not harm anyone else in the process. Dwight Eisenhower once said that "government cannot legislate morality." Nor can government compel people to live in good health.

[28] Davies, *New England Journal of Medicine,* p. 312.

Controlling Medical Costs

Total national medical-care costs can be viewed as:

1 The total amount spent for all medical and hospital services rendered in the United States
2 The costs borne by the individual people who receive U.S. health-care services

We have already discussed why medical costs are so high in both cases. We will now discuss some suggestions that have been made to lower or to stabilize health-care costs.

Total national health costs can be reduced in two important ways: by technology, and by personnel and education.

Centralizing Technology. Medical technology has increased the efficiency of health-care services. At the same time, the fact that physicians prefer to practice medicine in their private offices results in an overinvestment in some types of equipment compared to the smaller investment necessary if fewer devices were used more often in centralized facilities. If medical practice no longer centers around the private practitioner and basically becomes a clinic and outpatient service, then medical technology will be more efficiently used at lower costs. However, the concept of private medical practice is an important part of the doctor–patient relationship. Some centralization of medical facilities has already been undertaken in group medical practice, which is becoming increasingly popular among doctors. Yet technological centralization is not a real option in the rural areas of America, where in many small towns having even one physician is considered quite advantageous.

Personnel and Education Policies. Medical education has long focused more on cure than on prevention; its goal has been to produce traditional health-care practitioners—predominately physicians and registered nurses. Many of our most common and most severe medical problems (heart disease and some kinds of cancer, for example) are preventable in that they result from or are aggravated by poor personal habits such as smoking. In some respects, the medical profession's concentration on producing highly trained physicians and specialists has been a misallocation of resources. Paramedical professionals could handle many routine medical problems and procedures in places where physicians are scarce. Many paramedical aides could be trained with the same resources that are currently used to educate only one physician.

Managing Cost Distribution

A financial crisis looms in the health-care industry: The potential costs of treating illness are greater than the ability of most individuals or families to pay for them. Several dozen national health insurance plans and amendments have been presented in Congress in the last five years. They vary in degree of inclusiveness, deductibility, cost-effectiveness, and coinsurance. In the interest of brevity, we will examine only the features of the two most extreme forms of coverage here: the American Medical Association plan and the Kennedy–Griffiths plan. This

THE COSTS OF AGGREGATE NATIONAL HEALTH INSURANCE PLANS

The following data is derived from a July 1974 report to Congress by the Secretary of the Department of Health, Education and Welfare. No allowance is made for additional health care services rendered as a result of greater accessibility under alternatives to the present system. Inflation will naturally raise totals, but not the relative composition of costs.

Aggregate Cost (in billions of dollars)

	$112.8	$103.0	$116.0
Out-of-pocket costs	18%	29%	8% / 3%
Private health insurance costs (including Medicare coverage paid by beneficiaries)	45%	34%	89%
Federal, state, and local government spending for health care	37%	37%	
	AMA Plan	Present	Kennedy–Griffiths Plan

Source: *Consumer Reports* (February 1975), p. 123.

analysis is drawn from a February 1975 examination of national health insurance plans in *Consumer Reports*. [29]

The AMA Plan. This plan, proposed by the American Medical Association, is based on the voluntary purchase of private health insurance. According to this plan, the federal government would pay some premium costs for the poor. Persons with higher incomes would be eligible for tax credit under the plan. Preventive medicine would not be covered by this plan. The AMA plan would require $50 deductible for each hospital stay and coinsurance of 20% for the first $500 in hospital expenses. Participating insurance companies would be required to meet federal standards in terms of basic coverage, but few cost-control or cost-effectiveness measures would be built into the plan. The AMA plan would be administered by the participating insurance companies and overseen, as always, by state insurance regulators. Consumers would not be directly involved in the administration of the AMA plan.

The Kennedy–Griffiths Plan. Named after its original sponsors, Senator Edward Kennedy of Massachusetts and Representative Martha Griffiths of Michigan, the K–G plan is an income-tax financed, mandatory participation plan that would pay virtually all personal health-care expenses except some prescription drugs, some psychiatric care, and adult dental care. The K–G plan would

[29] "National Health Insurance: Which Way To Go," *Consumer Reports* (February 1975), pp. 118–24.

contain zero deductibility and zero coinsurance. No insured person would have to pay any out-of-pocket costs. The Kennedy–Griffiths plan proposes budget controls over hospital and other health-care services, a review of major surgical procedures, and educational funding for health-care professionals. The K–G plan would not rely on health insurance companies to serve as intermediaries, and consumers would participate in regional but not local administration of the plan.

Would National Health Insurance Work?

The dozens of health insurance bills now being considered by Congress propose numerous methods of health insurance funding and operation. *Consumer Reports* strongly favors the Kennedy–Griffiths plan, but *CR*s preferences and reasoning are not beyond criticism. According to *Consumer Reports,* no health insurance plan would increase the total health-care bill in the United States; it would only shift medical-care costs from out-of-pocket expenses for health insurance, doctor bills, and perscription drugs to expenses funded from other sources such as income and payroll taxes. But this is not true. If medical care were indeed free—as it would be under the Kennedy–Griffiths plan—many poor people could receive medical care who are currently denied it. If costs escalated drastically, taxes would have to be raised accordingly.

Shifting the burden of health insurance costs from individuals and families to the federal government via compulsory tax-base financing would substantially improve the quality of available health care in the United States. The poor would be better-served; the wealthy, perhaps no less well-served. It is true that the Kennedy–Griffiths plan's zero deductibility and zero coinsurance would encourage some people to overuse medical services, and some physicians would profit considerably from increases in their practices, as would other providers of health-care services. Administrative control would revert to Washington. Hopefully, sufficient controls would be placed on health-care spending under any medical insurance plan to avoid the waste and mismanagement that are so often characteristic of large federally funded programs.

Any national health insurance plan will be an improvement compared to the current medical care system in America, which actually lags behind other nations in reducing infant mortality, in controlling heart disease, and in prolonging the useful years of life. The benefits are there; only the costs need to be controlled. Federal regulation has been a mixed blessing in the past, and there is no reason to believe that a national health insurance plan could not be turned against the consumers it has been designed to help. If and when a national health insurance plan is implemented, consumers may have to protect their interests from the very agencies created to safeguard them.

Professional Standards Review Organizations

A large part of the cost of medical care in the United States is due to the lack of competitive checks on the charges levied by hospitals and physicians. There is some cost review under federal Medicare and Medicaid programs, as there is in a more limited fashion under Blue Cross and Blue Shield plans. But a rigorous examination of medical charges may be obtained through Professional Standards Review Organizations (PSROs).   Physicians are often inclined to use quite expensive treatment methods when less expensive methods may work equally well.   We have already noted that the frequency of surgical procedures can vary, depending on geographical area.   Since 1970 the Foundation for Health Care Evaluation has been reviewing the work of physicians and hospitals in Minnesota.   At one surveyed hospital in St. Paul, the average patient's stay was reduced from nine to seven days and bed occupancy declined from 87% to 71%.   This is an example of how PSROs can reduce health-care costs and improve the use of medical resources.[30]

PSROs may force physicians and hospitals to practice "consensus" medicine.   In such cases, unusual therapy and preventive treatments are often considered "irregular" and are eliminated.   PSROs may therefore encourage doctors to practice medicine that is "safe" for review—not medicine that is best for the patient.   Thus PSROs offer economic efficiency at the possible expense of the freedom of physicians to practice what they personally believe to be best for their patients.   HEW plans include the expansion of PSRO activities from federally financed health services to all health-service delivery systems throughout the country.   A continuous review of the health-care industry's work would probably result in more and improved medical services, but such a review could also jeopardize the confidentiality of patient records and the privacy of the doctor–patient relationship.   Like so many other issues in consumer economics, important political and social issues underly the economic problems posed by the PSRO.

PATIENT RIGHTS

Hospital patients can become victims of their keepers.   In bed, drugged and perhaps attached to a number of bottles and tubes, the patient is utterly at the mercy of the hospital staff.   Too often, hospital personnel fail to treat patients as human beings, robbing them of their dignity, bringing them tasteless meals, waking them at absurd hours to take their temperatures or sometimes even to give them sleeping pills, and in some cases practically holding patients hostage until their bills are paid.   In any other context such activities would be considered illegal.   Remember that no hospital can keep a healthy person from walking out, whether the bill is paid or not.   A hospital that does this is guilty of false imprisonment and can be sued for appropriate damages.

Some hospitals do recognize the patient's need for respect and have appointed ombudsmen to support patients' rights and to attend to their personal

[30] Claude E. Welch, "Professional Standards Review Organizations—Problems and Prospects," *New England Journal of Medicine* CCLXXXIX (August 9, 1973), pp. 291–95; Claude E. Welch, "PSROs—Pros and Cons," *New England Journal of Medicine* CCXC (June 6, 1974), pp. 1319–22; David E. Willett, "PSROs Today: A Lawyer's Assessment," *New England Journal of Medicine* CCXCII (February 13, 1975), pp. 340–43; and *The Wall Street Journal* (June 24, 1974), pp. 1, 14.

needs.[31] Such patient representatives can make hospital bureaucracy manage-able and bearable for the patient. The American Hospital Association (AHA) has even issued a patient bill of rights, a variant of which was adopted as law in Minnesota and became effective in August 1973. The Minnesota bill is an eight-point statement that must be presented to each patient on admission to a hospi-tal in that state. It entitles the patient to privacy, to respect, to be told which physician is supervising the case, to obtain current information about diagnosis and treatment, and to expect reasonable continuity of treatment. However, the Minnesota law does not include two important additional AHA guarantees: the right to refuse treatment to the extent permitted by law and the right to an expla-nation of the hospital bill.[32]

Patient rights are becoming a fervent issue. Hospital administrators endorse them, but the real test will be whether hospital personnel reveal by their conduct that they believe in patient rights.

TOWARD IMPROVING MEDICAL CARE

The United States does not have the best health-care delivery system in the world. Many European countries have lower rates of infant mortality and longer life expectancies. Improving health care in the United States is a compli-

[31] *Hospitals* (September 16, 1974), pp. 63–67.
[32] *Hospitals* (April 1, 1974), pp. 177–80.

cated problem that involves economic, medical, and political judgment. Physicians, hospitals, and the drug industry must all improve the efficiency of their services. Of all health-related industries, drug manufacturing firms are the most in need of reform, because they earn unusually high profits and devote far too much effort to monopolizing the drug market. Nursing homes reflect the low status of the aged and their problems. All too frequently these homes are staffed by incompetent personnel who, intentionally or unintentionally, abuse the elderly patients in their care. Hospitals, physicians, and dentists are improving the efficiency of their work, but they are also charging higher and higher prices for their services. The problem of health-care efficiency ultimately touches on the areas of insurance and preventive medicine. Here, efficiency can be regulated by government intervention, but citizens must question whether this efficiency is worth the potentially high price of the loss of both the individual's right to control his or her life and the physician's right to practice medicine as he or she thinks best.[33]

SUMMARY

1 The health-care industry grosses $60 billion a year, consuming 7% of the gross national product.

2 Medical care is becoming increasingly expensive due to the misallocation of physicians, the increased cost of medical technology, and the lack of competition in the health-services market.

3 Prescription drugs are expensive because dispensing fees are high and because drug manufacturers do all they can to limit competition in the drug market. An excessive portion of drug company research and development is spent on lavish advertising campaigns directed at doctors and in making trivially different compounds out of existing medicines. Much of the important basic research on prescription drugs is conducted free of charge by government-funded laboratories.

4 Most patent medicines are weak or ineffective compounds. Advertising is often the most expensive ingredient of analgesics and other drug compounds.

5 The individual can reduce personal drug costs by comparison shopping, by buying generic names, by encouraging government to permit or require pharmacists to advertise drug prices, and by demanding compulsory substitution laws that allow lower-cost generic drugs to be substituted for brand-name drugs.

6 About 10% of the population is over 65 years of age. Illness strikes the old much more frequently than it strikes any other age group. Poverty and illness are closely related conditions among the elderly: Illness causes poverty, and poverty makes it impossible to obtain adequate health care.

7 Incompetent personnel, greedy management, and abused patients are three all too common ingredients in most nursing homes today. Low pay encour-

---

[33] Eliot Richardson, "Perspectives on the Health Revolution," *New England Journal of Medicine* CCXCI (August 8, 1974), pp. 283–87.

ages rapid staff turnover and discourages well qualified people from entering the field. Nonprofit homes tend to provide better care than nursing homes that are run for profit.

8 The average cost per hospital patient per day exceeds $100. Other health-care costs are increasing so rapidly that prolonged hospitalization can imperil an individual's or a family's budget. Health insurance can help remove the financial risk from illness and injury.

9 Total health-care coverage is prohibitively expensive. The insured can achieve certain cost reductions by paying some costs through deductibles and coinsurance.

10 Blue Cross and Blue Shield pay out higher ratios of premiums as claims than do private, profit-making health insurance companies. This is because Blue Cross and Blue Shield are primarily group plans that incur small sales fees and offer standardized policies.

11 Health Maintenance Organizations (HMOs) are prepayment, insurance-like systems that deliver actual medical services instead of financial compensation and reimbursement.

12 Medicare covers hospital and medical services for participating persons over the age of 65. It is funded by contributions from the earnings of employees and self-employed persons and by medical-service premiums. Medicare costs are controlled by a $124 deductible in every 60-day benefit period and coinsurance for some portions of coverage.

13 Dental and drug insurance pose problems of administrative control. Dental insurers must urge people to improve their own dental hygiene; drug insurers must discourage people from excessive drug use.

14 Professional Standards Review Organizations (PSROs) are being encouraged by the Department of Health, Education and Welfare to monitor the efficiency of hospital and physician performance.

15 The recognition of patient rights represents an important improvement in hospital administration.

Suggestions for Further Reading

Cohen, Jerome B., and Hanson, Arthur W. *Personal Finance,* 4th ed. Homewood, Ill.: Richard D. Irwin, 1972, Chapter 10.

"National Health Insurance: Which Way to Go," *Consumer Reports,* February 1975, pp. 118–24.

Curtin, Sharon R. *Nobody Ever Died of Old Age.* Boston: Little, Brown, 1972.

Kennedy, Edward M. *In Critical Condition.* New York: Simon and Schuster, 1972.

Townsend, Claire. *Old Age: The Last Segregation.* New York: Grossman, 1971.

U.S. Department of Health, Education and Welfare, Social Security Administration, Office of Research and Statistics. *The Size and Shape of the Medical-Care Dollar.* Washington, D.C.: 1971.

U.S. Department of Health, Education and Welfare, Task Force on Prescription Drugs. *Final Report.* Washington, D.C.: February 7, 1969.

The Consumer Workshop

1 How can individuals or families anticipate and control their personal health-care costs?
2 Assemble a list of consumer criteria for nursing homes.
3 Many diseases can be prevented by practicing good health habits daily.   In terms of your family, friends, and environment, what present health hazards could easily be eliminated?
4 The doctor–patient relationship is personal in the sense that the consumer/patient has at least some control over the quality and the quantity of medical service rendered.   As a patient, how would you feel about having to depend on:
   1 A clinic
   2 An outpatient department in a hospital
   3 Someone else to mediate between you and your doctor
  Do you feel such changes in medical practice as HMOs, PSROs, and national health insurance would be worthwhile?   Explain your answers in depth.
5 Do individual or family lifestyles affect the amount and type of health-care insurance that is carried?   Discuss each of the following in terms of alternate lifestyles:
   1 Disability coverage
   2 General (routine cost) medical expense coverage
   3 Major medical coverage

22 CORPORATIONS AND THEIR SOCIAL RESPONSIBILITY

22

If the consumer movement and allied social protests such as the environmental movement were to single out their primary object of attack, it would be the abuse of corporate power. Examples are conspicuous: Strip miners rape the landscape; many types of heavy industry pollute the air and water; armament manufacturers conjure up new weapons to dazzle military leaders; businesses at all levels produce and market products that are singly or in combination deceptive, dangerous, unreliable, or simply wasteful.

Neil H. Jacoby[1] has provided a succinct list of the wrongs for which businesses are frequently indicted. Let's consider this list in its entirety:

1 The United States is dominated by 200 giant corporations.
2 Corporate conglomerates control—rather than are controlled by—their markets.
3 Large corporations operate for the benefit of their managers, not their stockholders.
4 Corporations control the government agencies that are supposed to regulate them.
5 The "military–industrial complex" inflates armament expenditures for private power and profit.
6 The multinational corporation is the modern instrument of imperialism and neocolonialism.
7 Corporate businesses exploit workers, cheat consumers, and degrade the environment.
8 Businesses conspire to raise prices and to suppress product improvements.
9 Corporate lobbying and campaign contributions corrupt public officials.
10 Corporations are ruled by self-perpetuating managements that are responsible to no one.
11 The "corporate state" has made Americans corrupt, disorderly, militaristic, and unjust.
12 In the "corporate state," material values always take precedence over moral, intellectual, and cultural values.

In this chapter, we examine Jacoby's criticisms of the corporate structure in the United States. Our objective is *not* to prove any of these accusations, but

---

* James Burnham, *The Managerial Revolution* (New York: John Day, 1941), p. 74.
[1] Neil H. Jacoby, *Corporate Power and Social Responsibility* (New York: Macmillan, 1973), p. 4.

rather to discuss the social, economic, and political problems that underlie corporate misdeeds. And we conclude by offering some suggestions to help solve these problems.

THE BIRTH OF THE CORPORATION

A *corporation* is a legal entity that is created and allowed to operate by a state or federal government. Historically, the first corporations (The East India Company and The Hudson's Bay Company) were created by the English Parliament to exploit world trade. During the early nineteenth century, the U.S. Congress and state legislatures created corporations on an individual basis. Only in the final decades of the nineteenth century did American state governments make the corporation a formal, legal entity.

To create a corporation today, a lawyer must file the appropriate papers with a state official, usually the Secretary of State, pay an incorporation fee, designate

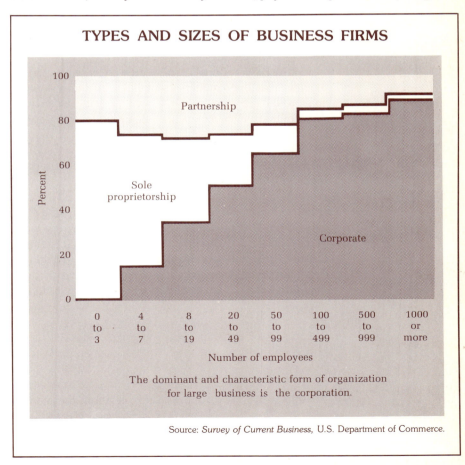

TYPES AND SIZES OF BUSINESS FIRMS

Partnership

Sole proprietorship

Corporate

Percent

Number of employees

The dominant and characteristic form of organization for large business is the corporation.

Source: *Survey of Current Business*, U.S. Department of Commerce.

corporate officers and directors, and establish a name for the corporation. A corporation is financed by investors who exchange their money for shares of corporate stock. The holders of common stock control the corporation. Any one person who holds 51% or more of the common stock controls the corporate enterprise. The corporate entity in effect legally becomes a "person" in that it pays taxes, appoints legal representatives, and can sue or be sued. Once established, a corporation acquires a personality of its own. It may be fair or unfair with its employees. It may or may not obey the law. It may attempt to corrupt government officials or it may become a scrupulously "good citizen."

CORPORATE MANAGEMENT

The personality of a corporation changes as the firm's management changes. In a business conglomerate however, certain structures and characteristics develop that tend to survive generations of managers. If the majority of the employees of a large corporation are members of one union, the corporation will initially oppose that union. However, this firm may acquire a corrupt, cozy relationship with the union (witness the relations of many coal mines and the prereform United Mine Workers).

Many corporations have become so large and have acquired so many stockholders that their management has become independent of the people who really *own* the company. No one person owns more than a 1–2% share of General Motors or American Telephone & Telegraph. Exxon and other Standard Oil spinoffs are obligated to no one; their administrative staffs are composed of independent executives. The law requires a corporate board of directors to be in charge of management and stockholders to participate in the election of the corporate directors. But the directors themselves control their own elections. Constructing a mailing list of all the stockholders in a giant corporation is a possible but a substantial undertaking. Paying postage to millions of stockholders, printing a statement as to why the directors may be corrupt, incompetent and analyzing stockholder ballots (called proxies) are not jobs for a loosely organized storefront protest group. To influence corporate management successfully requires a well-financed corporation or someone like Ralph Nader who can deftly use the press and Congress to the consumer's advantage.

CORPORATE PROFITS

What is profit? Is it good or bad? Is a firm that earns large profits an obvious exploiter, or is it simply efficient? Economists assign a simple definition to profit: *Profit* is the return received by a business enterprise in excess of its operating

"Keeping in mind Armstead vs. California, 1967, and Conway vs. Dade County, 1972, the Court finds, by a vote of 7 to 2, that the price of $1.79 for a pound of prunes is unfair and absurd."

costs; the calculation of profit results from *subtracting* total costs *from* total revenue. Total costs include operating costs, raw materials, wages, compensation for hired managers, and interest on money invested in the business. Total costs also include a normal return to stockholders, because they would invest their money elsewhere if the corporation did not produce a profit.

Yet this definition of profit would not be used by an accountant. In accounting, profits are calculated before payments are made to stockholders. To the consumer, profit is the gross markup over the wholesale cost—a viewpoint that is good enough for the grocery buyer but quite inadequate for the kind of social analysis we wish to make here.

Looking in from the outside, we assume that a firm efficiently purchases its raw materials and always pays the minimum price for them. We further assume that the firm's workers and managers are not overpaid: Each earns his or her worth in terms of average wages for service in the industry. The company is also assumed to acquire money from stockholders and bankers wisely, paying only what is necessary to induce investment. Finally, we impose a critical condition: If the business is profitable, many other firms will rush into the industry to compete for the profits; if the business fails, it will leave the industry, permitting the remaining firms to attract a greater number of customers and possibly to raise their prices. When these assumptions hold, a business or an industry earns no excess profits.

Unfortunately, these assumptions are too idealistic. Businesses are encouraged to dissipate tax liabilities by corporate tax laws that claim about 50% of an individual firm's profits. To avoid these taxes, companies award generous salaries to their chief executives. (Does the President of General Motors really need an annual salary of $800,000? Wouldn't $200,000 suffice?) Corporations may buy jet airplanes for top executives and furnish their corporate offices lavishly. Economists do not include such costs when determining excess corporate profits—but they are excesses.

The assumption that firms can quickly enter or leave a given industry is also idealistic. Few industries in North America are granted the condition of free entry and exit. The agriculture industry may be the only major exception. Farm profits depend on the weather, agricultural pests, and world food prices.

Profit and Firm Size

Most industries are not competitive. The finances and skill required to open another General Motors, Shell Oil, or IBM are prohibitive. If IBM and Xerox earn large profits, they do not attract many successful competitors. Small firms do enter and compete for smaller portions of their markets, but the corporate giants easily control a predominant portion of the industry. IBM and Xerox had average annual compounded growth rates of about 20% during the 1960s. The average for the entire industry was 10%, and for major railroads and some utilities the average was less than 5%. Was 20% excessive? Or were IBM and Xerox simply well run?

Large operations are the backbone of some industries. Passenger jets, automobiles, locomotives, and chemical compounds are all constructed on a large scale. Efficiency requires such firms to manufacture not only the finished products but also the subassemblies, so that these by-products can be sold if the main product produces valuable residual markets. The burden of environmental control falls heavily on the large corporation, but only large firms can afford to comply with such laws as the Environmental Protection Act.

Profit and Research

It has been said that large corporate profits contribute to much valuable research. Small firms, it is claimed, don't conduct expensive research to find answers to the fundamental questions that industrial progress demands. Supportive evidence is incomplete, but we can fairly point out that its very lack of clarity casts doubt on this claim. Western Electric may have invented the transistor, but what action has General Motors actually initiated (without government prodding) in terms of safety, engine efficiency, or *basic* automobile design since the 1930s? Why didn't Kodak invent the Polaroid process or the Xerox dry-copy process? Why can't American railroads with their billions of dollars of invested capital repair and maintain their tracks? Evidently, small firms are equally capable of making such research "contributions."

The Distribution Problem

Large corporations pose a difficult problem for consumer-oriented reformers. If a corporate conglomerate is widely owned and hires a great number of employees, laws designed to stifle its growth or to restrain its profits may hurt as many

people as they help. Let's consider AT&T, which has 15 million stockholders and hundreds of thousands of employees. If AT&T raises its prices, the company owners and employees benefit at the public's expense. If a strike compels AT&T to increase wages 20%, the public—not the company—may bear the financial burden. Such a cost/benefit calculation becomes a numbers game when it is applied to large corporations. We can easily say that a law should be passed if it helps 100 million people and hurts only a few hundred. But what if the law hurts 10 million low-income earners and produces only a slight benefit compared to this overall loss? This seldom-mentioned dilemma engenders many attacks on the large corporation.

CAN BUSINESS BE REGULATED?

Regulation of businesses becomes increasingly difficult the larger the operation. If a company has a single plant, sells in only one state or city, and hires its employees from a limited number of unions or a reasonably small geographic area, then the firm can be effectively regulated. Many electric utility companies fit this description.

However, large corporate conglomerates that spread across state and national boundaries are not as easily regulated. The largest firms in the United States are also those that are more geographically dispersed. The operations of

AT&T are so complex and its needs are so vast that it rivals the federal govern-ment as an unmanageable bureaucracy. This company is so readily identifiable with the national interest that the U.S. Congress and courts hesitate to compel it to obey some of the country's laws.

AT&T operates within the confines of the United States. However, corpora-tions such as Ford, General Motors, Exxon, Dow Chemical, and the Chase Man-hattan Bank are *multinational* in their operations. A giant car manufacturer can make its parts in any one of dozens of countries, assemble these parts in other countries, and sell the final products in a score of nations. The multinational corporation builds where governments are the most cooperative and the least restrictive, thereby avoiding tax laws and monetary controls with ease.

If an American multinational industrial concern that manufactures a product in the United States using foreign parts wishes to reduce its federal income tax, it can raise the prices it pays its foreign factories to export parts. This will reduce the multinational's profit based on U.S. operations and, accordingly, its tax bill. And the foreign factory will earn a greater profit on the parts it sells to the U.S. multinational. An IRS ruling states that foreign profits are not subject to federal taxes until they enter the United States, so these corporations maintain bank ac-counts in the Bahamas, Lichtenstein, and wherever else tax laws are lenient.

A multinational firm can literally shop around for the best terms in the world. If pollution controls are too restrictive in the United States, the multinational can manufacture in Mexico. If labor costs are too high in North America, the multi-national can assemble goods in Taiwan or Singapore. Thus the multinational acquires an existence independent of its host country.

Solutions Law enforcement has always had a localistic view of the world and its problems. Jurisdictions are local, regional, or national—not international. International law exists in theory but not in fact. No government today has the freedom of movement and the choice of legal systems of a large multinational. According to Richard Barnet and Ronald Müller:

> The global corporation has so many advantages vis-a-vis the nation-state, not the least its power within each nation-state to influence national policies, that effective regulation appears extremely difficult. Because its reach is so pervasive and its power so great, the corporation can be restrained only within the context of inter-national reform.[2]

To deal with the multinational, national governments must create an interna-tional agency capable of regulating these supranational corporations or, alterna-tively, equalize national laws so that these firms cannot shop around the globe for the lowest taxes and the most lenient treatment. This means that nations must come to terms with the problems of industrialization that they have avoided until now. Profit, taxes, pollution control, and rapid growth are often synon-

[2] Richard J. Barnet and Ronald E. Müller, "Global Reach" (*The New Yorker,* December 9, 1974), p. 148. This article was taken from Richard J. Barnet and Ronald E. Müller, *Global Reach: The Power of the Multinational Corporations* (New York: Simon and Schuster, 1975).

"When we want a
code of ethics,
Dalton, we'll ask for
a code of ethics."

ymous. If a nation establishes pollution controls today, corporate profits decline
and corporate tax revenues are reduced. If corporate tax laws are to be har-
monized, governments must establish and adhere to commonly accepted social
priorities. If they do not, then international corporate regulation will do little
more than increase job opportunities for specialized accountants whose task is to
abet the evasion of yet one more level of regulation.

Democratizing the Corporation

On both a national and a local scale, consumer representation on corporate
boards of directors has been one recommended method of democratizing corporations. This would probably do little harm, but it would probably do little
good either. Most boards of directors are rubber stamps: Few oppose management. Company presidents sit on one another's boards, and few board
members feel inclined to criticize one group when next week they themselves
may face the same criticism. The consumer representatives appointed to corporate boards thus far have been well-behaved moderates with fine credentials
and a cooperative mentality: Middle-class black ministers, upper-class socialites,
and successful yeasayers from university faculties can hardly be viewed as the
vanguard of a consumer revolution.

Strategies of Control

The traditional corporate control strategy of penalizing firms for their misdeeds
and rewarding them for acts of social conscience is difficult to apply to multinational corporations. For example, a worldwide firm can establish operations in
one country, collect its subsidy reward, and pollute other places where penalties

for its action do not exist. To some extent, this can be considered acceptable behavior. After all, pollution is less a problem in Nevada today than it is in New York. But pollutants drift and accumulate, and moving the pollution postpones the problem rather than corrects it.

The most helpful approach to the regulation of the multinational corporation may be to apply the traditional American style of antitrust legislation on an international scale. Then if a corporation consistently opposes public policy, it can be dispersed by the same government that created it, provided other governments cooperate. This is the basis of the Barnet–Müller solution.

Legislation to regulate multinationals need not encumber society with more laws. Many regulatory laws are contradictory, and others seem to have no real social purpose. To regain national control of international businesses each country must discard useless laws that actually shield multinationals from effective public control.

Societal control of the multinational—for that matter, of business in general—requires that governments have the clarity of thought to know what they want and to define their social purposes and the maturity to cooperate with one another. Ultimately, governments do speak for the societies that elect or tolerate them. They should exercise their moral authority and political power to ensure that powerful corporations do not defy the interest of people at large.

SUMMARY

1 The corporation is a legal entity that is treated as a ''person'' in law.
2 Corporate management is often independent of and beyond the control of a corporation's stockholders.

3 Accountants define profit as the residual earnings of a business after all operating expenses have been met.

4 Most industries are not particularly competitive. They are dominated by giant corporations that earn large economic profits and restrict firms that might compete away profits from entering the market.

5 The difficulties of regulating big business are compounded by the problem of distribution: A large corporation employs so many people that its earnings cannot be reduced without adversely affecting the livelihood of its employees.

6 Corporate regulation is also complicated by the business conglomerate that operates in many different jurisdictions, each of which has its own laws. A large firm is free to choose the jurisdiction in which the laws are most tolerant of its operations.

7 The multinational corporation is difficult to regulate, because it can conduct each phase of its operations in the country that has the least restrictive laws pertaining to the firm's activities. The multinational practically exists as an independent state.

8 To control the multinational corporation, governments must create an international agency to regulate these global firms or, alternatively, equalize national laws to eliminate tax breaks and havens of special treatment.

Suggestions for Further Reading

Barnet, Richard J., and Müller, Ronald E. *Global Reach: The Power of Multinational Corporations.* New York: Simon and Schuster, 1975.

Berle, Adolf A., and Means, Gardiner C. *The Modern Corporation and Private Property,* rev. ed. New York: Harcourt Brace Jovanovich, Inc., 1968.

Burnham, James. *The Managerial Revolution.* New York: John Day, 1941.

Jacoby, Neil H. *Corporate Power and Social Responsibility.* New York: Macmillan, 1973.

The Consumer Workshop

1 In what ways do large corporations and multinationals influence and direct your life? What buying, working, and living alternatives are created or restricted by giant enterprise?

2 Large corporations offer both societal advantages and disadvantages. Choose a large firm (say, Boeing or Xerox), obatin its annual report from your library, and analyze the social advantages and disadvantages of its operations.

3 Because multinational corporations operate on a worldwide basis, they have an advantage that governments do not: The multinational has a single set of goals. What steps would you recommend that governments take to achieve the regulation of multinational corporations?

4 Do you think that the national interests of the United States are furthered or hindered by multinational corporations? Explain your answer.

SENATE
CHAMBER

23

THE ISSUE OF
CONSUMER SOVEREIGNTY

23

> "It is a revealing fact that few planners are content to say that central planning is desirable. Most of them affirm that we can no longer choose but are compelled by circumstances beyond our control to substitute planning for competition."

F. A. HAYEK
The Road to Serfdom*

What goods and services do consumers want and need? How can they obtain them? What prices should they pay for them? How should products be produced? These are central questions of paramount importance to consumers that must be answered to achieve an understanding of any economy. In this chapter, we examine various proposed solutions to these problems. We also discuss market issues in greater depth, incorporating the concept of the "free" market in the capitalist system, and consider the usefulness of limitations on this so-called "free" market as well as some socialist alternatives. Our findings will depend on political values that we will state clearly here. Economics does not in itself dictate which market—capitalist or socialist—is best for all people at all times.

THE NATURE OF THE MARKET

The concept of a "market" is a timeless abstraction. A market can be something as concrete as the New York Stock Exchange or the corner grocery store, or it can be as vague as, say, the "market" for the undiscovered paintings of Leonardo da Vinci. The first type of market represents an ongoing trading process composed of many buyers and sellers, established prices, substantial volumes of goods or services, and known participants. The second example exhibits none of these characteristics, but it is also a market; a great amount of trading and negotiating would take place—in fact, often does take place—if a da Vinci is newly discovered or is even rumored to exist.

The Definition of a Market

The concept of a market is a broad one that must be comprehensively defined if it is to be understood. A *market* is an opportunity for exchange that may be specified by time, space, the goods or services to be traded, the participants, or even the commodities used to pay for these goods or services. There are markets for next year's wheat, for used locomotives, for books not yet printed,

* F. A. Hayek, *The Road to Serfdom* (Chicago: University of Chicago Press, 1944), p. 43.

for the right to be in the market (a seat on the stock exchange), even for money itself.   Our concept of a market encompasses all of these examples.

The Market Is Voluntary

It is important to keep in mind that the market we have defined here represents an opportunity for—not a compulsion to—exchange.   In our terms, the market is voluntary.   You may or may not exchange your potatoes for shoes—as you prefer.   If the price is right, you may want to sell your potatoes.   If it isn't, you'll probably haul your potatoes back home again.   The choice is yours.   *Exchanges* can also occur without a market in this sense.   If a large corporation orders the managers of two of its factories to trade inventory surpluses (say an overstock of cans in one factory for an overstock of screws in another), the market has actually been by-passed: Because they were told what to do, these managers had no choice in the matter.   And if a state bureaucracy reallocates all goods and services produced according to a master plan, no market process is involved because no element of choice is permitted.

The concept of choice rests on some important assumptions.   That a market exists or is allowed to exist presupposes that people know what they want, can evaluate the products or services that they are offered, and are good regulators of their own economic interests.   When these presumptions do not hold, market problems—and often consumer problems—arise that must be corrected.   Let's consider the defects in market processes and their implications for the concept of the market as we have defined it here.

Nonmarket Systems

It is possible for exchange to occur without the medium of a market.   Prehistoric societies often allocated work and rewards by traditional means that excluded a market.   The men hunted, and the women sewed and cooked; the children were taught by observation and ritual to follow their parents' exemplary roles.   In these societies, choice played no part in the production and consumption processes, and markets as they exist today were virtually unknown.   Perhaps due to their extremely limited needs and skills, freedom of choice as we know it was irrelevant to these people.   Societies struggling on the edge of existence are not faced with the abundant alternatives available to modern nations.   Within extended families, the accumulation of wealth in prehistoric society may have been either impossible or considered antisocial.   If a local grove of fruit trees produced an abundant crop, all members of the community were permitted to pick the fruit; specialists were not needed to perform tasks that the society considered unrelated to its survival.

THE MARKET SYSTEM IS NOT PERFECT

Critics frequently claim that market systems misallocate goods and services and misuse resources.   In most socialist literature, the distribution of the capitalist market system is criticized for placing too much income and wealth in the hands of too few. People who make no direct contribution to production but who merely *own* valuable land or mineral deposits (perhaps through inheritance) receive what critics of the capitalist system consider to be an excessively large share of the total national output. The objection to this inequity is valid, but it can be offset in any market system by taxing unearned rents or incomes.

Critics also feel that because the capitalist market system misallocates and overproduces nonessential goods and services, it should be replaced by a planned and regulated economic system that limits production to essential commodities. We will discuss this attitude in greater detail later in this chapter, but for the present we can say that this concept seems not only dull but unworkable. How can overseeing economic planners allocate aspirin if they can't predict who will have a headache? Or how can they distribute shoes proportionately when some people wear them out faster than others? Appointed planners could distribute any product in any amount, correctly or incorrectly, but a person with, say, a shoe surplus would soon find another person with, say, a shirt surplus and a market would reemerge. Adam Smith, the great social theorist of the late eighteenth century, noted that people have a natural tendency to barter and exchange.[1] It is precisely this individual tendency to adjust wealth and income to

[1] Adam Smith, *An Inquiry into the Nature and Causes of the Wealth of Nations* (New York: Random House, 1937), Bk. 1, Ch. 2, p. 13.

''Comrades, a laboratory in Odessa has come up with a fine, mild, fragrant soap, better than any ever devised by man. As you know, we are not allowed to identify this product by name for you, but if you happen to buy it, you will love it.''

ability and personal need that confronts the would-be economic planners of today who wish to eliminate the imperfections of the market by eliminating the market itself.

The Mechanics of the Market   Let's look briefly at the ways in which the market determines who is rewarded, how much of a product is to be produced, and what the relative prices of goods and services will be. Examining these points calls for some social theory, but the results of this discussion will be important in our later investigation of the broader concern of consumer sovereignty.

Who Is Rewarded?   In a market system, the distribution of goods and services depends not only on peoples' needs but also on their ability to pay. Because the ability to pay does not always coincide with personal need or usefulness of work performed, critics of the capitalist market system propose various reforms that range from subsidizing necessary commodities (such as milk) and grants to needy persons to creating new systems of reward, one example of which is Marx's "from each according to his abilities, to each according to his needs."

What Is Produced?   In a market system, how much of a product is to be produced is determined by monitoring the demand for a commodity and comparing it to the relative costs of producing various types of that commodity. If people are willing to pay a high price for a product that can be cheaply produced, ever greater amounts of the commodity will be manufactured until people are no longer willing to pay such a high price for it and/or until it costs too much to produce (perhaps because a crucial resource has practically been exhausted and has therefore become prohibitively expensive). In a large economy, millions of producers and marketers of goods and services constantly seek opportunities for profit and consumers try to purchase the most economical products. More efficient producers tend to charge lower prices to attract more business.

Prices.   A free market relies on price changes to reveal shifts in demand and supply, so that buyers and sellers can make sound economic decisions. Millions of commodities are assigned individual prices that indicate their relative values. Each production factor also has a specific price that enables producers to estimate its ability to contribute to profits.

In a nonmarket system, prices are unnecessary. If the state ultimately decides what products and services each person is to receive and produce, there is no need for prices. In large socialist economies such as the Soviet Union, economic overseers actually operate without "prices" as we know them, although Soviet planners go to great lengths to construct indicators of supply and demand that are prices in *every* aspect except name. Paradoxically, most socialist economies do price *consumer* goods. Why? Perhaps because economic planners realize that although they can predict total steel and coal production accurately, for example, they cannot anticipate the style of clothes that people will prefer or whether they will want to spend their extra income on the ballet, expensive cuts of meat, or trips to the zoo. So even socialist states price consumer goods to permit individuals to make choices after their basic needs have been met.

Market Problems

Thus far we have compared market and nonmarket alternatives in ideal forms to avoid two important problems:

1 How does the market react if producers supply the wrong goods and services?
2 What level of product quality is economically preferable?

A market economy provides one rather simple answer to both these questions: Overproduced or inadequate goods do not sell. They pile up in warehouses, and firms must either reduce their prices or their production runs to deplete this stock. (A firm that earns a less than anticipated profit on a product will probably commit fewer resources to that product and produce it in lesser quantities in the future.)

It is even harder to estimate the market in a nonmarket economy. Once economic planners determine how many automobiles are to be manufactured, for example, they can easily compute the amount of steel, headlights, and other materials and equipment required to produce them. But how can these overseers determine, say, whether people will prefer a new car to a new apartment or a smaller apartment to more frequent steak dinners? Sometimes goods are produced that can be sold at any retail price. The classic example of this is the Soviet glass factory that doubles its output quota of window glass by making the glass half the standard thickness. Here the problem of *quality* arises. Given a choice, consumers in a free market buy competing goods at the level of quality that they need and can afford. A nonmarket economy does not have the market economy's potential for self-correction. Errors must be administered away—a less efficient process than consumers' refusal to buy what they don't like or want.

MIXED ECONOMIC SYSTEMS

It would be naive to suggest that all production–consumption systems can be classified neatly as either market or nonmarket economies. Throughout history, most civilizations have functioned with a mix of market and nonmarket economies. We can find evidence of price regulation in ancient Babylon, of powerful manufacturer activist groups and monopolies in Augustinian Rome, and of specific industrial regulation in Elizabethan England. Highly unregulated markets did exist briefly in early Victorian Britain and in the United States before the Civil War. But the nonregulation of business yielded to the social problems it created and failed to solve. The legacy of market regulation—what today we can call the *mixed economy*—is the result of this failure.

It is also difficult to cite historic examples of pure nonmarket economies. During the latter part of the Bolshevik Revolution in Russia (1919–1921), Lenin

"'. . . and the government hopes to lower the cost so that every family can afford a pyramid'."

attempted to abolish the market system totally—an effort that failed dismally. Similarly, Fidel Castro sought to eliminate the monetary system in Cuba during the early part of his revolution—and he too failed. It is simply not possible for newborn, struggling governments to operate nonmonetary economies without the aid of computer and statistical services vaster than any yet constructed in even the most advanced and monetized economies.

A market system allocates work and rewards. For reasons to be explored later in our discussion of public goods, markets also have a great capacity for error. It is unrealistic to believe that consumers always act in their own best interests and can successfully correct economic inequalities. In a small, isolated nation that is entirely self-sufficient in raw materials, that consumes all its own production, and that has a truly equal distribution of income and wealth, the pure market system might be applicable. But in modern nations, wealth is highly concentrated, there are vast inequalities in economic power, and strong protest and special-interest groups often manipulate the economy for their own benefit. Do these economic imperfections mean that the market system is unworkable and the theory of the market is obsolete in the modern economy?

Galbraith's Analysis

In 1952, John Kenneth Galbraith tackled this question in *American Capitalism*. There Galbraith asserts that the market system does exist, does work, and does perform more or less efficiently in the modern economy. But he states that the main determinants of supply and demand are no longer individual consumers and workers; they have become the giant corporations, large labor unions, and overgrown government agencies that wield massive power in advanced economies and that balance one another's influence through what Galbraith calls "countervailing power."

As Galbraith sees it, U.S. Steel's preference for high steel prices is countered by General Motors' preference for low steel prices. American Telephone & Telegraph prefers to pay its lineworkers low wages; members of the International Brotherhood of Electrical Workers prefer to earn high wages. IBM wants to grow larger; the U.S. Department of Justice, in the interest of smaller competitors, wants it to reduce its current size. The voice of the individual consumer is rarely heard; powerful special-interest groups speak for the individual. If prices are not established on the basis of pure supply and demand, at least they are reduced to affordable levels as large organizations compete with one another.

We should not conclude, however, that price administration by "countervailing power" produces the same prices that would result from pure competition. Unions tend to support company demands when they are mutually beneficial. For example, the United Auto Workers and General Motors agree that higher tariffs should be imposed on imported cars to retain the better part of the American market for themselves. Maritime unions and large shipping conglomerates both prefer to keep shipping charges high: The more money for the company, the more money for the union.

State and Private Enterprise

The ratio of free enterprise to regulated or state-controlled enterprise varies from country to country and from industry to industry. Some economies are highly state-controlled. In both the Soviet Union and China, for example, all enterprises are state-owned except extremely small businesses. It is estimated that state-owned factories are responsible for 90% of the nonagricultural production in these two countries. Yugoslavia and Poland have a greater number of small enterprises: Only 70% of all nonagricultural output is state-controlled in these countries. Yugoslav factory managers are given some latitude in pricing their products and in determining their markets. Workers participate in management, making this country's mixed economy particularly interesting and almost unique in the world. In most partially socialized western economies, the state nationalizes basic or essential industries. In the United Kingdom, labor governments now regulate both basic *and* essential industries, so that the state can control up to 30% of all product output. In Britain, state enterprise includes the main airline, coal production, virtually all trains, some oil production, most iron and steel production, and a variety of manufacturers. In Sweden, long regarded as a partially socialized capitalist economy, government manages only 10% of total product output.[2]

---

[2] See John E. Elliott, *Comparative Economic Systems* (Englewood Cliffs, N.J.: Prentice-Hall, 1973), Chapter 17; William N. Loucks and William G. Whitney, *Comparative Economic Systems*, 9th ed. (New York: Harper & Row, 1973), Chapters 13, 24; Egon Neuberger and William J. Duffy, *Comparative Economic Systems: A Decision-Making Approach* (Boston: Allyn & Bacon, 1976), Chapters 12, 13, 15, 17.

Government and Business in the United States

In the United States it is often difficult to distinguish government from business. Government is reluctant to compete with the private economic sector, although a federal monopoly is maintained on the postal service, atomic weapons manufacture, and other goods and services that the government deems inappropriate for the private sector to supply. The federal government has also become the primary creditor of the railroad system and juggles laws to enable airlines such as Pan Am to survive. Government is so inextricably involved with business and so responsible for its continued health that we may well ask whether the American economy is not already a weak form of socialism in that the state is not the owner but the *creditor* of most major U.S. business enterprises.

Consumers in Mixed Systems

Advanced economies tend to formulate different kinds of mixed market solutions. The interests of powerful activist groups and corporate conglomerates often conflict with government policies. Individual citizens and consumers are practically powerless, although their interests and needs can be better served by concentrated representation. Naturally, the components of what has come to be called the "consumer movement" are the consumer-interest groups.

Some nations that are more socialized than the United States have political systems that do not tolerate or acknowledge legitimate special-interest groups that oppose government or state enterprise. Communist nations practice variants of Marxist ideology and recognize no conflict of interest between business enterprise and government. Open opposition to the goals or methods of government or state enterprise is discouraged, although a low level of complaint and correction can be channeled through government or party.

RESOLVING MARKET PROBLEMS

The processes of producing and allocating goods are imperfect in both market and nonmarket systems. In market systems, accurate product information may not be transmitted to the buyers, or the buyers may make wrong decisions even when their product information *is* adequate. In nonmarket systems, economic planners may incorrectly anticipate consumer choice or factory managers may diminish the quality of their work to meet established quotas, as in the case of the Soviet glass factory mentioned earlier. Traditionally, consumer studies have focused on the buyer's post-sale recognition that he or she has been the victim of a deceptive business transaction. More recently, consumer researchers have recognized that the average retail buyer may be a poor judge of the long-run costs of purchasing hazardous products or complex goods that could produce unknown side effects. We now turn to an examination of the post-sale corrective devices that are available to consumers in different market and nonmarket systems.

Due Process

The phrase "due process of law" has been handed down traditionally from medieval English history. These words are the citizen's defense against unjust seizure of property or liberty by the state. Due process allows people to tell their side of any controversial issue that involves goods, rights, or even life. This is an essential premise of English law and of all legal systems that descend from it, including U.S. law. Due process was considered to be such an important and basic right that it was incorporated in the Bill of Rights of the U.S. Constitution as part of the Fifth Amendment in 1791: "No person shall . . . be deprived of life, liberty, or property, without due process of law."

Following the Civil War, Congress believed that it was essential to extend and clarify the protection of due process offered in the Fifth Amendment. In 1868, the Fourteenth Amendment was proclaimed:

> . . . No State shall make or enforce any law which shall abridge the privileges or immunities of citizens of the United States; nor shall any State deprive any person of life, liberty, or property, without due process of law; nor deny to any person within its jurisdiction the equal protection of the laws.

The concept of due process as extended by the right to "equal protection of the laws" remains the primary defense of civil liberties in the United States today. The Fourteenth Amendment extends the right to a reputable legal defense to impoverished defendants in criminal cases. It also upholds the rights of citizens to present legal objections to being drafted; in doing so, it defeated attempts by General Lewis Hershey to use the draft system to force young men to fight in Viet Nam against their will without granting them legal recourse. The Fourteenth Amendment even assures the most obviously guilty perpetrators of consumer fraud, whether people or corporations, of the right to present a full defense before a court may fine or jail them.

English law may have been the basis for many legal systems, but the right to a full hearing is guaranteed in no country as firmly as it is in the United States. This right is extended at all levels of American government: No city can rezone without holding a zoning hearing that involves all concerned parties; no state can plan a highway or acquire land without many hearings and compensation reviews; no federal administrative agency, such as the Federal Trade Commission, can act unless some recourse for protest is extended to those affected before or after the action. In theory, every government action can be appealed to a court. A firm that objects to the denial of a license by a federal agency can appeal to a federal court to have its views heard. If the court upholds the federal agency, several other avenues of appeal may be available to the firm. Due process guarantees proper treatment for all defendants, yet due to the number of hearings or trials that may be required, it is also a cause of much delay in law reform. Although it tends to favor the person or the firm that can afford the most litigation, due process is the precious and essential foundation of personal liberty in the United States.

Limiting the Right of Contract

The *right of contract*—the right of the parties who enter into an agreement to establish any terms they wish—is carefully protected in the United States, where it is maintained via the standards of due process and equal protection. But the concept of due process is not as firmly rooted in all countries as it is in America. Canada has no formal constitution, although the document known as the *British North America Act* does establish the rights of the Canadian government. Due process as it exists in Canada arises from English common law and from various acts of Parliament. Canada can and does limit the right of contract. A person who is legally charged with an offense has fewer rights and fewer defenses in Canada than in the United States.

In theory, the Canadian government is more powerful than the U.S. government. The Canadian government can seize property, limit the right of contract, and enforce criminal laws much more freely than American government on any level. When leases are unfair to tenants, Canadian provincial governments can and do restrict the landlords' actions toward their tenants. In Manitoba, for example, a standard lease is extended that establishes the terms of residential occupancy throughout the province. Such a standard contract could not be lawfully enforced or even created by any U.S. state government. If it is believed that corporate acts are contrary to the public interest, the Canadian federal government can and does rearrange the affairs of the business in question.

It should be pointed out again that we are speaking in theoretical, not practical terms. The point to be made here is that in the United States there is a powerful right to construct any type of contract that does not in itself specify illegal actions; in Canada, this right is circumscribed by the absence of a vigorous concept of due process and of a standard of equal protection. In fact, the U.S. government prosecutes business for all forms of transgressions much more vigorously than the Canadian government. But American business law enters corporate board rooms through the "back door" of specialized regulation, not through the open "front door" of constitutional authority.

Public Advocacy   It is an established principle of American and English law that there are two primary ways to gain compensation for a wrong:

1 The state may criminally prosecute any person who violates the law
2 An individual may bring a civil suit against another person or a legal entity

In the first case, the state pays the trial costs; in the second case, the injured party must finance the suit. Many of the large corporations that are prosecuted can easily afford to defend themselves in court. Suing General Motors or the federal government can be a prohibitively expensive process that may be appealed for many years.

Criminal Law.   It is even more difficult for the injured consumer to obtain compensation. Criminal law requires proof beyond a reasonable doubt that the defendant has broken a specific law. A firm cannot be convicted for committing an immoral or an improper act; it must violate a specific law. In addition, the consumer must usually prove that the firm *intended* to break the law when it acted. Clearly, the rigorous standards of criminal law make it difficult to prosecute firms in most cases of consumer abuse. And criminal law provides no financial reward to the injured consumer—only punishment in terms of a fine or a jail sentence for the guilty firm.

Civil Law. On the other hand, civil law requires that the evidence presented in court only *favor* the plaintiff. To win financial compensation in civil court, a consumer is required to show only that the firm that caused the injury acted more incorrectly than correctly. This means that civil suits are easier to win because they are easier to prove. But consumers must finance their own civil suits, hire their own lawyers, spend time in court, and perhaps wait years before they receive any compensation.

The Ombudsman. Sweden has instituted an important and increasingly popular innovation to help the consumer. For the purposes of consumer compensation, it constitutes a third branch of law. An officer of the state, known as an *ombudsman,* is empowered to bring a court suit against the government and to encourage the state to intervene on behalf of the injured party. Ombudsmen are empowered to act on behalf of anyone in all kinds of matters; they are superagents with greater powers than those granted most government officials. However, the ombudsman is not a law enforcement official or a judge, but rather a type of government official who is authorized to help anyone afflicted with a government or a consumer problem.

The Canadian province of British Columbia extended the ombudsman concept in 1974. Under the British Columbia Trade Practices Act, this province ini-

"Say, that's not the ombudsman, is it?"

tiated a civil suit on behalf of a consumer who had been deceptively sold a defective car that had no reverse gear. British Columbia took the automobile dealer to court, paid the trial costs, and obtained $571 in compensation for the consumer. Although this represents a small case in a low-level court, it establishes a valuable and exciting precedent for consumer law.

Ombudsmen can be important defenders of consumer rights in the marketplace, and these officials rarely have the continual contact with a particular industry that can and has led to corruption in other government offices. The ombudsman can intervene quickly, unencumbered by a mass of internally generated rules and regulations. Operating as an individual federal or state "agency," an ombudsman can be a lightweight but a more effective defender of the consumer than such blundering giants as the U.S. Department of Agriculture. It is interesting to note that the ombudsman's power to intervene in all government processes was suggested in Ralph Nader's early proposals for a cabinet-level federal consumer agency.

PUBLIC GOODS: A MANDATE FOR GOVERNMENT CONTROL

Public goods belong to no one person and are used by many people. Highways, schools, public recreation facilities, and many government installations are all examples of public goods. If a person has an opportunity to own a small share in a particular good or service that he or she intends to use infrequently and cannot be sure that the other investors in the good or service will contribute their share of the costs, then he or she will be inclined to avoid making the investment or contribution to the public good. Nevertheless, public goods can represent an efficient way to use resources and a highly rational investment for each participant if each investor can be sure that the others involved in the project will contribute their own shares.

Consider an example of a public good. Owning a private art museum is beyond the personal resources of 99.9% of the population. Making voluntary contributions to establish an art museum can be risky, because no investor can be sure that the others will contribute. However, patrons readily pay small individual sums to spend an afternoon looking at treasures in an art museum.

Public Versus Private Transit

Public transit is one of the most obvious examples of a public good. The average family relies on—indeed is forced to rely on—the automobile for most personal travel, because a satisfactory public mass-transit system does not exist in most areas of the United States. People would save money, trouble, and exasperation if they could avoid the burdens of owning and operating a car. The automobile imposes huge costs on both the economy and the environment: the road system must be enlarged, more police officers must be hired, and the quality of our air deteriorates. These problems could be greatly reduced if a public transit system were available to everyone.

Public Versus Private Benefits

But note that although individual citizens save in terms of automobile-ownership expenses, the public also saves the costs of additional federal and state building programs to produce roads and cities to accommodate private cars. Public savings will be greater than private savings if automobiles are removed from the road in large numbers. Thus a public good may be financed by government *when it would never be financed by private persons who do not share directly or immediately in the savings that accrue to the public sector.* The political implication of this fact is that government should produce public goods and finance their production either by taxation or by charging special fees. Only government can do this, because the government must assume the burden of paying for the alternatives to public goods: air pollution, overgrown road and highway systems, and swollen police forces.

How can consumers retain their sovereignty as they allocate their incomes to *consentient* private goods ("Yes, I want the Oldsmobile; I'll pay this price for it") and *nonconsentient* public goods ("Because I was forced to pay for the beach through my taxes, I'll use it")? With cash in hand, we can express our preferences for various private goods. A decision to buy is a vote in favor of a particular item. On the other hand, public goods do not incorporate the aspect of personal decision; all consumers pay for public goods, whether they use them or not. Accordingly, public goods must be allocated and financed by *political* votes. A vote to issue bonds or to build a school is a political decision about a public good. So consumer sovereignty can be preserved if appropriate referendums are held to establish the acceptability of public goods and public finance.

Pricing Public Goods

A special category of public good is a commodity that is abundant for one or a few people or users but limited for consumers or users as a whole. Let's consider air and water: Business once treated these two valuable natural resources as free goods, using them as avenues of cheap waste disposal by pouring smoke into the air and filth into the water. Many nations "overfish" the oceans, drastically affecting their ecology. Oil-tanker operators fail to take maximum spillage precautions because any one firm can accrue only high expenses and questionable benefits for such efforts. But the loss of adequate, healthful water or air sources is a high cost for us all to bear.

If a valuable resource is underpriced, it will be overused. There are several ways of coping with this problem. The federal government can license the use of the resource, regulate it, ban it, or perhaps put a price on it. Unfortunately, it is impossible to control access to breathable air and prohibitively difficult and costly to "fence in" every body of water. Consumers cannot be sovereign over such vast natural resources, nor can they rely on manufacturers to allocate these resources effectively. Only if natural resources are regulated or sold as quasi-public goods can consumers retain sovereignty over them.

ECONOMIC CHOICE

Societies can choose one of a number of economic destinies. Should a developing economy strive to achieve a higher level of consumption and a lower level of capital investment? Britain appears to have done this after World War II, although now she is paying the price for choosing consumption over investment in terms of her current loss of productivity. Or should a society elect to increase investment and decrease consumption? Stalin charted this course for the Soviet Union in his Five-Year Plans. Should people work in urban areas, or should they be employed in diversified industries throughout the country? The Peoples' Republic of China favors the second alternative. And most importantly, should individual citizens be permitted to influence such matters in any way? Choice is a valuable good in itself—one for which people are often willing to pay quite a lot.

Despite their inefficient allocation of public goods, market systems do provide choices. Centrally administered economies cannot cope with the multitude of choices consumers must make, so they misallocate at least some of their production and manufacture goods that people don't want to buy.

Choosing between market and nonmarket economies then becomes a political question of what offers the greater sovereignty to the citizen or consumer. We could say that people select their goods poorly, tend not to invest properly, or misdirect their spending. Or we could say that the individual is the best judge of his or her own wants and needs.

It is easy to criticize almost any market for producing the wrong commodities. Grocery stores stock their shelves with junk food because people eagerly buy it. Billions of dollars are spent annually due to a contrived demand for cosmetics. Yet choice is a valuable part of our economic freedom. We could nationalize all goods and all production and vote daily to determine who gets what and who does what. That would be one democratic method of allocating effort and reward in a nonmarket economy. But buying goods and earning money accomplish the same result, except that those who have more to spend have more market power than those who have less to spend.

SUMMARY

1 A market is an opportunity for exchange. This concept rests on the assumptions that market participants have the choice of whether or not to exchange and that they are capable of evaluating the goods that are offered and their own personal needs.

2 Alternative nonmarket systems can be found in traditional societies that allocate work and reward by custom and in modern societies that presume consumers, if given a choice, cannot or may not make decisions that are in their own best interests.

3 Historically, societies have been a mixture of state-controlled and private enterprise. Most modern, advanced economies today are also mixed systems.

4 In his theory of "countervailing power," John Kenneth Galbraith holds that large firms and unions in the market administer prices on levels similar to the ones that would prevail if supply and demand forces were exerted by small producers and consumers. Government and the special-interest groups that comprise the consumer movement exert such countervailing power.

5 The Fifth Amendment to the U.S. Constitution ensures the right of due process to all persons within its jurisdiction. The Fourteenth Amendment to the Constitution extends this right with the mandate that all citizens receive "equal protection of the laws." These guarantees of a citizen's full access to all legal resources slow the process of regulation and reform, but they are a crucial affirmation of precious individual liberties.

6 The right to enter into any kind of lawful agreement is strongly protected by the standards of due process and equal protection in the United States. However, this right is rather weakly protected in Canada, and the Canadian government therefore can and does limit the right of contract.

7 Criminal law establishes punishment for an offender who has broken a specific law. The state pays the trial costs, but financial compensation for the injured party does not automatically result from conviction. Criminal law requires:
1 A precise description of the violation of a certain law
2 Proof beyond a reasonable doubt that a crime has been committed
3 Proof that the offender intended to commit the crime

8 In a civil suit, a person may be financially compensated for an injury, but he or she must finance the litigation. Standards of proof are much lower in civil law than they are in criminal law, and the evidence presented must only be favorable to the injured party for compensation to be granted.

9 An ombudsman is a government agent empowered to bring court suits against business or government on behalf of consumers and citizens. With no continuing responsibility to any particular industry, an ombudsman can assist consumers quickly without divided loyalty. The ombudsman combines the state-paid assistance found in criminal law with the opportunity for financial compensation found in civil law.

10 Public goods belong to no one person and are used by many persons. Mass-transit systems, national parks, and clean air are all examples of public goods. A public good may be financed by government when it would never be financed by private persons who do not share directly or immediately in the savings that accrue to the public sector.

Suggestions for Further Reading

Galbraith, John Kenneth. *American Capitalism.* Boston: Houghton Mifflin, 1956.

Galbraith, John Kenneth. *The Affluent Society.* Boston: Houghton Mifflin, 1960.

Hayek, Friedrich A. *The Road to Serfdom.* Chicago: University of Chicago Press, 1944.

The Consumer Workshop

1 Your lifestyle expresses the freedom of choice that society allows you. Give some concrete examples of the ways in which your lifestyle would be different in a nonmarket system?

2 The theory of countervailing power holds that large economic units balance one another. Do you believe that this theory is valid? Do unions and businesses really concern themselves with final retail prices during wage negotiations? Or do large economic conglomerates often attempt to achieve compromises at the expense of the consumer? Elaborate.

3 The right of due process makes it harder to police the market and to restrain business from abusing the consumer. Do you think business is currently too free to challenge the law via extended litigation? As a citizen, would you maintain, restrict, or extend due process as it applies to business?

4 Choice is itself a valuable commodity. Would you consider trading some or all of your potential and actual choices to obtain more goods and services for yourself or for others? (Note that income and sales taxes that transfer your purchasing power to others are actually transfers of choice: You receive less goods in exchange for the knowledge that others have more.)

5 You have just been appointed an ombudsman in charge of consumer problems. Rate what you consider to be the ten most important consumer problem areas in need of attention.

24

WHERE IS THE CONSUMER MOVEMENT GOING?

24

" What the consumer movement is beginning to say —and must say much more strongly if it is to grow— is that business crime and corporate intransigence are the really urgent menace to law and order in America. "

RALPH NADER*

Throughout this book, we have examined many market issues from the standpoint of what is often called "consumerism."   In conclusion, we view the consumer movement in perspective and attempt to assess its future direction.

THE CONSUMER MOVEMENT IN PERSPECTIVE

We have seen that the consumer's problems are intrinsically interwoven with thousands of diverse questions and issues.   The consumer's point of view can usually be found among the arguments surrounding each of these problems, but do all of these arguments really add up to the "consumer movement"?

Writing in the *Harvard Business Review,* Philip Kotler defines "consumerism" as "a social movement seeking to augment the rights and powers of buyers in relation to sellers."[1]   This description is broad, embracing practically every consumer issue.   Labeling consumerism a "social" movement in itself places it in a broad category.   We suggest that this definition is apt and correct: Within the consumer movement, there *is* a consensus that the buyer's rights must be increased in relation to the seller's rights as they currently exist in the market.

Origins of the Movement   In the last 100 years, the consumer movement has had three points of generation: the Populist and Progressive movements (1890–1910), Franklin Roosevelt's New Deal in the 1930s; and social activism of the late 1960s.

The first two eras of consumer reform were engendered by distinct economic problems.   The Populist and Progressive movements were reactions to the growth of corporate power in the form of trusts and large railroads; the New Deal attempted to deal with the Great Depression.   However, these movements died rather quietly when national concern shifted to World Wars I and II, respectively.

* Ralph Nader, "The Great American Gyp," *The New York Review of Books* **XI** (November 21, 1968).

[1] Philip Kotler, "What Consumerism Means for Marketers," *Harvard Business Review* (May–June 1972), p. 49.

MAJOR CONSUMER LEGISLATION, 1872–1975

1872 *Mail Fraud Act of 1872:* Made use of the mails for fraud a federal crime.

1887 *Interstate Commerce Act:* Ended discriminatory rail rates and established the Interstate Commerce Commission (ICC) to regulate them.

1906 *Food and Drug Act:* Established federal control of food and drugs in interstate commerce.

1914 *Federal Trade Commission Act:* Established The Federal Trade Commission (FTC) to control, among other things, unfair methods of competition and deceptive advertising.

1938 *Federal Food, Drug, and Cosmetic Act of 1938:* Strengthened the Food and Drug Act of 1906 by extending coverage to cosmetics. Required the prereleased clearance of new drugs and their toxicity levels; authorized packaging standards.

1953 *Flammable Fabrics Act:* Prohibited the shipment of flammable fabrics in interstate commerce.

1958 *Automobile Information Disclosure Act:* Required automobile manufacturers to post the suggested retail prices of new models.

1958 *Food Additives Amendment:* Amended the Food and Drug Act by prohibiting the use of food additives until proved safe.

1959 *Textile Fiber Products Identification Act:* Required textile fiber products to carry identifying labels.

1960 *Hazardous Products Labeling Act:* Required hazardous household chemicals to carry warning labels.

1960 *Color Additives Amendment:* Amended the 1906 Food and Drug Act to include safety standards for food colors.

1965 *Fair Packaging and Labeling Act:* Established procedures for standardizing package sizes and measures.

1966 *National Traffic and Motor Vehicle Safety Act:* Authorized the U.S. Department of Transportation to set safety standards for new and used automobiles.

1966 *Child Safety Act:* Made the marketing of potentially dangerous toys illegal.

1967 *Wholesome Meat Act:* Required states to raise their meat inspection standards to federal levels.

1967 *National Commission on Product Safety Act:* Established a commission to review hazardous household products and to make recommendations for protective legislation.

1968 *Consumer Credit Protection Act:* Required interest-rate disclosures and other interest charges to be specified on consumer loans and revolving charge accounts.

1970 *Fair Credit Reporting Act:* Regulated credit bureaus and the use of credit information.

1974 *Fair Credit Billing Act:* Established procedures for correcting billing errors on charge accounts.

1975 *Magnuson–Moss Warranty Act:* Clarified law and terminology on appliance and other product warranties and established restitution procedures.

THE CURRENT CONSUMER MOVEMENT

The consumer movement in its current form put down its roots in the late 1960s. Spurred by Ralph Nader's dramatic and compelling arguments for reforms in automobile design, product safety, pensions, and nursing homes—to name only a few of his interests—consumer protest has moved to the forefront of national concern.

Citizens are far better protected from their own and others' errors now than ever before. But technological advancement has drastically increased the possibilities for error. The Fair Credit Billing Act of 1974 is a response to the difficulties of correcting computer-caused errors. Food additive amendments were required to neutralize the capabilities of food chemists to make us believe that harmful food or nonfood is pleasant and nutritious.

Clearly, the major accomplishments of consumer reform during 1965–1975 seem modest compared to the needs for reform that the products of science and technology will undoubtedly bring in the coming decades.

DIRECTIONS FOR FUTURE REFORM

The future of reform is rooted in the needs and accomplishments of the present. Today three significant but broad currents of consumer reform can be identified:

1 Equalization of consumer market power with respect to business
2 Enhancement of consumer defenses in the marketplace
3 Improvement of consumer remedies for business misconduct

Equalization of Market Power

Caveat Emptor.   Traditionally, the consumer has lacked individual market power in dealing with business.   Formerly, the law held that the consumer was his or her only source of protection: *Caveat emptor* ("let the buyer beware") was the consumer's sole guideline.   Business was liable for misrepresentation only in cases of gross fraud, if at all.

"Let the buyer beware" may have been an adequate form of consumer protection when markets were smaller and products were bought and sold among neighbors and friends.   But technological advancements have created such diverse and complex products and such distant sellers that consumers can no longer simply familiarize themselves with the products on every store shelf in town.

Consumer reform means improving the consumer's position.   Labeling acts are designed to cut through advertising misinformation to give the buyer substantive product information.   Similarly, food and drug standards governing additives and product safety represent efforts to protect the consumer from characteristics and components of foods and drugs that cannot be detected by the naked eye.

Fair Trade Laws.   At one time, consumers were able to bargain, but this practice began to decline when merchandising transformed retailing from individual enterprises into impersonal, corporate enterprises.   Consumer bargaining was nearly extinguished under the New Deal by misguided laws that permitted manufacturers to fix retail prices.   Known as "fair trade" laws, these regulations were designed to prevent large retail chains from driving small businesses out of the marketplace.   These laws never worked, but they cost consumers billions of dollars before Congress invalidated "fair trade" in December 1975.

The propensity to give consumers greater market power and more product information is expected to continue.   Subsequent disclosure standards may even include markups.   In 1975, for example, Mexico passed a law requiring retailers to disclose their own purchase (wholesale) prices on all price tags.   Such a law, which would permit consumers to compare the values of retailer services, might be worth the U.S. Congress' consideration. Laws requiring food and cosmetic labels to include more extensive ingredient information would enable consumers to determine the safety of the substances they use. This ingredient information would be especially helpful to people with allergies.

Consumer Defenses in the Marketplace

Consumer defenses in the marketplace have been and will continue to be strengthened by law reform. For many decades, consumers were not treated fairly because the law governing transactions between consumers and business was the same as the law governing transactions between businesses. Until recently, consumers were expected to be as shrewd and expert in overall contract negotiations as business executives experienced in trading a narrow group of commodities.

Laws were developed to help businesses grow—not to assure that consumers got what they paid for. These laws were partial to business in all consumer–business transactions. Two important areas of buyer–seller relations exemplify this bias:

1 The theory of privity of contract
2 The doctrine of holder in due course

Privity of Contract. When two parties are related as *direct* buyer and seller in any contract, *privity of contract* is said to exist. If A buys a Ford from B that turns out to be a lemon, A can sue B to rescind the purchase contract and obtain restitution. However, in a state that requires privity of contract, A cannot sue the Ford Motor Company in Detroit because A had no direct relation with the Ford manufacturer. Therefore, according to the privity of contract theory, all performance warranties extend from the seller—in this case B, not Ford.

Privity of contract clearly impedes consumer action in suits for breach of warranty, product liability, and misrepresentation in advertising. This doctrine has been eroded by scores of laws that directly impose liability on manufacturers and permit consumers to place blame for defective products where it belongs—on the maker, not on the dealer (unless the dealer has also contributed to the misrepresentation or hazard). As Rothschild and Carroll diagnose privity of contract, "the doctrine is in the throes of terminal illness."[2]

Privity is being steadily eliminated by state legislature, courts, and the U.S. Congress as a barrier to liability. This process will probably continue until privity is a dead issue. However, the elimination of privity in itself will create problems, because it is unreasonable to presume that a manufacturer can know every situation in which its product will be used.

Holder in Due Course. The doctrine of holder in due course has been developed to assist commerce. As we explained earlier in Chapter 10, *holder in due*

[2] Donald P. Rothschild and David W. Carroll, *Consumer Protection* (Cincinnati: W.H. Anderson, 1973), p. 418.

course asserts that any financial obligation is collectable if it is properly transferred, no matter who holds it. If A gives an IOU to B and B sells the IOU to C, then the holder in due course (C) is entitled to receive payment from A.

Holder in due course is a useful and necessary doctrine in banking and in many areas of commerce. Unfortunately, it presents a problem to consumers who buy merchandise in credit transactions, because the buyer is liable to pay for the purchase even if the goods are defective. The doctrine of holder in due course had been reversed by 21 states by the end of 1974, and it will undoubtedly continue to be attacked as a barrier to consumer justice. Many federal laws that guarantee product performance already have denied or infringed on the doctrine. Eventually, holder in due course will probably be eliminated as a functional law affecting consumer transactions.

Consumer Remedies for Business Misconduct

One of the most active areas of consumer reform in the last ten years has been the improvement of consumer recourse regarding business misconduct. Today consumers have more avenues available to them to obtain financial compensation for fraud, nondelivery of merchandise, warranty evasion, and many other deceptive business practices than were ever open to them in the past. For this reason, businesses can now be held to a higher standard of responsibility toward the consumer.

In Chapter 23, we commented extensively on the role of due process in American law. We learned that due process guarantees full rights of trial and appeal to almost all persons and businesses. In practice, due process extends enormous advantages to business firms that have sufficient financial resources to litigate issues throughout years—even decades—of hearings, trials, and appeals.

Government can limit the advantage that the wealthy corporation has in court in four ways:

1 By allowing consumers to sue *en masse* (as a class)
2 By having government actively assist consumers in court
3 By steering corrective action away from the courts and toward administrators who can act more directly than the courts can
4 By limiting the doctrine of due process

Class actions. The difficulty facing any single consumer who wishes to obtain restitution in court is the high cost of judicial procedures in terms of both time and money. Counsel must be hired (paid perhaps $50 per hour for pretrial investigations, research, and the actual trial work), court transcripts must be purchased, and expert witnesses must be engaged, and even a simple legal suit can cost thousands of dollars to implement. A successful plaintiff may recover some of these costs, but substantial amounts of time and effort are still spent in arriving at a judicial solution.

In response to the obvious difficulty of requiring each consumer to pay his or her own legal costs, the U.S. Congress has passed several class-action statutes.

"Good heavens—not *another* class action suit!"

A *class action* is a lawsuit initiated by a class of plaintiffs, each having a similar legal issue or financial matter to resolve. By law, the class of plaintiffs must be of a known size. For example, the class could be comprised of tens of thousands of people who bought a particular brand of defective washing machine during 1965–1972, if it is clearly established who is and who is not in the class.

An important current issue is what entitles a person to join a class action. Federal courts fear they may be faced with thousands of elaborate cases in which individual class members have lost rather small sums of money. Recently, class-action regulations have restricted the initiation of such suits to cases in which each class member has incurred a loss of more than $50. But there is good reason to expect that class-action rules will be liberalized to permit a greater number of suits. A class action gives consumers the collective power of a corporation and permits them to present and solve their own grievances in the courts. This means that consumers do not have to take all their problems to the legislature. Legislatures have the final say in most forms of judicial procedure, so that they can be expected to act on their own behalf to ensure that consumer class-action suits are taken to court.

The Role of Government Lawyers. In many situations, the consumer is the lonely victim of a particularly severe abuse. The abuse may be too specific to assemble a class of plaintiffs, and the burden of trial costs may be too great for the consumer to bear alone. In such cases, federal and state governments appoint a competent attorney to represent or assist the consumer. The attorney may be a so-called "poverty lawyer," a government lawyer who enters the case as a friend of the court (and of the consumer), or a government lawyer who acts as the plaintiff's own lawyer.

The U.S. Supreme Court already recognizes that anyone charged with a crime is entitled to counsel, but this rule has not yet been extended to civil matters where one citizen sues another. The courts and legislatures are reluctant to initiate a legal program that would subsidize lawyers without limit and clog the courts with trivial litigation.

For these reasons, it seems unlikely that government will ever agree to pay for everyone's legal fees. If government funds the plaintiff's case, it can hardly do less for the defendant. It seems much more likely that government will enter important civil cases more often as a friend of the court and discretely aid consumers in critical cases.

Nonjudicial Solutions. In Chapter 23, we pointed out that due process gives every corporation its day in court. However, because a trial can be time-consuming, some form of nonjudicial arbitration or regulation may be preferable. But preserving the speed and efficiency of administrative decision making is more easily said than done. Federal regulatory agency procedures have become as unwieldy and costly as the process of trial and appeal, but administrative action is still *potentially* faster and more decisive. The efficiency of administrative solutions should encourage legislatures to make this alternative more available to consumers in future years.

Limits to Due Process. The main impediment to quick and low-cost alternatives to judicial solutions is due process itself. The U.S. Constitution guarantees due process as a right and a defense against arbitrary action by the state. Consumer problems could be solved quickly by government if the state represents the consumer and if due process is not required by law. Of course, without due process, a government hostile to consumers and their problems could easily side with business and impede consumer recourse.

We will not attempt to predict the fate of due process here. It will probably be tested in consumer law and in other areas of consumer action in the coming years. In every test, the courts must decide whether the value of due process as a defense against arbitrary government is worth the cost of due process as an economic obstacle to consumer justice.

GUARDING CONSUMER POWER

The essence of consumerism, as Philip Kotler notes, is that it is a *social movement.* The inherent danger in formalizing consumer policies in government administrations and bureaucracies is stagnation. Most regulatory bodies in the federal government drown in their own paperwork, and any bureaucracy that separates itself from the final beneficiaries of its work—the consumers—can become a mockery of reform.

Regardless of what future reforms consumers achieve, it remains imperative that they never allow the movement to fall into the hands of bureaucrats who are more concerned with procedure than with result. Having struggled so hard to attain their power, consumers must now learn to keep it and to use it wisely.

SUMMARY

1 Consumerism is a social movement that aims to develop the buyer's rights and powers.
2 Three periods have generated consumer activism: the Populist and Progressive movements (1890–1910); the New Deal in the 1930s; and the social activism of the late 1960s.
3 Future consumer reform may occur in three areas:
  1 Equalizing consumer market power:
    • Abolition of *caveat emptor* ("let the buyer beware")
    • End of "fair trade" and other business price fixing
  2 Enhancing consumer defenses in the marketplace:
    • End of privity of contract
    • End of holder in due course doctrine
  3 Improving consumer remedies for business misconduct:
    • Possible broadening of the role of class-action suits
    • Possible direct legal government aid to consumers
    • Creation of nonjudicial alternatives
    • Limitation of due process if courts and Congress permit

Suggestions for Further Reading

* Buskirk, Richard H., and Rothe, James T. "Consumerism—An Interpretation." *Journal of Marketing* **XXXIV,** October 1970, pp. 61–65.
* Hermann, Robert O. "Consumerism: Its Goals, Organization, and Future," *Journal of Marketing,* **XXXIV,** October 1970, pp. 55–60.
U.S. Department of Health, Education and Welfare. *State Consumer Action Summaries.* Published annually.
* Nader, Ralph, "The Great American Gyp." *The New York Review of Books* **XI,** November 21, 1968, pp. 27–34.
Executive Office of the President, Office of Consumer Affairs. *Guide to Federal Consumer Services.* Washington, D.C.: U.S. Government Printing Office, 1971.

The Consumer Workshop

1 List and discuss your own concerns about the current direction of the consumer movement. To what issues and/or problems do you think the movement should address itself more intensively? Additionally?

*Note: These references are reprinted in Barbara B. Murray (ed.), *Consumerism: The Eternal Triangle* (Pacific Palisades, Calif.: Goodyear Publishing Company, 1973). *See also* Ralph M. Gaedeke and Warren W. Etcheson (eds.), *Consumerism* (San Francisco: Canfield Press, 1972).

2 How can a person or a group transmit his/her/its concerns to consumer-action groups? In other words, what communication devices and tactics will induce others to consider what you view as a consumer problem?

3 Traditionally, business firms and consumer-action groups have held opposing views of consumer wants and needs. Is this opposition necessary and healthy? Or should an alternative be sought in cooperative reform? What are the advantages and the disadvantages (risks) of each route to reform if consumer groups and business continue to establish different goals for the consumer?

4 The values and concerns of consumers are being built into current law and government administration. How could shifting the power of reform from grass-roots organizations to government bureaucracies endanger the consumer movement?

APPENDIX: FEDERAL AND STATE AGENCIES THAT HELP THE CONSUMER

The following list of federal, state, and local government offices to contact in connection with consumer problems is necessarily brief. For further information, consult any good directory of government offices in a local library or courthouse and/or refer to the excellent *Guide to Federal Consumer Services* issued by the Office of Consumer Affairs of the Executive Office of the President.

FEDERAL AGENCIES AND WHAT THEY DO

Agency	Activity
CIVIL AERONAUTICS BOARD (CAB) Office of Consumer Affairs Civil Aeronautics Board Washington, D.C. 20428	Regulates airline ticket prices; controls unfair or deceptive advertising for air travel; handles complaints.
DEPARTMENT OF AGRICULTURE Office of Information Department of Agriculture Washington, D.C. 20250	
Agricultural Marketing Service Department of Agriculture Washington, D.C. 20250 (or any local office)	Inspects meat, poultry, and their products; approves labels prior to use; sets grade standards; egg inspection.
Food and Nutrition Service Department of Agriculture Washington, D.C. 20250	Administers Food Stamp Plan; operates and funds school lunch programs.
COMMERCE DEPARTMENT National Bureau of Standards Department of Commerce Washington, D.C. 20234	Administers Refrigerator Safety Act, Flammable Fabrics Act, Fair Packaging and Labeling Act.
INTERSTATE COMMERCE COMMIS-SION (ICC) Interstate Commerce Commission Washington, D.C. 20423	Regulates rates and operating territories of surface interstate common carriers (rail, bus, truck, water, and pipeline).
OFFICE OF CONSUMER AFFAIRS (OCA) Office of Consumer Affairs New Executive Office Building Washington, D.C. 20506	Channels consumer complaints to appropriate agencies; aids in the formation of executive policies regarding consumer problems.

Agency	Activity
NATIONAL CREDIT UNION ADMINIS-TRATION (NCUA) National Credit Union Administration Washington, D.C. 20456	Charters and regulates credit unions for qualified groups; insures member accounts.
EQUAL EMPLOYMENT OPPORTUNITY COMMISSION (EEOC) Equal Employment Opportunity Commission 1800 G Street, N.W. Washington, D.C. 20506 (or any local office)	Prohibits discrimination in hiring, firing, promotion, job ads on the basis of race, sex, religion, or national origin.
ENVIRONMENTAL PROTECTION AGENCY (EPA) Director of Public Affairs Environmental Protection Agency Washington, D.C. 20460	Administers Clean Air Act, Solid Waste Disposal Act, Federal Water Pollution Control Act.
FEDERAL COMMUNICATIONS COMMIS-SION (FCC) Office of Reports and Information Federal Communications Commission Washington, D.C. 20554	Assures that broadcasters and cable TV systems operate in the public interest with respect to content, commercial time, and amplification.
FEDERAL DEPOSIT INSURANCE CORPORATION (FDIC) Federal Deposit Insurance Corporation Washington, D.C. 20429	Insures bank accounts, examines state member banks and corrects any unsound banking methods; oversees trust-fund abuse cases.
FEDERAL HOME LOAN BANK BOARD (FHLB) Director Federal Home Loan Bank Board 101 Indiana Ave, N.W. Washington, D.C. 20552	Insures and regulates state and federally chartered savings and loan associations.
FEDERAL POWER COMMISSION (FPC) Federal Power Commission Washington, D.C. 20426	Regulates interstate electric-power and natural-gas rates and services at the wholesale level.
FEDERAL RESERVE SYSTEM Board of Governors Federal Reserve System Washington, D.C. 20551 (and regional offices)	Regulates the money supply, Truth in Lending laws, and bank-holding statutes; supervises member banks.

Agency	Activity
FEDERAL TRADE COMMISSION (FTC) Federal Trade Commission Washington, D.C. 20580 (*Regional offices:* Los Angeles; San Francisco; Atlanta; Chicago; New Orleans; Boston; Kansas City (Mo.); New York; Cleveland; Falls Church (Va.); Seattle)	Regulates unfair business practices and anticompetitive business behavior; administers Wool Products Labeling Act, Fur Products Labeling Act, Textile Fiber Products Labeling Act, Fair Packaging and Labeling Act, Truth in Lending laws, Magnuson–Moss Warranty Act.
DEPARTMENT OF HEALTH, EDUCATION AND WELFARE (HEW) Office of Consumer Affairs Department of Health, Education and Welfare Washington, D.C. 20201	Coordinates HEW consumer programs.
Food and Drug Administration 5600 Fishers Lane Rockville, Maryland 20852	Enforces laws to prevent distribution of misbranded or adulterated foods, drugs, and cosmetics; assures drug safety.
Social Security Administration 6401 Social Security Building Baltimore, Maryland 21235 (or any local office)	Funds and disburses payments to persons and their families in the event of death or disability; helps pay health-care expenses for people over 65.
DEPARTMENT OF HOUSING AND URBAN DEVELOPMENT (HUD) Department of Housing and Urban Development Washington, D.C. 20410	Provides funds to build and improve housing; enforces antidiscrimination laws; provides flood-insurance programs; enforces laws against interstate land-sales abuses; aids mobile-home buyers.
DEPARTMENT OF THE INTERIOR Office of Information Department of the Interior Washington, D.C. 20240	Manages conservation programs for public lands, including national parks; administers mine-safety acts.
DEPARTMENT OF JUSTICE Justice Department Washington, D.C. 20530	Handles prosecutions for other federal agencies; plays a major role in antitrust law enforcement.
DEPARTMENT OF LABOR Department of Labor Washington, D.C. 20210	Monitors labor conditions; enforces equal-pay and certain antidiscrimination laws as they relate to employment.

Agency	Activity
UNITED STATES POSTAL SERVICE Chief Postal Inspector U.S. Postal Service Washington, D.C. 20260 (or any local post office)	Enforces laws against mail fraud and misuse of mails; handles problems regarding money orders, nondelivery, damage in transit.
SECURITIES AND EXCHANGE COMMISSION (SEC) Securities and Exchange Commission Washington, D.C. 20549	Regulates trading in stocks and bonds; monitors operations of stock exchanges; sets standards for disclosure of information regarding marketed securities.
DEPARTMENT OF TRANSPORTATION Federal Aviation Administration Washington, D.C. 20590	Licenses and certifies aircraft, pilots, carriers, airports; establishes and enforces air safety and navigation laws.
Federal Highway Administration Department of Transportation Washington, D.C. 20590	Develops highway transportation; administers interstate system of highways and highway trust funds.
National Highway Traffic Safety Administration Washington, D.C. 20591	Insures that all cars manufactured or imported after January 1968 meet federal motor vehicle safety standards; requires date and disclosure tags on vehicles.
DEPARTMENT OF THE TREASURY Secretary of the Treasury Washington, D.C. 20226	Oversees the Internal Revenue Service; taxes and inspects alcoholic beverages; operates the Customs Bureau; insures deposits in national banks; replaces lost or stolen savings bonds.
VETERANS ADMINISTRATION (VA) Veterans Administration Washington, D.C. 20420	Provides benefits and services to veterans and their families due to death or disability; provides medical care and education loans.

STATE AGENCIES

ALASKA
Attorney General of Alaska
Pouch "K", State Capitol
Juneau, Alaska 99801

ARIZONA
Consumer Fraud Division
Office of the Attorney General
159 State Capitol Building
Phoenix, Arizona 85007

ARKANSAS
Consumer Protection Division
Office of the Attorney General
Justice Building
Little Rock, Arkansas 72201

CALIFORNIA
Consumer Fraud Section
Office of the Attorney General
600 State Building
Los Angeles, California 90012

Director
Department of Consumer Affairs
1020 N Street
Sacramento, California 95814

COLORADO
Office of Consumer Affairs
Attorney General of Colorado
503 Farmers Union Building
1575 Sherman Street
Denver, Colorado 80203

CONNECTICUT
Commissioner
Department of Consumer Protection
State Office Building
Hartford, Connecticut 06115

DELAWARE
Consumer Protection Division
Office of the Attorney General

1206 King Street
Wilmington, Delaware 19801

FLORIDA
Attorney General of Florida
State Capitol
Tallahassee, Florida 32304

Division of Consumer Affairs
Florida Department of Agriculture and
    Consumer Services
The Capitol
Tallahassee, Florida 32304

GEORGIA
Georgia Consumer Services Program
Department of Family and Children Services
15 Peachtree Street, Room 909
Atlanta, Georgia 30303

HAWAII
Director of Consumer Protection
Office of the Governor
602 Kamamalu Building
P.O. Box 3767
250 South King Street
Honolulu, Hawaii 96811

IDAHO
Consumer Protection Division
Office of the Attorney General
State Capitol
Boise, Idaho 83707

ILLINOIS
Consumer Fraud Section
Office of the Attorney General
134 North LaSalle Street
Chicago, Illinois 60602

INDIANA
Attorney General of Indiana
219 State House
Indianapolis, Indiana 46204

Consumer Advisory Council
Indiana Department of Commerce
336 State House
Indianapolis, Indiana 46204

IOWA
Consumer Fraud Division
Office of the Attorney General
1223 East Court
Des Moines, Iowa 50319

KANSAS
Consumer Protection Division
Office of the Attorney General
The Capitol
Topeka, Kansas 66612

KENTUCKY
Consumer Protection Division
Office of the Attorney General
The Capitol
Frankfort, Kentucky 40601

Executive Director
Citizen's Commission for Consumer Protection
State Capitol
Frankfort, Kentucky 40601

MAINE
Consumer Protection Division
Office of the Attorney General
State House
Augusta, Maine 04330

MARYLAND
Consumer Protection Division
Office of the Attorney General
1200 One Charles Center
Baltimore, Maryland 21201

MASSACHUSETTS
Consumer Protection Division
Office of the Attorney General
State House
Boston, Massachusetts 02133

Executive Secretary
Massachusetts Consumers' Council
State Office Building
Government Center
100 Cambridge Street
Boston, Massachusetts 02202

MICHIGAN
Consumer Protection Division
Office of the Attorney General
Law Building
Lansing, Michigan 48902

Special Assistant to the Governor for
Consumer Affairs
1033 South Washington Street
Lansing, Michigan 48933

Executive Director
Michigan Consumer Council
525 Hollister Building
Lansing, Michigan 48933

MINNESOTA
Special Assistant Attorney General for
Consumer Protection
Attorney General of Minnesota
102 State Capitol
St. Paul, Minnesota 55101

Office of Consumer Services
Department of Commerce
State Office Building, Room 230
St. Paul, Minnesota 55101

MISSISSIPPI
Assistant Attorney General for
Consumer Protection
Attorney General of Mississippi
State Capitol
Jackson, Mississippi 39201

Consumer Protection Division
Department of Agriculture and Commerce
Jackson, Mississippi 39205

MISSOURI

Consumer Protection Division
Office of the Attorney General
Supreme Court Building
Jefferson City, Missouri 65101

NEW HAMPSHIRE

Assistant Attorney General for
    Consumer Protection
Office of the Attorney General
State House Annex
Concord, New Hampshire 03301

NEW JERSEY

Office of Consumer Protection
1100 Raymond Boulevard
Newark, New Jersey 07102

NEW MEXICO

Consumer Protection Division
Office of the Attorney General
Supreme Court Building
P.O. Box 2246
Santa Fe, New Mexico 87501

NEW YORK

Consumer Frauds and Protection Bureau
Office of the Attorney General
80 Centre Street
New York, New York 10013

Chairman and Executive Director
Consumer Protection Board
380 Madison Avenue
New York, New York 10017

NORTH CAROLINA

Consumer Protection and Antitrust Division
Office of the Attorney General
P.O. Box 629
Raleigh, North Carolina 27602

NORTH DAKOTA

Consumer Protection Division
Office of the Attorney General
The Capitol
Bismarck, North Dakota 58501

OHIO

Consumer Frauds and Crimes Section
Office of the Attorney General
State House Annex
Columbus, Ohio 43215

OKLAHOMA

Administrator
Department of Consumer Affairs
Lincoln Office Plaza, Suite 74
4545 Lincoln Boulevard
Oklahoma City, Oklahoma 73105

OREGON

Assistant Attorney General for Antitrust and
    Consumer Protection
Office of the Attorney General
322 State Office Building
Salem, Oregon 97310

Assistant to the Governor for Economic Development and Consumer Services
State Capitol Building
Salem, Oregon 97301

PENNSYLVANIA

Bureau of Consumer Protection
Pennsylvania Department of Justice
Durbin Building
2–4 North Market Square
Harrisburg, Pennsylvania 17101

RHODE ISLAND

Special Assistant Attorney General for
    Consumer Protection
Office of the Attorney General
Providence County Court House
Providence, Rhode Island 02903

Executive Director
Rhode Island Consumers' Council
365 Broadway
Providence, Rhode Island 02902

SOUTH DAKOTA

Office of Consumer Affairs
Attorney General of South Dakota

State Capitol
Pierre, South Dakota 57501

TEXAS
Antitrust and Consumer Protection Division
Office of the Attorney General
P.O. Box 12548
Capitol Station
Austin, Texas 78711

Office of Consumer Credit
P.O. Box 2107
1011 San Jacinto Boulevard
Austin, Texas 78767

UTAH
Assistant Attorney General for
    Consumer Protection
Office of the Attorney General
State Capitol
Salt Lake City, Utah 84114

Administrator of Consumer Credit
403 State Capitol
Salt Lake City, Utah 84114

VERMONT
Consumer Protection Bureau
Office of the Attorney General
94 Church Street
Burlington, Vermont 05401

Family Economics and Home
    Management Specialist
Terrill Hall, Room 210
University of Vermont
Burlington, Vermont 05401

VIRGINIA
Assistant Attorney General for
    Consumer Protection
Office of the Attorney General
Supreme Court
Library Building
Richmond, Virginia 23219

Special Assistant to the Governor on Minority
    Groups and Consumer Affairs
Office of the Governor
Richmond, Virginia 23219

Administrator, Consumer Affairs
Department of Agriculture and Commerce
8th Street Office Building
Richmond, Virginia 23219

WASHINGTON
Consumer Protection and Antitrust Division
Office of the Attorney General
1266 Dexter Horton Building
Seattle, Washington 98104

WEST VIRGINIA
Assistant Attorney General for
    Consumer Protection
Office of the Attorney General
The Capitol
Charleston, West Virginia 25305

Consumer Protection Division
West Virginia Department of Labor
1900 Washington Street East
Charles, West Virginia 25305

WISCONSIN
Assistant Attorney General for
    Consumer Protection
Office of the Attorney General
Department of Justice
Madison, Wisconsin 53702

Bureau of Consumer Protection
Trade Division
Department of Agriculture
801 West Badger Road
Madison, Wisconsin 53713

WYOMING
State Examiner and Administrator
Consumer Credit Code
State Supreme Court Building
Cheyenne, Wyoming 82001

COMMONWEALTH OF PUERTO RICO AND THE VIRGIN ISLANDS

Attorney General of Puerto Rico
P.O. Box 192
San Juan, Puerto Rico 00902

Consumer Services Administration
P.O. Box 13934
Santurce, Puerto Rico 00908

Executive Director
Public Services Commission
Charlotte Amalie
St. Thomas, Virgin Islands 00801

SOME LOCAL AGENCIES

CALIFORNIA

Secretary
Los Angeles Consumer Protection Committee
107 South Broadway
Los Angeles, California 90012

Secretary
Bay Area Consumer Protection
  Coordinating Committee
Box 36005
450 Golden Gate Avenue
San Francisco, California 94102

Director
Santa Clara County Department of Weights and
  Measures and Consumer Affairs
Division of Consumer Affairs
409 Matthew Street
Santa Clara, California 95050

FLORIDA

Director
Consumer Protection Division
1351 N.W. 12th Street
Miami, Florida 33125

Consumer Affairs Officer
Division of Consumer Affairs
Department of Public Safety
220 East Bay Street
Jacksonville, Florida 32202

Director of Consumer Affairs
264 First Avenue North
St. Petersburg, Florida 33701

ILLINOIS

Commissioner
Department of Consumer Sales and Weights
  and Measures
City Hall
121 North LaSalle Street
Chicago, Illinois 60602

Secretary
Chicago Consumer Protection Committee
U.S. Court House
Federal Office Building, Room 486
219 South Dearborn Street
Chicago, Illinois 60604

KENTUCKY

Supervisor
Division of Weights and Measures and
  Consumer Affairs
Metropolitan Sewer District Building, 2nd floor
Louisville, Kentucky 40202

LOUISIANA

Secretary
Consumer Protection Committee of
  New Orleans
1000 Masonic Temple Building
333 St. Charles Street
New Orleans, Louisiana 70130

MARYLAND
Consumer Protection Division
Prince Georges County Court House
Upper Marlboro, Maryland 20870

MASSACHUSETTS
Chairman
Boston Consumer's Council
Office of the Mayor
Boston City Hall
Boston, Massachusetts 02201

Secretary
Boston Metropolitan Consumer
  Protection Committee
Federal Trade Commission
John Fitzgerald Kennedy Federal Building
Government Center
Boston, Massachusetts 02203

MICHIGAN
Secretary
Detroit Consumer Protection
  Coordinating Committee
Immigration and Naturalization Building
333 Mt. Elliott Avenue
Detroit, Michigan 48207

MISSOURI
Chairman
Citizens Consumer Advisory Committee
7701 Forsyth Boulevard
Clayton, Missouri 63105

NEW JERSEY
Director
Camden County Office of Consumer Affairs
Commerce Building, Room 60
#1 Broadway
Camden, New Jersey 08101

NEW YORK
Director, Consumer Affairs
City Hall
Long Beach, New York 11561

Commissioner
Office of Consumer Affairs
160 Old Country Road
Mineola, New York 11501

Commissioner
City of New York Department of
  Consumer Affairs
80 Lafayette Street
New York, New York 10013

OHIO
City Sealer of Weights and Measures
City Hall
Columbus, Ohio 43215

OREGON
Deputy District Attorney in Charge of
  Consumer Protection
600 County Court House
Portland, Oregon 97204

PENNSYLVANIA
Secretary
Philadelphia Consumer Protection Committee
53 Long Lane
Upper Darby, Pennsylvania 19082

Consumer Protection Office
City Hall, Room 121
Philadelphia, Pennsylvania 19107

The foregoing list of federal, state, and local consumer advocates and agencies has been compiled from publications of the Office of Consumer Affairs; from the Executive Office of the President publication *An Approach to Consumer Education for Adults* (January 1, 1973), pp. 36–37; and from the *Consumer Education Bibliography* (September 1971), pp. 38–44, prepared in conjunction with the New York Public Library.

PICTURE CREDITS

INDEX

Note: Agencies, laws, and other entities of the U.S. government are indexed under the first descriptive word of the name or title. (E.g., for the U.S. Department of Transportation, *see* Department of Transportation.)